WAR OF TITANS

War
of
Titans

*Blake's Critique of Milton
and the Politics of Religion*

Jackie DiSalvo

University of Pittsburgh Press

Published by the University of Pittsburgh Press, Pittsburgh, Pa. 15260
Copyright © 1983, University of Pittsburgh Press
Feffer and Simons, Inc., London
Manufactured in the United States of America

Library of Congress Cataloging in Publication Data

DiSalvo, Jackie.
  War of titans.

  Includes bibliographical references and index.
  1. Blake, William, 1757–1827—Criticism and interpretation.   2. Milton, John,
1608–1674—Influence—Blake.   3. Epic poetry, English—History and criticism.   4.
Religion in literature.   I. Title.
PR4147.D57 1983   821'.7   82-11136
ISBN 0-8229-3804-9

Parts of chapter 9 were first published, in slightly different form, in "Blake Encounter-
ing Milton," in *Milton and the Line of Vision*, ed. Joseph A. Wittreich (Madison: The
University of Wisconsin Press; © 1975 by the Board of Regents of the University of
Wisconsin System), pp. 143–84.

Contents

Acknowledgments

*A*lthough *it was only a decade* and a half ago that I began studying Blake and Milton, the cultural context that inspired my explorations now seems as distant as the golden age Blake always evoked in resistance to the low, dishonest decades of the early nineteenth century. Contemporary Blake scholars seem inclined to shift our focus from that prophet of liberation to the poet as a reincarnation not of the Milton who championed "mental war" against all tyrannies, political and religious, but of the frustrated revolutionary brooding bitterly upon the limits of our fallen condition. In contrast, *War of Titans* holds to the biblical injunction to repeat a "man-saving myth" "in season and out of season" and to trust that history which buries our hopes also brings them back to life. My work, therefore, openly acknowledges its legacy from a time when many of us proposed not only to understand the world but also to change it.

My first debt, therefore, is to those friends who discussed these ideas with me over the years as if our lives depended upon them. They include my associates at the University of Wisconsin, 1965–1972, in that "shadow university" where we sat in continuous session at a mostly informal, interdisciplinary seminar discussing literature, politics, philosophy, economics, psychology, history, and so forth—determined, as it were, not to disband until we had fully comprehended the roots of our culture and the possibilities for reconstructing it. So many participants in that conversation come to mind, but let me at least recall by name Roger Keeran, Elizabeth Bouchard,

Michael Strong, Steve Levine, Mark Demming, Susan Gutwill, Brian Peterson, Joyce Peterson, David Mintz, and Margaret Blanchard.

Next I mention my fellow faculty and students at what was, before it was undone by the new agendas of the eighties, Livingston College at Rutgers University. Let this be one short elegy for that brief and wonderful experiment in a multicultural, socially concerned educational community where visionary teachers served the intellectual hungers of black and white working-class students. Watching my students penetrate Blake's obscurities and embrace his voice as that of their own aspirations, I could imagine him finally becoming for us the popular prophet which he wished but failed to be in his own time. I should also acknowledge, in particular, the intellectual influence of Michael Klein and of Gillian Parker Klein, a fellow Miltonist. I want to recognize, in addition, the benefits I derived over several decades from participation in the Grail, an international family of women who showed me what it might mean to bring the female experience to bear upon possibilities of community, social change, and spiritual culture. Moreover, I am aware that one inherits the riches of black culture so unconsciously in America that one rarely stops to notice it, but I must say that without having witnessed the flowering there, out of popular genius, of a culture where sensuous joy, spiritual and political vision are merged, I wouldn't have really known what Blake was talking about.

I have been fortunate in having had such excellent teachers and scholars to assist me in my work. What a gift it was to discover Milton with a man who loves him and knows as much about him as anyone I've found. I refer to John Shawcross, a scholar who has always embodied the spirit of *Areopagitica,* earning the love of Miltonists for having made us into one of the warmest and most tolerant intellectual fraternities in America. Professor Shawcross's encouragement of my first investigation of Milton's social vision in *Samson Agonistes* enabled the first germination of these ideas. I was assisted further by the historian Harvey Goldberg, who introduced me to the historiography of the English civil war and inspired me—and thousands of others—by a vision of history which attempted to bring to light the traditions of the powerless in their long struggle for justice and community. Of the historians I discovered, the most important for me was Christopher Hill, whose works taught me more about the contradictions carried along in our culture and society than anything else I have ever read. I am thankful to him for reading this book in manuscript and offering me critical encouragement as I pursued its publication. I would like to mention as well the Blake scholar Leslie

Tannenbaum, who, as a reader of the manuscript, made a number of felicitous suggestions.

However, the scholar who has been most central to this enterprise is Joseph Wittreich. His grasp of the nature and significance of the Blake-Milton relationship within a radical prophetic and apocalyptic tradition gave me my moorings. His vast knowledge of the scholarship continually informed my ignorance; his painstaking and repeated reviews of the manuscript were indispensable, though helpless in countering my most resilient stylistic perversities. While many of my friends became alienated from academia, my own involvement with scholarship, despite many other concerns, continued to deepen, thanks largely to Professor Wittreich. He satisfied the foremost need of an aspiring junior scholar and the impossible dream of a feminist one—a mentor who was not a patriarch. With admirable negative capability, he could appreciate my determination to be controversial, even when his own views were the ones I contradicted; he did not seek to impose Urizenic boundaries on the passionate female Orc in me. No doubt I should have heeded his advice more often—my mistakes are my own—but the fact that I exist at all as a scholar reflects his ability to offer me guidance without constraint. Therefore, as Milton said to his father, let it suffice for me to say "that with a grateful mind I remember and tell over your constant kindnesses."

Three other individuals played fundamental roles in the final preparation of this manuscript. My long-standing friend and intellectual companion Constance Pohl was part of the ferment in which the project was born and saved me from chaos in the end by bringing her competent editorial skills to the task of suggesting the final reorganization and rewriting necessary to bring clarity to so complex an argument. In addition, I was blessed in my editor Jane Flanders at the University of Pittsburgh Press, whose "enormous labors" on the final version sorted out baroque complexities of style and saved me from a score of minor embarrassments. Her friendly enthusiasm for the project was the only thing that could have gotten me through the last stages; working together was a delight. Finally, I want to thank my sister, Patricia DiSalvo, who took on the ordeal of typing and repeatedly retyping the manuscript with her characteristic hard work, patience, good cheer, and selflessness.

Lastly, something must be said generally about my working-class family, for although I hardly spoke to them about this book, their influence is on every page. *War of Titans* is not only about Blake's assertion of plebeian values against those of middle-class England; as its depth it is about the hidden injuries of class, and the hidden decencies and potentialities of the American working class and its consciousness as I have felt them in my life. This book implicitly celebrates my father's years of selfless communal service, my mother's never fully realized or appreciated intelligence and talent, my sister's sanity, spunk, growth, and loyalty through changing times, and, above all, my brother's sensitive and rebellious spirit. Moreover, knowing like Milton that I too have lived "out of the sweat of other men," I am grateful to all my other "brothers and sisters" whose work in the fields, in mines, offices, and factories allowed me the leisure to study in libraries. In celebrating Blake the unschooled artisan who dared to reassess boldly the culture of the elite, I dedicate this book to his belief in the far better world which might come to be when their as yet undetonated imagination explodes upon the stage of history.

Textual Note

Quotations of Milton's poetry are taken from *The Works of John Milton*, ed. Frank Allen Patterson et al., 18 vols. (New York: Columbia University Press, 1931–39); quotations from Milton's prose are taken from *Complete Prose Works of John Milton*, ed. Don M. Wolfe et al., 8 vols. (New Haven, Conn.: Yale University Press, 1953–82). Quotations of Blake's works are taken from *The Poetry and Prose of William Blake*, ed. David V. Erdman, rev. ed. (New York: Doubleday, 1970). Citations in parentheses give an abbreviated title followed by page numbers, or book, plate, and line numbers. The following abbreviations are used:

CM   "Columbia Milton," the Patterson edition of Milton's works
YP   "Yale Prose," the Wolfe edition of Milton's prose
PB   the Erdman edition of Blake's poetry and prose
PL   *Paradise Lost*
SA   *Samson Agonistes*
A   *America   a Prophecy*
FR   *The French Revolution*
FZ   *The Four Zoas*
J   *Jerusalem*
M   *Milton*
MHH   *The Marriage of Heaven and Hell*
U   *The Book of Urizen*
VDA   *Visions of the Daughters of Albion*

WAR OF TITANS

1

Critical Introduction

In the year 1900, Paradise Lost, a poem which had loomed for centuries over the Western imagination, was declared a "monument to dead ideas,"[1] and thereupon a generation of critics proceeded to give it a proper funeral. That funeral turned out to be rather more like an Irish wake, producing one of the greatest brawls in literary history. As one Miltonist summarized the situation, "If Milton's poetry, in our time, has ceased to beget poetry, the arguments entrenched in his poems have not ceased to beget arguments. Not only are there two opposing camps of critics, incessantly in conflict, but within each of these camps there is continual sniping."[2] Milton, aroused often enough in his life from retirement by the clamor of controversy, revived to the heat of the debate going on above his unaccomplished grave. While that debate has in recent years become more subdued, its issues have not been resolved and, as Christopher Hill has put it, "The splendid thing about Milton is that he is still alive enough to be highly controversial."[3]

Emerging from these polemics was evidence for such incompatible readings of *Paradise Lost* and for so many and such various Miltons as to rival the most bizarre cases of multiple personality in the journals of psychoanalysis. Or, by another analogy, one sometimes feels in Milton studies like a participant in a TV game-show, hoping for some critical master of ceremonies to draw the curtain, terminate the charades, and announce, "Will the real John Milton please stand?" Fortunately, there is a critical master in whom such perceptions of the Milton enigma find their precedent and resolution. For the sense of a Milton lost and a Milton regained, a Milton "self-divided," "A mournful form double" (*M* 14:37), and a Milton hidden behind veils of criticism was anticipated by William Blake long ago. The moment of the bard's greatest resurrection was that in which he entered William's foot to be reborn in his epic and pictorial vision as a Milton liberated from the vagaries of history, the obtuseness of his readers, and the contradictions of his own world view.

As we emerge from the wasteland of New Criticism (not without some useful skills learned in the wilderness), we return to those insights without which literature withers: that the artist is not just a craftsman sharing tricks of the trade but, as Wordsworth tells us, "a man speaking to men"; that his art expresses a broader human experience for which the word "culture" must be reserved; that this culture is the continuous creation of all generations, and, consequently, literature communicates our common history and is incomprehensible outside our shared traditions.

These points must be reiterated as we undertake a study of Blake, who should be excluded from that "tradition of the new" in which it has sometimes been fashionable to locate him.[4] This view was revived with new sophistication in Harold Bloom's *Anxiety of Influence* which interprets English poetry since the romantics as a quest for liberation from tradition in general and, in particular, from the influence of "the great Inhibitor, the Sphinx who strangles even strong imaginations in their cradles: Milton."[5] For Bloom, literary influence is primarily an obstacle provoking the battle of individual genius against its antecedents for the guerdon of originality. Thus he extols Blake as an exemplary "strong poet" who, partly by perverse distortions, is able to liberate his own vision from Milton's.

Bloom is undoubtedly right about the iconoclasm of much modern poetry, although the causes are to be found more in the nature of an atomized, liberal society than in his oedipal dynamics. But he is dead wrong about Blake. Like other romantics, Blake faced this social and intellectual isolation with alternate exaltation and dismay. Far from being iconoclasts, romantic artists hoped, as M. H. Abrams demonstrates, to renovate the Milton tradition by turning it in the fires of their own experience and so to save the meaning of biblical symbols from the wreckage of ecclesiastical doctrine.[6] Too often, of course, they became what they beheld and could translate that vision only into the terms of individual psychology.

Since their time, we find among the widely acknowledged characteristics of our culture a radical discontinuity from decade to decade, as well as from generation to generation, the artist's isolation from a supportive audience, the absence of a common poetic language, and an inability to create an epic vision which could render our collective experience comprehensible—rather, we note the importance of mock-epic since Joyce.

But, from the first, Blake stood against these conditions, determined to overcome this loss of a unifying vision, and to lay the basis for a renovated epic tradition that may yet bear fruit. (Indeed, in Third World writers like Neruda, Fuentes, and Marquez it already has borne fruit.) In *The Four Zoas* Blake portrays the closing of the Western gate of the tongue, consequent upon the Eternals' fall into anarchy, as the main barrier to Eden. The egotistical and discontinuous world of his culture is portrayed as a contingent, not an absolute, reality, a creation of the fallen Urizen whose claim to being "self-begotten" is just an apology for his destruction of our common life.

Nevertheless, it is Bloom who reminds us, correctly, that "criticism is the art of knowing the hidden roads that go from poem to poem"[7] and who notes that "Milton is the central problem in any theory and history of poetic influence" and that "the relationship of Blake and Milton is the key to such a theory of influence."[8] However, if one realizes that these roads pass through life—history—a quite different theory from Bloom's emerges. I find more useful guidelines to the nature of that poetic encounter in Joseph Wittreich's *Angel of Apocalypse: Blake's Idea of Milton*, which offers the following premises: (1) Milton's poetry is the context for Blake's—that is, Blake is Milton's "first 'fit' critic"; (2) both build upon the "central traditions of Western culture"; and (3) both share, as A. L. Morton writes, "a tradition of revolution."[9]

Blake's poetry is scarcely comprehensible outside its Miltonic context, so this has received increasing critical attention. An awareness of Miltonic sources has informed the works of Denis Saurat,[10] Northrop Frye,[11] Harold Bloom,[12] John Beer,[13] Leslie Brisman,[14] and Florence Sandler.[15] Wittreich[16] and Frye[17] have attended to Blake as a critic. S. Foster Damon was, of course, the first writer to appreciate Blake as a critic of Milton and as "apparently the first man to understand what Milton was writing about." Damon acknowledged that Blake, despite "his great admiration, disagreed with some of Milton's conclusions" and proposed that a Miltonic analogue might be sought for every one of Blake's major poems.[18]

An understanding of Blake's place, along with that of other romantics, in a Milton tradition has begun to replace the earlier image of the poet as an iconoclastic genius who created a totally unique, private mythological system, rather than be "enslav'd by another Mans" (*J* 10:20). Thus Kathleen Raine has called for "a deeper understanding of Blake through knowledge of his traditional roots".[19] She follows

Saurat, who had sought sources for Milton's unorthodox ideas down the esoteric bypasses of heterodox mysticism. But much of Milton's and Blake's inspiration lay well within the mainstream, for the nineteenth-century radical agreed with his precursor that "all he knew was in the Bible,"[20] "the Great Code of Art" (PB 271). This is clearly why Blake was "happy to find a Great Majority of Fellow Mortals who can Elucidate [his] Visions" (PB 677), for "the Beauty of the Bible is that the most Ignorant & Simple Minds Understand it Best" (PB 657). Blake's poetry may never, alas, achieve the accessibility of popular art that he sought, but its obscurity diminishes as secular academics discover the rich vein of symbolism he shared with uneducated evangelicals.

Herbert Grierson instructed us some time ago that the biblical tradition in which Milton and the romantics find their common antecedents is prophecy.[21] The "line of vision" was shared in various ways by Dante, Chaucer, Langland, Shakespeare, and Spenser, and Blake assures us that it was bequeathed to him by Milton.[22] Moreover, as Abrams remarks, it was Spenser's and Milton's "preoccupation with Apocalypse" that "had important consequences for their Romantic successors in the prophetic tradition."[23] Its importance for Blake has been shown in the commentaries of Frye, Bloom, and William Halloran. Michael Fixler, A. L. Morton, William Kerrigan, and Austin Dobbins have advanced ambitious arguments that the Book of Revelation is not just a source, but the organizing vision behind Milton's epics; and now Wittreich has shown it to be the link between Milton's epics and Blake's.[24]

Moreover, the Book of Revelation, with its prophecy of a "final conflict" between a liberating Christ and all satanic oppressors, was at the core of a "revolutionary tradition." This particular oxymoron has been the stumbling block upon which many critics of Blake and Milton have foundered. Blake inherited his own millenarian faith from the Puritan poet who had once believed that Jerusalem was about to arise in England's green and pleasant land. The romantics appreciated this Milton whom they saw as the chief model of the revolutionary poet-prophet, the great "bard" of what Shelley called "the last national struggle for civil and religious liberty."[25] From the iconography of Blake's portraits of Milton, his illustrations of Milton's poetry and poetic commentary, Wittreich has established that it was this revolutionary Milton who became Blake's "Awakener," his "Angel of Apocalypse." It was in order to restore the image of that fiery prophet, clouded by eighteenth-century orthodoxy, that Blake composed his epic tribute. *Milton* is thus the culmination of an alternative tendency in eighteenth-century criti-

cism which, according to Marcia Pointon, resulted in "the crystallization of the concept of Milton the man as a great revolutionary,
nonconformist protagonist of liberty which was current in the early
nineteenth century."[26]

Milton's politics underlie much of what must be seen as the politics of Milton criticism. It is worth recalling with K. L. Sharma that
"prejudice against the man" has often been "involved with . . . prejudice against his political and religious ideas," which "in England . . .
can easily be seen in critics from Johnson to F. R. Leavis."[27] Johnson's
distaste for the "surly republican" was inherited by that Anglican
Tory, T. S. Eliot, and the New Critics in whom there were "hidden
ideological biases to which both Milton and Blake pose[d] a challenge."[28] By the same process Milton has found enthusiastic support-
ers among such liberals and radicals as Thomas Hollis, William
Hayley, Henry Fuseli, Percy Shelley, and, recently, Christopher Hill.
Some critics tried to assimilate him to their own orthodoxy, repeating
the error which Wittreich has seen in eighteenth-century conservatives, wont to draw Milton in their own image. Thus, an ahistorical
New Critical approach to Milton's theological symbolism came to
reinforce the wrong, or at least one-sided, historical readings which
had obliterated Milton's radicalism by divorcing assumptions he
shared with orthodox humanism and Puritanism from their revolutionary context.[29]

Edgell Rickword once observed that we note that Milton's "ideal
values have become platitudes of the pulpit, the speech-day and the
election campaign, at the price of slurring over the fact that he
narrowly escaped the halter and the disembowelling knife, because
he endeavoured to embody his ideas of liberty, to have them realized
as tangible relations in an actual human society." And Rickword goes
on to say that the "seeming paradox, or historical dirty trick" which
rendered Milton "laureate of the victorious middle class" cannot be
overlooked.[30] Shelley was disturbed by it, remarking that "Milton's
poem contains within itself a refutation of that system, of which by a
strange and natural anti-thesis, it has become the chief popular
support."[31] Blake saw deeper and found here the clue to Milton's
many apparent ambiguities.

With this in mind, I would add to any Blakean guidelines for a
Milton criticism this emphasis on the contradictions in Milton's
poetry. Doing so affords one the opportunity to appreciate and illuminate further the insights of a great deal of Milton criticism. One
might perhaps even be able to resolve some of those seemingly
irreconcilable debates over *Paradise Lost* which finally prove nothing
so well as the fact that there is something particularly double-edged

about the poem itself. Every issue of central importance in that epic has been found by some critic to be laden with conflicting meanings. Satan is too often an irresistibly attractive rebel, while God is a tyrannical bore, and despised royalist trappings are granted to both by the notorious "defender of regicides."[32] Romantic love, so close to the heart of Eden, seems also to provoke Adam's fall. The lovers, moreover, are called to a life of temperance in a quite sensuous paradise.[33] At the same time, banishment might seem almost a relief to the passivity of their existence there, a "fortunate fall" into a more human experience; it is the devils, by contrast, who enjoy energetic acts of construction.[34] Again, while reason is elevated, the desire for knowledge is repeatedly rebuked and rendered suspect by its role in Eve's temptation.[35] Furthermore, history is written off in the last books as vanity of vanities by a man who for twenty years made revolution his priority. The catalogue of prospective incongruities is almost interminable, ranging to the most minute details of poetic association. If Milton is consistent in anything, it is in what Harold Fisch calls approvingly his "heroic capacity for inconsistency."[36]

Too often, however, such observations have become accusations. Thus A. J. A. Waldock once contended, "In the poem as it is there is a fundamental clash: it is a clash between what the poem asserts, on the one hand, and what it compels us to feel, on the other." Waldock and his followers have argued that this "embedded ambiguity at the heart" of *Paradise Lost* amounts to a major artistic failure. Surely, the conflicts in Milton's poem have their aesthetic manifestations, but to lay it all upon Milton's alleged "inexperience in the assessment of narrative problems" seems a hopelessly simpleminded solution to the major ideological debates inspired by the poem.[37] Critiques of Milton's artistry have called forth demonstrations of the brilliant architectonics of his epics. If the conflicts have never been resolved, it was not because Milton failed to bring conscious genius to the task.

Yet other explanations of the enigma have seemed at best partial, as with Basil Willey's identification of philosophic problems (Milton caught on the horns of a Cartesian dilemma)[38] or Tillyard's Freudian suggestion that the poem is disturbed by eruptions from Milton's unconscious.[39] Nor does the whole truth lie in Maurice Kelley's and now Hill's postulate that censorship demanded Milton's inconsistencies, requiring that he be "capable of maintaining . . . incompatible trends of thought when his individual views conflicted with a more generally accepted doctrine."[40] Least satisfactory, however, has been a kind of neotheological scholarship—albeit knowledgeable or even brilliant—like that of C. S. Lewis or Douglas Bush, which tends to blame all incongruities upon the ignorance or moral turpitude of the reader. Or one thinks here of the ingenious logic of Stanley Fish who treats the poem's sharp dichotomies as a magnificently calculated plot to trap the reader into such misinterpretations as would prove one's need for salvation.[41] Even Milton in his most aristocratic mood was never quite that arrogant.

No, a more fundamental dilemma is involved, and its explanation lies somewhere in Rickword's tale of an apostate Milton converted within a century—within decades even—into a bulwark of political and intellectual orthodoxy. The problem does not rest, I think, solely with the errors of his interpreters.[42] Instead, I would argue that Blake put his finger on it precisely in his picture of a divided Milton "who wrote in fetters when he wrote of Angels of God, and at liberty when of Devils & Hell because he was a true Poet and of the Devils party without knowing it" (*MHH* 5). At the heart of Milton's epic lies a contradiction aesthetically reflected in the magnetism of his Satan and the repulsiveness of his God. The real problem, however, is not aesthetic, but political and ideological. Blake focuses upon the confusion of sympathies involved when a poet of the "Devils party," a revolutionary, centers his epic around a civil war in which he has identified the rebels with the denizens of hell. Here, Blake is not so far from some of Milton's contemporaries who perceived a political purpose in his poem. For example, when his friend Theodore Haak read his German translation of the early books to the Hanoverian pastor, H. L. Benthem, he was convinced, according to Christopher Hill, "that Milton's poem was really about politics in Restoration England, after a republican Paradise had been lost."[43]

In quest of this political Milton, one has had to turn mainly to historical studies focused primarily upon his prose, by Arthur Barker, Edgell Rickword, William Haller, Don Wolfe, Zera Fink, A. S. P. Woodhouse, George Sensabaugh, and Florence Sandler.[44] For a long time we had only two studies which touched upon the political significance of *Paradise Lost* (*Milton's Royalism* by Malcolm Ross and *Chariot of Wrath* by G. Wilson Knight), as well as the mostly literary studies by Wittreich and Fixler of *Paradise Regained*.[45]

Now, since this book was largely completed, we have had Christopher Hill's ground-breaking work, *Milton and the English Revolution*. Hill is a giant in his field, and this work was inspired by my reading of his marvelous studies of Milton's period. His new work adds decisive weight to my argument for the political significance of *Paradise Lost*. Hill, moreover, had already provided me with the framework for that reading. The problematic character of Milton's allegiances becomes comprehensible within Hill's analysis that there were *two* revolutions in the seventeenth century, one made by the bourgeoisie against the monarchy, which ultimately succeeded, and one by the more egalitarian lower classes whose goals have not yet been realized. In that conflict lay the germs of the dilemma which would forever plague liberal society. If Milton remains a focus for our cultural fascination, it is because he was the first to be so profoundly plagued by it.

Despite this perspective shared with and learned from Hill, my own work differs from his in several respects. Hill attempts to document the assumptions that Milton shared with the plebeian left and thus to reveal "Milton the radical." I am looking at him instead from the strict line of demarcation drawn by that one crucial assumption that differentiates him from many of those radicals and from their true heir, William Blake. Again, Hill has clearly identified this distinction with Milton's desire "to preserve the authority of the Bible because (among other things) he wanted to preserve private property and class distinctions."[46] On almost every question, from sexual mores to the millennium, it is this issue of class perspective that informs Blake's critique of Milton.

Again, Hill and I differ on our historical vantage point. As the masterful historian of Milton's own circumstances, Hill judges him, within the strategic exigencies of the Interregnum, quite accurately as very radical indeed. But Milton as the spokesman for a new elite as well as the scourge of an old one, would have quite a different impact on later generations than on his own. By adopting Blake's critical position of hindsight and by focusing on that legacy, this study decidedly weights the dialectic in a way that highlights the limitations, not of Milton, but of his vision. Milton's political stance for his own time was extraordinary, a fact that can be readily grasped if one thinks of what the outcome would have been if I had instead compared Milton's work to that of an earlier poet like Spenser.

Finally, my study differs from Hill's in my intent, which is that of a literary critic using historical awareness, as opposed to that of a historian examining literary documents. Hill keeps his eye on the man as a whole, I, on the poem as a whole. He grasps in Milton's rhetoric a political message for his own audience; I am interested in what the historical tensions within Milton's epic contribute to its meaning for a modern reader. Within his focus, Hill gives us an original, insightful, and poignant reading of Milton's struggle with revolutionary defeat and hope in *Paradise Lost* and offers dozens of suggestions about possible political overtones in many of Milton's lines. My own purpose is to explore through Blake an ideological dimension of the epic which forces us to refocus our approach to every issue in it.

An inquiry into poetic influence presumes, finally, a theory of history. And no poet was more conscious of influence than Blake, who made the "enormous work" of understanding his roots the center of his major poems. *The Four Zoas,* as I read it, attempts to construct from the Bible and other sources the first consciously historical epic of social and cultural evolution. In its historical concerns, this study will be interested, not only in Blake's immediate context, but also in his position in relation to Milton within the the larger historical overview which *The Four Zoas* provides. And, it was not merely because accident made him a Christian, an Englishman, and thus heir to a Miltonic legacy, that Blake was led to make a concern with the vision of *Paradise Lost* the fulcrum of his own poem. Rather, he was doing what epic poets must do: proposing a myth for a new culture by challenging the myth of origins that he had inherited. Blake's emphasis on Milton recognizes the Puritan poet's central concern with transforming earlier traditions in order to give the otherwise invisible, unconscious assumptions of the capitalist era their first fully articulated form. Milton not only expressed the liberating aspects of the bourgeois revolution, but also succeeded for Blake in "giving a body to Falshood that it may be cast off forever" (*J* 12:13). History is not merely the past; it is also dragged along with us in our institutions and consciousness. Unlike those critics who would have had us reenter a seventeenth-century mentality where Milton sits as in a museum, Blake seeks to demonstrate how much of that Miltonic consciousness already informs our own.

Although many artists stand in this relation to us, Blake significantly focuses upon that "sublime Puritan," for it was, after all, the seventeenth-century English bourgeoisie that first wrapped history into a ball and rolled it towards the overwhelming questions of human development. Hence, the "Three classes of Mortal Men take their fixed destinations / And hence they overspread the Nations of the whole Earth" (*M* 6:32–33). There is no society in the world today that is not being defined by its relation to the values and institutions of Milton's England. Milton's works remain so very much alive in our own century because they express not universal wisdom, but the particular contradictions of the world in which we still live.

I agree with Hill that Milton's work should be seen in the context of his "dialogue with the radicals," a dialogue which touched precisely upon these questions of class and politics in the reassessment of Judeo-Christian tradition. By emphasizing their disputes I hope to show that it is that confrontation, rather than a failure of artistry, that disturbs the unity of *Paradise Lost.* When criticism focuses on poetry more as craft than as vision, it tends to overemphasize artistic consistency and internal harmonies in isolation from the question of what conflicts a poet was trying to resolve. Words are not magic, and too thorough a synthesis may do a disservice to reality. If anything, the enormous tensions of Milton's epic are only a greater testimony to the poetic genius which could, through its grand Christian paradoxes, hold together such conflicting social consequences. Well trained in oratorical strategies, Milton knew he must state his opponent's position before delivering his own refutation. With remarkable thoroughness, therefore, he articulates those controversies of the day which he seeks to resolve through his theological vision. Notwithstanding the grandeur of his attempt, it was inevitable that the democratic, antipatriarchal, and irreligious views which he assigned to the enemies of God, despite the massive intellectual and artistic weight Milton heaved against them, should eventually touch a responsive chord in readers approaching the poem from a new social and ideological perspective and should reorient their reading of the poem. It may even be that this subversion was abetted by Milton himself, when the "liberty" in his liberalism pushed his beliefs to the brink of their dialectical inversion, producing the confused sympathies of *Paradise Lost*. In spite of, or even because of all this, I believe the poem remains what Frank Kermode has called it, "the most perfect achievement of English poetry, perhaps the richest and most intricately beautiful poem in the world."[47]

The historical reversals that would reshape our reading of Milton's poem had already begun in Blake's day with the outbreak of Jacobin agitation. In the late eighteenth century Milton's pleas for liberty would be revived alongside the more radical demands of plebeian revolutionaries, while across the Channel in France a liberal revolution would occur under conditions that give rise to egalitarian economic aspirations which would define the political future. Blake's place in all this and the effect of this history upon his poetry was definitively established years ago in David Erdman's *Blake: Prophet Against Empire*.[48] What Hill and Edward P. Thompson have since argued is that this political role made Blake the direct descendant of those lower-class radicals of the seventeenth century.[49] The result has been to cast Blake in an ambivalent relationship to the liberalism that was so radical in Milton, a stance not unlike that which Marx and his followers would adopt towards the democratic movements in Europe. This dialectic provoked Blake to take at once the most appreciative and combative attitude towards his prophetic ancestor, his aim being both to fulfill and supplant the Miltonic legacy and, in his revisions of Milton's poems, "to rectify the errors of a thinker he loves, whose influence on him is immense."[50]

A futher distinction might clarify this ambiguity; as Wittreich demonstrates, Blake has unqualified admiration for Milton as a model of the radical artist, the transmitter of the line of prophecy. However, Blake is locked in fiercest battle with significant aspects of Milton's politics and ideology. Blake embraces the revolutionary, but criticizes the revolution. Since history is not linear, but dialectical, it is for Blake no more a matter of merely repudiating than it is of simply developing Milton's vision. In Hegel's terms, Milton must be *aufgehoben*—negated and absorbed. The bard must undergo a kind of ideological fission in which all that was liberating can be disentangled from what has proved stultifying. He must be severed from his "Selfhood" so that the "Emanation" can be redeemed—that is, the revolution accomplished. Since it is not just a matter of updating Milton, but of resolving conflicts already implicit in his own era and vision, Blake cannot simply write a coda, a sequel or a commentary; rather, he must enter the Miltonic cosmos and completely reorganize its relationships. Because Milton's epic expresses something beyond its theological doctrines—a social content which, secularized throughout the centuries, has survived its religious expression— Blake as a prophetic poet "Striving with Systems to deliver Individuals from those Systems" (*J* 11:5) could carry on his struggle to transform that society through an effort to transform Milton's myth.

In offering this proposition, we must immediately add that, for Blake, politics signifies far more than the vicissitudes of government. Blake's political vision is based on his conception of all life as social, and his perception that in making history human beings also make themselves. Nowhere, in fact, have these processes been so well documented as in the example of the seventeenth century's bourgeois saints. Their social revolution required nothing less than reconstruction of the character structure of an entire class, reformation of religious institutions and beliefs, and transformation of the family into a crucible in which these new citizens might be molded. We find evidence for this psychological revolution in the spiritual diaries and autobiographies of the seventeenth century wherein pious individuals recorded their daily struggle to "reform" themselves according to these new ideals in the face of onslaughts from the demons of outmoded feudal attitudes. Literature is a kind of diary of the race, or at least of its articulate sectors. It is the interior of history, recording alterations in modes of thought and feeling that accompany changes in social relations. *Paradise Lost* is, on one level, a polemic endorsing these new values of the middle class, but also a sensitive recording on the seismograph of Milton's consciousness of the enormous cultural trauma involved in its creation. These dimensions are explicitly explored by Blake in *The Four Zoas* when he explores the psychic structure of bourgeois civilization and the implications of Milton's conflation of his vision of the Puritan revolution with an epic revolving around a familial drama, the conflict of a rebellious woman and a satanic son with patriarchal authority. Subtitling his own epic "The torments of Love & Jealousy in The Death and Judgement of Albion the Ancient Man," Blake analyzes in it the implications of love, marriage, sex roles, and the socialization of children in the culture he inherited from Milton. From this broad vantage point I hope to be able to incorporate some of the many psychological and ideological insights already provided by critics of *Paradise Lost* and *The Four Zoas* into a new historical and materialist framework.

Although Blake stated, "I must create my own System or be enslaved by another Man's" (*J* 10:10), he was well aware that he did not create in a vacuum but at least partly by his selections and assessments within a common legacy. *The Four Zoas* approaches this "terrible eternal labour" (*J* 12:24) by following *Paradise Lost* down into the vast biblical and mythical catacombs which support it in order to trace the institutions and ideologies of modern England back to their ancient roots. Believing that humanity is primarily the embodiment of its history, Blake recounts in the story of Albion, the Eternal Man, and of "his fall into Division & his Resurrection to Unity" (*FZ* 4:4), the entire social, cultural and psychological history of the human race from its dim origins, recorded in ancient myth, to its present struggles and future possibilities.

That epic makes continuous, overlapping reference to Genesis and to *Paradise Lost* because Blake identified those works with two crucial events in human development. The first was expressed in the seminal myths of a loss of paradise and a war in heaven and involved the transformation of tribal society into "civilization." In Blake's reworking, that fall appears as a multidimensional catastrophe involving the destruction of egalitarian social relations, sexual harmony, and the unified consciousness of an Edenic primitive world. Genesis is accused of celebrating this disaster by attributing divine sanction to the values of the hierarchic civilizations of Israel, Babylon, Egypt, Greece, and Rome, built upon its ruins. Finding those same myths at the heart of *Paradise Lost*, Blake speculated that a second great cataclysm, experienced by Milton, deepened while altering the directions of the first. For Blake, the seventeenth-century revolution of the English middle class adapted and built upon religious, social, and familial institutions forged in that ancient civilization.

What makes Blake's linkage more interesting than obvious is that his dialectical and dynamic historical view sets this Genesis-Milton tradition against a countermovement which similarly conflates Milton and the Apocalypse. For Blake, "all that has existed in the space of six thousand years" is "Permanent and not lost or vanished" (*J* 13:59–60). However triumphant that civilization, primitive experience is never entirely obliterated, but survives—not only on the peripheries, but also within the mainstream—revived in a countertradition he traces through the Jewish prophets, the mythic Prometheus, Jesus, and both occult wisdom, and the millenarians' dream of reestablishing Eden upon earth.

Milton's revolutionary contradictions are thus seen to be manifest in the ways in which he assimilates that apocalyptic tradition to the strictures laid down by Genesis. Milton articulated the significance of a crucial historical conjuncture. Not only was he central in the forging of the liberal values which would underlie industrial society; at the same time, even as Puritan was meeting aborigine in the New World, Milton unconsciously reflected the beginning of a great unraveling of Old World, European culture down to its primitive roots. In his polemics for the values of his rising class, he had already uncovered the fissures within all of Western history. *Paradise Lost* expressed a unique cultural epiphany, a vantage point from which the Blakean prophet could survey both past and future, a juncture at which the ancient streams of Judeo-Christian culture were diverted through the Puritan experience into the new channels of the modern order. In Milton, Blake found both alpha and omega.

In *The Four Zoas* Blake develops his commentary on Milton, Genesis, and the Apocalypse. He weaves a continuous thread of parody, allusion, and inversion within a syncretic mythology which merges those sources with Greek, Norse, and Celtic myths, ancient history, and contemporary ethnography. From these materials, Blake builds his epic of history. Some of this context has already been noted. John Broadbent's *"Paradise Lost": Introduction* suggests anthropological themes bequeathed by Milton to Blake.[51] Northrop Frye notes Blake's concern with historical cycles. Fred Whitehead provides an excellent reading of *The Four Zoas* vision of ancient history which is in some respects like mine.[52] As I read the epic, it surveys all of history with Nights I–IV depicting the rise and fall of ancient civilization; Night V, the appearance of a radical Christianity and its subsequent distortion under feudalism; Nights VI–VIII, the rise of modern England on Miltonic foundations; and Night IX, the revolutionary future.

In this context, one can finally reconcile the Blake of Frye's *Fearful Symmetry*, delineating a "universal" human consciousness through the re-creation of world mythology and the Blake of Erdman's *Prophet Against Empire*, mythologizing the daily news in almost topical verse. For Blake's epics offer two kinds of syntheses: a reading of history in (at least) three historical frameworks—ancient, Miltonic, and contemporary—and a dialectical analysis linking sociopolitical contexts to the creation of human culture and psychology. By now, with so many interpretations of Blake's symbols worked out, it is necessary to define a perspective in which those many levels can be seen to cohere in a single, unified design.

I believe that this study goes a good part of the way towards accomplishing that task. While acknowledging a debt to Frye's deciphering of the myths, I propose to find in historical dialectics a more adequate syntheses than that offered by Frye's abstract, archetypal analogies. I intend to utilize the many parallels between Blake's and Marx's understanding of the social origin of ideas, within the context of Engels's reminder that they had never intended to imply that "the economic condition is the cause and alone active, while everything else is only a passive effect" but instead that "political, juridical, philosophic, religious, literary, artistic, etc. developments are based upon economic developments," though "all these react upon one another and upon the economic base."[53]

Of course, I should stress that my approach is only partly comprehensive; significant differences remain between Blake's views and Marx's, even if one avoids a narrow constriction of the latter. Blake is, after all, a unique puzzle. Any interpretation which reads him solely as class-conscious or materialist, or, by contrast, solely as a mystical, Platonic, or psychological visionary, leaves something out. Always something of an oxymoron, he appears to be a class-conscious, materialist mystic—whatever that might be. While I was preparing this work, a synthesis of Blake's political vision and his exploration of "higher states of consciousness" was beyond my comprehension. I have thought about it deeply and continuously since, and hope to write about it in the future. At this point, I simply wish to make it clear that I think these historical readings are ultimately consistent with Blake's spiritual vision but do not circumscribe it.

It says something about Blake's performance as a prophet that one must call not only upon Marxism, but also upon so many modern and controversial disciplines even to understand him. With regard to my selection, since I am not myself a historian, I purport neither to uncover new data nor to provide a comprehensive analysis of the many controversial issues involved in an exploration of Blake's historical vision. Rather, I have selected interpreters whose insights ‿re congenial to Blake's own perspective and, therefore, can illuminate it. My task has only been rendered possible by the fact that the periods involved have been so brilliantly treated by historians noted for their scholarly excellence as well as their political radicalism: George Thomson on ancient history, Christopher Hill on the English Revolution, and E. P. Thompson on Blake's era. To complement Blake's own interest in woman's liberation, a movement which was born in his time through the work of his friend, Mary Wollstonecraft, my work has drawn on an increasing body of literature on the family and woman's social role, as well as the critical light that the woman's movement has shed on our culture's biases. Another relevant context has been mythography, which was a major element in Blake's intellectual environment, leading him (as it later would lead Bachofen, Frazer, and Engels) to challenge orthodox views of prehistory and religion. This iconoclasm has persisted in such modern mythological scholars as Jane Ellen Harrison, Robert Graves, and Joseph Campbell, whom I have consulted. Doubtless, Blake was also influenced by an incipient ethnography; thus I have drawn upon the evolutionary anthropology pioneered by Lewis Henry Morgan and continued by Robert Briffault, Vera Gordon Childe, Leslie White, and Eleanor Leacock. Similarly, as Blake benefited from enlightenment critiques of the Bible, I have had access to historical and sociological readings.

Indeed, one should not be surprised if in pursuit of Blake's prophetic wisdom, one is led somewhat afield from the reigning consensus to an alternative tradition in scholarship as well as culture. Then, inquiries into prehistory, biblical ideology, the social history of popular movements, psychohistory, the forgotten acts of women, and the story of human evolution, gathered in many cases from the partly obliterated and largely unattended sources of myth and cult, from primitive cultures and submerged popular traditions—all can converge in an interpretation of Blake's remarkable epic.

PART I

Art Against Ideology

2

Milton and the Line of Prophecy

"Are not Religion & Politics The Same Thing?"   (J 57:10)

*W*hen in Book V of *Paradise Lost* Milton turns from the narration of human to celestial events "By lik'ning spiritual to corporal forms" (*PL* V.573), he anticipates the charge that he leaves the sphere of truth for a fantasy realm whose details he could have known neither through experience nor Scripture. Accordingly, he suggests through Raphael, "what if Earth / Be but the shaddow of Heav'n, and things therein / Each to other like, more then on earth is thought?" (*PL* V.574–76). Ironically, the Platonic doctrine that earth simulates an ideal model is turned here into its opposite, into a justification for visions of heaven extrapolated from Milton's own mundane experience. Since he then proceeds to depict a war in heaven remarkably like the civil tumults he had just been through in England, a further conclusion might logically be deduced—that the theological vision of *Paradise Lost* is a projection of England's revolutionary tragedy. If such a conclusion might have seemed alien to Milton himself, it would not to his interpreter, William Blake, for whom Milton served as the model of the revolutionary poet. However, in reading *Paradise Lost* politically, Blake came to revise the epic in his own poetic works where he became the challenger of Milton's religion and politics.

Blake explored the politics of Milton's religion, and religion in general, through the humanistic inversion by which he turned Milton's correspondences of heaven and earth on end. In *The Four Zoas* the divine appears as but a shadow of the human:

Then Man ascended mourning into the splendors of his palace
Above him rose a Shadow from his wearied intellect
. . . .
Man fell upon his face prostrate before the watry shadow
Saying O Lord whence is this change thou knowest I am nothing
. . . .
Idolatrous to his own Shadow.   (*FZ* 40:2–12)

Some fifty years later, similar sentiments would be voiced by Karl
Marx:

Man makes religion, religion does not make man. In other words,
religion is the self-consciousness and self-feeling of man who has either
not yet found himself or has already lost himself again. But *man* is no
abstract being squatting outside the world. Man is *the world of man,*
the state, society. This state, this society produce religion, a reversed
world-consciousness, because they are a reversed world.[1]

This text could almost be a prospectus for *The Four Zoas,* the epic in
which Albion has lost himself in a fall that is, at the same time, the
creation of Urizen as God, an inversion symbolized by the image of a
capsized Atlantis. Moreover, for Blake, as for Marx, this catastrophe is
no purely metaphysical mishap; rather, Urizen's ascension as both
God and king links the ideological reversal implicit in the rise of
religion to the development of social domination. Urizen's web of
religion arises as the ethereal reflex of his repressive civilization;
consequently, Blake would have agreed with Marx:

The criticism of religion is therefore in embryo the criticism of the vale
of woe, the halo of which is religion. Criticism has plucked the imaginary flowers from the chain not so that man will wear the chain
without any fantasy or consolation but so that he will shake off the
chain and cull the living flower. The criticism of religion disillusions
man to make him think and act and shape his reality like a man who
has been disillusioned and has come to reason, so that he will revolve
around himself and therefore round his true sun. Religion is only the
illusory sun which revolves round man as long as he does not revolve
round himself.[2]

Even the imagery here is incredibly Blakean, for Albion falls into
Vala's realm of torment by mistaking the flowers for the truth. His fall
is also a physical dislocation of the four Zoas from their places in an
eternal abode, a transposition of center and circumference in which
Urizen's ascent as sun-god is a displacement of the illumination that
properly belongs to human consciousness itself.

The goal of *The Four Zoas* involves man's finding himself again,
but he must do so against the twin demons of his own false conscious-

ness and his worldly oppressors. The ambiguity is stated in the headnote from Ephesians (6:12) with which Blake begins his epic: "For we wrestle not against flesh and blood, but against principalities, against powers, against the rulers of the darkness of this world, against spiritual wickedness in high places." Blake quotes in Greek; while the translation quoted here, the King James, appears to stress the workings of spiritual or psychic "powers," another emphasizes the contention "with dominion, with authority, with the blind world-rulers of this life." In radical Christian tradition, the misery of the oppressed had often been attributed to the reign of the powers and principalities of "this world," a demonic social order which would have to be overthrown by a divine redeemer. With Blake, we need not choose between spiritual and political conflicts. Rather, he turns the ambiguous biblical text to his own dialectical vision in a prophecy which will analyze how false consciousness, promoted by "spiritual wickedness in high places," has allowed these world rulers to reign. Thus, in the apocalyptic "Night the Ninth" of his epic, the overthrow of religious mystery will accompany dethronement of the tyrants whose emanation and whore religion has been. Consequently, Blake anticipates the Marxian project in which "criticism of heaven turns into criticism of the earth, the criticism of religion into criticism of right, and the criticism of theology into the criticism of politics."[3]

Milton: Millenarian Prophet

The Four Zoas opens with the proclamation of "long resounding strong heroic Verse / Marshalld in order for the day of Intellectual Battle" (*FZ* 3.2–3). In this warfare, Blake would consider himself only the latest champion in a long tradition of prophets culminating in Milton. Milton is Blake's true ancestor insofar as he too, battling against prelacy and monarchy, embraced criticism of theology as a criticism of politics and attacked, at once, spiritual wickedness in high places and the principalities and powers of his world. Blake derives the dramatic encounter between Los, the "Eternal Prophet" (*FZ* 4.70), and Urizen, the "primeval Priest" (*U* 2.1), which is at the heart of all his epics, from Milton's Puritan opposition to the bishops of English state-religion, as well as from those ancient Hebrew sources which were their common inspiration. In approaching their relationship we must understand, on the one hand, how Milton served as the model of a revolutionary poet, and, on the other hand, how an ideological breakthrough caused Blake to become the prophetic challenger of Milton's own religion and politics.

Milton left no doubt that he was assuming a prophetic mantle in his poetry as well as his prose. In a passage noted by Blake (PB 635) from *The Reason of Church-Government,* Milton compared his inspiration to Isaiah's calling "by devout prayer to that eternall Spirit who can enrich with all utterance & knowledge & sends out his Seraphim with the hallow'd fire of his Altar to touch and purify the lips of whom he pleases." In this same work, abandoning the "quiet and still air of delightfull studies" "to imbark in a troubl'd sea of noises and hoars disputes," (YP I.820–22). Milton compares himself to that reluctant scourge of the Hebrew establishment, "the sad prophet Jeremiah." Lamenting with his forebear, "Wo is me my mother that thou hast born me a man of strife and contention" (YP I.803), he plunges in 1642 into the struggle against the bishops which was to trigger the English civil war.

It was in this revolutionary context that Milton rediscovered the conceptions of spiritual warfare which Blake was to inherit. He finds himself in the company of Jesus, who "came not to bring peace but a sword" (Matt. 10:34), and the apostles who found "in the discharge of their commission that they are made the greatest variance and offence, a very sword and fire both in house and City over the whole earth" (YP I.802). His own polemical vocation is seen as a charge from Saint Paul "that [he] might'st warre a good warfare, bearing [himself] constantly and faithfully in the Ministery, which in the I to the Corinthians is also call'd a warfare" (YP I.758–59).

Behind this conception lay the images of a millenarian tradition based upon the Book of Revelation whose prophecy had possessed a perpetual fascination for Christian revolutionaries. In its final battle, Christ would defeat a reincarnation of Satan called Antichrist, after which he would establish a reign of peace and justice—a millennium in which he would rule with his saints upon earth. Milton identifies his own prophetic mission with that of John of Patmos (Rev. 11:9–10) whom "that mysterious book of Revelation which the greatest Evan-gelist was bid to eat, as it had been some eye-brightning electuary of knowledge, and foresight, though it were sweet in his mouth, and in the learning, it was bitter in his belly; bitter in the denouncing" (YP I.803). He calls up the image of the conquering Christ as evidence that the true faith has not only spiritual power but political significance too for undoing the mischief that an anti-Christian prelacy does in the state: "The Gospell being the hidden might of Christ, as hath been heard, hath ever a victorious power joyn'd with it, like him in the Revelation that went forth on the white Horse with his bow and his crown conquering, and to conquer" (YP I.850).

While the sword proceeding from the mouth of Christ is a sword of truth, Puritans would find in the Book of Revelation a prophecy of actual military confrontations as well. Milton shared with his compatriots this belief in an Antichrist at large in England with whom the battle predicted in Scripture was at hand. William Haller documents the cosmic conflict depicted in Revelation 12 as the central metaphor of reforming Puritan preachers.[4] They saw a continuing battle being fought out not only in the Christian soul, but also in a social world which was "a great field of God in which Michael and his angels fight the dragon and his angels." Sermons like Richard Bernard's "Bible Battells," John Downame's "The Christian Warfare," and William Gouge's "The Whole Armour of God" had accustomed Puritans to conceive of their spiritual task in political and military terms.[5] Bernard had concluded that "God is pleased to be called a man of war"[6] and that the just, confronted with the forces of Satan himself, were prepared to rout such enemies in a most militant manner.

Increasingly in the seventeenth century, this biblical imagery took on literal connotations. Scholars like Thomas Brightman and Joseph Mede studied Revelation with an eye to its contemporary significance, and hundreds less scholarly ventured predictions that the millennium would soon begin in England.[7] Milton himself, in his early enthusiasm, had spoken of Christ as a "shortly-expected King" (YP I.616). Preachers had proclaimed that Parliament's cause was God's cause, and the government of Charles I with its Romish bishops was a fifth column of the papist Antichrist. "I do not conclude that Prelaty is Antichristian," Milton writes, "for what need I? the things themselves conclude it" (YP I.850). The New Model Army had marched forth inspired by military examples in the *Souldier's Pocket-Bible* to fight the "Lord's Battells" against an anti-Christian aristocracy. The Fifth Monarchy Men believed that God had willed the beheading of Charles I in order to clear the throne for "King Jesus."[8]

In this context, Milton's declaration in *Areopagitica* of a commitment to fight the "wider wars of truth" (YP II.562) is an engagement to revolutionary struggle. He consistently defines his own role in relation to the actual battles involving his countrymen. The metaphor of "intellectual war" conveyed to Blake has behind it Milton's perception of the concrete relationship between his polemical battles and those of Cromwell's army. Thus in the *Second Defence* he justifies his choice of a literary vocation over a military one:

> For I did not avoid the toils and dangers of military service without rendering to my fellow citizens another kind of service that was more

useful and no less perilous. . . . Having from my early youth been especially devoted to the liberal arts, with greater strength of mind than of body, I exchanged the toils of war . . . for those labors which I better understood . . . that truth defended by arms be also defended by reason.

(YP IV.552–53)

When we recall that Milton is functioning here as a spokesman somewhat analogous to our secretary of state, writing the defenses partly to dissuade Europeans from providing military aid to the monarchy, we realize that we are dealing with more than a metaphor.

Moreover, Milton understood perfectly well, as did Cromwell, that a conviction of the righteousness of one's cause was the crucial weapon in the arsenal of revolutionaries, for he had noted in his *Commonplace Book* that "the cause of valour [is] a good conscience" (YP I.374). His task, therefore, was an integral aspect of the actual civil wars, inspiring the parliamentary forces, winning them allies from among the uncommitted and neutralizing potential opposition. His combative prose furnishes the army's deeds "so gloriously performed under God's guidance with a defence against jealous slander (a duty second in importance to theirs alone, and one in which the sword and implements of war are of no avail, but which requires other weapons)" (YP IV. 305). In the context of interregnum England, images of spiritual warfare provide a justification for, not an alternative to, political struggle.

Clearly it is this radical Christian tradition that Blake wishes to call back to life in *Milton* when he evokes the bard with images of the apocalyptic Christ appearing in his chariot of fire and sings,

> I will not cease from Mental Fight
> Nor shall my Sword sleep in my hand:
> Till we have built Jerusalem
> In England's green & pleasant Land. (*M* 1.13–16)

Blake understood, of course, that images of heavenly warfare had acquired quite opposite meanings, for, as he writes in *The Marriage of Heaven and Hell*, "this history [of the conquest and fall of Satan] has been adopted by both parties" (*MHH* 5). Saint Augustine had muted the revolutionary impact of the Book of Revelation by declaring the city of God to be a present rather than a future reality, existing in a visible church compatible with the existing social order upon which it exerted a reforming moral influence. Once the tensions between the kingdom of God and the kingdoms of earth had thus been softened, feudalism was able to claim the church as an ally of the state. Then, the conquering Christ was reinterpreted as the arm of divinely appointed authorities suppressing the demonic revolts of chronically disobedient men.

These antagonistic versions of Christian symbolism underlie the antinomies of *The Marriage of Heaven and Hell*, where the Gospel has been so inverted by angels of the ecclesiastical establishment that its true meaning must now appear as a Bible of Hell. Within this context Blake offers his dialectical evaluation of Milton. In presenting the Messiah as a "governor," a punitive "accuser" (as Satan is called in the Book of Job), Milton himself perpetrated such a reversal. The very crux of Milton's vision, Blake grasped, lay in that unique conjunction in *Paradise Lost* where a revolutionary version of the war in heaven merges with its repressive opposite. Nevertheless, Blake insists, Milton's radical sympathies broke through, for he "wrote in fetters when he wrote of Angels & God, and at liberty when of Devils & Hell." Stalemated in debate over the validity of this aesthetic observation, criticism has usually overlooked the significance of Blake's political metaphor which, in identifying Milton as one who was "a true Poet and of the Devils party" (*MHH* 5), suggests that the tensions in his art derive from his revolutionary allegiances.

The implication would not have been lost on some of Milton's own contemporaries who were accustomed to seeing opponents of the established order as in league with Satan himself. Richard Baxter, a moderate Puritan divine, had characteristically complained that "all this stir of the republicans is but to make the seed of the serpent to be the sovereign rulers of the earth."⁹ The radical print shop of Giles Calvert from which issued so many of the radical diatribes of the civil war was denounced as "the forge of the devil from whence so many blasphemous, scandalous pamphlets for many years past have spread over the land."¹⁰ Milton's own detractors made it clear what they believed to be the source of his works. He earned his place as a divorcer in the devil's party as definitively catalogued by Thomas Edwards in *Gangraena, or A Catalogue and Discovery of Many of the Errours, Heresies, Blasphemies and pernicious practices of the Sectaries of this time.* An attack on the *First Defence* branded Milton and his parliamentary allies as "inhuman creatures inspired by the Devil,"¹¹ while a Restoration attack was entitled *Salamasius His Dissection and Confutation of the Diabolical Rebel Milton.*¹²

Although by Blake's time the growth of rationalism had enabled a discussion of politics in other than religious language, the evangelical revival of the 1790s led to similar methods for discrediting the radical opposition. In the turbulence of the reform agitation of that day, the tavern keepers of Manchester were persuaded to deny their meeting rooms "to any club or societies . . . that have a tendency to put in force what the Infernals so ardently devotedly wish for, namely the destruction of this country."[13] Blake must have had many friends similarly considered demonic by the righteous defenders of George III—for example, that sinister atheist Paine whom Blake defended against Bishop Watson as "either a Devil or an Inspired man" (PB 603).

The Politics of Paradise Lost

Blake's emphasis on the connection between politics and poetry in Milton is faithful to the Puritan's own attitude towards his literary vocation. Milton's plan to write an epic is not conceived in aged retreat, but at the height of his political passion. In *The Reason of Church-Government* he projects a work that will be "doctrinal and exemplary to a Nation" (YP I.815) and will both celebrate and help to create his nation's greatness so "That what the greatest and choycest wits of *Athens, Rome,* or modern *Italy,* and those Hebrews of old did for their country, I . . . might doe for mine" (YP I. 812). Emphasizing the role of the poet in preparing the consciousness of his compatriots for political action, he affirms, "These abilities . . . are the inspired guift of God . . . and are of power beside the office of a pulpit, to imbreed and cherish in a great people, the seeds of vertu and publick civility" (YP I.816). The work he conceives will "celebrate . . . the deeds and triumphs of just and pious Nations" and "deplore the general relapses of Kingdoms and States from justice" (YP I.817).

Composition of this epic, although consummated during the Restoration, must have proceeded through all the years of revolutionary tumult. Moreover, when Milton looks back over this polemical prose from the vantage point of 1654, he sees it more as a fulfillment of his epic mission than as a digression from it. For "just as the epic poet . . . undertakes to extol, not the whole life of the hero whom he proposes to celebrate in his verse, but usually one event of his life (the exploits of Achilles at Troy, let us say, or the return of Ulysses, or the arrival of Aeneas in Italy) . . . so let it suffice me too . . . to have celebrated at least one heroic achievement of my countrymen" (YP IV.i.685). Thus as the inspiration behind the poetry and the prose is the same, so we might conclude that the same great event underlies the intellectual warfare of the *Defences* and the heavenly warfare of *Paradise Lost.*

This was, in fact, a more common assumption in the eighteenth and early nineteenth centuries than it is today. Milton's politics then was still too lively an issue to be ignored, and the tendency of Milton criticism to divide into warring camps occurred along more admittedly partisan lines, with a Tory antagonist like Dr. Johnson on one side and such Whig enthusiasts as Thomas Hollis and Francis Blackburne on the other. John Toland, one of Milton's early biographers, believed the design of *Paradise Lost* was "to display the different Effects of Liberty and Tyranny."[14] In 1763 and 1764, a debate raged in the *London Chronicle* over the nature of the poem's political allegory. According to a Tory advocate, "Milton by the rebellious spirits under the conduct of their infernal chief meant to characterize the Parliament's forces under Cromwell." Faced with the obvious conflict between such a reading and Milton's stated views, the writer goes on to interpret the poem as a recantation. It must signify "a confutation of the error of his pen," for "how could he better refute the good old cause he was such a partisan of and such an advocate for than by making the rebellion in the poem resemble it, and giving the same characteristics to the apostate angels as were applicable to his rebel brethren?"[15] A Whig charges in rebuttal that "the Tory plan, where man assumes a right of dominion over man, was nearer related to Satan's aim of setting himself in glory above his peers."[16] This writer then proposes a series of connections between Abdiel and Milton, Nimrod and Charles I, Bacchus and Charles II, and even the Messiah with Cromwell.

A purely allegorical approach to *Paradise Lost* is obviously too limited, but the fundamental insistence made by this earlier criticism on a unity of art and politics in Milton is sound. Our own era has tended to attribute to Milton a far more total recantation, a retreat in his poetry from all the political concerns to which he had dedicated his life. It is undoubtedly true, as Christopher Hill documents, that for many partisans of that good old cause, the Restoration occasioned a turning inward. But it is also true, as Mao Tse-tung was never loath to point out, that defeated political tendencies often retreat into culture, not as a mode of surrender, but of survival, as a means of preserving their goals for revival at a more opportune moment. There is little reason to believe that the man who was still producing plans for a commonwealth on the eve of Charles II's recall to London, when the most militant were silent and in hiding, would ever really wave good-bye to all that and turn detachedly to the "deeper" questions of metaphysics. The failure of the revolution doubtless changed the political emphasis of Milton's epic, but that failure did not render it apolitical. *Paradise Lost* is best read as a criticism of certain aspects of the civil war, as an effort to encourage attitudes that would be indispensable to the achievement of "liberty" at some future time.

Religion and Politics in the Interregnum

Any other interpretation misses, as Blake surely did not, what was at stake politically in the arena of theology and ethics. Marx has written that in epochs of social transformation such as Milton's,

> with the change of the economic foundation the entire immense super-
> structure is more or less rapidly transformed. In considering such
> transformations, a distinction should always be made between the
> material transformation of the economic conditions of production,
> which can be determined with the precision of natural science, and the
> legal, political, religious, aesthetic, or philosophic—in short, ideologi-
> cal forms in which men become conscious of this conflict and fight it
> out.[17]

In few fields of scholarship has that insight borne more fruit than in the analysis of what, significantly, has alternately been termed the "Puritan" and the "bourgeois" revolution of seventeenth-century England. Scholars such as R. H. Tawney, C. H. George, A. L. Morton, Michael Walzer, Keith Thomas, Don Wolfe, and, especially, Christopher Hill have demonstrated the connections between a ris-ing middle class and alterations in politics, religion, and even human psychology.[18]

There was a great deal going on in Milton's period which indicates that his contemporaries were aware, even if we are not, of the political and social significance of conflicting ideas. With ideology, for cen-turies, having been under the domination of the church, with the Bible having been the common library of lords and peasants, masters and servants, aristocrats and commoners, it is no wonder that their battles should take place on theological turf. Until that time, the church had possessed a complete monopoly over the entire realm of communications, for the local parish had been simultaneously the center for worship, education, and the dissemination of news. Its control was clearly a question of political power. Queen Elizabeth, as the saying went, used to "tune her pulpits"; parsons were instructed to end their sermons with admonishments toward obedience to the crown. Similarly, the concern of James I for imposing religious orthodoxy did not stem merely from a personal religious fanaticism, but from an indisputable political logic—as he summed it up suc-cintly, "no bishops, no king."

Such were the conditions that so inflamed Milton's contempt for the prelates, "whose Pulpit stuff . . . hath bin the Doctrin and per-petual infusion of servility and wretchedness to all thir hearers" (YP III.344). It was in this context that his espousal of religious toleration could lead to such revolutionary politics. Thus, battles raged over whether there should be a ritual priesthood or a preaching ministry; whether only Scripture or also sermons at services; whether congregations could be allowed to choose their ministers, or a Christian his congregation; whether sermons might be followed by discussions or given by the laity and, if so, did that mean by servants? By women? At stake was the question of whether others besides the aristocratic bishops would be allowed to take ideological weapons into their own hands. We must imagine a time when civil control had broken down, and the people were not only demonstrating and petitioning Parliament but also organizing into armed militia, so that the fears of the upper classes were well justified. Thus, to Milton's dismay, everyone from the royalist nobility to the Presbyterian Parliament agreed that a centralized church must impose its moral and theological discipline upon the people. Let the "rabble" speak for itself, conservatives warned, and before you know it, democratic ecclesiastical doctrines will teach "some *Wat. Tylers* Chaplaine, to preach againe upon that text: *When* Adam *dolve and* Eve *span* / Who was then a Gentleman?"[19] Which, of course, is exactly what happened.

Parliament could not defeat the king without mobilizing the support of a broad population hitherto excluded from the public arena. Lay persons began to organize themselves into independent congregations where discussion easily passed from religion to politics— the more lowly the congregation, the more unorthodox and incendiary the views. Soon the countryside was being canvassed by hundreds of "mechanick preachers" who spread their own versions of Christian liberty. They took as their precedent the apostles, described by William Dell as "poor, illiterate mechanic men" who "turned the world upside down,"[20] which these radicals in their turn proceeded to do. For, from the perspective of the lower classes, the Bible seemed to offer a message quite different from that received by the appointed parsons of the established church. Consequently, as Dell explains, the respectable came "to abuse the precious saints of God with these and other reproaches": "Oh, these are the men that would turn the world upside down, that make the nation full of tumults and uproars, that work all the disturbance of church and state. It is fit such men and congregations should be suppressed, . . . that we may have truth and peace and government again."[21]

Therefore, laws were passed making it illegal for "intruders," who found themselves moved by the spirit, to rise and refute the sermons of the official clergy. And a Blasphemy Act was adopted to suppress lower-class sects who were spreading radical ideas of an indwelling spirit, economic equality, and moral liberty, that old demonic trilogy: atheism, communism, and free love.

The intellectual war was raging, and it resulted in literal battles for the pulpit as well. For example, nowhere did this ferment get further out of hand than in the New Model Army where it had been legitimized by Cromwell's practice of recruiting common men along ideological lines, "a plain russet-coated captain that knows what he fights for, and loves what he knows."[22] Soon these zealous soldiers of Christ had organized themselves into independent congregations of "armed saints." Nothing better typifies the unity of religion and politics at this time than the manner in which, in the process of routing the royalist foe, this rank and file marched about the countryside tearing down altar rails and other symbols of hierarchic religion and climbing into pulpits to preach their own version of the Gospel.

It was, furthermore, an increasingly radical Gospel they preached. By 1648, army congregations had yielded political councils pledged to achieving by force of arms a Christian liberty based on manhood suffrage and a democratic constitution. In 1649, some such soldiers entered a church at Walton-on-Thames and announced that tithes, the Sabbath, ministers, magistrates, and the Gosepl itself were abolished by Christ who would now speak directly through his saints. Their Gospel was apparently that Good News so revered by lower-class believers, for on perhaps the same spring Sunday in the same rural parish, the communist Gerrard Winstanley led his followers out to dig upon its waste in common and so bring back Eden upon the earth.[23]

In the early 1640s, while Thomas Edwards was hysterically hunting down these heresies and arguing in *Gangraena* for suppression of the sects, Milton was enthusiastically battling for their freedom. Looking out upon the ideological ferment others would call anarchy, he expostulates in *Areopagitica* that "the time seems come, wherein . . . all the Lords people are become Prophets" (YP II.555–56). It is with this echo from the Book of Numbers that Blake will introduce the bard's return as the inspirer of true poetry in his epic *Milton*.

The Line of Prophecy from Milton to Blake

The Puritan faith in prophecy is based upon a doctrine of direct inspiration from the Bible which had a dual significance. Against a public, legal, ritualistic Catholicism, which offered mankind salvation through the collective efforts of the church, this doctrine fostered a meditative introspection that located grace in the heart of the individual believer. In Milton, this idea verges upon the belief in every man as his own church. Such a conception underlies his vision of the vatic poet in "Il Penseroso" (169–72)—a solitary genius, conversing with spirits amid the "dim religious light" and ethereal choirs of a cathedral of the mind. Aspiring to "The Hairy Gown and Mossy Cell, / Where [he] may sit and rightly spell, / Of every Star that Heav'n doth shew, / And every Herb that sips the dew," Milton describes his own quest for more than natural knowledge in images of astrology and magic. Thus his "prophetic strain" tends to become the province of a spiritual elite which abandons the mundane considerations of ordinary life for "ecstasies" of a higher wisdom, hermeneutic mysteries that unveil spiritual significances beneath the hieroglyphs of nature.

Inheriting this sense of prophecy from the romantics, we have tended to overlook its social significance. For when the Puritans claimed that "every one is made a king, priest and prophet,"[24] it was because they thereby overthrew in a single tenet the weight of the orthodoxy of centuries and cleared the slate for more relevant ideologies. Now a rising class of people would be able to find a new ethos written in their hearts which released them from the proscriptions of the old order. Unsurprisingly, the inner voice spoke to them of the economic, political, and religious freedom that was their prime desire.[25]

Moreover, as Christopher Hill documents, during the revolutionary decades, the role of prophet became "almost a new profession . . . as interpreter of the stars, or of traditional popular myths, or of the Bible."[26] Amid such momentous changes, the obscure predictions of a book like the Apocalypse were studied not only by scholars like Pareus, Mede, and Milton, but also by artisans and vagrants who, suddenly propelled into public life, turned to the Bible as the only tool they had "in order to understand and so be able to control what was going to happen."[27] Prophets held forth in barns and pubs and on village greens. Itinerants like Arise Evans or the Fifth Monarchy Men arose to interpret their world by biblical lights. And these beliefs, if nothing else, confirmed their own desires and gave them revolutionary confidence; for as John Selden noted, "Dreams and Prophecies do thus much good; They make a man go on with boldness and courage, upon a Danger or a Mistress."[28] The Puritans prophesied the fall of their enemies while mobilizing to overthrow them.

This highly politicized conception of prophecy is taken over by William Blake who placed it at the center of a native English tradition inherited from the Hebrews by ancient minstrels and perpetuated by Milton. In this tradition, the bard was, above all, an antagonist to tyrants. Blake celebrates such insurgent art in his engraving of Gray's *The Bard*, a tale in which Edward I has ordered the execution of those Welsh poets who through their lays kept alive a spirit of resistance.

One escapes to predict the downfall of Edward's line, to "weave the warp, and weave the woof, / The winding sheet of Edward's race." "Weaving the winding sheet of Edward's race by means of sounds of spiritual music . . . and articulate speech," Blake extols as "a bold, and daring, and most masterly conception" (PB 531–32).

When Blake returns poetry to its Miltonic norms, therefore, he is returning to what he sees as a native English tradition of radical art from which most eighteenth-century artists had deviated. Milton's literary revival was just one element in the reclamation of a popular legacy that accompanied the return of the people's own voice to public affairs in the 1790s movements. After the Restoration, that voice had been silenced, and the literary culture of the eighteenth century, as we have come to know it, was left to in-fighting between the landed and moneyed classes. Since between them the major issues had already been settled, the dialectic receded in art, and little remained but for the elegant poets of the court and the country estate to embody the compromise of 1688 in complacently universalized and classicized verse. With Pope singing, "*Whatever is, is right,*" "mental warfare" disappeared from literature as from politics.

Blake's condemnation of these poets for setting up "the Stolen and Perverted Writings of Homer & Ovid: of Plato & Cicero against the sublime of the Bible" (*M* 1), moreover, is no mere arbitrary aesthetic prejudice. From Bunyan to Blake, from Christian's allegorical conflicts with such aristocratic opponents as the Lord Carnal Delight, the Lord Luxurious, the Lord Desire of Vain Glory, my old Lord Lechery, and Sir Having Greedy, to Blake's socialist Jerusalem, the radical tradition had survived within the language of Christian dissent. Historian E. P. Thompson argues that the hopes of the Puritan left, when they could no longer be realized in the kingdom without, persisted at least as hopes in a kingdom within, nurtured in the Nonconformist chapels. Salvaging from the radical program of their failed revolution only liberty of conscience, this, at least, enabled humble believers to maintain "a kind of slumbering Radicalism—preserved in the imagery of sermons and tracts and in democratic forms of organization—which might, in any more hopeful context, break into fire once more."[29]

The Revival of Religious Radicalism

Among the lower classes, the ideas of the seventeenth-century revolutionaries must have survived to form the subculture from which Blake drew his inspiration. After all, as A. L. Morton points out, it had only been three or four generations since the followers of

Cromwell and Lilburne had walked about London. The city of Blake's boyhood must have contained many old men whose acquaintances had seen and talked with the earlier radicals.[30] Memories would have been embodied in religious, if not political, offshoots. John Wesley noted in his *Journal* of 1768 that he found in a Somerset woollen town "a mixture of men of all opinions, Anabaptists, Quakers, Presbyterians, Arians, Antinomians, Moravians and what not."[31] Sects like the Sandemanians continued the primitive Christian practice of community of goods and at least one member of their congregation, Thomas Spence, was inspired thereby to preach a radical Jacobin gospel which eschewed monarchy, aristocracy, and private property in land. Similarly, the Moravians kept Winstanley's communist faith. In 1774 they set out to create the first Shaker communes in America.[32]

The language of millenarianism also survived. According to Thompson, "The Bolton Society from which the Shakers originated was presided over by Mother Jane Wardley who paced the meeting room 'with a mighty trembling', declaiming 'Repent. For the Kingdom of God is at Hand. The new heaven and new earth prophesied of old is about to come.' "[33] Muggletonians still congregated in London where Blake might have known them. They were the followers of Lodowick Muggleton and John Reeve who had declared themselves in the 1650s to be the "two witnesses" of the Apocalypse. It is significant that Blake uses the image in *Milton* (22:55–66) and that he identifies the witnesses as Wesley and Whitfield whose Methodism brought the Christian promise of salvation out of the established churches into the communities of oppressed miners and weavers. With the return of political radicalism, a Christian symbolism which had preserved the aspirations of the lowly in an otherworldly guise began to reveal its implications for this world again. When Thomas Hardy, a shoemaker and the secretary of the radical London Corresponding Society, recalled his trial for high treason, it was in the language of the Book of Kings, so pregnant with meaning to ordinary Englishmen: "What portion have we in David? neither have we inheritance in the son of Jesse; to your tents O Israel. . . . So Israel rebelled against the House of David unto this day."[34] Blake may have refrained from joining his fellow engraver, William Sharp, in becoming a disciple of the dubious prophets of his own time, Johanna Southcott and Richard Brothers, but both he and Brothers denounced the English state for its counter-revolutionary attacks against France and regarded repression of reformers at home as the Great Beast of the Book of Revelation.[35]

Nor is it surprising in this context that, under the impact of events in America and France, when a movement revived in England to complete the aborted democratic revolution of the previous century, Milton should be among its greatest heroes. "Milton! thou shouldst be living at this hour," Wordsworth exclaimed in a moment of political fervor. And when Dr. Richard Price hailed those auspicious events abroad and called for English counterparts, he pointed to Milton as the forerunner of "those revolutions" in which men were "now exulting" because he had instructed them in the ways of liberty and inspired them for "the overthrow of priestcraft and tyranny."[36] In this spirit, Blake complements Wordsworth's invocation with his own call for Milton to be resurrected through a new outburst of revolutionary art based upon a radical reading of the Bible.

Milton's World Turned Upside Down

Part of the movement which harkened to Milton's polemical voice and absorbed his politicized Christian symbols would nevertheless reject the limitations of his liberal program and the sober middle-class saints with whom it had once been associated. By Blake's era, as Christopher Hill puts it, Milton's nation of prophets had become a nation of shopkeepers.[37] When radicalism revived in the late eighteenth century, it would be under the auspices of those who had been Milton's leftist opposition, the great-great-grandchildren of the artisan Levellers. In the constitutional societies, these English sansculottes, barred from political life with Cromwell's suppression of the army rank and file, once again came into their own. Now humble mechanics might be not only a radical fringe tailing after the bourgeois leadership. In France, the *menu peuple* were a powerful enough force to overthrow a government and impose the Jacobin program of 1793. In England the same were organizing and educating themselves in societies for parliamentary reform that boasted of enlisting "members unlimited" and demonstrated in masses of over a hundred thousand strong for the old Leveller program of universal manhood suffrage. Again the stirrings of class struggle threw all conventional ideas into question. Thompson recounts how Paine's *Rights of Man* struck with an ideological force unprecedented since the spread of the Gospel itself and, according to the frightened upper classes, was soon in the hands of "every cutler in Sheffield."[38]

During Blake's years, moreover, the inchoate "lower classes" of preindustrial England had begun to develop into something more than a motley collection of dislocated peasants, vagabonds, servants, and itinerant laborers. In the first quarter of the nineteenth century, a working class emerged, forged in the socialized labor of the new factories and the cooperation of its own trade unions and friendly societies. Out of the experience of this working class, a new program for freedom arose. That "new song" is first articulated by Blake as an apocalypse of liberated common labor through the persona of a "prophet" who forges his vision in iron amid the din of industry and hence provides a link between an earlier and later radicalism.

Prophecy and Class Consciousness

Behind Blake's particular conception of prophecy there is another which arises from Milton's but goes beyond it. Henry Parker had enunciated it in the Puritan revolution when he proclaimed that "vox populi was ever reverenced as Vox Dei."[39] This tradition was related also to a belief that "God hath chosen the weak things of this world to confound the things that are mighty" (1 Cor. 1:27). When Milton interprets this text, as in his *Treatise of Civil Power*, it becomes a metaphor, a contrast between a laity's conscience and the political authority of a state church. More radical implications could, however, be found there. One tenet of the millenarian tradition which Milton ignores held that the poor would be God's agents in the final crisis when they would actually supplant their superiors. "The voice that will come of Christ's reigning," Thomas Goodwin preached, "is like to begin from those that are multitude, that are so contemptible, especially in the eyes and account of Antichrist's spirits and the prelacy."[40] The idea was taken up by Leveller Richard Overton who writes "that it must be the poore, the simple and meane things of this earth that must confound the mighty and the strong."[41] When Overton voices these sentiments in *An Appeale from the degenerate Representative Body the Commons of England . . . to the Body Represented, the free people in general . . .* (1647), that is, to the rebellious rank and file of the New Model Army, we are dealing with ideas of prophecy, government, revolution, and, indeed, "the people" which go far beyond the limits of Milton's views. The author of *Areopagitica* came to lose some of the enthusiasm of those early years when he had hoped all the Lord's people might be prophets, but it should also be noted that he never considered all people to be the "Lord's people," but instead only the saintly elite of a reforming middle class—certainly never the broad audience addressed by Overton. It was inherent in the nature of Milton's revolutionary faith that he could only become increasingly appalled at the claims made in God's name by the untutored multitude.

Blake argues, consequently, that Milton must himself be redeemed; his perception of prophecy must be purged of its supernatural connotations and be both democratized and humanized. He dramatizes this conversion in plate 32 of *Milton* where the poet "oft sat upon the Couch of Death & oft conversed / In vision & dream beatific with the Seven Angels of the Presence" (*M* 32:1–2). Blake calls upon him to turn his back "upon these Heavens builded on cruelty" (*M* 32:3), that is, upon the privilege of an elite sanctioned by special access to divine wisdom. The angels explain, in a critique of such supernatural religion, that they only received their celestial or "Druid" form after Satan had "made himself a God &, destroyed the Human Form Divine" (*M* 32:13).

Blake's true prophet must eschew Miltonic appeals to God and acknowledge an inspiration that derives from the "Human Form . . . combined in Freedom & holy Brotherhood" (*M* 32:14–15), which Blake interprets marginally as Parker's "multitudes Vox Populi." The metaphysical delusions that ascribe the truth to transcendent realms remove it from the reach of ordinary people. Blake brings heavenly inspiration back down to earth in order to democratize it and locate its prophetic impulse in the political clarity of the common man. For, he writes, "Every honest man is a Prophet he utters his opinion of both private & public matters Thus If you go on So the result is So" (PB 606–07). Prophecy becomes the understanding of the ways of history by those who have no reason to distort. On this simple peg, William Blake will rest his harp.

Milton's vision had been based upon a political idealism, which, as idealism, had been unconscious of its own class biases; Blake's, as he expresses it in *Visions of the Daughters of Albion*, is class consciousness itself:

> Does he who condemns poverty, and he who turns with abhorrence
> From usury: feel the same passion or are they moved alike?
> How can the giver of gifts experience the delights of the merchant?
> How the industrious citizen the pains of the husbandman.
> How different far the fat fed hireling with hollow drum;
> Who buys whole corn fields into waste, and sings upon the heath:
> How different their eye and ear! how different the world to them!
> (*VDA* 5:10–16)

The world appears differently to those who would only live and labor in it, sharing its gifts, and to those merchants, usurers, and hirelings who view everything as commodities to be turned into profit. For the farmer, the corn field is his home, his community, his ancestors' legacy, a cultivated and personalized bit of nature whose fruitfulness is his harvest of life. For the hireling, it is just a piece of real estate, and its human families are only so many rents. The profiteers claim their gains in righteous complacency as the reward of the "industrious citizen" and, while turning abundance into waste and driving the poor into destitution, pass judgment on their want. Blake understood that such ideological reversals were at the heart of a culture built upon exploitation. "With what sense," he asks, "does the parson claim the labour of the farmer?" (*VDA* 5:17). No sense at all, he suggests; its justification must be manufactured:

> What are his nets & gins & traps. & how does he surround him
> With cold floods of abstraction, and with forests of solitude
> To build him castles and high spires. where kings & priests may dwell.
>
> (*VDA* 5:18–20)

"State Religion"

The English parson provides an apt symbol of the process by which exploitation is defended and mystified. He was usually the son of a local landlord who paid his son's way through the university and then bestowed upon him a "living" provided by tithes extracted from his tenant farmers. The parson's right to the tenants' earnings was guaranteed by the state into which the church was thoroughly integrated. With rare exceptions, such preachers would, in return, urge upon their parishioners belief in a divine sanction for the status quo. Thus they provided intellectual foundations for an order of privilege, building "castles & high spires. where kings & priests may dwell" (*VDA* 5:20).

Such a man, for example, was Blake's enemy, Bishop Watson of Landaff, who, having become wealthy on tithes, was moved to preach his notorious sermon "On the Wisdom and Goodness of God in having made both Rich and Poor." Blake lambasted the bishop's *Apology for the Bible*, insisting that, since Christian ministers had degenerated into mere mouthpieces for the powerful, the prophetic spirit was henceforth to be found among radical unbelievers. "It appears to me Now that Tom Paine is a better Christian than the Bishop," Blake concluded, but declined to publish his thoughts because "to defend the Bible in this year 1798 would cost a man his life" (PB 609,601).

Similar experiences with counter-revolutionary bishops had inspired the distinction which pervades Milton's prose between the true prophet and those false prophets who had taunted Elijah (YP I.903) and against whom Christ had warned his apostles (YP I.931). To a great extent Blake's ideological critique draws upon Milton's ideas and images. From Milton he takes the attack on tithes and the denunciation of those "Dishonest Designing Knaves who in hopes of a good living adopt the State religion" (PB 605). Judging "that pride and covetousnesse are the sure markes of those false Prophets which are to come," in *An Apology against a Pamphlet [Apology for Smectymnuus]* Milton castigates the worldliness of those bishops "Who possesse huge Benefices for lazie performances. . . . Who ingrosse many pluralities under a *non-resident* and slubbring dispatch of soules" (YP I.952) and turn the church from its task of spiritual edification to the gratification of the clergy's own avarice and ambition. He also anticipated Blake's attack on the collaboration of priests and tyrants in the image in *Eikonoklastes* of the Whore of Babylon (that "spiritual Babel" of the prelates) who fornicates with the kings of Europe, an image repeated in *The Four Zoas* where Blake depicts the church as "Harlot of the Kings of Earth" (*FZ* 111:6).

Liberty of Conscience—Political and Economic

If the language is the same, nevertheless the analysis diverges, with Blake going far beyond Milton's antagonism toward Erastianism. For Milton, the literal enemy is "state religion," the privileged status of the Anglican church, while Blake extends that opposition to all political perversions of intellect. Where Milton condemns the bishop's subordination of a spiritual ministry to their pursuit of riches, Blake charges that all clamoring for profit, even within the secular spheres of merchant and banker, ultimately produces a corrupted culture. Where Milton draws a line between true and false religion, Blake finds a line between classes. Thus Blake alleges in *The Everlasting Gospel* that the respectable tend to remold Christ in their own image. "Was Christ gentle," he rebukes, "or did he / Give any marks of Gentility?" (PB 514). Different classes, he contends, worship what amount to being different gods: "Both read the Bible day & night / But thou readst black where I read white." "The Vision of Christ that thou dost see / Is my vision's Greatest Enemy," and, to underline his social meaning, he adds slyly, "Thine has a great hook nose like thine / Mine has a snub nose like to mine" (PB 516).

The difference in emphasis reflects the poets' dissimilar experiences in performing their prophetic functions. Milton had found his ability to instruct his people in liberty threatened by the spiritual hegemony of the state church with its nefarious censors who "had almost brought Religion to a kinde of trading monopoly" (YP III.348–49). Presumably, the end of ecclesiastical repression and the advent of religious toleration, a free trade in spiritual beliefs, would remove all obstacles to his vocation of enlightening his fellows.

Blake, as a man of no property bound to labor for others for his survival, found other barriers. His critique of culture must reflect at least in part the difficulties, described by David Erdman, that he had in pursuing prophetic art. Blake bemoaned his problems in the sarcasms of his *Public Address* and his annotations on Sir Joshua Reynolds of the Royal Academy of Art.[42] Blake continually faced the choice of neglecting his art to support himself through engraving other people's designs or submitting his radical vision to the curtailment of wealthy patrons. He eschewed "Liberality," calling for "a Fair Price & Proportionate Value & a General Demand for Art" (PB 626) and decrying the fact that such patrons "have left him to shift for himself, while others, more obedient to an employer's opinions and directions, are employed" (PB 528). To his dismay, the government refused his proposals for public subsidy of the arts; the general public, whom he saluted as "the true Encouragers of real Art" (PB 570), lacked resources, and those affluent connoisseurs who had them, preferred innocuous landscapes and sycophantic portraits. The indifference with which English society greeted Blake's "Republican Art" (PB 707) was his equivalent to Milton's having been "Church outed by the Prelats" (YP I.823). Since Blake now faced a censorship that no longer was confined to the deliberate repression of church and state, but was embedded in the functioning of a market society and particularly the requirement that those without property should sell their labor, he formulated the first economic, the first working-class critique of culture.

Revising Milton

Blake's experience of working-class conditions led him beyond Milton's analysis. The fact that by Blake's time Puritanism had passed out of the camp of the devils into that of the ruling angels, where it became part of their artillery against the laborers, urged a thorough reevaluation of the Miltonic vision. Blake views Milton, therefore, as a prophetic poet who, like Los, had become assimilated to Urizen. The bard of liberty, who had battled so zealously against bishops and kings, nevertheless had evolved a vision that was to serve as the covering cherub for a new set of oppressors, barring humanity's reentry into Eden via social revolution. Seeing the ruling-class elect "making War upon the Lambs Redeemed; / To perpetuate War & Glory, to perpetuate the Laws of Sin," Blake exclaims that "Milton's Religion is the cause" (M 22:44–45,39).

Blake's allegation that Milton was of the devil's party "without knowing it" can be understood in this light. Blake is not charging that Milton's true views were repressed, but rather that his commitment to revolution was only partial. In mystifying the biases of his class, the "elect," as universal and eternal truth, Milton succumbed to a false consciousness which led both to the contradictory allegiances of his poem and to the repressive implications of his ideology. Blake announces in *The Marriage of Heaven and Hell* his commitment to expunge these false doctrines which deface Milton's prophetic creations by evaluating them from the perspective of Milton's demonic enemies.

Blake appreciated Milton as a visionary poet and a revolutionary one, but repudiated the bias and limits of his revolution. Milton may have espoused a poetry of intellectual battle, but his polemic was double-edged, directed not only against the forces of feudalism and its Presbyterian compromisers, but also against the extreme left in which Blake found his own roots. The principles of Milton's revolution were challenged in his own day by such lower-class radicals as the Levellers and Diggers, Blake's real antecedents.

The principles of Miltonic liberty—free conscience and free trade—in Milton's case had merely involved unexamined contradictions. By the nineteenth century, they had evolved into the politics of complete hypocrisy, the classical liberalism of the political economists. Although Milton's struggle for civil liberties was still relevant, and his own rebellious spirit continued to inspire radicals, much of his liberal ideology, revolutionary in its own day, had since been assimilated by Blake's reactionary opposition. The time had come for a new prophet.

Mind-Forg'd Manacles

Now the need for prophecy was particularly urgent because by the turn of the nineteenth century, the world view of the middle class was, for the first time, seriously impinging upon the consciousness of the workers themselves. In the previous century each class, existing in some considerable social isolation, had essentially retained its own distinctive life style and outlook. The Anglican church had never really bothered to elicit the participation of the workers, who retained a basic orientation of "us" against "them." Middle-class sobriety exerted little influence on those either above or below them. According to G. Rattray Taylor, it was during the years when Blake was writing his prophecies, from 1790 to 1810, that this situation began to undergo drastic change, and the pall of bourgeois morality spread over the entire culture.[43] The Protestant ethic had originally evolved as the expression of a life style conforming to the interests of the bourgeoisie. Now, in its support for the Methodist campaign, the middle class was trying to impose "godly discipline" upon its employees.

Blake viewed with horror this encroachment of bourgeois attitudes upon the working class—attitudes which threatened to turn a generation of chimney sweepers into their own worst enemies. "I went to the Garden of Love," he writes, "And saw what I never had seen: / A Chapel was built in the midst, / Where I used to play on the green" (PB 26). Seeing the chapels, the factories and the "mind-forg'd manacles" of bourgeois ideology where they never had been before, Blake comprehended them as part of a common system. The contraries of the *Songs of Innocence and of Experience* are already an expression of Blake's recognition of a conflict of social perspectives, two cultures and even two Christianities whose assumptions clash in the poems. Thus we find, in "The Little Vagabond" (PB 26), the alehouse of working-class culture with its warmth, its gaiety, its community, its fusion of body and spirit in sensuous exhilaration, set against the repressive church with its authoritarian, ascetic, and self-centered values.

Finding aspects of both cultures anticipated in the ideas of Milton, Blake sought to build his argument upon a dialectical analysis of the Puritan's symbols. The difference was one of perspective here too. As a child of the bourgeoisie, Milton, critical thinker though he was, did not challenge its fundamental premise—class society itself. Raising all his profound questions within those constraints, he could only describe a fall which was a universal double bind requiring divine salvation. Blake, on the other hand, watching the intrusion of the bourgeois world view from the quite different perspective of a working-class culture, could see that fall as a historical development, could challenge its assumptions and prophesy its end. Blake could watch capitalism's growth as it drastically altered earlier modes of life. The relationship between labor and capital would not have been just a theoretical abstraction, for him; workers saw factories replace their little workshops and large estates their farms, observed their bosses moving into larger and larger establishments as a result of their toil, while they suffered in poverty. For the same reason, Marx could elaborate a whole social analysis on the growing power of capital because he saw it changing everything—environment, ideas, people themselves—and not as a fait accompli. When Milton first articulated the attitudes of the rising middle class, it was not at all clear what their dominance would imply. For Blake, watching the process from a different historical vantage point, its implications were becoming terrifyingly obvious.

Blake is often portrayed as an isolated visionary, but revolutionary prophets are never really originals. More often, they are the articulators of insights which have only circulated within a subculture for which they finally win recognition. If Blake's tradition is hard to place, it is because he was, to a great extent, a spokesman for the inarticulate. His roots lie in a long underground tradition of radical Christianity in the leftist and working-class communities of London. Like Albion, "struggling" as he falls "to utter the voice of Man" (*FZ* 44:18), Blake gives his era's most conscious expression to the horror of an anguished lower-class populace as capitalism attempted to swallow them into the vortexes of its own ideology.

Milton's revival in Blake signified the need of a rising working class to confront and sort out the progressive and oppressive aspects of its legacy from the bourgeois revolution and its Christian traditions. That revival—of Milton in Blake and Milton through Blake—will, I believe, prove to be the enduring form of the Puritan poet's artistic bequest long after his neo-orthodox apologists take their place on the shelves of infrequently circulating books in library basements. As for those who would have buried Milton earlier in the century, they lacked Blake's dialectical insight into the fact, dramatized in the continual resurrections of his epic personages, that history not only buries the past, but also brings it back to life. Milton remains alive to us because we, like Blake, are still wrestling with his legacy, still battering against its obstacles and building upon its foundations.

Such revivals have nothing in common with the faddism artificially stimulated by the market such as fashion's periodic readjustment of the hemline, Madison Avenue's various juiced-up versions of the "good old days," or even academia's fastening upon this or that kind of "relevance" through which to rejuvenate itself. For the process underlying the revivals of Blake and Milton, one must look instead to historical recrudescences such as the outbreak of the "spirit of '93" in the Paris Commune; the resurrection of Frederick Douglass and of Nat Turner since the rebellions of Selma and Harlem; the emergence of a host of once-forgotten women—from Mary Wollstonecraft to the suffragists—in the contemporary women's movement; and the repeated return of the oft-proclaimed "outmoded nineteenth-century orthodoxies" of Karl Marx, despite recurrent and allegedly successful attempts to bury them. There are traditions that have only a past, and there are traditions that have a future. Ironically, it was T. S. Eliot's inability to distinguish between the two which led the notorious "traditionalist" to celebrate only the funeral of his culture in *The Waste Land* and to become a pioneer of modernist art, while Blake, alleged iconoclast, sang the resurrection and the life of a "wisdom of ages."

Blake's having consciously placed his relationship with Milton in a larger historical dialectic makes their relationship unlike any other literary alliance I can think of. Blake's poetry cannot be comprehended outside its Miltonic context, and Milton is never better comprehended than through his follower. Milton and his characters walk again in the later poet's works, where he continues Milton's dialogue with the radicals in *Paradise Lost*, clarifying the implications of a polemic already begun and giving Milton's leftist opposition the chance for a fuller and fairer rebuttal. Having once read Blake's version, however, we can never read Milton's epic in the same way again. Blake intensifies our awareness of its contradictions and redirects our sympathies. If, when we hear the words of Satan or Eve, we sometimes think we are hearing Blake, it is because at that moment they are speaking for revolutionary forces that are actually reborn in Blake's work. Because, as epic writers, Blake and Milton have articulated social forces beyond themselves, chronology at certain points becomes irrelevant, and these two amazing poets appear to speak as the great protagonists of each other's poems.

3

Blake's Philosophy: A "New Church" of the "Active Life"

The philosophers have tried to understand the world; our point is to change it.
—Marx

From the chimney sweeper's cry to the later prophecies' visions in "the darksom air," all Blake's art is a protest against the condition of Albion's children. These "myriads of Eternity" (*FZ* 92:28) have been cast, like Luvah, into furnaces of affliction and bound to labor at the mill like slaves. "Believe Christ & his Apostles," Blake warns, "that there is a Class of Men whose sole delight is in Destroying" (*M* 1). The question that engages him from the *Songs* through *Jerusalem* is why the multitudes of London allow themselves to be reduced to "multitudes of lambs" for sacrifice, and why Albion, collective humanity, gives up his scepter and sleeps while such men reign. The answer emerging from the prophetic works is a monstrous system identified finally as "Religion hid in War, a Dragon red and hidden Harlot / Each within other" (*J* 89:53–54). Thus Blake symbolized how the prostitution of culture to established powers combined with their repressive violence, in England as in Babylon, to maintain the status quo, both by bemusing people's consciousness and threatening their lives.

In contrast to this, for Blake as for Milton before him, the poet must rouse men to throw off their oppressors by passing a last judgment upon them. For Blake, a last judgment is "not for the purpose of making Bad Men better but for the Purpose of hindering them from oppressing the Good with Poverty & Pain by means of such Vile Arguments & Insinuations." For "this is A Last Judgment when Men of Real Art Govern & Pretenders Fall" (PB 551). "All Life," he argues, "consists of these Two Throwing off Error & Knaves from our company continually & receiving Truth or Wise Men into our

Company Continually. . . . No man can Embrace True Art till he has Explord & Cast out False Art" (PB 551).

Blake's claims for art appear excessive unless we realize that by "the labours of Art & Science" (*J* 77) he means the entire sphere of culture and production, an arena involving a conflict not merely between principles but between individuals. The struggle for true art is nothing less than the overthrow of the dominion of the "rulers of the darkness of This World" in the entire sphere of communication, education, and ideas. False art is a "hireling" art which serves the interests of the powerful—the art of "Sr Joshua & his Gang of Cunning Hired Knaves" which, because it is "obedient to Noblemens Opinions," is "applauded & rewarded by the Rich & Great" (PB 625,632). Blake would suspect that from the rituals of Babylonian state religion to television stations owned by the Chase Manhattan Bank, such culture has served to distort reality and pervert the people's understanding. Thus it keeps them divided from each other, reconciled to their masters, and incapable of altering their condition. By contrast, "the Arts & Sciences," when honestly practiced, become a true medium between people, stimulating that communication which restores their unity and their power to act. As such, these arts affect "the Destruction of Tyrannies or Bad Governments" (PB 625).

In light of these principles, Blake leveled his scorn at two variants of false art: one which glorifies the powers that be and the other which evades the sphere of social combat for an escapist realm of nature or fancy. In the former group he classed Dante, whom he alleged was "an Emperor's—a Caesar's—Man" (PB 624), and the entire tradition of heroic martial epics deriving from "silly Greek & Latin slaves of the Sword" (*M* 1). Blake's repudiation of the classics is more political than aesthetic; in his mind they had sanctified conquest and empire. Thus he writes, "it is the Classics! & not Goths nor Monks that Desolate Europe with Wars": "Sacred Truth has pronounced that Greece & Rome as Babylon & Egypt: so far from being parents of Arts & Sciences as they pretend: were destroyers of all Art. Homer Virgil & Ovid confirm this opinion. . . . Virgil, says . . . Let others study Art: Rome has somewhat better to do, namely War & Dominion" (PB 267). Blake thought it no coincidence that the eighteenth-century laureates of English imperialism should look to this heritage for models. He harkens back to Milton's celebration of Christian, rather than to Homeric heroism, for his sources.

Being "the liberty both of body & mind to exercise the Divine Arts of Imagination" (*J* 77), art was, for Blake, incompatible with an economic and social order that forced its people to "spend the days of wisdom / In sorrowful drudgery to obtain a scanty pittance of bread"

(*FZ* 92:30–31) and that yielded only a "devastation of the things of the Spirit" (*J* 77). Moreover, since all human existence in Albion was interdependent, it was folly for the poet to pursue an expression of his own imagination that did not consider the plight of his fellows. Such art, Blake believed, ultimately betrayed its accommodation to a world of oppression, since "he who will not defend Truth, may be compelld to defend / A Lie" (*J* 9:29–30).

Blake may have satirized such art, as David Erdman suggests,[1] in *Tiriel* whose "pleasant gardens of Har" appear as a kind of perverted Eden, a prison-paradise where Har and Heva live in perpetual childhood: "Playing with flowers. & running after birds they spent the day / And in the night like infants slept delighted with infant dreams" (PB 274). The image of Har singing "in the great cage" (PB 276) suggests a poetry that offers no real rejuvenation; it can, as Donne wished, "build in sonnets pretty rooms" but only at the expense of blinding itself to the bars on the windows. Thus Blake excoriated all those painters of pretty landscapes who neglected history and society in favor of naturalistic description. Focusing on a nonhuman realm, they could avoid questioning the social origins of existing conditions or seeing the apocalyptic possibilities inherent in them. Under the influence of a sensationalist philosophy, they ignored the world beyond their immediate perceptions. In celebrating nature, such empiricist art by analogy celebrated the "natural" validity of things as they are. Blake lashed out at the artists who came under its influence—Rousseau, Reynolds, Gainsborough, and, to some extent, Wordsworth—as among those who "worship the God of this world" by acquiescing in his kingdom of empire, slavery, and war.

Disavowing any attempt to build an "artifice of Eternity" within the empire of Urizen, Blake, through his persona Los, the "eternal prophet," must sing not merely in his cage but of it, constructing a representation, in all its terror, of the bastille in which people really live. Blake dramatizes this function of art in Los's unrelenting struggle to bind Urizen, "Giving a Body to Falshood that it may be cast off forever" (*J* 12:13). Such art, committed to proving the historical origins and implications of oppressive ideologies, characterizes *The Four Zoas*. In this work Blake depicts the history of human consciousness from the fall of tribalism through the rise and degeneration of Christianity to the present. By Night VI we have reached the present, with Urizen's exploration of his dens having brought us to the virtual dead end of modern materialism. Blake's negation of this world view has sometimes led critics to assume that in *The Four Zoas* he was reviving some "perennial philosophy" of religious idealism. This chapter will argue, to the contrary, that he moves to a far more dialectical conception which resembles in many ways Marx's theory of *praxis* rooting truth neither in sensations of things nor in mental ideas but in human activity. Having clarified this critical conundrum, I hope to move in the next chapter to consider the proposition that Night VII A, generally regarded as describing a breakthrough in Blake's individual consciousness, celebrates as well his contribution to the contemporary advance toward a historicist view of society and culture of which *The Four Zoas* itself is the greatest literary product.

"Night the Sixth": The Bourgeois Philosophers

By Night VI, we have arrived at the era of industrial capitalism with Urizen, its master, wandering "among fiery cities & castles built of burning steel" (*FZ* 70:30). Much of this section explicates the dead end of a bourgeois world view incapable of seeing beyond the chaos it has created. Urizen, caught amidst his vortexes in which "nor down nor up remaind" (*FZ* 72:17) is powerless to give any direction to the industrial hell of "wheels without wheels" which he has set in motion, for he is trapped within the unchallenged laws of his own system.

Anticipating Marx and Engels in identifying Bacon, Newton, and Locke as the philosophers, par excellence, of the developing capitalist order,[2] Blake delivers his indictment of the Urizenic bourgeoisie in Night VI. In this nightmare vision, he traces their mechanical materialism, empiricist epistemology, and the utilitarian social doctrines built upon them to the self-interest of those bent upon accumulating material wealth without regard for the human costs. Thus he writes in *Jerusalem*:

I see . . . Humanity in deadly sleep
. . . .
For Bacon & Newton sheathd in dismal steel, their terrors hang
Like iron scourges over Albion.
. . . .
I turn my eyes to the Schools & Universities of Europe
And there behold the Loom of Locke whose Woof rages dire
Washd by the Water-wheels of Newton. black the cloth
In heavy wreathes folds over every Nation; cruel Works
Of many Wheels I view, wheel without wheel, with cogs tyrannic
Moving by compulsion each other: not as those in Eden: which
Wheel within Wheel in freedom revolve in harmony & peace.
(*J* 15:6,11–20)

The philosophic and psychological implications of Blake's analysis have been expounded at length, but our understanding is incomplete if we overlook the thoroughly social emphasis of his critique. The iron scourges, for example, must immediately evoke the "yron flaile" of Talus in Book V of *The Faerie Queene*. There, at the center of Spenser's discussion of justice and the social order, we confront a giant who preaches the doctrine of return to a golden age of equality. He is identified with the "lawlesse multitude" who, when they rise up "in tumultuous rout / And mutining to stir up civill faction," are routed by Talus's iron flail, Spenser's symbol for the repressive force that necessarily accompanies "justice" in his aristocratic world. Blake is suggesting that in the bourgeois order these "mundane philosophers" play an equally repressive role.

Moreover, this imagery is unmistakably industrial, focusing our antagonism on a particular economic order rather than matter in the abstract. The symbolic "Loom of Locke" merges this traditional figure of fatalism—the loom—with a depiction of that horrific textile industry which gave birth to British capitalism and such accompanying scourges as child labor, the Negro slave trade, the slums of Manchester, and the general degradation of English workers in "dark Satanic Mills." Fatalism here reflects a social condition of which Lockean thought and capitalist economics are but two aspects. Since the weaving in the textile industry had meant a destruction of human life, Blake views its product as a black funeral bunting which "in heavy wreathes folds over every Nation."

This industrial imagery is continued in the image of a mechanized factory, the "cruel Works" (read: "a manufacturing establishment") which has reduced men to slavery as appendages of its machines, its "cogs tyrannic / Moving by compulsion each other." Here Blake is judging mechanical materialism by its social origins and consequences; by merging materialist and social imagery ("cogs tyrannic"), he suggests a relationship between the external interactions of Newtonian physics and the coercion of factory discipline. The alternative, therefore, appropriately appears to be neither a non-material spiritual realm nor an idealist philosophy; rather, it implies a different society based upon a liberating technology where like "those in Eden . . . Wheel within Wheel in freedom revolve in harmony & peace"—freedom, harmony, and peace being decidedly social virtues.

The Newtonian Cosmos

If we return now to Urizen's exploration of his bourgeois kingdom in Night VI, we find a similar congruence between ideological and social phenomena. Urizen's philosophy, as it is exposed here, is clearly that which Marx would reject as mechanical materialism. This philosophy, derived from Bacon and elaborated by Hobbes and Newton, put forth the following premises: (1) that reality is composed of stable, irreducible material particles, (2) that each thing has its own fixed properties independent of anything else, (3) that motion and change are the result of external causes, and (4) that such change is reducible to the simplest mechanical motions of particles, their change of place resulting from the action of external forces upon them.

An isolated being wandering in circles amidst vague spaces, "rocky masses frowning in the abysses revolving erratic / Round Lakes of fire in the dark deep the ruins of Urizens world" (*FZ* 72:4–5), Urizen inhabits such a Newtonian universe. It is a world modeled upon the astronomical heavens where material globes spin their solitary paths in the "horrid bottomless vacuity" (*FZ* 70:23). Thus Urizen ascended

> From heaven to heaven from globe to globe. In vast excentric paths
> Compulsive rolld the Comets at his dread command the dreary way
> Falling with wheel impetuous.   (*FZ* 75:28–30)

The things which inhabit this waste—"a wide world of solid obstruc- tion" (*U* 4:24)—are of impenetrable solidity, "hiding themselves in rocky forms" (*FZ* 68:4). Viewed as a whole, this world of tiny particles (all alike) appears, as Northrop Frye suggests,[3] to be a dense fog, or a sandstorm, images pervading Night VI, along with their concomi- tants, "Snows eternal & iron hail & rain" (*FZ* 74:20) and "clouds / Of smoke" (*FZ* 70:25–26). Viewed in their cumulative density by an endless process of simple addition, they appear as "A dreary waste of solid waters" (*FZ* 69:2) or "hills of stor'd snows" (*U* 3:32). This is the world reduced to its simplest inanimate elements: dust, smoke, clouds, rain, sand.

Urizen's errant travels are an appropriate example of movement in this world, restricted to simple alterations of position in space in which new arrangements involve no new entities, where the more things change the more they remain the same. Such motion is the product of simple, repeatable mechanical operations and is depicted by Blake as fundamentally cyclical, like the motion of the planets in Newton's heavens. Thus Urizen pleads, "Can I not leave this world of Cumbrous wheels / Circle oer Circle" (*FZ* 72:22–23). Since things possess no inner dynamic, they are also shown to move as a result of the external coercion of Urizen's "dread command"—the first cause of this abyss. Finally, Blake captures the reduction of all complex processes to simple mechanical ones in his image of "Caverns rooting downwards their foundations thrusting forth / The metal rock &

stone" (*FZ* 74:12–13). This inverted image of "ungrowth" is the opposite of the organic process by which life, a higher form of organization, emerges from the inanimate earth, the symbol of an alternative ontology based upon conceptions of development.[4]

Lockean Paradoxes

In addition to negating the Newtonian world, equally important for Blake is rejecting the Lockean world view that was its counterpart. A world of impenetrable particles has no way of accommodating human subjectivity; thus an unbridgeable gulf is established between the human subject and the objects of perception. In Locke's reduction of perception to simple sensation, reality stops at the skin, tapping a kind of Morse code on the nerve endings; consciousness becomes a series of physiological spasms.[5] If worlds of matter and mind do not interact with each other, the consequence is that, in fact, all we can know are our own sensations: "Beyond the bounds of their own self their senses cannot penetrate / As the tree knows not what is outside of its leaves & bark" (*FZ* 70:12–13).

Empirical philosophy immediately produced a series of paradoxes. Its impetus was to challenge the general principles authorized by custom, religion, and abstract philosophy and to appeal to the demonstrable certainties of actual experience. Instead, by imprisoning each perceiver in the uncertainties of his own sensations, Locke's psychology led immediately to Hume's skepticism. Hume argued that human beings could know nothing about the connections between things; causal relationships dissolved upon analysis into a series of discrete sensational moments, just as things dissolved into discrete particles in space. We are left with no ability to form any ideas about reality at all. Finally, Kant proposed that reality is a completely unknowable *ding an sich* and commenced to develop relationships from the internal structures of the mind instead. Empiricism had in a short time produced its idealist opposite, for as J. H. Randall writes, "If we start out with Locke's assumptions, we are bound to wind up with Kant's belief that whatever certainty our science may have, it does not give us any light on the basic structure of the world; in other words, that the mind of man cannot know reality as it exists, if, indeed, there be such a world at all apart from man's mind."[6] And so, to the present day, with its subatomic physics and the consequent "uncertainty principle" of Heisenberg, science remains in this cul-de-sac.

Blake acknowledges and rejects this development when he calls upon humanity

To cast off the idiot Questioner who is always questioning,
But never capable of answering; who sits with a sly grin
Silently plotting when to question, like a thief in a cave;
Who publishes doubt & calls it knowledge; whose Science is Despair.
                                                              (*M* 41:12–15)

The Social Consequences

The interesting point in Blake's characterization of this skeptical philosophy is that he immediately attributes it to social motives. Of the "idiot Questioner," he says:

[His] pretence to knowledge is Envy, [his] whole Science is
To destroy the wisdom of ages to gratify ravenous Envy;
That rages around him like a Wolf day & night without rest
He smiles with condescension; he talks of Benevolence & Virtue
And those who act with Benevolence & Virtue, they murder time on
   time.   (*M* 41:16–20)

"Envy" signifies here its broadest meaning—greed, covetousness, and possession—whose social consequences appear as theft, conflict, and repressive "murder." The new philosophy, dating from Hobbes, was applied to society with disastrous consequences, resulting by Blake's time in that philosophy of capitalism par excellence, the utilitarianism of Jeremy Bentham to which Blake may well be alluding here. (John Stuart Mill would later call Bentham "the great questioner of things established.")[7]

As a social philosophy, the world view of the English empiricists took up the role played a century earlier by faith in another kind of individual experience, the inner light. Both the old faith and the new doubt proposed to liberate people from the doctrinal and moral restraints of the old order. However, the "conscience" of the Puritans was very revolutionary in validating their hopes for a world as yet unborn.[8] Skepticism, on the other hand, deriving its principles from the "facts" of a world already dominated by the bourgeoisie, accomplished the opposite, the elimination from philosophy of any hopes or values that might conflict with things as they are; this reduction of thought to reportage completely validated the status quo. Hence Blake's "science of despair."

In fact, morality became a completely problematic matter from this perspective. The liberal philosophers reduced society to its component parts as Newton had decomposed nature, leaving only isolated individuals with their drives and passions. Nassau Senior, a utilitarian himself, described the liberal philosophy as one based upon an arbitrary definition of man as a being who invariably does that by which he may obtain the greatest amount of necessities, conveniences, and luxuries with the smallest amount of labor and physical self-denial.[9] Man, in sum, is recreated in the capitalists' own image as homo economicus, taking care for the main chance. Newton's world of self-sufficient particles is the reflection in nature of a middle class which, in the gospel according to Samuel Smiles, proclaimed itself free of any social bonds whatsoever. Society in the bourgeois definition was a very limited contractual relationship between self-sufficient individuals, its sole purpose being to restrain their otherwise natural tendency to invade and destroy one another.

From the full implications of this Hobbesian paradigm, subsequent thinkers sought to retreat. Throughout much of the eighteenth century, therefore, attempts were made to reconcile social morality and some limited political community with the implications of the doctrine of individualism that had been the starting point of bourgeois philosophy and economics alike. As Blake observes, these thinkers went on at great length, and with some dubious sincerity, about the compatibility of such principles with "benevolence" or "sympathy." Bernard Mandeville arrived at the conclusion that private vices in the end yielded public benefits, an idea which, for Adam Smith, meant that the individual capitalist's unmitigated greed virtually became an "invisible hand," an instrument of Providence for bringing about national wealth and well-being.

In fact, the entire moral dilemma, as Alasdair MacIntyre observes, did not lie in reality or nature at all, but arose from the exigencies of a particular social experience:

> So if I eat to sate my hunger or do my job well in order to succeed, I do not necessarily act from self-interest. It is only when I am in a situation where food is short or my rising in the world requires a disregard for the legitimate claims of others that to consult only my hunger or my ambition becomes to act from self-interest. The notion of self-interest therefore has application not *to human behaviour in general but to a certain type* of human situation, namely, one in which behavior can be either competitive or noncompetitive.[10]

For the rising middle class, consequently, the easiest solution was simply to redefine virtue to conform to its economic circumstances and predilections, what Carlyle would call "doing as one likes." This end was accomplished with some cleverness. For example, charity was transformed from the highest Christian virtue into the worst of crimes, a selfish sentimentality which would drag the poor into an abyss of idleness, indulgence, and dependency. And so the "wisdom of ages," which had dreamed of the holy community, preached the subordination of material accumulation to moral ends, and asked whether the body was not more than raiment and life more than meat and drink (*J* 77), was abandoned by the Manchester savants to "gratify ravenous Envy" and protect the rate of profit.

The Mind of Urizen: Projection and Rationalization

Similarly, most philosophic and scientific "laws" propounded by these bourgeois thinkers originated as a projection of this social experience and became, in circular fashion, their justification. For instance, their conception of an atomized world corresponded to the reality of a society and economy directed by the wills of numerous capitalists who believed themselves to be self-propelling atoms undetermined by any larger social fabric. Their belief that all could be explained by mechanical laws conformed to their reduction of all reality into commodities exchangeable in the marketplace according to laws of supply and demand. The dismissal of humanity from nature which was implied by mechanical materialism accompanied the actual reduction of human labor to a commodity. Humanity itself was wrenched from the old collectivities of family, village, and guild, and forced to peddle itself from factory to factory like so many yards of cheap English goods. Thus Urizen finds human beings in his world indistinguishable from the particles of a lifeless environment in which they are tossed about like so many specks of sand (in conformity, of course, with the laws of gravitation).

> On racks & wheels he beheld women marching oer burning wastes
> Of Sand in bands of hundreds & of fifties & of thousands strucken with
> Lightnings which blazed after them upon their shoulders.
>
> (*FZ* 70:21–23)

This world "involvd in clouds / Of smoke with myriads moping in the stifling vapours" (*FZ* 70:25–26) can only be the industrial world of Manchester, Birmingham, and Leeds with their armies of female wage slaves and their blazing furnaces. There Urizen's capitalist materialism is in the process of turning human culture into chaotic matter and humanity into rocks and beasts:

> over rocks
> And Mountains faint weary he wanderd. where multitudes were shut
> Up in the solid mountains & in rocks which heaved with their
> torments
> Then came he among fiery cities & castles built of burning steel
> Then he beheld the forms of tygers & of Lions dishumanizd men.
>
> (*FZ* 70:27–31)

Once human beings are reduced to things, they too can be explained by the mechanical laws to which the political economists now sought to reduce all social relationships. According to Richard Altick, "Benthamism was Newtonian mechanism applied to ethics."[11] Blake's "science of despair" anticipated Carlyle's "dismal science," the new political economy which made the study of society an analysis of things. Urizen's book of brass, consequently, inscribes iron laws of both nature and society:

> Urizen answerd Read my books explore my Constellations
> Enquire of my Sons & they shall teach thee how to War
> Enquire of my daughters who accursd in the dark depths
> Knead bread of Sorrow by my stern command for I am God
> Of all this dreadful ruin.   (*FZ* 79:20–24)

The laws which follow (*FZ* 80:1–21) are an explicit parody of the ideas of the utilitarians and, especially, as Mark Shorer has noted, those of Malthus.[12] Urizen proceeds from his intellectual explorations of the laws of science in Night VI to an assertion of his laws of repression in Night VII A where he begins a direct assault on the rebellious Orc. The imagery, however, remains the same:

> For Urizen fixd in Envy sat brooding & coverd with snow
> His book of iron on his knees he tracd the dreadful letters
> While his snows fell & his storms beat to cool the flames of Orc.
>   (*FZ* 78:1–3)

Again we must conclude that Urizen's whole philosophy emerges from a mind obsessed with preserving his power. Engels's comments on the political bias of Newton's world of law are relevant in this respect:

> But what especially characterized this period is the elaboration of a peculiar general outlook, in which the central point is the view of the *absolute immutability of nature.* In whatever way nature itself might have come into being, once present it remained as it was as long as it existed. The planets and their satellites . . . circled on and on in their prescribed ellipses for all eternity. . . . The stars remained for ever fixed and immoveable in their places, keeping one another therein by "universal gravitation." . . . The five continents of the present day had always existed, and they always had the same mountains, valleys, and rivers, the same climate, the same flora and fauna. . . . The species of plants and animals had been established once for all when they came into existence. . . . All change, all development in nature was negated. Natural science, so revolutionary at the outset, suddenly found itself confronted by an out-and-out conservative nature, in which even today everything was as it had been at the beginning and in which—to the end

of the world or for all eternity—everything was to remain as it had been since the beginning.[13]

Applied to social life, this philosophy offered a complete justification of the status quo which, it was argued, arose not from human dominion, but from immutable natural laws. Poverty became an inescapable "fact," like earthquakes or floods. Wages could not be raised; hours could not be shortened; starvation was a working-out of the laws of population. The statistics of human suffering were collected in utilitarian blue books where, it was shown, they compared favorably with statistics on expansion of trade. It was never quite explained why, in this "moral arithmetic," one person's gain should so cancel another's misfortune. Anyway, nothing could be done about "it." Thus John Stuart Mill would prove that trade unions could do nothing to raise the standard of living, as Nassau Senior had demonstrated that (since all profits derived from the last hour) legislation of a ten-hour day would be a sure catalyst of economic collapse. Such causes were well intentioned but misinformed; they disregarded the "facts" of economic law.

Meanwhile, the laborers suffered the cracking of the whip of productivity in the factory, the bitterness bred by want in family relations, and the collapse of minds and bodies subjected to too much exertion and too little nourishment. They experienced the shredding of human solidarity provoked by thrusting human labor onto a competitive market and the degradation of poverty-induced crime. These human consequences did not significantly impress the utilitarians. Unlike Blake, these first social scientists would not form all the lineaments of fear, anxiety, and strife into a picture of the mangled social body. Rather, their data was compounded, as by contemporary Urizens, into indexes of acceptable unemployment, fluctuations in prices and increments of profit—the lives of persons disguised in the movement of things and attributed to the inscrutable laws of the market.

Blake's attack on empiricism is very close to Dickens's assault in *Hard Times* on a "philosophy of fact" which appears explicitly as the doctrine of capitalist Gradgrinds and Bounderbys. Thus, in a lesson on "National Prosperity," the innocent pauper Sissy Jupe is queried by a fact-obsessed schoolteacher: "Now this schoolroom is a Nation. And in this nation, there are fifty millions of money. Isn't this a prosperous nation? . . . and an't you in a thriving state?" Sissy's naive rejoinder cuts through all the philosophers' hypocritical objectivity: "I said I didn't know. I thought I couldn't know whether or not it was a prosperous nation or not and whether I was in a thriving state or not, unless I knew who had got the money, and whether any of it was mine. But that had nothing to do with it. It was not in the figures at all."[14] Similarly, such misguided science is criticized when Louisa Gradgrind, a manufacturer's daughter schooled in its principles, discovers in her first confrontation with an actual, suffering human laborer that all such thought had erred when it attempted to treat human beings in the same terms as quantifiable commodities:

> She knew from her reading infinitely more of the ways of toiling insects than of these toiling men and women. Something to be worked so much and paid so much and there ended; something to be infallibly settled by the laws of supply and demand; something that blundered against those laws and floundered into difficulty; something that was a little pinched when wheat was dear and overate itself when wheat was cheap; something that increased at such rate of percentage, and yielded such another percentage of crime, and such another percentage of pauperism; something wholesale of which vast fortunes were made; something that occasionally rose like a sea, and did some harm and waste (chiefly to itself), and fell again; this she knew the Coketown Hands to be.[15]

This fallacy of bourgeois thought would be denounced by Marx as a "fetishism of commodities":

> A commodity is, therefore, a mysterious thing, simply because in it the social character of men's labour appears to them as an objective character stamped upon the product of that labour because the relation of the producers to the sum total of their own labour is presented to them as a social relation, existing not between themselves, but between the products of their labour. . . . There it is a definite social relation between men, that assumes, in their eyes, the fantastic form of a relation between things.[16]

Marx goes on to state that this mystification is an analogy to that of "the mist enveloped regions of the religious world."[17] In presenting Urizen as creator both of the traditional religious and the Newtonian world, Blake had made the same point, that both are inadequate substitutes for the real world of human activity, and both are reflections of Urizen's self-interested point of view.

The bourgeoisie had accomplished an enormously clever ideological feat when it tried to substitute for the sanctions of feudal society, superstition, custom, and metaphysics an appeal to experience for vindication of bourgeois principles. What these apologists neglected to observe was that it was only their own very limited class experiences that they consulted. Thus Blake portrays the Newtonian universe not as the real world, but as a construct of Urizen who, in *The Book of Urizen*, simply creates nature in his own image.

Where bourgeois philosophers claimed to be finding in society the continuation of natural laws, Blake sees an opposite process, their projection onto nature of the assumptions by which they governed their own social life. The atomism and mechanism of their static universe was imposed upon it by the bias of its perceivers, for Urizen is a "self-contemplating shadow" (*U* 3:21). The passivity and individualism of Lockean perception was a consequence of a real breakdown in communication and community and the resultant loss of the power of human beings to master their world. The source of all motives in self-interest was not a fundamental fact of human nature, but only of that particular society. Urizen's world is self-begotten and "Self-closd" (*U* 3:3):

> And a roof, vast petrific around,
> On all sides He fram'd: like a womb;
> Where thousands of rivers in veins
> Of blood pour down the mountains to cool
> The eternal fires beating without
> From Eternals; & like a black globe
> View'd by the sons of Eternity, standing
> On the shore of the infinite ocean
> Like a human heart strugling & beating
> The vast world of Urizen appear'd.   (*U* 5:28–37)

This world is completely solipsistic.

Urizen's much-vaunted laws are simply rules of his own making in which he has imprisoned himself:

> Restless turnd the immortal inchain'd
> Heaving dolorous! anguish'd! unbearable
> Till a roof shaggy wild inclos'd
> In an orb, his fountain of thought.   (*U* 10:31–34)

However, it is not sufficient to see this Newtonian vision of the world as merely an erroneous world view, for it is the product of Urizen's furious activity as well as his deformed consciousness:

> He dug mountains & hills in vast strength,
> He piled them in incessant labour,
> In howlings & pain & fierce madness
> Long periods in burning fires labouring.   (*U* 5:22–25)

Likewise, Urizen's world, as depicted in Night VI, is both a distorted version of nature and a realistic picture of industrial England. This reading is comprehensible when we recall that throughout the poem Urizen is both a priest and a king, the architect of an oppressive society and a false ideology. In Night VI he is the English bourgeois exploring a Newtonian cosmos and an industrial order which are both the products of his own subjective experience. For Blake, that is precisely what it means to be in the ruling class: having the power to impose one's own will on society, on one's environment, and on human consciousnes, and, at least for a time, having the power to create a world, and not only a world view, in one's own image.

Blake and Marx: Philosophers of Praxis

In developing an alternative to such static and oppressive consciousness, Blake forged a perspective which, despite real differences, in significant ways coincides with Marx's philsophy of praxis, the attempt to root perceptions and ideas in active human experience. Both Blake and Marx looked at ideas strategically, challenging them, first and foremost, in terms of the sort of human existence they envisioned or implied. Blake develops his vision in the persona of the poet-prophet whose role it is to enable the people to assert their own view of experience against that of tyrants in order to reconstruct their world.

The two social critics tackled fundamentally the same problems: both sought to build their world view on the revolutionary assumption that humanity and its ideas are not fixed entities; both believed that human beings and their ideas are created by themselves in the active, collective, historical process in which they (some more than others) make their world. With this premise, both challenged the dichotomies which had characterized Western civilization, dividing God and humanity, humanity and nature, subject and object, thought and sensation. Blake's effort, of course, is part of a wider romantic attempt to replace enlightenment attitudes with more dialectical conceptions of experience. However, his particular plebeian emphases suggest a general orientation more anticipatory of Marx with whom he shares several social assumptions: the insistence that such a reconciliation be accomplished in action as well as in thought; the emphasis on a collective, rather than merely individual breakthrough; the belief in the important role of the lower classes and their political struggles in this process; and the identification of this apocalyptic resolution with both social revolution and the technological transformation of nature.

To say all this is not to deny the significant differences between Blake's vision and Marx's. Unlike Marx, Blake asserts an apparently mystical conception of the active power of the mind itself, emphasizing the subjectivity of perception, and giving a strategic primacy to cultural revolution. But, even here, the degree of difference can be seen to diminish somewhat, once the class content of Blake's epistemology is given proper weight and his analysis is located within his lifelong insistence upon the influence of class biases on perception. This chapter will try to offer some clarification of Blake's philosophy, its activism and its peculiarly materialist mysticism, as a necessary preliminary to my main argument: that the Blakean prophet makes a breakthrough to something like Marx's theory of historical evolution in Night VII A of *The Four Zoas* and that the epic as a whole recounts that history.

Blake's anticipation of a kind of Marxist historicism has been obscured by the fact that the two thinkers came to their respective views from such different directions. Marx proceeds from scientific materialism, while Blake develops out of that critical idealism which had sustained the social vision of the radical Judeo-Christian tradition. Hence it is crucial that we distinguish Blake's sources from his use of them. Each thinker recasts his traditions in a specifically humanistic, historical form. Marx emphasizes human activity in nature over the laws of subhuman matter, while Blake removes from idealist conceptions of "spirit" their suprahuman and ascetic connotations. Each is eager to counter reactionary tendencies which see human fate as determined by forces outside ourselves, be they laws of nature or of God. Thus Blake repudiates Newton's necessitarian doctrines because, in reducing human activity to a reflex of subhuman forces, they create "hindrance & not Action" (PB 555). Similarly, Marx refuses to interpret the human condition in relation to divine or merely psychic forces, lest people be prohibited or distracted from the task of altering their social conditions.

Consequently, Blake and Marx reject both abstract philosophy and physical science as the basis for a theory of knowledge, emphasizing instead the value of active human experience. In a remark which reminds us of Blake's attack on Urizenic abstraction, Marx decries philosophies in which "productions of the human brain appear as independent beings endowed with life, and entering into relation both with one another and the human race."[18] And when Blake criticizes scientific method, it is because experience is limited there to the catalogued sensations of a passive perceiver, whereas for him, "As the true method of knowledge is experiment the true faculty of knowing must be the faculty which experiences" (PB 2). For Marx, scientific knowledge is valid to the extent that it is understood to report repeatable human interactions with nature. The search for the thing-in-itself, a truth believed to inhere either in ideas or objects, can only produce skepticism. Ultimately all human beings can know are the effects of their own activity: "The question whether objective truth can be attributed to human thinking is not a question of theory but is a *practical* question. In practice man must prove the truth, that is, the reality and power, the this-sidedness of his thinking. The dispute over the reality or non-reality of thinking which is isolated from practice is a purely *scholastic* question."[19]

Blake's conclusions are, in some respects, the same, for the primary distinction underlying his intellectual critique is one of activism versus acquiescence. He seeks a world view which gives full play to humanity's conscious powers and which would reject all defenses of the social conditions that inhibit such powers. Thus he remarks that "the Whole of the New Church is in the Active Life" (PB 595) and "the hindering of act in another, This is Vice but all Act is Virtue" (PB 590). In *The Four Zoas* the Fall means that "Human Nature shall no more remain nor Human Acts / Form the rebellious Spirits of Heaven" (FZ 11:23–24). In fact, the world remains unfallen only so long as it is under the dominion of human creativity. In Eden, Albion, unfallen human nature and an unfallen community, lives harmoniously with his Emanation, Jerusalem, the heavenly city, an environment transformed by his creative activity.

This Eden signifies simultaneously a social condition and a higher state of consciousness. In the latter sense, so long as the Zoa, Urthona, remains undivided from his Emanation, Enitharmon, the human imagination is virtually omnipotent:

> For Los & Enitharmon walkd forth on the dewy Earth
> Contracting or expanding their all flexible senses
> . . . .
> At will to stretch across the heavens & step from star to star
> . . . .
> While round their heads the Elemental Gods kept harmony.
>
> (FZ 34:9–15)

Here both nature and the gods are subsumed in human experience. In recognizing the faith expressed here in the powers of consciousness, however, we should at the same time remember that Urthona, the unfallen Los, is a craftsman through whose labors humanity actually becomes the Earth-Owner by being the functional creator of his environment.

Urthona's fall will, therefore, be a disaster on every level of culture, a story which we will recount later. For now let us note that it involves Urthona's fragmentation into a Spectre who embodies a split-off subjectivity as, at the same time, the fallen Los finds himself alienated from an "objective" world of space-time, now estranged in his Emanation, Enitharmon. Moreover, once Urthona's ability to mold reality is lost, Urizen usurps his place as a kind of subjectivity gone wild. He imposes the most solipsistic delusions upon reality and all the Emanations separate into a completely hostile and intractable material world. Sometimes Enitharmon herself dramatizes these splits into two aspects of inhuman reality. On the one hand, she flees sensuous experience for the abstracted world of religious mystery, becoming Urizen's queen of heaven, crying, "the God enrapturd me infolds / In clouds of sweet obscurity" (*FZ* 34:24–25). On the other hand, her heavens are also Newton's, so she signifies as well the degeneration of the natural world into dead matter: "Enitharmon remains a corse such thing was never known" (*FZ* 22:25).

Blake's analysis of Urthona and his fate anticipated Marx's idea of a "praxis" or practice which alone could prevent the division of reality into false opposites:

> The chief defeat of all hitherto existing materialism . . . is that the thing, reality, sensuousness is conceived only in the form of the object, but not as human sensuous activity, practice, not subjectively. Hence, it happened that the active side, in contradistinction to materialism, was developed by idealism, but only abstractly since, of course, idealism does not know real sensuous activity as such . . . "revolutionary" . . . practical-critical activity.[20]

Materialism and Idealism

Marx's insight here into the limitations of antecedent forms of materialism and idealism provides a framework for understanding his differences with Blake, who rejected precisely this "objectivity" of materialism to develop the active side of human life preserved in more idealist thought. In Blake's own terminology, however, he stands against Marx as a "contrary," emphasizing other aspects of the same reality, not as a "negation," canceling all the insights of such materialism.

Nevertheless, before we can weigh their differences precisely, we must speedily dismiss vulgar misreadings of Marx as an economic determinist who preaches a gospel that man does live by bread alone. Engels was forced to correct this error in a later edition of their jointly written works, pointing out that their real position was that economic conditions set the limits within which other aspects of human life could develop, not that economics alone was significant:

> According to the materialist conception of history, the *ultimate* determining element in history is the production and reproduction of real life. More than this neither Marx nor I ever asserted. Hence if somebody twists this into saying that the economic element is the *only* determining one, he transforms that proposition into a meaningless, abstract,

senseless phrase. . . . We had to emphasize the main principle vis-à-vis our adversaries, who denied it, and had not always time, the place or the opportunity to give their due to the other elements involved in the interaction.[21]

Marx modified Newtonian materialism in two ways: by stressing the evolutionary possibilities within nature against conceptions of immutable law, and by shifting the focus from the gravitational bombardments of things to the consciously directed physical activities of human beings in the material world. This is consistent with his goal which was to liberate human action from the debilitating effects of poverty and servile labor. Marx himself had clearly affirmed a role for consciousness in history against eighteenth-century determinists; in his words, "The materialist doctrine that men are products of circumstances and upbringing, and that, therefore, changed men are the products of other circumstances and changed upbringing, forgets that it is men that change circumstances and the educator himself needs educating."[22]

With these sentiments Blake could heartily concur, for indeed he made "educating the educator" his life's work. There is a need, however, to reexamine precisely how he viewed consciousness. No question in Blake is more vexed than that of his "idealism." Those who are accustomed to criticism stressing Blake's assertions of the primacy of mental reality (Kathleen Raine now claiming him an unqualified Neoplatonist) will suspect that I have located Blake in rather odd company unless some finer distinctions are introduced.[23] We must, therefore, consider Blake's affirmation of the powers of subjective consciousness, his espousal of the spiritual life within the framework of biblical and Christian language, his rejection within these contexts of their traditional supernaturalist, dualist, and ascetic implications, his apparent contempt for the "natural man" of Generation, and his celebration of the New Jerusalem of a higher state of consciousness.

Too often Blake's assertion, "As the Eye—Such the Object" (PB 634), is extracted from the context of his whole work and read only as a trumpeting of individual subjectivity. In assimilating Blake to Bishop Berkeley, or Thomas Taylor, one has to overlook a whole universe of Blakean views which he does not share with them. Blake did attribute to consciousness the power of constructing its own world, but invariably he speaks of collective consciousness and class subjectivity. Much of his emphasis upon the act of perception appears in the context of his encouraging the people to trust their own emotionally informed experience in opposition to the abstractions through which their "betters" would have them interpret it. Blake did insist that what people think possible will determine what they see. But he was primarily concerned with those biases described above in *Visions of the Daughters of Albion* as distinguishing the views of oppressor and oppressed. He rarely discusses the limits of any thinker completely apart from an analysis of their social prejudices. This conjunction is particularly evident in his annotations to *The Works of Sir Joshua Reynolds* from which Blake's epistemology is often extracted. The limits of Reynold's "eye" are inseparable from his obedience to "Noblemans Opinions in Art & Science" (PB 632). What irks Blake particularly is the way in which Lockean ideas obscure the principles of selection behind an allegedly "realistic" art.

When Blake proclaims his own vision, he is invariably juxtaposing his concrete, radical, lower-class perspective to the truths touted by the elite. He is surely not alleging that the fact that perception is mental and individual means that the world it reports is not real or that it cannot testify to a common experience of that world. Blake believed reality to be accessible to those who had no reason to censor or distort it; however, in a world where much censorship had already occurred, reality was not necessarily so easily accessible. Consciousness needed to be developed, freed from false biases, for "A fool sees not the same tree that a wise man sees" (*MHH* 7). Moreover, the world itself had been deformed by the elite, so intellectual effort was necessary to penetrate present realities to see the potentialities lying within them.

The belief that human beings could achieve common wisdom was, furthermore, an indispensable component of prophetic faith. The world is a "subjective" rather than a purely "objective" world, not because it is merely illusion, a reflection of perverse individual fantasies, but because it is a collective human creation, a creation of a consciousness which involves as much social interdependence as the common life which is also a creation, one with which all consciousness is invariably bound up.

Forgetting this holistic view, critics miss much of the significance of Blake's proclamation of the power of imagination in his *Vision of the Last Judgment*:[24]

> What it will be Questiond When the Sun rises do you not
> see a round Disk of fire somewhat like a Guinea O no no
> I see an Innumerable company of the Heavenly host crying
> Holy Holy Holy is the Lord God Almighty.   (PB 555)

Blake is affirming mental powers here, and for him the air did swarm with spiritual presences of some sort. But there is more at stake than a contrast between Lockean observation and his individual visionary experience. For what Blake evokes here is that century-old vision of the poor who are inspired by the Book of Revelation to look to the heavens for affirmation of their ultimate rise to glory, a hope which he contrasts with the mercenary vision of a bourgeoisie which sees everything reducible to money. The subjectivity which Blake celebrates is that "wisdom of ages" in which collective human experience and desire had been articulated and preserved as myth.

The problem with bourgeois thought, for Blake, was that it attempted to suppress most people's experience and replace it with abstractions primarily reflecting the selfish interests of the bourgeoisie. It was Urizen's ideology, not Blake's, that imprisoned people in their own individual minds. Various forms of idealist metaphysics and religion, as well as rationalist abstraction and Lockean empiricism, all conspired to prevent human beings from seeing through the atomization of bourgeois society to their common social plight. Thus Urizen aproaches his children and finds that

> His voice to them was but an inarticulate thunder for their Ears
> Were heavy & dull & their eyes & nostrils closed up
> Oft he stood by a howling victim Questioning in words
> Soothing or Furious no one answerd every one wrapd up
> In his own sorrow. (*FZ* 70:39–43)

From Dualism to Dialectics

When critics extract from Blake a statement such as "Mental Things are alone Real" (PB 555) and make it the touchstone of his whole vision, they fall into precisely those dangers of abstraction which Blake seeks to avoid. World like "mental," "natural," "body," and "soul" are all given unique interpretations in Blake's dramatic use of them, and readers must proceed cautiously when removing statements from their poetic context, lest they lose half his dialectic of spirit and sense, vision and action. In his most explicitly conceptual treatment of the problem, Blake prevents this misconception by giving us two apparently contradictory statements to brood upon. Insisting that the greatest error perpetrated by religion has been the assumption that "Man has two real existing principles Viz: a Body & a Soul," he goes on to explain: "Man has no Body distinct from his Soul and that calld Body is a portion of Soul discernd by the five Senses, the chief inlets of Soul in this age." While arguing that body and soul are one, this remark suggests that soul is the ultimate reality and body a perceptual illusion. But this impression is checked when Blake adds, "Energy is the only life and is from the Body and Reason is the bound or outward circumference of Energy. Energy is Eternal Delight" (*MHH* 4).

Blake's concept of energy moves his thought beyond the dichotomies of idealist and materialist philosophies. By translating "spirit" as "energy," he divests it of its ususal nonmaterial connotations, anticipating something like post-Einsteinian physics in which matter and energy, particle and wave, are interchangeable, and the cosmos is pervaded by powerful energies undetected by normal vision. Human perceptions are relative in such high-energy physics where there exists, though the eye may not see it, "a World in a Grain of Sand / And a Heaven in a Wild Flower" (PB 481). Within such conceptions, Blake could affirm levels of human activity which are also invisible and which go beyond the gross dynamics of lever and pulley. Consciousness is active, both in directing human goals and in itself functioning as a transformer or receiver of these subtler energies, sending and receiving signals along invisible air waves.[25]

At the same time, since energy is "from the body," Blake's spiritual vision rejects the supernaturalism and asceticism of idealist religion. He shifts the meaning of concepts derived from Platonic and Gnostic traditions such as "mind," "spirit," "body," "nature," and "corporeal," and reinterprets religious language to avoid dualistic implications. His seemingly theological passages become comprehensible only within that tradition of radical Christian incarnationalism expounded by Thomas Altizer.[26] The idea that God became man is interpreted to mean that humanity can become God, that the creative powers constitute a divine element in human nature. Thus Blake responded to Henry Crabb Robinson's query whether he believed Jesus to be divine: "He is the only God and so am I and so are you." Believing Jesus to have proclaimed the Good News of all people's divinity and not his alone, in the *Everlasting Gospel* Blake has him state, "Thou art a Man God is no more / Thy own humanity learn to adore" (PB 511). True Christianity does not worship what is more than human, but whatever makes humanity more. As Blake tells us in *The Marriage of Heaven and Hell:* "The worship of God is. Honouring his gifts in other men each according to his genius. and loving the greatest men best, those who envy or calumniate great men hate God, for there is no other God" (*MHH* 22–23). At this blasphemy, the orthodox angel who has been interrogating the poet turns blue, exclaiming, "Thou Idolater is not God One & is he not visible in Jesus Christ?" To which Blake retorts, as a kind of Christian atheist, "If Jesus Christ is the greatest man, you ought to love him in the greatest degree" (*MHH* 23). Contrarily, Blake's antagonism to the deists' "atheism" derives from their repudiation of Jesus, which he sees as a negation of the divinity present in human beings and active in history.

Blake consistently rejects the escapist supernaturalism which he calls "mystery," and even has the prophet Isaiah return to correct misinterpretations which may have occurred when he said that God had spoken to him, for, in his words, "I saw no God, nor heard any . . . but my senses discover'd the infinite in every thing" (*MHH* 12). Blake's Christianity must therefore be understood within his historical vision (which we shall explore later) that from the time of Paul two opposite tendencies had continued under the same name: a revolutionary humanist gospel, with Jesus as its chief prophet, and a supernaturalist mystery cult dependent upon a divine savior.

Blake's Isaiah goes on to comment that "the voice of honest indignation is the voice of God" (*MHH* 12), and the test to which Blake puts spiritual, like scientific, philosophies is their ability to resist the impoverishment and enslavement of Albion's children. Unlike all those quiestistic and ascetic idealists who had sought to free the mind from the illusions of sensual existence, Blake insists that humanity would come to experience "the whole creation" as "infinite and holy . . . by an improvement in sensual enjoyment" for which "the notion that man has a body distinct from his soul, is to be expunged" (*MHH* 14).

In addition, Blake realizes that this apocalypse will require more than just the elimination of ascetic ideologies. Since spirit is energy and from the body, the human energies of sexuality and labor must be liberated. For the oppressed masses, this means an improvement in their material conditions, in food, shelter, clothing, and the conditions of labor. Blake would have agreed with Marx about the effects of material degradation on human beings, the effects of spending "the days of wisdom / In sorrowful drudgery to obtain a scanty pittance of bread" (FZ 92:30–31). He never doubted that social and economic improvement was the prerequisite of cultural advancement, for "it is the same with Individuals as Nations works of Art can only be produced in Perfection where the Man is either in Affluence or Above the Care of it Poverty is the Fools Rod" (PB 551). In *The Four Zoas*, as I hope to show, he attempts, like Marx after him, to trace the effects of human impoverishment and enslavement on the evolution of human consciousness.

Blake wishes to distinguish not between God and man, soul and body, but between the different levels of human experience. He repudiates the mechanical materialists' imprisonment in "Single vision & Newton's sleep" (PB 693) where matter remains inanimate and chaotic, a Urizenic cloud of dust and bed of slime. He also argues that a fully human life must go beyond the organic life of "generation," restricted to the vegetative functions of growth and the animal functions of eating, sleeping, and reproducing.

Along with these materialist reductions, however, he also abjures the alienation of a human being in a bodiless spectre, locked in the mind, divided from others and the world. In traditional categories, natural life means sensuous existence, while spiritual life is relegated to a nonmaterial realm. But Blake's metaphoric use of these concepts draws different distinctions. Sometimes, spiritual man lives a communal existence, while "natural man" is the atomized egotist who turns to the material world merely to accumulate things, forgetting that the body is "more than Raiment" (*J* 77). The unfallen Albion is presented in the opening vision of *The Four Zoas* as living in "the Universal Brotherhood of Eden / The Universal man." There too Blake alludes to Jesus's association of the divinity of humanity with its solidarity when he prays "that they all may be one; as thou, Father, art in me, and I in thee, that they also may be one in us" (*FZ* 3:5–6; John 17:21–22). Here spiritual existence belongs to those who live in a poetic state of consciousness in Albion, the liberated community, and Jerusalem, the environment they have collectively and imaginatively transformed.

The more pointed question to be raised about Blake's philosophy is a strategic one. To what extent is he identifying liberation with a personal breakthrough in consciousness, as many critics suggest, rather than a historical transformation of social institutions? For Blake, surely all have the right to expanded states of consciousness as their birthright in the poetic genius, and the prophet must witness to such possibilities even against the times. Nevertheless, it would be a mistake to assimilate Blake to contemporary ideologies which pose psychological transformation as an alternative to political change. Ever since Freud, especially in America, there has been a recurrent tendency for some intellectuals to trace all problems to mental ones, either in individual character or cultural heritage.

In fact, Blake seems always to want us to read his lines both ways. In doing so, he was exhibiting a tendency of the romantics, pointed out by M. H. Abrams, to take over from biblical exegesis an allegorical method which allowed an elaborate parallel between spiritual biography and historical events:

> A striking index to the psycho-historical parallelism in Christian thinking is the early appearance and elaborate development of the

distinction between the "letter" and the "spirit" of Biblical narrative, the same text being taken to signify, in its literal sense, an outer event of sacred history, and in one of its several "spiritual" or "allegorical" senses, an inner event which may occur within the soul of every man.[27]

It was also true, however, in the traditions of Christian radicalism, that the "spiritual" events of biblical passages, like those of Revelation, were held to have historic, prophetic significance. Too often, Blake's history is read primarily as a symbol of inner realities, as though he were working the same transmutations upon epic as Wordsworth was. Even Abrams's "polysemantics of simultaneous reference to the outer history of mankind and the spiritual history of the individual,"[28] is used to suggest a disjunction between those two frameworks. Similarly, Frye's multileveled reading of Blake's symbols ignores his interest in historical causality and posits only abstract, analogical connections between them.

These ambiguities are central to the comprehension of Blake's apocalyptic vision of the building of Jerusalem. In the preface to chapter 4 of *Jerusalem*, a great deal depends on what is read literally, and what metaphorically. "To Labour in Knowledge," Blake states, "is to Build up Jerusalem," and then goes on to identify the "spiritual" and "mental" gifts of the imagination with the "labours of Art & Science." Critics like Abrams, who read "labours" and "build" metaphorically and "mental" and "spiritual" literally, find here a view of Jerusalem as a paradise within to be achieved through strictly intellectual and artistic processes.[29] If, conversely, the "labours of Art & Science" be taken literally, Blake's vision goes beyond a personal, interior liberation. Rather, spiritual freedom appears to be achieved through the emancipation of labor for those "Mental Studies & Performances" which would include conscious and practical efforts to reconstruct the world as Jerusalem, as a new social and environmental order.

In conclusion, then, Blake shares with Marx an emphasis on the relationship of ideas to social and historical practice, but differs from him in two significant ways. First, Blake acknowledges higher powers of consciousness in tune with invisible fields of energy, and second, he places a greater emphasis on the cultural dimension in his vision of social change than is found in Marx's subsequent strategy. Blake's attitude towards the possibilities of consciousness and its potential alteration in the course of social development will distinguish his historicism from historical materialism. He seems to be suggesting that extraordinary states of consciousness might be recaptured from the priests of mystification and put at the service of revolutionary goals. Moreover, however acutely aware Blake was—as composer of the first and greatest industrial poetry—of the connections between production and culture, still, he had nothing like Marx's scientific ecnomics nor an awareness of the organizing strategies these connections implied. Because he was a cultural worker, Blake's revolutionary vision stressed ideological considerations. He emphasized "intellecutal war," but consistently located those battles within popular struggles, rather than seeing them as taking the place of social change.

A full synthesis of Blake's mysticism and his politics is beyond our scope; Blake's position grants him few peers and even fewer comprehending commentators, for mysticism and political action are both matters of experience and one less engaged by them than Blake will invariably get him wrong. At any rate, the goal of this study lies elsewhere. I propose only to try to show that *The Four Zoas* attempts to sketch the collective evolution of the human spirit, the interior of history, as it is felt, suffered, and created by people bound within the dialectics of social development.

4

Blake's Epic Art: "Historical Facts . . . Written by Inspiration"

> *The greatest wisdom would be to understand that every fact is already history.*
> —Goethe

According to a popular contemporary myth, revolutionary enthusiasm is a stage through which many artists pass before ultimately arriving at resigned disillusionment and deeper wisdom. Many critics believe to have found this pattern in Blake. His increasing emphasis on the creative Los as against the rebellious Orc in the later prophecies has been read as a shift of allegiance from revolution to the liberation of individual consciousness, an apotheosis to be achieved primarily by art.[1] There has been a tendency, in other words, to assimilate Blake to Wordsworth.

One of the key pieces of evidence advanced for this theory has been Blake's alleged substitution of Night VII A, with its symbols of an apocalyptic breakthrough in consciousness, for the earlier Night VII B, with its explicit allusions to the French Revolution. The assumption is problematic on a number of counts. Not all analysts (not Frye or Margoliouth, for example), accept the contention that Night VII A is a substitute for, rather than an addition to, the earlier version.[2] Moreover, there is ample evidence for continued political zeal in other passages—for example, the exuberant, revolutionary Night IX. David Erdman has suggested, therefore, that what we have in Night VII A is only the record of Blake's temporary change of heart to a more quietistic Christianity, inspired by the peace of 1803.[3]

Still another reading is possible if we abandon the assumption that Night VII A is a psychomachia congruent with a transformation of *individual* consciousness. We might consider instead that in it Blake is groping toward that one breakthrough in thought which was eventually to have as great an influence in changing human society as a score of social uprisings. What Blake formulates here, I am suggesting, is not an alternative to revolution, but its indispensable companion—a theory of history which is his own equivalent to what would later appear as historical materialism. In this reading, the two versions of Night VII are intimately related.

The failure of the French Revolution might have led Wordsworth and Coleridge to abandon revolution altogether. It led Marx and perhaps Blake to search for a revolutionary theory that could explain such failures and identify the characteristics that must differentiate a new and successful insurgency from the limitations of its aborted antecedents. It is Marx's conscious analysis of how such struggle evolves in relation to particular historical circumstances that would henceforth distinguish Marxism from the mere insurrectionism of Blanqui, Bakunin, and others. Similarly, Blake seems to be saying that the fires of Orc, however necessary they may be to the revolutionary process, are not sufficient. Unless an analysis of the sources of tyranny guides that struggle beyond the overthrow of particular tyrants to the complete restructuring of institutions and ideologies, it will be impossible to prevent new rulers from arising upon old thrones. In his dramatization of Los's reintegration with the Spectre of Urthona and subsequent reconciliation with Enitharmon and Orc in Night VII A, Blake may be describing the discovery of a new and thoroughly historical philosophy whose grasp of the dynamics of human development finally offers the possibility of their conscious mastery.

The first product of this new consciousness, I shall argue, is *The Four Zoas* itself, an epic of human history from the fall (in Blake's depiction of Genesis) of tribal communism to the apocalyptic possibilities of a new egalitarian social order. Before tracing Blake's vision of history, however, let us turn to his explication in Night VII A of the theoretical breakthrough which is the prerequisite for the historical reversals of Night IX.

Night VII A: Discovering History

After spending Night VI trapped in the vortexes of Urizen's self-serving philosophies, we witness a breakthrough to a class-conscious historical vision in Night VII A. This event is dramatized in the reintegration of the fallen Urthona—his reabsorbtion of his Spectre in Los, Los's reunion with his Emanation, Enitharmon, and their collaboration to liberate their abandoned child, Orc. Since Urthona represents simultaneously the Edenic world's capacity for intellectual and social harmony, this struggle for his revival takes place in both politics and thought. While *The Four Zoas* as a whole demonstrates the social and cultural restoration, Night VII A introduces the intellectual shift which began in the early nineteenth century and whose implications for the future Blake was the first to realize.

Since the knowledge of human praxis is history, the breakthrough in *The Four Zoas* occurs appropriately at the time when the other characters abandon Urizen's ideology of mechanical relations governed by eternal laws and discover that, in fact, his universe is a historical, human creation. The beings who have come to "dwell in dim oblivion" (*FZ* 73:10) wish to shake themselves out of an amnesiac state in which they have been stumbling like somnambulists, so the Spectre and Enitharmon commence to dredge up memories out of their fading dreams. They reveal that the "World of Solid darkness" in which they have been "Shut up in stifling obstruction rooted in dumb despair" (*FZ* 74:17–18), far from being eternal, had never existed until Urizen overthrew Eden and usurped dominion over a hell of his own creation. The resulting leap of consciousness coincides, as I will try to show, with the nineteenth century's formulation of a revolutionary, historical ideology.

With Urthona's fall, the unity between man and nature, human experience and ideas, individual and society is shattered. Then, the Spectre of Urthona appeared as what Frye calls "the isolated subjective aspect of existence in this world, the energy with which a man . . . copes with nature."[4] He is now separated from a community kept alive only in the social vision of Los. As a prophet, Los is heir to those Hebrews who molded a vision of their people's history in order to provoke their social conscience and inspire their common destiny. Frye identifies him with "the imaginative control of time,"[5] that is, with the historical consciousness he creates with his chains of days and years and his armies of fifty-two weeks. At this point, however, Los's voice has been silenced. His subjective will has been absorbed in the individualistic obsessions of his Spectre, while the alienation of his emanation, Enitharmon, has deprived him of any real power over the material world. Enitharmon has, instead, become the mistress of Urizen, serving an inhuman metaphysics, alternately supernatural and mechanistic. The Spectre, in like manner, has been trapped in the futile pursuits of both personal fantasy and purposeless productivity.

The sole remaining active force is the child of Los's and Enitharmon's ancient union, the revolutionary Orc. The product of developments in society and the material world, it is Orc who finally challenges Urizen's reign, an unmistakable allusion to the French Revolution. Orc's revolt has within it "visions of sweet bliss far other than this burning clime . . . visions of delight so lovely that they urge thy rage" (*FZ* 78:35,38). However, by the time of this writing Blake has concluded that the vision arising from the masses needs and desires is not itself sufficient for a successful revolution. Orc's power is limited: "I rage in the deep for Lo my feet & hands are naild to the burning rock / Yet my fierce fires are better than thy snows" (*FZ* 79:1–2). Without a highly developed consciousness to direct his rebelliousness, Orc can fall prey to Urizenic ideology or degenerate into a mere lust for power. But this was exactly what happened in the French Revolution. Erdman suggests[6] that Blake intended the revolution's deviation into Napoleonic war and empire after the coup d'état of the 18th Brumaire in his image of Orc's metamorphosis into his serpent form, "turning affection into fury & thought into abstraction / A Self consuming dark devourer rising into the heavens" (*FZ* 80:47–48).

Nonetheless, it is highly significant that, whatever his reevaluation of the outcome of that revolution, Blake retains it through all his versions of *The Four Zoas* as the catalyst which provokes the intellectual synthesis that occurs in Night VII A. If theory is necessary for a successful revolution, it is still action that will inspire liberations of consciousness. In fact, the cultural consequences of the French Revolution were enormous. Its massive assault on the status quo exploded all forms of static philosophy and gave birth to the dialectical orientation towards thought and history which characterized both the romantic poets and the nineteenth-century German philosophers. In fact, even the failure of that revolution bore theoretical fruit, provoking a host of thinkers, such as Marx and Blake, to probe the dynamics of history so that—they hoped—future revolutions might be better understood and more successfully concluded. The revolution's effects on the intellectual are dramatized by Blake when the Spectre of Urthona is moved at the end of Night VI to take a stand in defense of Orc against Urizen.

The Spectre of Urthona and Romantic Reconciliation

Blake's portrayal of the Spectre can be seen to constitute a criticism of much that M. H. Abrams has descried as essential to romanticism. It was, Abrams argues, the romantics' "cardinal concern . . . to help redeem man by fostering a reconciliation with nature, which, because man has severed himself from his earlier unity with it, has become alien and inimical to him." He attributes to the romantics

concepts which have evolved into the reigning diagnosis of our own age of anxiety: the claim that man, who was once well, is now ill, and that at the core of the modern malaise lies his fragmentation, dissociation, estrangement, or . . . "alienation." The individual . . . has become radically split in three main aspects. He is divided within himself, he is divided from other men, and he is divided from his environment; his only hope for recovery . . . is to find the way to a reintegration which will restore his unity with himself, his community with his fellow men, and his companionability with an alien and hostile outer world.[7]

This precisely is the Spectre's consciousness. He knows himself as a divided and contradictory being, haunted by memories of a lost unity in which he lived at one with his Emanation, Enitharmon:

> Where thou & I in undivided Essence walkd about
> Imbodied. thou my garden of delight & I the spirit in the garden
> Mutual there we dwelt in one anothers joy revolving.   (*FZ* 84:5–7)

The Spectre's memory of his fall into division is an important step in the movement back toward integration. His yearning for a lost community where once he "Livd / Drinking the joys of Universal Manhood" (*FZ* 84:10–11) will be crucial to the revival of Los's social power. He describes the lost Eden where he lived with Enitharmon and their transmutation into fallen beings, when she was projected as a divided part of himself and Los was left as a deformed counterpart (*FZ* 84:1–35). In this world, accordingly, we do not find permanent self-sufficient particles buffeted by external forces, but the constant metamorphoses of one thing into another—the mutual interdependency of subject and object and the interpenetration of desire and reality within a humanized environment. Urthona is able to offer some resistance to Urizen and, at least temporarily, defend Orc at the end of Night VI because his vision of the world as process and change and his protest against the status quo in the name of a lost harmony legitimizes the demand for revolution.

Harold Bloom once observed that the Spectre of Urthona is the "fearful selfhood" that "haunts Romantic poetry."[8] It is in this predicament that Blake captures the Spectre. As individual self-consciousness, devoid of social power, his longing for unity can only take the form of a romantic eros whose frustrated intensity leads it into greater isolation. The paradigm for this dilemma, at least for poets like Keats and Shelley, is romantic love:

> Thou knowest that the Spectre is in Every Man insane brutish
> Deformd that I am thus a ravening devouring lust continually
> Craving & devouring but my eyes are always upon thee O lovely
> Delusion.   (*FZ* 84:36–39)

Blake identifies the limits of any romantic quest for individual wholeness in the Spectre's disastrous attempt to unite with Enitharmon. Since she represents all forms of alien objectivity, both estranged nature and religion's metaphysical spirits, we might understand these lines as a criticism of all attempts to overcome the dualism of subject and object outside of social change. Blake's depiction of their intercourse amid "the intoxicating fumes of Mystery" (*FZ* 85:5) represents his rejection of all such forms of the "Apocalyptic marriage of mind and nature"[9] as merely new forms of escapist religion. Abrams's characterization of romanticism as secular Christianity turns out to be all too apt. We should remember that in Blake's vision only Albion, the redeemed human community, can be wedded to Jerusalem in Eden. All other unions, though they represent a progression from the completely dichotomized realm of generation, can achieve only the transitory unity of Beulah, the "married land" of most romanticism. For the romantics replaced the dualism of man against nature with a threefold dialectic of humanity-in-nature and nature-in-humanity, emphasizing a vital force which suffused and united all organic life and all consciousness. But Blake's Eden is fourfold, nature-in-humanity-in-society, for it recognizes the extent to which the forms of collectivity, in consciousness as our common myths or in action as the production of our material existence, mediates the development both of the individual and nature.

Abrams's argument is that romanticism represents a secularization of a Christian legacy. This is true, but it means too that the romantics inherited the dichotomy which plagued Christianity from its inception: visions of a collective, revolutionary apocalypse versus a private, interior redemption. Abrams's insight that the romantics were inspired by the French Revolution, but translated its impetus primarily into a psychological and interior dialectic, is also true, but one has to share some of their biases to celebrate it, and one must certainly exclude Blake from a "visionary company" defined by such quietism.

As much as Blake admired Wordsworth as a poet, Wordsworth's articulation of the romantic marriage of mind and nature so infuriated the radical poet that it "caused him a bowel complaint which nearly killed him." Wordsworth writes in *The Recluse* (63–68):

> How exquisitely the Individual Mind
> (And the progressive powers perhaps no less
> Of the whole species) to the external World
> Is fitted—& how exquisitely too,
> Theme this but little heard of among Men
> The external World is fitted to the Mind.

To which Blake exlaims, "You shall not bring me down to believe

such fitting & fitted I know better & Please your Lordship" (PB 656).
He then goes on to quote a few lines further where Wordsworth hears
"Humanity in fields & groves / Pipe solitary anguish" and "sorrow
barricadoed evermore / Within the walls of cities" (76–80), to which
Blake protests, "does not this Fit & is it not Fitting most Exquisitely
too but to what?" (PB 656). Clearly there can be no reconciliation
while social life still creates such misery. To find harmony in such a
world is mere acquiescence to the status quo, a romantic revival of
mystery's old promise of individual salvation.

Abrams acknowledges a limitation in the romantics' social vision:
"The Romantic poets were not *complete* poets, in that they represent
little of the social dimension of human experience; for although they
insist on the importance of community, they express this matter
largely as a profound need of the individual consciousness."[10] The
social basis for their perspective is revealed in Blake's identification
of the Spectre with the alienated intelligentsia. No longer a mere
fraction of the dominant classes, but frequently forming a new inter-
mediate stratum of their own, artists were even further dislodged
from adaptation to the existing society by the catastrophic events of
the French and industrial revolutions. The indifference the new market economy shows towards all culture, values, and human feelings
caused these intellectuals to reject their society's claim on their
allegiance. Against the self-congratulation and complacency of its
prosperity, they weighed the human consequences: a divided self out
of touch with both emotional and bodily sensitivities, demoralized
by the meaninglessness of its activity and caught up in relationships
which only revealed how psychic conditioning and social circumstances had already destroyed all possibility for such relationship.
Artists, philosophers, and moral visionaries found themselves with
no role in a pragmatic world, excluded from the bourgeois centers of
power and usually estranged from the rising working-class movement which offered the most serious challenge to bourgeois hegemony. Here the romantics would be divided between those like
Shelley, Hazlitt, Ruskin, and Morris who sought to forge links with
the radical movement and those who offered purely aesthetic, philosophic or psychological alternatives to the bourgeois world. As the
case of Wordsworth and Coleridge shows, however, the dichotomy
lay as much within these thinkers as between them.

Ideological and social biases clashed. The romantics' determination to reexamine philosophic premises was partly a response to the
limitations of the enlightenment ideology that inspired the French
Revolution. However, their desire to transcend "mere" social and
material change was as much a result of their own social position

which increasingly locked them up in an ivory tower divorced from both the material capability of the bourgeoisie and the collective power of the workers. Continually meditating upon their condition, seeking intellectual and emotional answers to historic questions yet becoming no more capable of changing that condition, they fell deeper and deeper into the pit of subjectivity.

In addition, we noted earlier that Blake's Spectre signified an alienated productivity as well as an estranged creativity, and perhaps also the diversion of intellect into purely technological concerns, "a pursuit of the instrumental and mechanical for its own sake."[11] The social disaster involved in the Spectre's intercourse with Enitharmon, then, also involves the ravages performed by individual will on the material world in the Industrial Revolution. This is conveyed in the imagery preceding this interlude in Night VI and follows it in Night VII B. This context is, in fact, the real source of the intellectual's alienation. It explains why, no matter how much Blake may share the romantics' aversion to dualism, their dismay at a world alien to the human affections, and their proposal that art pursue reintegration, his vision must be differentiated from all that would provide solutions outside of complete economic and social revolution.

Blake rejects any reunion of subject and object, Spectre and Emanation outside the collective, historical world of Los. The fall of Urthona, having been a social as well as a psychic split, cannot be overcome, except through the restoration of power over nature to an egalitarian community. Blake's revolutionary apocalypse cannot be equated with those philosophies which keep everything of the dialectic except that which counts most—its historic, human content. So this apocalypse will not be merely a Wordsworthian identification with nature, nor the translation of religious doctrines into an equally abstract psychological mythology, nor the aesthetic transmutation of perceptual objects into paradises of words and colors, nor any form of sexual mysticism which proposes to obliterate all the abrasiveness of daily life in the momentary fusion of an orgasm. Though he shares romanticism's repugnance toward the dichotomies of modern life, Blake's vision is closer to Marx's in this respect than to the visions of Keats, Wallace Stevens, Hegel, Jung, or D. H. Lawrence. He might have agreed with Marx's criticism of Feuerbach's own "Natural Supernaturalism":

He overlooks the fact that after completing his work, the chief thing still remains to be done. For the fact that the secular foundation detaches itself from itself and establishes itself in the clouds as an independent realm is only to be explained by the self-cleavage and the self-contradictoriness of this secular basis. The latter must itself, therefore, first be understood in its contradiction and then, by the removal of the contradiction, revolutionized in practice.[12]

The Decline and Revival of Prophecy

The real breakthrough comes, therefore, not as a reunion of Spectre and Emanation (mind and nature, body and spirit, thought and experience), but of the Spectre and Los, individual and social consciousness. Los represents the survival in thought of a community which, in fact, had been shattered. He keeps alive a radical, popular vision in opposition to the world view which a Urizenic elite tries to portray as indistinguishable from reality itself. Since they also control much of reality and create the world in their own image, this independence is difficult to attain. Los accomplishes it by revealing the historical limits of the Urizenic universe, undermining its claims as "nature" by proving it the creation of specific human beings in the service of specific interests under concrete and transient conditions.

> Yet ceasd he not from labouring at the roarings of his Forge
> . . . .
> At the sublime Labours for Los. compelld the invisible Spectre
> To labours mighty, with vast strength, with his mighty chains,
> In pulsations of time, & extensions of space . . .
> With great labour upon his anvils & in his ladles the Ore
> He lifted, pouring it into the clay ground prepar'd with art;
> Striving with Systems to deliver Individuals from those Systems.
>
> (J 10:62–11:5)

In "forming under his heavy hand the hours / The days & years. in chains of iron round the limbs of Urizen" (FZ 52:29–53:1), Los is establishing the historical limits of Urizen's power against the ideological attempt to declare it eternal, probing its origins in order that he might prophesy its end.

Resistance to assimilation is extremely difficult, however, particularly in nonrevolutionary periods when the prophet stands alone in contradicting the claims of the status quo:

> In terrors Los shrunk from his task. his great hammer
> Fell from his hand his fires hid their strong limbs in smoke
> . . . .
> Pale terror seizd the Eyes of Los as he beat round
> The hurtling Demon. terrifid at the shapes
> Enslavd humanity put on he became what he beheld.
>
> (FZ 55:16–22)

Los falls prey to what Marx calls the "illusion of the epoch," the tendency for the ideas of the ruling class in each era to become the ruling ideas. Similarly, in the *Book of Urizen* (13:40) we find "The Eternal Prophet & Urizen clos'd" in complete collaboration. The specific event alluded to in *The Four Zoas* seems to be Christianity's decline from an apocalyptic into a mystery cult. As such, however, the event symbolizes all failures of revolutionary, apocalyptic vision.

For Blake, facing the enormous temptation to "eschatological despair" posed by a failed revolution, the other key historical antecedent would have been Milton's experience.[13] In such a situation, the Puritan bard had faced a severe crisis and had not acquiesced. He had held on to his apocalyptic faith—only in an attenuated form, however. After the Restoration, Milton could only uphold the millennium as a fideistic contradiction of history, rather than its perpetual possibility; history is revealed in the final books of *Paradise Lost* as a cycle of frustration. The pathfinder had wound up in the wilderness full or raw hope and courage, but with little of the prophetic illumination remaining which in the prose had pointed the way forward to Jerusalem. As Blake finishes the story, Milton spends the next hundred years still trying to figure it all out, "pondring the intricate mazes of Providence" (*M* 2:17) into which he had stumbled in *Paradise Lost* until finally he turns to Blake for the salvation granted by historical hindsight.

Now Blake and the romantics were faced with Milton's dilemma once again. Bloom is right to see in Los's impotence Blake's anticipation of "the crisis in Wordsworth's and Coleridge's creative lives,"[14] for he was well aware of such dangers. Like Milton, the romantics were all concerned with the pursuit of "genuine freedom" (*Prelude* XIV.132), as they too lived in an age of revolution. However, for Wordsworth and Coleridge questions of liberty and power led to contradictions which drove them to disillusion and despair, "the melancholy waste of hopes o'erthrown" (*Prelude* II.448). Having expected the French Revolution to bring back "the bowers of Paradise" (*Prelude* XI.120), they could not understand how it resulted instead in the Napoleonic empire. Coleridge snapped his "squeaking trumpet of sedition,"[15] and both went from a revolutionary defense of individual liberty to supporting the established church and the repressive state as the only props for that same individualism against the threats of the democratic mob. But this social process was not new. In the English Revolution as in the French, liberty had turned into tyranny and libertarians into oligarchs. Cromwell had no sooner finished killing the king than he had turned to the elimination of the democratic Levellers. Presbyterians had gone from being martyrs of conscience to becoming "Oppressors in their turn" (*Prelude* XI.206), just as in France. So Wordsworth, according to Abrams, had recognized his "error in fixing upon an external political means, the French Revolution, his hopes for achieving universal freedom and equality." Like Milton, some romantics now turned instead to a "paradise within . . . happier far" (*PL* XII.587). Abrams documents with approval their transposition of concepts taken from social history, ideas of "slavery," "tyranny," "mastery," and "conflict" "into non-political areas, as metaphors of mind."[16]

Blake's obsession with Milton derives from his perception that much of what has been going on across the Channel had already been played out on Albion's rocky shore under the eyes of the Puritan poet. Blake hopes that he might learn from Milton how to avoid a similar fate and extract from an analysis of Milton's contradictions a purified prophetic light by which to guide his contemporaries. Here Blake's interest in Milton parts company with those of his fellow romantics who believed it sufficient to revive the Puritan's libertarianism and unnecessary to go beyond it. Their achievement, as Abrams realizes, will be to secularize Milton's vision. They will not transcend its political limitations. Wordsworth declares, "Milton! thou shouldst be living at this hour," but Blake recalls the bard "To cleanse the Face of [his] Spirit by Self-examination" (*M* 40:37) in a historical reevaluation of the significance of Milton and his revolution.

In this scrutiny, I will argue, Blake will seek to divest his own prophecy of the individualism inherent in both Milton's and the romantics' conception of liberty. Theoretically, this advance occurs with the reunion of the Spectre and Los, which places the individual quest for redemption once again within the context of social revolution and, at the same time, infuses social conscience with the energies of a reviving will for change. Blake keeps alive the promise of revolutionary romanticism so that the suffering individual, no longer "wrapd up / In his own sorrow" (*FZ* 70:42–43), will make common cause with others, and individual aspirations will motivate collective achievements. People will burst forth from their isolating shells just as "Los embracd the Spectre first as a brother / Then as another Self" (*FZ* 85:29–30), proclaiming,

> Glory Glory Glory to the holy Lamb of God
> Who now beginneth to put off the dark Satanic body
> Now we behold redemption Now we know that life Eternal
> Depends alone upon the Universal hand & not in us
> Is aught but death In individual weakness sorrow & pain.
>
> (*FZ* 104:6–10)

Divided humanity will find their wholeness in each other, and those who have been laboring at the mill like slaves, simply by joining their own hands will bring forth that universal hand to build Jerusalem.

Before this can happen, however, Los must realize that the Spectre's desperate solitude is itself a new manifestation of social life and human historical creation, a consequence of the prophetic error or building bourgeois individualism. Thus Los recognizes himself in the Spectre, who addresses him: "Not as another but as thy real Self I am thy Spectre / Tho horrible & Ghastly to thine Eyes" (*FZ* 85:38–39). This is the moment which will inspire the Puritan's confrontation with his selfhood in *Milton*, a whole new epic. There as Los he cannot simply uphold a biblical vision in the abstract; he must struggle with the deformed consciousness of his own time and by revealing its social basis free himself from the false assumptions which have threatened to paralyze him. Like the other romantics, Blake was inspired by the French Revolution to explorations of intellect, but where they often sought solutions to social problems in individual consciousness, he must find the answer even to such individualism in history. Once he forges that link, the Spectre, having been absorbed into Los, disappears from the poem, and Los takes up his labors anew.

His first task is to "Unbar the Gates of Memory" (*FZ* 85:37) and revive historical consciousness. As Northrop Frye interprets this episode:

> The Spectre of Urthona . . . gives him a sense of the passing of time which his imagination creates into a vision of the meaning of history. The latter is the reason why Blake puts the union of Los and his Spectre directly after his account of the Orc cycle. The passing of such a cycle increases the conscious awareness in the imaginative view of life, as Hebrew prophecy was inspired by the decline of Egypt and Babylon.[17]

Los must now begin to explore the vistas opened by the Spectre's revelation that the existing world had fallen from a prior Eden and possesses within itself dynamics of metamorphosis. Once released from Urizen's frozen universe by a sense of its past development, he can revive an understanding of its teleology and progress. With his newly incorporated Spectre, Los commences building Golgonooza which begins to open up the possibility of "new heavens & a new Earth" (*FZ* 87:9).

From Fatalism to Commitment—The Return to Orc

Temporarily, however, this work is stymied by the obstacles represented by Enitharmon and her vision of an unchanging material universe which continually traps humanity within its circle of destiny:

> But Los stood on the limit of Translucence weeping & trembling
> Filled with doubts in self accusation beheld the fruit
> Or Urizens Mysterious tree for Enitharmon thus spake
>
> When In the Deeps beneath I gatherd of this ruddy fruit
> It was by that I knew that I had Sinnd & then I knew
> That without a ransom I could not be savd from Eternal death
> That Life lives upon Death & by devouring appetite
> All things subsist on one another thenceforth in Despair
> I spend my glowing time.   (FZ 87:13–21)

A history of scarcity and want in nature—which, without the aid of human creativity, remains barren—has produced this fatalistic vision. In the absence of increasing abundance, all beings are locked into an eternal struggle for survival at each other's expense. Religion had accepted this vision of the universe and, ignoring humanity's unaccomplished tasks, had condemned sinful human nature. The salvation religion offered was purely external, "a ransom" which would redeem human beings from nature and from their own humanity rather than inspire Los's task, the salvation of nature and humanity by their own conscious powers. Unless Los can enlist the cooperation of Enitharmon, he remains only a voice crying in the wilderness, lamenting the abuses of Urizen.

However, once Enitharmon can be coaxed into leaving Urizen's camp for Los's own, the alienated material world can come into Los's hands, and he can acquire once again the hammer and furnace of Urthona, with their power actually to change reality. Then prophecy will no longer be limited to moral remonstrance, but will propel real material developments that constantly open up new possibilities for human expansion. This discovery is the other side of Urizen's demonic industrialism depicted in the previous book, the apocalyptic potential offered by technology for converting the material world into a form of human gratification. Enitharmon's move from Urizen's Newtonian world to Los's universe of change signifies Blake's discovery that nature is not static but evolving, particularly when it can be continually infused with a human purposefulness which lifts it out of the realm of necessity into the service of human freedom.

The problem then is how to remove technology from Urizen's hands. The only serious challenge to his power has been mounted by the fiery Orc, but Enitharmon recoils from that confrontation, believing that from Orc's material desperation can only arise new versions of lust, greed, and destruction. The Orc cycle, as we have seen, has just culminated in the degeneration of the French Revolution, which seems to confirm Enitharmon's fears that historical action is also condemned to a cyclical hopelessness in which nothing new can be created, and rebellion can yield only more oppression. She fears, moreover, that Los's social criticism merely gives aid and comfort to such insurgency. If the abused masses are not restrained, she feels, they will not "redeem us but destroy" (*FZ* 87:60), creating through their revolution an orgy of vengeance—"fit punishment for such / Hideous offenders" (*FZ* 87:55–56). Enitharmon dreads all conflict because she cannot yet see any difference between the unrelenting violence of repression needed to sustain an unjust order and the cleansing effect of a revolutionary struggle which removes the causes of injustice and conflict. Los, however, points out to her that the oppressed masses do not simply represent a negating mob aroused by Urizen's persecution, but also a survival of the positive values of human solidarity symbolized by Jesus: "look! behold! take comfort! / Turn inwardly thine Eyes & there behold the Lamb of God / Clothed in Luvahs robes of blood descending to redeem" (*FZ* 87:43–45).

Los appeals to Enitharmon to abandon her counter-revolutionary fears and instead join him in forming a vision that can guide the rebellious lower classes beyond the Orc cycle to real freedom:

> Lovely delight of Men Enitharmon shady refuge from furious war
> Thy bosom translucent is a soft repose for the weeping souls
> Of those piteous victims of battle there they sleep in happy obscurity
> They feed upon our life we are their victims.　　　　(*FZ* 90:5–8)

Enitharmon encompasses the dead past, the bodies of all who suffered individual death and now "sleep in happy obscurity." She contains within her bosom also all the struggles and efforts which seem to have come to naught, all defeats and losses. From that perspective, humanity remains a victim of history, which itself appears as a series of dead ends whose legacy of failure and despair weighs upon the living.

Los proposes that from this historical substance he and Enitharmon create a new vision, one which will reveal that the dead live on through their creations; for though individuals die, their works live in collective humanity. The struggles of the past can thus be seen to have been neither final victories nor defeats, but rather contributions to those later generations who will build on the sacrifices of those who preceded them:

> 　　　Stern desire
> I feel to fabricate embodied semblances in which the dead
> May live before us in our palaces & in our gardens of labour

Which now opend within the Center we behold spread abroad
To form a world of Sacrifice of brothers & sons & daughters.
(*FZ* 90:8–12)

Through such an understanding, even the failures of the past can be
made to serve the present in its tasks of liberation. Setbacks are
acknowledged, but the emphasis is on overcoming them through an
increasing understanding of their roots in insufficiently radicalized
institutions and ideologies. Such an ideology opens up the potential
for an even more thoroughgoing revolution and thus serves "To comfort Orc in his dire sufferings" (*FZ* 90:13).

Los finds that, through this alliance with the rebellious masses and
material reality, he once again acquires Urthona's potential for mas-
tering his world: "look my fires enlume afresh / Before my face
ascending with delight as in ancient times" (*FZ* 90:13–14). Erdman
writes of such metamorphoses that

> Los walking the earth is a transformed Orc and holds the visionary
> power to become transformed into Urthona. He is Poetic Genius who
> can see beyond the gates of sense and the horizon of the present.
> Because he is conscious of the loss of Eden he can guide mankind to it:
> "I know I am Urthona keeper of the Gates of Heaven, / And that I can at
> will expatiate in the Gardens of bliss" (*J* 82:81–82).
> "At will"—but Orc must supply the will.[18]

Los takes his vision of history directly from the class struggle of Orc
against Urizen:

> So Enitharmon spoke & Los his hands divine inspired began
> To modulate his fires studious the loud roaring flames
> He vanquishd with the strength of Art bending their iron points
> · · · · · · · ·
> From out the ranks of Urizens war & from the fiery lake
> Of Orc bending down as the binder of Sheaves follows
> The reaper in both arms embracing the furious raging flames.
> (*FZ* 90:25–31)

Los cannot do without Orc's furious raging fires—"the prophet without the rebel is impotent."[19] Conversely, without Los's guiding hand
to produce "sweet moderated fury" (*FZ* 90:22), mere insurrection
would only consume itself in costly, bloody, and futile upheavals.
Only through a profound grasp of history's dynamics—the sources of
oppression, the dangers of false consciousness and the real possibilities for change—can Orc resist the usurpations which threaten
to transform him into his satanic opposite.

The Birth of Historicism

Blake's vision here of the breakthrough to a thoroughly historical world view captures the tendency of European thought as it would develop from the Enlightenment to the time of Marx. Rationalists like Hume, Voltaire, and Gibbon had studied history to show the progress of their age of science over the dark centuries of superstition.[20] At the same time, world explorations had revealed a whole primitive stratum behind recorded history, provoking an interest in comparative culture. This new sense of the scope of human experience would lead to Schiller's conception of a universal history encompassing all human experience in a single, interrelated vision; in this atmosphere were written the first real world histories (although some ventures had been made in the Renaissance).[21] At the same time, the historical impetus was spurred by a rising nationalism that promoted antiquarian studies whose end was to demonstrate the unique cultural origins of various European communities. Such a climate inspired Bishop Percy's *Reliques of Ancient English Poetry*, as well as the republican antiquarianism of a Thomas Hollis and other of Blake's contemporaries who celebrated a lost republic of freeborn ancient Britons.

Perhaps the most advanced historical conception was that of the Scottish philosopher, Adam Ferguson. Growing up between the still tribal Highlands and the commercial Lowlands, he was able to forge the first scientific theory of social evolution.[22] The Enlightenment had generally been prevented from seeing this by a conviction that bourgeois society conformed to the laws of nature itself and needed no historical explanation. But as early as 1767, Ferguson had tried to explain its origins in his *Essay on the History of Civil Society*. Meanwhile, in eighteenth-century Naples, Vico had conceived of historical development as a spiral, an apt image for Blake's own dialectical vision. This evolutionary perspective was considerably aided by the revolution in France. Herder and Hegel developed philosophies of historical development—Hegel, like Blake, finding the dynamics of history to provide a better paradigm for reality and thought than the laws of Newtonian physics. Soon French bourgeois historians such as Guizot, Thierry, and Mignet would elaborate a vision of class struggle in their accounts of the middle class's triumph over feudal aristocracy.[23]

We should not be surprised in this context to find historical concerns also at the center of Blake's poetic and pictorial art. Even his apprenticeship as an engraver was spent copying antiquaries for James Basire and exploring what he believed to be the traces of an

egalitarian civilization which, having preceded the English monarchy, might be hoped to survive it. In his old age, we find Blake
still sketching spiritual visitants from the past such as Wat Tyler,
Herod, an Egyptian taskmaster, and English royal figures, whose
resemblance to people of his own day confirmed his continued
faith in a past that lived on in the present.

Blake located his own art within that native English school of
"Historical & Poetical artists like Barry & Mortimer" (PB 570) who
ignored the current fashion of portrait and landscape painting and
chose instead subjects from English history which they invested
with contemporary moral and political significance. James Barry
was an enthusiast for Irish independence, women's rights, republican government, and the abolition of slavery. He appears in
Blake's marginalia as a kind of alter ego, *"the really Industrious,
Virtuous, & Independent Barry"* who *"is driven out to make room
for a pack of Idle Sycophants"* (PB 565). Blake protests that "while Sʳ
Joshua was rolling in Riches Barry was Poor & Unemployd except by
his own Energy" (PB 625), which he devoted to covering the halls of
the Society of Arts with murals. Barry had declared himself a champion of "the true sublime style of historical art," and, according to
Erdman, during the years from 1800 to 1809, Blake's hopes for a
prophetic role before a wide audience were tied up with the pros-
pects of Barry's proposal for publicly supported, socially relevant art.
Barry had hoped to get Parliament to establish a national gallery of
art to be adorned with pictures from English history so he might
"decorate Westminster Hall with giants."[24]

Blake, who committed his own art to "the historical fact in its
poetical vigour; so as it always happens" (PB 534), seems to have that
dream before him in his depiction at the climax of Night VII A of Los
laboring at his fires:

> Los drew them forth out of the deeps planting his right foot firm
> Upon the Iron crag of Urizen thence springing up aloft
> Into the heavens of Enitharmon in a mighty circle
>
> At first he drew a line upon the walls of shining heaven
> And Enitharmon tincturd it with beams of blushing love
> It remaind permanent a lovely form inspird divinely human
> Dividing into just proportions Los unwearied labourd
> The immortal lines upon the heavens till with sighs of love
> Sweet Enitharmon mild Entrancd breathd forth upon the wind
> The spectrous dead Weeping the Spectres viewd the immortal works
> Of Los Assimilating to those forms Embodied & Lovely
> In youth & beauty in the arms of Enitharmon mild reposing.
>
> (*FZ* 90:32–43)

In this shift from epic metamorphosis to a rare moment of overt autobiography, we find that Los's furnaces are burning in the poet's own workshop where he and his wife Catherine work in friendly collaboration. The product of these labors and thus of the whole leap of consciousness in Night VII A is, in the most immediate sense, *The Four Zoas* itself and Blake's engraved prophetic books.

The basic idea for such a universal history had already been crystallized in the Judeo-Christian scheme of salvation which moved from the Fall to a future Apocalypse. In Night VII A, Urizen's circle of destiny is overthrown by a movement opened up backward through the Spectre's and Enitharmon's memories of an unfallen world and forward through Los's revolutionary vision. In Blake's narrative the industrial revolution of Night VI has ultimately increased mankind's potential for changing nature, and the French upheavals at the start of Night VII A have indicated both the masses' potential to move history and the transience of Urizen's supposedly eternal institutions. These developments, once comprehended and directed by Los, bring forth the new incarnation of Jesus that opens Night VIII. Blake identifies it with the long-anticipated Second Coming, for "Then All in Great Eternity Met in the Council of God . . . / And Enitharmon said I see the Lamb of God upon Mount Zion" (*FZ* 99:1,17). Blake's comprehension of this event as the culmination of advances in production and politics puts him ahead of even the Utopian socialists and at the very threshold of Marxism. For, as Eric Hobsbawm writes, "In Marx," through a similar conception of history, "the gap between the wish and its fulfillment, the present and the future, is at last closed."[25]

Like Marx's, Blake's reading of history led to revolutionary conclusions because it denied the institutions of his own society any ancient authority and, rendering them recent human creations, made them completely subject to human alteration. Here Blake found himself in opposition to eighteenth-century historians who, having dismissed feudal forms as the product of backwardness and superstition, were happy to announce that history proved the inevitability of middle-class society. In his description of the "Ancient Britons," a lost fresco which presumably testified to the superiority of primitives, Blake announces as the intent of his works to refute these historians:

> The reasoning historian, turner and twister of causes and consequences, such as Hume, Gibbon and Voltaire; cannot with all their artifice, turn or twist one fact or disarrange self evident action and reality. Reasons and opinions concerning acts, are not history. Acts themselves alone are history, and these are neither the exclusive property of Hume, Gibbon nor Voltaire, Echard, Rapin, Plutarch, nor

Herodotus. Tell me the Acts, O historian, and leave me to reason upon them as I please. (PB 534)

He challenges these writers here because they deny the existence of an egalitarian golden age and, "being weakly organized themselves, cannot see either miracle or prodigy" by which such an era might be restored. Blake protests that the opinions of anyone "who does not see spiritual agency, is not worth any man's reading; he who rejects a fact because it is improbable, must reject all History' (PB 534). "Miracle" usually denoted divine intervention in history, but since "all deities reside in the human breast" (*MHH* 11), by this and by "spiritual agency" Blake upholds the ability of collective humanity to create its own destiny. From this perspective, the greatest miracle is revolution, a total redirection of time; consequently Tom Paine was a "worker of miracles," for "Is it a greater miracle to feed five thousand men with five loaves than to overthrow all the armies of Europe with a small pamphlet?" (PB 606).

Blake's Apocalypse: Unveiling History

This perspective will also differentiate Blake's art from much of the other social criticism found in nineteenth-century art—the magnificent, but only reformist, indictments by novelists like Dickens. Blake understood that merely to delineate oppression was not sufficient to make one a revolutionary artist. The prophet must also show the way out. In his epoch, any honest observer could record the shadow of dark satanic mills encroaching on the English landscape. Similarly, in our age, as that economic system becomes moribund, the mere journalistic eye yields its indictment. An overriding image of contemporary art is wreckage; a dominant literary mode is negation and irony; even film, once primarily a preserve of romantic fantasies and righteous combats, increasingly projects images of catastrophe and despair. Often, the main challenge our artists are able to muster against the "system" is the futile moral indignation of a single, unarmed individual, hurling himself defiantly in the path of the tanks.

Blake's art, by contrast, set out to show the hidden weaknesses, rather than the apparent strengths, of the oppressors. Recall that it is Urizen, the tyrant, who pronounces himself almighty, omnipotent, omniscient, and eternal and places himself at the center of a self-constructed universe buttressed by myths of necessity. His stature diminishes as soon as we begin to view him from Blake's prophetic stance. Then he appears as a Johnny-come-lately on the historical scene, strutting about in outsized royal robes, furiously trying to upstage the Eternal Man and promulgating his commands with a divine bluster in which we invariably detect the hollow ring of a huckster. Blake shows us that Urizen lives, from the moment of his usurpation, insomniac, anxiety-ridden, and tormented with a fear that in the womb of history his present slaves will develop into his future conquerors, "that Prophetic boy [who] Must grow up to command his Prince" (*FZ* 38:6–7).

This vision of an ultimate reversal renders *The Four Zoas* an apocalypse. It is interesting, by way of contrast, that in our own day "apocalypse" has primarily come to signify a holocaust without any corresponding triumph. Florence Sandler points out the Blake develops its literal connotation as an "unveiling."[26] The prophet assaults the forms of "this world," first of all, by revealing their contingency. Thus the revolutionary climax of *The Four Zoas* begins when Los tears away from the existing order its claim to objectivity. "His right hand branching out in fibrous Strength," Los "Siezd the Sun. His left hand like dark roots coverd the Moon / And tore them down cracking the heavens across from immense to immense" (*FZ* 117:7–9). The present system, hitherto guarded by a veil of natural legitimacy, is thus revealed as subject to human transformation and the apocalyptic trumpet sounds, "thundering along from heaven to heaven" (*FZ* 117:11).

With this breakthrough we also find "The foundations of the Eternal hills discoverd" (*FZ* 117:17); in liberating the future, the prophet also circumscribes the past, tracing the hidden origins of reigning institutions until they cease to appear eternal. In uncovering how they came into being, he discovers how they might be ended. For this reason revolutionary visions of apocalypse have traditionally focused on the myth of a primal fall. Present oppression is rendered ephemeral when viewed as a departure from ancient conditions and a prelude to their eventual restoration. When Blake welds together Genesis and Revelation in *The Four Zoas* he is following a typical revolutionary logic and taking his place in a long lower-class tradition that extended from the peasant revolts to Milton and the radical Puritans. A corresponding logic would soon lead Marx and Engels from the "secular apocalyptic"[27] of the *Communist Manifesto* to their probings of *The Origin of the Family, Private Property and the State.*

In defining its usable past, any interpretation of history adopts a stance toward the central intellectual conflicts which have pervaded it. This process of selection and modification creates a tradition. The tendency of T. S. Eliot and, recently, of Harold Bloom to brand Blake as an iconoclast misses his point. Eliot, by merging the entire past into an elite and primarily aristocratic tradition, disregards Blake's argument that there was no single tradition, but rather a popular legacy of the masses which diverged significantly from the culture of their superiors. In a revolutionary period, therefore, traditions are not discarded but rather reevaluated and reorganized. Previous biases are rejected, and the villains of old stories become heroes in the retelling. We live in just such a period and should understand this reversal. Establishment intellectuals may continue to present themselves as the heroic defenders of "civilization" or, as they like to put it, "Western civilization"—that crystallization of all humanistic achievement, soaring from its Judeo-Christian and Greco-Roman foundations. However, this view has been increasingly challenged as Westerners witness the emergence of a Third World where most of humanity has existed outside those boundaries, experiencing only a fairly recent and somewhat dubious influence from the West. Something began to shift as early as Blake's antiquarianism which has flowered in our century's growing enthusiasm for "primitive" and non-Western art. Blake understood that this split also went right through the center of Western civilization itself. Under the weight of the imperialist edifice it has been expected to support, that great tradition has for some time been showing its cracks. Malcolm X called black Americans to an exodus from Christianity as a "slave religion"; women's liberationists grant Crete cultural supremacy over Athens and Jerusalem; Palestinians question the nature of Joshua's victory at the battle of Jericho, and, in the darkened movie houses of U.S. ghettoes, audiences sometimes root for the Indians against the cowboys.

For Blake, over a century and a half ago, the fissures were already apparent. The French Revolution had knocked a hole in the dominant culture, opening a tunnel to the future from the underground past. At the same time, the explorations of the empire in the colonies were casting a new light on "precivilized" cultures. When Blake came to compose his epic of human history, it was with a conviction that not only beyond, but right within the tradition touted by Urizen, there was an opposing heritage which had been craftily obscured over the centuries, but which he might uncover. Following Blake's intellectual labors and those of his poetic persona Los is like watching the travail of a Blake Wrecking, Salvage & Construction Company hacking away at the facades of our culture. John Beer had commented that "to read *The Four Zoas* now is like walking through an ancient city which has seen several civilizations. Here a group of pillars indicates a temple, there a frieze survives in isolation, elsewhere we enter a Christian basilica."[28] What Beer intended only as a metaphor for the fragmentary artistic condition of Blake's work might be an unconscious insight into its real content. For, in this epic, Blake is an archaeologist of consciousness, chipping off artifacts of the tradition in order to reconstruct the evolution of culture.

Epic as Revisionism

The site where Blake found his Tell el Amarna was *Paradise Lost*. Here he was inquiring into how the past survived in the present, and there was Milton, having written an epic to guide his society in terms of a Genesis thousands of years old and based upon mythical materials over a millennium older than itself. Genesis can be classed with a group of similar stories discovered throughout the world by anthropologists and designated as "myths of origins," which E. O. James, the historian of religion, explains as follows:

> The many stories about the way in which the present order of events came into being which recur all over the world, are certainly not the result of an innate inquisitiveness regarding the way in which the natural order has arisen. . . . What happened in "the brave days of old", and at the creation of the world, is of practical importance because it has had a permanent effect on the subsequent behaviour and the structure of society.[29]

Bronislaw Malinowski expresses a similar point of view:

> Myth . . . is not an explanation in satisfaction of scientific interest, but a narrative resurrection of a primeval reality, told in satisfaction of deep religious wants, moral cravings, social submissions, assertions, even practical requirements. . . . It is always used to account for extraordinary privileges or duties, for great social inequalities, for severe burdens of rank.[30]

Milton had originally planned to write an epic based on the legends of Arthur, celebrating the English nation. By the time he came to write, he and the Puritan radicals had broken too drastically with feudal institutions and ideas to find models in Camelot. Clearing the board of such historical precedents, Milton turned to Hebrew sources, using the biblical fable of prehistory to create a myth of origins for the new social order struggling to be born. Into these largely prefeudal realities, he projected the values of his own society. It was for the same reason that such bourgeois philosophers as Locke and Rousseau would create their no less mythical "state of nature," peopled with beings whose institutions and predilections were remarkably like those of the rising middle class.

In order for Los to manifest "The foundations of the Eternal hills discoverd" (*FZ* 117:17), Blake first had to confront Milton's recasting of the long-established theory of origins found in Genesis as the definitive past. Blake did not assume the problem to be simply one of orthodoxy, as did the enlightenment thinkers who dismissed religious traditions as superstition while unconsciously incorporating many of their central assumptions into their own works. Rather, Blake felt there were reasons why a particular orthodoxy was still relevant, and began to seek in Genesis the origins of the institutions and values upon which Milton's culture continued to rest. In his quest for the meanings behind the myths, Blake found much of what Marx and Engels would later discover in analogous researches—the origins of those political and familial structures which the modern world had inherited from the ancient one and had adapted to its own necessities.

It is worth recalling French Fogle's point that while "Milton may never have achieved the heights as a historian that he achieved as a poet, . . . it was not for lack of serious attention to the refinements of or of sustained effort in the practice of the art of history." Moreover, Milton's interest in Genesis was itself prompted by the historical questions left unanswered by the civil war. In order to "assert Eternal Providence, / And justifie the wayes of God to men" (*PL* I.25–26), he had "to discover a pattern in history which would render intelligible the slow unfolding of God's inscrutable plan."[31] Thus the final books of *Paradise Lost* are no afterthought. Rather, this panorama, as well as the richly allusive context of biblical and historical analogues in which Milton locates humanity's primal acts, indicates that his biblical poem is still motivated by the same mundane concerns that once inspired him to project an epic on the history of Britain. Blake is one of the few critics to recognize Milton's achievement in these terms, observing that "If historical facts can be written by inspiration Miltons Paradise Lost is as true as Genesis. or Exodus" (PB 607). As true, and no more—Blake challenges the reading of history offered by both the Bible and Milton.

At the same time, Blake inherited from Milton the typological method of interpreting biblical events, which presumed that they were inherently symbolic, for God had written history as a sublime book of man's instruction. Eric Auerbach describes the approach as establishing a connection between two historical persons or events "the first of which signifies not only itself but also the second, while the second encompasses or fulfills the first."[32] The Fall had traditionally provided a rich endowment of types, leading to such conceptions as Christ as a "new Adam." J. M. Evans shows that "in this case the relationship between the type and its fulfillment is both analogical and causal, for the persons and events involved in the Fall story both foreshadowed and made necessary the persons and events involved in the Redemption."[33]

Such a perspective surely informs Milton's treatment of history in Books XI and XII as "a rich storehouse of illustrations of moral principles"[34] and a series of types revealing God's ways and works. Consequently, all the events in Milton's narrative are depicted either as echoes of mankind's fall (and repentance) or prefigurings of God's redemption. For example, Adam's succumbing to Eve is repeated when the daughters of Cain seduce the once-pious sons of Seth; and his fault in bringing "Death into the World, and all our woe" (*PL* I.3) is actualized in Cain's murder of Abel and the subsequent history of violence and ambition.

Frye has analyzed Blake's use of this typological method, which Abrams tells us released the Bible's symbols from the orthodoxy of a literal reading for the romantics' secular purposes.[35] We should note, in addition, that *The Four Zoas* might be seen as a retelling not only of Genesis but also of Milton's version of universal history in Adam's vision. From Milton's account, Blake takes such biblical incidents as the seduction by idolatrous goddesses, the flood, the usurpations of Nimrod and the building of Babel, the enslavement in Egypt, the proclamation of the Mosaic law, the wandering in the desert, the establishment of monarchy and the temple, the fall of Jerusalem, and, finally, the birth and death of Christ.

If Blake's borrowing has not been noticed, it is no wonder, for Milton's relatively straightforward narration of the events is almost unrecognizably transformed in Blake's revision. Blake carries much further Milton's conflation of events, particularly their association with materials from pagan myth and literature, altering the scriptural account to accommodate his own vision of history. Unlike Milton, Blake took as his goal neither moral instruction, nor a celebration of divine salvation, but an explication of the meaning of history itself where humanity works out its own fate. Thus the defection of Adam and Eve from God is itself illuminated, or rather allegorized, to symbolize the whole history of human injustice. In doing so, Blake diverges from most romantic uses of biblical symbols which dehistoricize them, extracting them from their contexts as expressions of feeling or ideas. What attracted Blake about typology was that actions thereby became symbols of other actions; thus he retains their fundamentally historical character and instead of offering us merely history as symbol, he presents biblical history as expressive of real events which have been forgotten or lost and as prefiguring the whole history of humankind.

Blake bases his vision on the Bible, for it was there that the poetry of history originated—"The Hebrew Bible & the Gospel of Jesus are not Allegory but Eternal Vision or Imagination of All that Exists" (PB 544). And "all that exists" is the summation of human acts. When he offers it pictorially from the hindsight of his "Vision of the Last Judgment," he calls it "a History of Art & Science the Foundation of Society Which is Humanity itself" (PB 551). The problem was that the Bible offered a biased account which sorely needed revision. Joseph Campbell compares its purpose to that of an origin myth like that found in Genesis:

> The world is full of origin myths, and all are factually false. The world is full, also, of great traditional books tracing the history of man (but focused narrowly on the local group) from the age of mythological beginnings . . . to a time almost within memory . . . . just as all primitive mythologies serve to validate the customs, systems of sentiments, and political aims of their respective local groups, so do these great traditional books. On the surface they may appear to have been composed as conscientious history. In depth they reveal themselves to have been conceived as myths: poetic readings of the mystery of life from a certain interested point of view.[36]

Blake acknowledged this subjective factor when he declared that "The Jewish & Christian Testaments are An original derivation from the Poetic Genius" (PB 3) and determined to bring his own plebeian imagination to disentangling its real vision from certain interested points of view. Hence he stated that while he and his enemies "Both read the Bible day & night," they read black where he reads white (PB 516). However, Blake had "warmly declared" to Henry Crabb Robinson that "all he knew was in the Bible." As Florence Sandler points out, Blake had been influenced by the Enlightenment's critique of the Bible and proclaimed that Voltaire and Paine had been "commissioned by God" to expose its errors.[37] He determines, therefore, to read it in its "infernal or diabolical sense" (*MHH* 24), using the corrosive of his own ideological sensitivities for "melting apparent surfaces away" and expunging the false doctrines insinuated by angelic apologists to reveal the true story beneath.

In addition, Blake maintained that "the antiquities of every Nation under Heaven, is no less sacred than that of the Jews" (PB 534), a conclusion urged by the prolific mythographers of his time. Works like Paul Henri Mallet's *Northern Antiquities* and Jacob Bryant's *New System of Analysis of Ancient Mythology* (which Blake illustrated) had opened up a vast range of mythological materials, adding Welsh, Norse, Celtic, and even Hindu tales to the already accessible classical myths. Still, within the limits of Renaissance sources and a theological bias toward showing the superiority of Scripture, *Paradise Lost* had already provided a comparative mythology. Throughout his epic, Milton had located biblical symbols alongside their pagan analogues in a rich and continuous inlay of allusions. The connections forged in this process raised questions which cried out for historical answers barred to Milton himself by his obligation to uphold Genesis's literal truth. Blake would later make that leap, using myth to expand and contest biblical explanations and to unfold (as Engels did after reading Bachofen's mythological analyses) a theory of social evolution.

In noting these poets' great epic syntheses, we should realize that their originality in incorporating and revising their prototypes was only a variation of what epic poets usually do. For the essence of the genre lies in the renovation of traditions. In analysing *Paradise Lost*, Joan Webber remarks that "in almost every instance literary epic both praises and subverts" the values of its culture.[38] In other words, the epic imagination selects and adapts what is usable in materials inherited from its antecedents to create a gestalt for its own culture. As an encyclopedic form, the epic compiles traditional materials, retells familiar stories, and reorganizes a cultural legacy from a perspective of contemporary significance. Thus, in George Thomson's analysis, the Homeric epics incorporate myths derived from a primitive tribal stage into legends about the brigand chiefs of early conquests and then remold both these layers into works celebrating the Mycenean monarchies which arose on those historical foundations.[39] By this account, Northrop Frye is absolutely right in treating the Bible as an epic. Over the centuries, the Old Testament was composed by generations of poets and editors who combined layers of oral tradition, including tribal memories, Mesopotamian myths, historical chronicles, and ritual poetry into an apotheosis of the developing Hebrew nation. That heritage, radically recast by Christian Testament and commentary, provided the symbolic framework for the Western consciousness.

Since epic is reformulation of tradition from a contemporary perspective, it can be, as Wittreich indicates, the vehicle for either a conservative or a radical vision.[40] Revolution and tradition are not inherently opposed; the question is which traditions are upheld and whether they are mustered in defense of a reactionary society or a new and progressive one. Milton and Blake both wrote revolutionary epics, looking to the past for validation of the changes they hoped to advance. Heir through the Renaissance to a classical legacy never fully assimilated by Christian vision, Milton sought to sift it and reconcile it to his Judeo-Christian legacy and to bring both to bear on his celebration of the new social order then in conflict with feudal culture. Over a century later Blake would take up the task again, and evoke those and other traditions to evaluate the culture Milton had partly helped to create from the perspective of other, rising social forces. He turns to *Paradise Lost*, then, for far more than literary borrowing, as the definitive articulation of his society's assumptions and the repository of its history and consciousness, as the conduit for the materials from which he might create the myth that explains our myths.

PART II

A Myth of Origins

5

Milton and Genesis: Mythological Defamation

"*P*aradise Lost is supposed to justify God's ways; instead it seems perpetually to call them into question."[1] Thus Joan Webber sums up an increasingly common experience of Milton's readers—one first articulated by William Blake. We should realize that the contradictions were not only Milton's; many of the tensions were already built into the Genesis symbols themselves, ready to be exploited to express Milton's ambiguous vision. For, as Joseph Campbell points out, there is an ambivalence inherent in many of the basic symbols of Genesis which no amount of stress on the official interpretation can suppress.[2]

In Milton's orthodox reading of the Judeo-Christian Fall, God offers his angelic and human creatures paradises which they ungratefully forfeit by rebelling against their all-wise and just creator. Within his text, however, Milton also presents a satanic polemic against these allegations in which the real cause of the Fall is God's illegitimate assertion of authority. Moreover, the poet lends this demonic version much unintended support by weaving into his narrative allusions to two prebiblical mythological complexes which parallel but contradict the biblical story in a number of interesting ways. In one motif, Milton's Father God appears as an interloper in a garden which myth consistently associates with Eve-like goddesses of earth. In the other, where the biblical war in heaven appears analogous to the battles of Zeus against the Titans, Milton's God might also be seen as the usurper of an ancient order which, it was suggested, was not lost but overthrown. Moreover, by reuniting these originally related myths (the Titans having been identified with Gaia, Mother Earth), Milton allows Satan a rather substantial theological argument which threatens to undercut Milton's own biblical religion.

Our procedure in this chapter will be, first, to take note of this mythic strata in Milton's epic and particularly in Satan's polemic against Milton's God. Here we will see how Eve becomes assimilated to the goddesses of old, and the devils to gods of pre-Olympian religion. Then we will consider how Genesis itself, in the context of its sources and analogues, must be considered a polemic. We will note that it reflects a tendency, also common to Babylonian and Greek mythology, to suppress the woman-centered fertility cult of primitive tribes in favor of the worship of a royal father. For clarification, we will consider scholarly arguments that this confrontation of religious perspectives reflected historical transitions from clans practicing horticulture, in which women were held in high esteem, to new social, economic, and family institutions. Hence the lowered status of women would be reflected in the traditions of mythological defamation—of Eve, Pandora, Venus, and others—carried on by Milton.

These biblical and mythological contexts evoked in *Paradise Lost* become crucial in Blake's reconstruction of that vision in *The Four Zoas*. This chapter, therefore, provides a preface to a consideration in chapters 7 and 8 of Blake's rejection in his own historical epic of both "matriarchal" and patriarchal mythologies and his identification of the Fall with a historical degeneration celebrated in the reactionary politics of Genesis.

Milton's Eve in the Garden of the Goddess

As one examines the fabric of mythological allusions in *Paradise Lost*, Eve breaks out of her role as wife and daughter, subordinate to Adam and to the Father God in Milton's narrative, and joins the company of the goddesses of paganism. Thus Adam smiles on her "as *Jupiter* / on *Juno* smiles" (*PL* IV.499–500) and awakens her as gently as "*Zephyrus* on *Flora* breathes" (*PL* V.16). She is persistently compared to Venus, proclaimed "more lovely fair / Then Wood-Nymph, or the fairest Goddess feign'd / Of three that in Mount *Ida* naked strove" (*PL* V.380–82). Moreover, she is associated with Venus's symbolic flowers, the myrtle and the rose. Flowers generally "at her coming sprung" (*PL* VIII.46), as they do for the goddess of love: "With Goddess-like demeanour forth she went; / Not unattended, for on her as Queen / A pomp of winning Graces waited still" (*PL* VIII.59–61). Indeed, it seems that, just as all the ancient goddesses were once seen as manifestations of a single reality, so in

Eve all their attributes are summed up: "like a Wood-Nymph light / *Oread* or *Dryad*, or of *Delia's* Traine . . . but *Delia's* self / In gate surpass'd; . . . To *Pales*, or *Pomona*, thus adorned, / Likeliest she seemd . . . or to *Ceres* in her Prime" (*PL* IX.386–95).

The garden is, in addition, most consistently associated with the gardens of the ancient goddess of fertility where the Hours, the goddesses of the seasons, danced out the cycle of the year and thus "Led on th' Eternal Spring." Similarly, it was in "that faire field / of *Enna*, where *Proserpin* gathring flours" (*PL* IV.268–69) was kidnaped by Hades and condemned to serve each winter as his underworld bride, returning for the fertile months in an obvious symbolic enactment of the seasonal round. Eve's arbor is like the arbor of Pomona, the garden of Venus and Adonis, and that orchard of golden apples which was given by Mother Earth to Hera and presided over by the Hesperides, the nymphs of the West.

This association between Eve and nature goddesses is intensified by the fact that Milton has portrayed nature as a female embodiment of his paradise, "where Nature multiplies / Her fertil growth, and by disburd'ning grows / More fruitful" (*PL* V.318–20). In *Milton's Earthly Paradise*, Joseph Duncan notes that "in none of the other literary interpretations of Paradise is Nature so strongly personified, so dynamic and so lavish. . . . Milton's Nature is so strongly personified that she is almost another character."[3] Thus we enter into the garden as into "A Wilderness of sweets," where nature appears as a Venus-Aphrodite, goddess of eroticism and fertility:

> for Nature here
> Wantond as in her prime, and plaid at will
> Her Virgin Fancies, pouring forth more sweet,
> Wilde above rule or Art; enormous bliss. (*PL* V.294–97)

The garden is, moreover, so animated with its flowing veins, its breathing winds, that, as Isabel MacCaffrey writes, its version of nature often comes close "to older mythical versions of nature's body in primitive legend."[4]

Such a garden—alive, erotic, fertile, and nurturant—is strongly identified with Eve who is thus greeted by Raphael:

> Haile Mother of Mankind, whose fruitful Womb
> Shall fill the World more numerous with thy Sons
> Then with these various fruits the Trees of God
> Have heap'd this table. (*PL* V.388–90)

At one point Milton's syntax completely merges the maternal and nurturant activities of Eve and her garden so that "Whatever Earth all-bearing Mother yields . . . She [Eve] gathers, Tribute large, and on the board / Heaps with unsparing hand" (*PL* V.338,343–44). This maternal association is underlined by Milton's repeated observation of the milky quality of Edenic nourishment, as Eve "tempers dulcet creams." When Milton adds that our general mother "nor these to hold / Wants her fit vessels pure" (*PL* V.347–48), associations point to Eve's own maternal bosom. These overlapping identifications are even thicker in the passage directly following the celebration of "wanton" nature when Adam sits in

> his cool Bowre, while now the mounted Sun
> Shot down direct his fervid Raies, to warme
> Earths inmost womb, more warmth than *Adam* needs;
> And *Eve* within, due at her hour prepar'd
> For dinner savourie fruits, of taste to please
> True appetite, and not disrelish thirst
> Of nectarous draughts between, from milkie stream.
>
> (*PL* V.300–06)

The reader's unconscious easily skips over Milton's syntax to connect the sun mounted over earth's womb to perhaps "more warmth than *Adam* needs" within Eve (inverting Milton's words) and imagines the "milkie stream" flowing simultaneously from the body of Mother Earth and Mother Eve as she leans over Adam sitting at their cosmic table. Milton presses these sexual identifications upon us as Adam enters their "sacred and sequesterd" bower to make love in what appears to be, with its sensuously textured floral walls, simultaneously the womb of earth and the womb of Eve.

Adam, Satan, and the Fall into Paganism

Adam certainly is unable to separate the delight of the garden from that of Eve, for he exclaims, "what seemd fair in all the World, seemd now . . . in her summd up, in her contain'd" (*PL* VIII.472–73). To Raphael's dismay, Adam's love for Eve begins to approach the awe of worship as he rhapsodizes,

> Authoritie and Reason on her waite,
> As one intended first, not after made
> Occasionally; and to consummate all,
> Greatness of mind and nobleness thir seat
> Build in her loveliest, and create an awe
> About her as a guard Angelic plac't.   (*PL* VIII.554–59)

His sin is therefore chastised by Christ as not only disobedience but also idolatry: "Was shee thy God, that her thou didst obey?"

(*PL* X.145). As Frye comments, "For Adam . . . the most immediate idol is the fallen Eve, the fairest of creatures, and for his descendants idolatry becomes a debased form of woman worship, or taking woman, along with Mother Nature to which in this context she belongs, to be numinous."[5]

Satan's approach to Eve characterizes him as an even more full-blown pagan. When he echoes Adam's inflation of her, it is no mere romantic idealization; from his perspective Eve *is* a goddess. In her dream he suggests that the knowledge hidden in the forbidden fruit is the revelation of her real identity. "Taste this," he says, "and be henceforth among the Gods, / Thy self a Goddess" (*PL* V.77–78). Thus he addresses her as "sovran Mistress," "universal Dame," "Empress of this fair World," insisting that her "Celestial Beautie" reveals her as "Queen of this Universe" who therefore "shouldst be seen / A Goddess among Gods, ador'd and serv'd / By Angels numberless" (*PL* IX.522,612,568,540,684,546–48). In Satan's arguments, the allusions to Eve as a goddess become more than mere ornamentation, or—as Milton mostly intended them—foils for the greater sublimity of Eve's innocence; they become part of an argument against God's authority as creator of the universe in deference to the procreative earth:

> the Gods are first, and that advantage use
> On our belief, that all from them proceeds;
> I question it, for this fair Earth I see
> Warm'd by the Sun, producing every kind,
> Them nothing.   (*PL* IX.718–22)

In his temptation of Eve, as John Carey and Alastair Fowler note, Satan is "inviting her to participate in a satanic or pagan epic—complete with the machinery of jealous gods."[6] In fact, Milton's elaboration of creation shows God's role in establishing the universe by fiat almost completely overshadowed by Mother Earth's vivid, procreative activity:

> The Earth was form'd, but in the Womb as yet
> Of Waters, Embryon immature involv'd,
> Appeer'd not: over all the face of Earth
> Main Ocean flow'd, not idle, but with warme
> Prolific humour soft'ning all her Globe,
> Fermented the great Mother to conceave.   (*PL* VII.276–81)

Similarly, the creatures, though called forth by divine command, do not show either the effects of divine activity or conscious design, but spring parthenogenetically from the female earth, who "strait / Op'ning her fertil Woomb teem'd at a Birth / Innumerous living

Creatures, perfet formes, / Limb'd and full grown: out of the ground up rose" (*PL* VII.453–56).

Milton's Demons and Pagan Gods

Here Milton's poetry unintentionally buttresses a heretical version of creation and points to the devils as proselytizers of an alternative religion. Thus they are accused of promulgating a pagan myth which traces the origin of the universe to the Goddess:

> Among the Heathen of thir purchase got,
> And Fabl'd how the Serpent, whom they calld
> *Ophion* and *Eurynome*, the wide-
> Encroaching *Eve* perhaps, had first the rule
> Of high *Olympus*.   (*PL* X.579–83)

Milton allows us some remarkable associations here, as he himself connects Eve to the creatrix of the earliest known Greek myth of origins (to be discussed later) and reminds us that the serpent had once been considered not a passing demonic persona but her fellow divinity. We shall soon consider the development of Greek religion from a pre-Olympian cult of nature to a later version organized around the worship of Zeus (the Latin Jove), a royal father reigning at the head of a divine hierarchy which he himself has established upon Mount Olympus. Satan appears to be an adherent of what has been described as a premonotheistic, even pre-Olympian cult, alternately described as "animism," "vitalism," or "Zoism" (from the Greek *zoa,* or animal), which, if it worshiped any divinity at all, worshiped one dispersed throughout the universe and identified particularly with the fructifying powers of earth.

The "Devils party" will therefore appear a rather prodigious party, for Milton includes in it all such primitive nature deities, not merely metaphorically, but historically.[7] Apparently, he reports, the vagabond demons, upon being cast down from heaven, "got them new names" and

> By falsities and lyes the greatest part
> Of Mankind they corrupted to forsake
> God thir Creator, and th' invisible
> Glory of him that made them, to transform
> Oft to the Image of a Brute, adorn'd
> With gay Religions full of Pomp and Gold,
> And Devils to adore for Deities.   (*PL* I.367–73)

The prestigious company that follows includes Moloch, Ashtoreth, Thammuz, Horus, Isis, and Osiris, Dagon, Saturn, Rhea, and Titan.

The association of the devils with pre-Olympian cults is under-lined by the continual analogy running through *Paradise Lost* between the war in heaven and the battles of Zeus against the giants and the Titans. This story, told in Hesiod's *Theogony,* evokes the transitions from earlier to later generations of Greek deities. In the beginning Gaia, Earth (or Eurynome), existed alone, and gave birth to Uranus (Saturn), her first son-lover, and to the three hundred-handed giants; then, with Uranus as father, she gave birth to the Titans, planetary deities. Two of these, Rhea and Cronus, having castrated Uranus and assumed sovereignty, gave birth to Zeus, Demeter, Hera, Hades, and Poseidon. Led by Zeus, these future Olympians began a series of wars against Gaia and the Titans, led by Atlas and other elder divinities. First Zeus defeated the Titans and banished them to Tar-tarus (except for Atlas, bound to carry the earth on his shoulders), then retreated to Olympus. A second war began when Gaia gave birth to a new brood of twenty-four giants with serpent tails who attempted to avenge the fate of the Titans; they hurled rocks at Olympus where Zeus now sat enthroned over a new clique of deities—his siblings, children, and various mates—and from which he hurled his thunderbolts. When these giants were also defeated, Zeus was forced to battle Gaia's next child and champion, Typhon, the hundred-armed monster. Mounting his heavenly chariot, Zeus pursued the serpentine beast, who fended off thunderbolts by flinging mountains at them. Zeus finally won by dumping Mount Aetna on Typhon, leaving him to fume forever in volcanic rage. The rule of the Olympians did not go unchallenged, however; it was again contested by Prometheus (the son of a Titan, brother to Atlas) who revolted and was then punished by being chained to a rock, the prey of eagles.

The numerous allusions to this myth in *Paradise Lost* invariably associate God with Zeus and the devils with his opponents—the Titans, the Giants, Typhon, and specifically Atlas and Prometheus. Thus in Milton's war in heaven we find such details as the devils hurling hills in their defense and Christ pursuing them with thunder-bolts in his divine chariot and propelling their nine-day fall into a Tartarean hell. Satan is twice compared to the rebels against Olym-pus, first as he lay prone in hell "As whom the Fables name of monstrous size, / *Titanian,* or *Earth-born,* that warr'd on *Jove,* / *Briarios* or *Typhon,* whom the Den / By ancient *Tarsus* held" (*PL* I.197–200) and later when he "Collecting all his might dilated stood, / Like *Teneriff* or *Atlas*" (*PL* IV.986–87). Beelzebub is described with "*Atlantean* shoulders" (*PL* II.306); the fallen angels cause a "*Typhœan* rage" (*PL* II.539) in hell, and Belial fears that another assault on heaven might lead the devils to fates such as those of Typhon or

Prometheus, as if "this Firmament / Of Hell should spout her Cataracts of Fire . . . threatning hideous fall / One day upon our heads; while we . . . Caught in a fierie Tempest shall be hurl'd / Each on his rock transfixt, the sport and prey / Of racking whirlwinds (*PL* II.175–82).

Milton's adaptations of the Greek war in heaven, by favoring Zeus-Jove against the satanic Titans, reveals his polemic to be not only that of Christian monotheism against classical polytheism, but more strenuously a polemic against those earlier forms of paganism which revered the Goddess and her "earth-born" children, the chthonic gods of nature. The Hebrew Jehovah and the Greek Zeus had in common their opposition to such nature worship. For Christian humanism with its great respect for the classics, such analogies showed both that the Spirit had let a little light shine outside the chosen through human reason as well as through revelation, and that the universal movement of paganism toward more elevated religious conceptions buttressed the authority of scriptural faith.

On the other hand, Zeus's credentials as a supreme deity were sufficiently questionable—even Milton acknowledged that "*Jove* usurping reign'd" (*PL* I.514)—that it could reflect ill on the Christian God to be too closely compared with him. Here are two stories, in many ways remarkably similar, except that in one the all-powerful deity reigns from eternity and enters into heavenly war only to put down a nefarious revolt, while in the other the supreme being is clearly himself the upstart, battling his way to supremacy solely through force of arms. Now, to some—Satan, for one—these myths might look like the same story told from opposing points of view. Thus Satan persists in reducing God to the "Thunderer" (*PL* II.28) that he resembles (*PL* I.93,174,258). Satan usually goes out of his way to avoid acknowledging any superiority in God beyond that of political and military power. He is not the Creator; he is "Heav'ns high Arbitrator" (*PL* II.359), "the King of Heav'n" (*PL* II.316), "Heav'ns all-ruling Sire" (*PL* II.264), or merely "the Conqueror" (*PL* I.323). Rather, Satan insists upon the complete equality of his crew as "Deities of Heav'n" (*PL* II.11). For him, the battle in heaven is analogous to the revolt of the Titans against the illegitimate attempt by one of their number to establish a new order among them. The rebellion began when "A third part of the Gods, in synod met / Thir Deities to assert, who while they feel / Vigour Divine within them, can allow / Omnipotence to none (*PL* VI.156–59) and dared pursue "Enjoyment of [their] right as Gods" (*PL* VI.452).

Thus if *Paradise Lost* calls the ways of God into question, it is no accident; Milton has constructed the poem around Satan's polemic against that God's credentials and has made the devil no mere criminal, but rather an ideologue and a heretic. Satan's position is not uniform, since Milton's Puritan strategy is to have the demon articulate all the myriad "satanic" blasphemies which the Christian poet seeks to combat. The nature of this Christian bias, however, is manifest in a kind of general coherence demonstrated by Satan's heresies, as modes of *a*theism. Religious historians have argued, as indeed Blake does, that mythological polytheism in its earlier forms often expressed metaphorically what was essentially a *non*theistic philosophy. Similarly, the polytheistic Satan, linking ancient and modern heresies, seems to voice, alternately, a kind of "pre-Christian vitalism"[8] or pantheism, which reveres the creative powers of earth, and a mystical humanism, found both in primitive shamanism and seventeenth-century antinomianism, which emphasizes a "vigour Divine within" (*PL* VI.158) and the dignity of a "Goddess humane."

The Veiled Goddess in Genesis Myth and Symbol

The relationships between the garden of Eve and those of the ancient goddesses, between her serpent tempter and pre-Olympian deities, were not a creation of Milton's art, but his unwitting disclosure of a mythological cover-up accomplished by editors of the Pentateuch. In the next pages, we can begin to explore the contradictions in Genesis exposed by Milton and to examine the coherent vision implicit in the underlying symbols taken over by the Bible from more ancient religious cults.

Let us note before proceeding that the Judeo-Christian story of origins combines four separate mythological themes. First, there is the story of an all-powerful, patriarchal God who created the world and rules over it. In a kind of rebellious tension with this rule are the figures of the two interrelated motifs of that alien mythology woven throughout *Paradise Lost*. In the one, the Mother of All Living appears in her garden of fruit trees accompanied by her serpent lover. In the other, we find a cosmic battle through which the monarchic father god overthrows either a mother goddess, a serpent-dragon, a serpentine goddess, or some combination thereof. In Milton's version these themes have been reconnected, as the battle is returned to the place in the creation story that it had occupied in widespread mythology (and had retained even in some of the biblical psalms and in Revelation). Finally, in place of the decline of the Goddess, we find another kind of fall, a fall from a primitive state of bliss into one of sorrow, characterized, interestingly, by increasing misery in labor and a decline in the status of women. This fourth motif behooves us to consider, later in this chapter, what connections might exist, in cultures which believed such myths, between changing religious symbols and changing economic, social, and gender relations.

The most striking characteristic of the analogues and sources for Genesis is that in them creation is identified not with the power of a father god, but with the procreative powers of woman, associated mythically either with the fertile earth or the primeval ocean from which it emerged. Thus one of the most ancient creation myths, belonging to the Pelasgian people of pre-Hellenic Greece, reads (in Robert Graves's reconstruction) as follows: The Great Mother rose from Chaos; the wind of her advent became a serpent and impregnated her; she thereupon took the shape of a dove, and laid the World Egg which the serpent coiled about and hatched.[9] Out of that egg tumbled all of the universe and its creatures; man sprang directly out of the soil of the earth. This, of course, is the story of Eurynome and Ophion which Milton attributes to devilish propaganda, which alleged that the Goddess and her serpent-lover, rather than the royal father, "had first the rule / Of high *Olympus*" (*PL* X.582–83). The Pelasgian version goes on to report that there was a falling-out over sexual politics when Ophion claimed to be himself author of the universe, whereupon Eurynome bruised his head with her heel and banished him to the caves of the earth—suggestive details that will merit investigation.

Now, however, let us note similar motifs in other Greek myths which record that originally all things are born from Gaia, Mother Earth, without male partnership; she later mates with her sons, the first of whom, Uranus (sky), fathers the Titans and soon comes into conflict with Gaia and her children. In yet another very ancient Sumerian version, a goddess Nammu (primeval sea) is the original mother who gives birth to the masculine heaven and the feminine earth; these are pictured as a cosmic mountain whose summit is heaven and whose base, hovering above the watery abyss, is the female earth. Primeval female waters also characterize the Babylonian *Enuma Elish* in which the original creatrix is a goddess, Tiamat, a water monster personifying the ocean's salt waters and the generator of the other gods. She propagates the universe through intercourse with her lover-son, Apsu, the sweet waters:

> When on high the heaven had not yet been named
> Firm ground be had not been called by name
> Naught but primordial Apsu (male, sweet waters), their begetter
> And Mummu-Tiamat, she who bore them all,
> Their waters commingling as a single body; . . .
> Then it was that the gods were formed within them.[10]

E. O. James remarks that "it was the life-giving mother who was the dominant figure in Near Eastern religion. . . . From India to the Mediterranean . . . she reigned supreme." Scholars such as Robert Graves and Joseph Campbell have argued that the primitive agrarian cultures of the Bronze Age formed a kind of mythogenetic zone in which this relatively homogeneous world view was diffused over a broad geographical area.[11] Campbell relates this mythic complex to the rise of a Neolithic culture based upon grain agriculture and stock breeding which is now believed to have first appeared in the Near East as early as 9000 B.C., displacing hunting and food-gathering cultures. Archaeological artifacts of a Goddess culture have been found in the remains at Catal Hayuk in Turkey dating back to 6500 B.C. and are fully developed in the High Neolithic cultures (4500–3500 B.C.) in Mesopotamia from which this culture is believed to have spread eastward and westward, a millennium later reaching Egypt, then Crete, and eventually the Pacific coast of Asia and the Atlantic coasts of Europe and Africa.

This Goddess culture involved a whole complex of interrelated symbols found on primitive artifacts (such as ancient Greek seals, fragments of painted pottery, clay figures) as well as in myth and its literary reflection. Repeatedly we find the association of the Earth Mother with a serpent in a garden of sacred trees fructified by sacred waters. The motif appears in the Epic of Gilgamesh who visits a paradise presided over by the goddess Siduri to procure the plant of immortality, only to have it stolen by a serpent, as well as in the myth alluded to by Milton in which the nymphs of the Hesperides preside over a tree of golden apples planted by Mother Earth and guarded by the dragon Ladon.

These symbols, moreover, have been traced back to ancient rituals which comprised not so much the worship of a goddess as a magical relationship to Earth with her crucial fertility conceived as female. The figure most frequently associated with Earth is not a husband, but a son, often also a lover, identified with the fruits of the earth and their seasonal cycle of death and rebirth. We are familiar with this figure in the form of the Syrian Thammuz or Greek Adonis, whose passage to the underworld in the barren months was dramatized in a cult in which he had to die that the earth might be fruitful again.

This figure often appears as a serpent lord. The ancient heroes and gods of the Greeks were frequently half-human, half-snake—as for example Cecrops, the Titans, Erechtheus, and the Zeus Melicheus. The symbolic significance of the snake, as Jane Ellen Harrison explains, lies not only in its phallic associations but also in its connection, through its periodic sloughing of its skin, with the seasonal cycle.[12] Thus the importance of the *ourobouros*, the snake pursuing its own tail, as a symbol of the never-ending cycle of nature. In addition, in the association of serpents with caves, holes in the earth which figured prominently in the rituals of rebirth, snakes came to be thought of as inhabiting the womb-tomb of Mother Earth as did the spirits of dead ancestors. It was believed that in each new birth, each new harvest, the dead were reborn; thus the snake came to be seen almost as a receptacle in which these ancestral and fertility spirits lived.

The fruits of earth, on the other hand, were inevitably associated with fruit trees. A common symbol is the half-human, half-snake son of Earth bearing a fruit-filled cornucopia. "Primitive man," as Harrison puts it, "in general . . . is intensely concerned with the fruits of the Earth—not at first with the worship of Earth in the abstract, but with the food that comes to him out of the Earth. It is mainly because she feeds him that he learns to think of the Earth as Mother." "All trees tend to be sacred or possessed by an unseen life, but above all fruit trees are sacred, they are the foci of eager collective attention. Long before agricultural days and the sanctity of grain came the sanctity of natural fruit trees."[13] Frequently we find the tree, sometimes snake-entwined, appearing as a world axis in a garden located at the center of the earth, from which four rivers flow to the four quarters.

These symbols of an earth goddess in an orchard "paradise" with her serpentine son-lover have all been traced to a common ritual source in the new year festival which in ancient times commemorated the planting season. As this was a fertility celebration, it is possible that sometimes it involved an annual pairing of the adolescent initiates of two exogamous clans, thus integrating human reproduction into the seasonal fructification of nature.[14] In known versions of the cult, a representative of the new year was usually married symbolically to a representative of the Goddess and the pair enacted a ritual intercourse. As Vera Gordon Childe explains it:

> The early Oriental civilizations periodically celebrated . . . a sacred marriage, the nuptial union of a "king" and a "queen" who on this occasion represented divinities. Their union . . . magically insured . . . the fertilization of the earth. . . . But the seed must die and be buried before it can sprout and multiply. A human representative of the grain, a "corn king," was once slain and buried. His place was taken by a young successor who should stand for the growing crops till he too must die.[15]

The triumph of the new year over the old was dramatized in the new king's conquest of the old—in the triumph, that is, of life over death, a symbolic death and resurrection. The event usually culminated in a sacrifice of a sacred animal or the king himself, not as a gift to a god, but, as the word "sacrifice" originally signified, to "make sacred" the plants and participants who received the sacred blood and flesh and absorbed its fructifying powers. In these rites the community recognized its "marriage" to nature, and organized itself to meet the demands of production and reproduction.

This celebration of procreation, agriculture, the food chain, and the return of human life to nature helped to reconcile people to the cycle of life and death. The fact that the individual lived off the lives of other creatures and would pass into future generations was accepted as evidence of the metamorphoses of an eternal life, ultimately maternal and benign. At the same time, these rituals offered an intensification of that mana, or daimonic energy, through demonstrations of physical prowess and sexual potency, the consumption of particularly energizing ritual foods and intoxicants, and the participation in ecstatic dance and music.

We cannot help recognizing in these rites the sources of later religion: athletic competition to select the prime exemplars of communal vitality, often a combat between the "king" of the old year and of the new; the apparent "resurrection" of the life force in this new "year daimon," his "coronation" through investment with such life symbols as anointing oils, a crown of leaves, a staff from a live tree, blood-colored robes; his ritual intercourse or "marriage" to a representative of the Goddess; the ritual "sacrifice" of the old king or his animal substitute, often the bull, who came to be associated with such dying and rising gods as Osiris, Thammuz, and Dionysius; processions with this deified sacrifice through the fields and orchards, and, finally, a communion banquet through which the people achieved unity with the sacred force of life—the divine—by consuming the mana-filled sacrifice.

As Campbell, Harrison, Graves, and others explain, most of the symbols identified with the Goddess cult find their meaning in relation to this celebration of the cycle of life. She is a sea goddess, because life emerges from the womb of waters; because the sea is wild and dangerous, she is often represented as a sea beast or dragon. As goddess of earth from which life comes and to which it returns, she is also queen of the underworld, and her children are chthonic, "earthborn" gods. She is a moon goddess because of the links between the menstrual cycle and the phases of the moon. The "death" and "resurrection" of that moon also associates it with her child, the moon-bull, and with other creatures like the ram and the stag whose horns image the crescent moon. She is the double goddess of life and death. She is also the triple goddess of the female cycle: the prematernal (not asexual) maid or virgin (Persephone, Athene, Diana), the mother (Demeter, Aphrodite, Hera), and the crone (Hecate) whose passage through the cycle invests her with wisdom and magical power. As triple goddess, she reigns in heaven, the sea, and the underworld, and the three lunar phases. All cycles fall under her influence: the tides, the lunar months, the days of light and darkness, the seasons, the ages of humanity. She is also Lady of the Wild Things, identified with the animal fertility of the snake, the dove, the cuckoo, the pig, the cow, the sheep, the goat, the bee, and the fish. As goddess of the garden of fertility, the source of "eternal spring," she is identified with all vegetation, but in particular the fruit tree, the apple—particularly the seed-filled "Chinese apple," or pomegranate—with grain, the grape-vine whose intoxicating fruit figured so centrally in her Dionysian rites, and even the mushroom and other hallucinogenic plants. These animals, plants, and heavenly bodies are also the forms assumed by her son-lover, fruit of her fertility—the bull-god, snake-god, moon-god, goat-god (Pan), fish-god, wine-god.

The Goddess Cult in the Bible

Genesis draws upon this heterodox tradition of myth and cult. The Jews were among those pastoral peoples who poured into the Near East in the second millennium B.C. For a long time they continued to live their pastoral lives in the hills of Canaan alongside the agrarian people settled there. With David's conquest of the Amorite city of Jerusalem, the Hebrew monarchy absorbed many elements of its religious practice, and, during the exile in Babylon, the Jews were undoubtedly exposed to its literary traditions and mythical symbols. The Bible reflects the many stages of Hebrew development, and Genesis itself has been shown to be a highly artificial document produced by generations of priestly scholars. This is particularly evident in the repetition of the creation story (Gen. 1–2:4) celebrating a God designated as Elohim and the following story of the Fall referring to Yahweh. That "Yahwist" strand is believed to derive from an original account, upon which others built, probably put together during the reign of Solomon from "poetic and cultic narratives which previously had circulated orally and without context among the people."[16] The final, composite document, including the first chapter's ritualistic version of creation, was probably assembled by a priestly redactor in post-exile Jerusalem, perhaps as late as the fourth century B.C., and seems to have been influenced by exposure to Babylonian religion.

T. H. Robinson argues that Jewish ritual had at one time contained elements very similar to the new year festival. For example, he contends that during the Feast of Tabernacles sacred images of Yahweh and a female counterpart, Anath (a Babylonian fertility goddess), were removed to a bower of greenery in which, after they were symbolically married, the death and resurrection of Yahweh was dramatized. Raphael Patai cites other examples of Goddess worship in his book, *The Hebrew Goddess*.[17]

Thus we find Genesis full of references to the Goddess cult.[18] The association of the woman and the serpent, the banishment of that serpent to the underworld, and even the detail of her bruising his head with her heel all echo the primitive Pelasgian creation myth. Moreover, the name of Eve, Hawwah, is the name of the Goddess herself, Mother of All Living. Similarly, the creation of Eve from Adam's rib has Mesopotamian associations. In Sumerian script, *TI* means both life and rib; a Sumerian goddess called NIN TI could, therefore be interpreted either as Lady of Life (Mother of All Living) or Lady of the Rib. Both meanings seem to have influenced the conception of Eve in Genesis, which contains other allusions to the Goddess as well. Some have speculated that the suggestion of the origin of the universe in primeval waters recalls the association of the Goddess with the fecund ocean. The biblical Tehom (deep) is a proper name, probably an allusion to the Babylonian Tiamat. Others suggest that the Hebrew *tohu-wa-bohu* (waste and void) contains a demythologized reference to Bahu, the Babylonian Great Mother. At any rate, the image of the Spirit of God moving over the water carries a connotation of a brooding bird (Christian iconography envisions the Holy Spirit here as a dove) and recalls Eurynome brooding over the waters to hatch the universal egg. The impregnating role of the wind also echoes that Pelasgian myth. Finally, the creation of man out of the female earth, the *adamah*, has numerous mythical analogues with accounts of parthenogenetic birth out of the womb of Mother Earth.

The garden, of course, has connections with numerous gardens of the Goddess, the word paradise itself simply connoting an orchard. The earliest reference to it occurs in the Sumerian isle of Dilmun presided over by the goddess Ninhursag. It is described as a dwelling of the gods where no raven croaked, no dove drooped its head, no beast ravined and where there was neither sickness, old age, nor sorrow. Like the Genesis paradise, it is fed by "waters of abundance" arising from a stream which proceeds from the source "whence issue all the streams of the earth."[19] Such dwelling places of the gods exist as well in the Epic of Gilgamesh and the Ugaritic poems of Canaan. The very name Eden means pleasure and echoes the idea in the Gilgamesh epic of a rural pleasance (*hissu*) of the gods.

Milton and the Subtext of Genesis

We can now return to our consideration of Milton's exploitation of the parallels between Genesis and ancient myth with greater precision and significance. Milton deliberately identifies his "delicious Paradise" (*PL* IV.132) with these Mesopotamian sources by declaring it an "*Assyrian* Garden" (*PL* IV.285) and locating it near the Tigris and Euphrates rivers (*PL* IV.71). Moreover, Milton's comparison of this garden to that of "reviv'd *Adonis*" (*PL* IX.440) recalls the rites of returning spring associated with that dying and rising god, a Greek version of Thammuz, consort of the goddess Ishtar. These rites are directly recalled in his depiction of the rites in which "Universal *Pan* / Knit with the *Graces* and the *Hours* in dance / Led on th' Eternal Spring" (*PL* IV.266–68), an allusion heightened by the following identification of Eve with the seasonal myth of "*Proserpin* gathring flours" (*PL* IV.269).

At the same time, Milton's association of Eden with "*Hesperian* Fables" (*PL* IV.250) underlines the idea of a sacred grove of numinous fruit:

> His farr more pleasant Garden God ordaind;
> Out of the fertil ground he caus'd to grow
> All Trees of Noblest kind for sight, smell, taste;
> And all amid them stood the Tree of Life,
> High eminent, blooming Ambrosial Fruit
> Of vegetable Gold.   (*PL* IV.215–20)

Within this Greek context, however, not only the garden but also the serpent appears benevolent, a guardian of Hera's potent fruit. The tree of life then appears to be the symbol of fructifying power around which so many ancient rites centered. The apples, identified with the ambrosial fruit of the gods, are those gifts of the benevolent goddess through which she shares her life-giving mana with mankind. The serpent's real character is no different from those cherubim, also dragonlike, who at the end of *Paradise Lost* are left guarding the source of life. Milton gives the clue to the serpent's identity by repeating his own self-proclamation that he is Ophion, the consort of the goddess Eurynome, creatrix.

In fact, the details of Genesis confirm this identification, the "subtil" nature of the serpent signifying his special sapience; he alone of the beasts can speak because he was, in ancient cult, the oracle of the Goddess. Other mythologies also identify the serpent with wisdom; in kundalini yoga the image of the serpent-entwined tree symbolizes the powerful energies which the yogi learns to move up his spine to his brain. To understand these dimensions of the serpent symbol, we must realize that in ancient cultures this kind of knowledge involved intuition into both natural and mental processes.

As Campbell explains, it was because the serpent seemed to express the invisible power of natural and human life that he offered wisdom. For the same reason, he was a symbol of immortality, the eternal forces of life which prevailed through the cycles of death and rebirth, forces which were therefore worshiped as divine. Similarly, at the center of the garden of the Goddess is a tree of life bearing mana-filled fruit which is the source of both divine life and divine knowledge. The two trees are, therefore, the same in origin—the knowledge of good and evil signifying simply the knowledge of all things.

In this light, the entire episode of the Fall regains its significance, for what is at stake is no minor infraction against a fastidious overseer, but a rebellion against the whole premise of monotheism in favor of a religion of participation in godhead itself. In the cults surrounding this tree, human beings, by eating the fruits of the Goddess in a sacred feast, achieved participation in a divinity here conceived as the fructifying, female powers of nature. They did so, as well, by ritual intercourse which connected their own fertility with that of the earth. This origin accounts for the persistent sexual connotation of the "forbidden fruit," an emphasis which Milton intensifies by presenting the fall of Eve as a kind of seduction, especially through the allusion to the seduction of Ophias by Jupiter Capitoline in the form of a serpent (*PL* IX.509–10). The event recalls many similar exploits of Zeus and cannot help but suggest that we are observing the communion of Eve, not with a devil, but with a god.

Lest we miss the point, Milton states it overtly in Satan's interpretation of the event. He not only dwells on Eve's divinity, but also invites her to participate in divine immortality and divine sapience by "participating God-like food" (*PL* IX.717). She turns to the "Sacred, Wise, and Wisdom-giving Plant, / Mother of Science" (*PL* IX.679–80) as a source of divine power. The garden once again has become the orchard of the fertility goddess, and Eve and the serpent, their divine identity asserted, are elevated by their own interpretation to the center of pagan magical cult. At the climax of the Fall is an act of ancient worship:

> So saying, from the Tree her step she turnd,
> But first low Reverence don, as to the power
> That dwelt within, whose presence had infus'd
> Into the plant sciential sap, deriv'd
> From Nectar, drink of Gods.   (*PL* IX.834–38)

It is no wonder that Adam waits to welcome her back "and her rural labours crown / As Reapers oft are wont thir Harvest Queen" (*PL* IX.841–42).

Mythological Defamation in the Bible

In order to understand the metamorphoses which the symbols of the fertility cult have undergone, we must consider the fate of that Neolithic culture from which they derived. Here we must take into account two mutually reinforcing developments. On the one hand, by 3200 B.C. village societies began to give way to the rise of kingly cities, first in Sumer, then Egypt, Crete, and Greece, and these new hierarchic cultures began to bring forth new symbol systems and religious ideas. On the other hand, this process was effected and intensified by a second cultural shift promoted by waves of invasions in the third and second millennium B.C. Pastoral peoples, semi-nomadic herders of cattle or of sheep and goats, with values totally alien to the Neolithic planters, began pouring into the Near East and Mediterranean areas from northern grasslands and the Syro-Arabian desert. By 3000 B.C. these invaders had begun to establish their own states; by 2500 B.C. they had come to rule in Mesopotamia where Sumerian society gave way to the Babylonian Empire. In Greece and Crete between 2500 and 1300 B.C., there followed "a long period of interplay and adjustment between settled agricultural and intrusive pastoral-warrior folk," as Joseph Campbell describes it, precipitating "a veritable Gotterdammerung and the end of the world age of the people of bronze."[20]

A process, both similar and different, occurred when nomadic tribes later to become the Hebrew nation arrived in Palestine in the second millennium B.C. and settled in the hills outside its already developing city-states. The stories of the Hebrew patriarchs from Abraham to Moses seem to be an attempt to replace a complex history of invasion, settlement, assimilation, and exclusion with a simple legend of national destiny. In fact, various tribes probably coalesced into a federation around the "covenant with Yahweh" but continued to live in a tribal structure in both conflict and accommodation to the Canaanite cults of Baal (master) and the Goddess. Probably, Genesis and Exodus were not written until after the ninth century B.C., when the Hebrew monarchy had conquered those cities and unified Palestine under their rule, so as to legitimize claims to this "promised land."

The conflict of these two cultures, agrarian and nomadic, then came to be symbolized in the struggle of the Yahweh cult against the "idolatry" of Goddess-worshiping "pagans," that is, "peasants." Nevertheless, the Bible itself tells us how frequently such idol worship was practiced by the Jews themselves, with the Goddess and her fertility rites repeatedly ensconced in the Jerusalem temple itself; as late as the sixth century B.C. the reformer King Josiah had to take down the altars "which Solomon the king of Israel had built for Ashtoreth" and break down "the houses of the cult prostitutes . . . where the women wove hangings for Asherah" (2 Kings 22).

Genesis reflects a long period of marriage and divorce between its religion of the Supreme Father and its neighbors' Goddess worship. What Milton's conflation of pagan and biblical myth reveals, despite his attempt to distinguish "true" meanings from demonic "fables," is that a great number of symbols had been yanked by the Bible's priestly editors out of their original context and given a new and contrary meaning. This is why in their biblical context the symbols of Genesis appear so arbitrary. There is no reason within its framework why the Fall should be identified with a woman, a serpent, or a fruit tree, and this has led to a situation in which allegorical interpretation could impose virtually any meaning on the story of the Fall, constrained only by the more definitive and less primitive connotations involved in the idea of the biblical creator and judge. Similarly, the judgment itself has always had the potential of appearing somewhat arbitrary, justifying the entire misery of the human condition on so apparently trivial a fault. At the same time, the meanings inherent in the obfuscated mythical strata have made the idea of a lost garden paradise a source of ceaseless inspiration for the Western imagination.

What has obviously occurred in Genesis is that the priestly editors of the Pentateuch have taken the myths of the Mother of All Living revered by Neolithic planters and placed them under a ban and interdiction. The Great Mother in her garden of perpetual fecundity has been demoted to a disobedient daughter and subordinate wife. The snake who was her consort, receptacle of the immortal spirits buried and reborn in her womb, has been turned into a demon whose ability to speak as the oracle of her wisdom and to dispense the fruits of her benevolence is now only a source of temptation. The tree of life, with the waters of life flowing from its base, has been taken from her and made the private property of the Supreme Father. Those fruits have become fruits of evil, even as her single tree of life, the world-axis of the natural order, has been overshadowed by another tree identified instead with the moral order, whose fruits are guilt and fear. In the earlier versions, the sacred orchard of fruit trees, located at the source of the rivers and presided over by Mother Earth and her serpent lover, carried no suggestion of guilt, temptation, danger, or pun-

ishment. In Genesis, Hebraic priests, apparently eager to stamp out
fertility worship imported into Israel from Canaan, have placed the
Great Mother and the serpent of reincarnation under a shadow of
gloom and condemnation which, according to Campbell, has prevailed ever since "Nobodaddy" usurped the preeminence of the Goddess, "made her serpent lover crawl and locked the Tree of Life away
for all time":

> In the context of the patriarchy of the Iron Age Hebrews of the first
> millennium B.C. the mythology adapted from the earlier Neolithic and
> Bronze Age civilizations of the lands they occupied and for a time ruled
> became inverted, to render an argument just the opposite to that of its
> origin. And, a second point, corollary to the first, is that there is
> consequently an ambivalence inherent in many of the basic symbols of
> the Bible that no amount of stress on the patriarchal interpretation can
> suppress.

"There is," he adds, "a like inversion of sense in the legacy of
Greece."[21] Campbell terms this phenomenon "mythological defamation," "the employment of a priestly device . . . which has been in
constant use ever since. . . . It consists simply in terming the gods of
other people demons, enlarging one's own counterparts to hegemony
over the universe, and then inventing all sorts of great and little
secondary myths to illustrate, on the one hand, the impotence and
malice of the demons, and, on the other, the majesty and righteousness of the great god or gods." Robert Graves, the first to explicate the
massive underpinning of goddess symbolism in English poetry in his
pioneering book, *The White Goddess*, calls this same tendency "ico-
notrophy," "the deliberate misrepresentation by which ancient ritual
icons are twisted in meaning in order to confirm a profound change of
the existing religious system."[22]

Iconotrophic Aspects of Paradise Lost

We should not be surprised, therefore, to find that when Milton
embeds Eve in a garden of goddesses, "Her self, though fairest unsup-
ported Flour" (*PL* IX.432), he calls upon negative associations akin to
the attitudes of Genesis. Eve is, for example, metaphorically linked to

> that faire field
> Of *Enna*, where *Proserpin* gathring flours
> Her self a fairer Floure by gloomie *Dis*
> Was gatherd, which cost *Ceres* all that pain
> To seek her through the world.   (*PL* IV.268–72)

A fertility myth like the legend of Adonis, in which Proserpine's
removal from the earth to the underground once symbolized the

passage of the seasons, has been turned in this context into a moral allegory. Proserpine now suggests Eve succumbing to a seducer from a demonic underworld and by her dereliction bringing "all that pain" into the world. The temporary loss implied by the ritual mourning for Adonis or Proserpine has been transformed into a vision of total catastrophe.

Milton draws Eve into another damning analogy when he presents her to Adam,

> in naked beauty more adorn'd,
> More lovely then *Pandora*, whom the Gods
> Endowd with all thir gifts, and O too like
> In sad event, when to the unwiser Son
> Of *Japhet* brought by *Hermes*, she ensnar'd
> Mankind with her faire looks, to be aveng'd
> On him who had stole *Joves* authentic fire. (*PL* IV.713–19)

Milton is retelling the story recorded by Hesiod in which Zeus avenged himself upon Prometheus and his brother Epimetheus, sons of the Titan, Japhet, and the last generation to rebel against Zeus's power. According to this tale, Zeus ordered the gods to create and adorn a woman whom he presented to Epimetheus as a gift. However, once he succumbed to her seduction and married her, she opened her jar and unleashed upon him all the evils that would thence plague mankind—sickness, old age, labor, vice, and so on. In fact, Pandora meant Giver of All Gifts and was the name of the goddess who dispensed the benevolence of nature. In the hands of Hesiod, she has been reduced to a sexy doll whose "gifts" are the pretty face, shapely body, and fancy clothes identified with feminine appeal in an order in which women have been reduced to sexual objects. These gifts are at the same time the penalties which await men who succumb to such deceitful charms. Her jar, once a funerary urn containing the sacred spirits inhabiting her bosom awaiting rebirth, now contains only the source of death, not life. The import of this story, which robbed an ancient goddess of her matriarchal dignity and put her in her place in the patriarchal order, parallels the misogynistic theme of Genesis in blaming all humanity's troubles on a woman.

The significance of Proserpine's association with Hades and Pandora's marriage to a Titan is revealed in Milton's development of the even more sinister aspects of femininity in his portrayal of the sinful Eve's doppelganger, Sin herself. Sin is depicted as Hecate, that full-fledged devotee of barbaric fertility magic, the "Night-Hag" who "when call'd / In secret, riding through the Air she comes / Lur'd with the smell of infant blood, to dance / With *Lapland* Witches" (*PL* II.662–65). In fact, this goddess of the underworld is just another version of Proserpine, an aspect of "the original Triple Goddess, supreme in Heaven, on earth and in Tartarus."[23] Hesiod, although he maligns Pandora, reveals Hecate's origins as a gift-giver. As a moon goddess she is mistress of fertility rites through which, according to Hesiod, she has the power of granting every mortal his heart's desire. With the denigration of those ancient rites, her creative powers are transformed into destructive ones, and she is invoked only in rites of black magic. It is this context in which Milton locates her, his imagination undoubtedly having been stirred by the seventeenth-century obsession with witches, often identified by their accusers as participants in a satanic cult resembling the old pagan agrarian rites. At the same time, Sin, as the "Snakie Sorceress" (*PL* II.724), like the dragon-goddesses of ancient myth is the mother of a monstrous brood of subhuman creatures: Hydra, Chimaera, the Giants, Furies, and Gorgons of chthonic religion, creatures here transformed into demons.

Structuralist analysis of myth advise us to discern the common elements and relationships which emerge when several variants are compared. In juxtaposing thus the stories of Eve, Pandora, Milton's Sin, and Hecate, we find that in each we are directed to a structure in which Milton's two primary mythic complexes, the garden of the Goddess and the war in heaven, with its rebellious demons, appear as one. Thus Sin, as a hellish Hecate, is both an analogue for the seductive, sinful, and magic-prone Eve and at the same time a consort of the Titanic Satan. Their relationship as lovers and thereby co-conspirators against heaven, suggests similar dimensions in the relationship between Satan and Eve. Hecate, as the goddess who ruled the underworld is, of course, a manifestation of Gaia, mother and lover of her Titanic brood. She reigns in that Tartarus to which the Titans were exiled, like Sin in hell. Sin's incestuous relationship to Death evokes those stories in which the Mother of All Living mated with the sons to whom she had parthenogenetically given birth. Similarly, Eve's association with Pandora, a goddess directly linked to Zeus's conflict with a second generation of Titans, Epimetheus and Prometheus, underscores again the nature of Eve's alliance with Satan. Through such analogies, Eve as goddess finds her place among the elder generation of numinous beings who resisted the impositions of Zeus-Jehovah.

Historic Denigration of the Goddess

The denigration of the Goddess implied in these tales is part of a fate which was pronounced upon most of the female deities of the ancient world who almost universally fell under the shadow of new male gods. The most common means of suppressing them was simply to marry them off. Thus Hera, whose temples long predate those of Zeus, falls like so many goddesses of the Creto-Aegean world under his amorous domination. Others, like Aphrodite and Athene, being maiden goddesses whose worship was so notoriously unconnected to man or marriage, required more drastic forms of subjugation. Of Venus-Aphrodite, who had long been supreme at Corinth, Sparta, and Thespiae, Jane Ellen Harrison remarks: "She is the Bride of the old order: she is never wife, never tolerates patriarchal monogamy. . . . In Homer it is evident that she is a newcomer to Olympus, barely tolerated, an alien." Unable to reduce her to an Olympian housewife, the Hellenic Greeks slandered Aphrodite's sexual rites as adulterous indiscretions. Milton's connecting Eve with such a temptress, of course, is not without ominous undertones.

Athene presented similar problems. Harrison proclaims the myth of her birth from Zeus's head "a desperate theological expedient to rid an earth-bound Kore [maiden goddess] of her matriarchal conditions,"[24] and George Thomson explains: "She had never been married because in Pelasgian times there had been no marriage, but in the new age this was taken to mean that she prefers virginity. She had never had a mother because as mother-goddess she was herself the embodiment of motherhood, but now she has become the favorite daughter of Zeus the Father. . . . As divine president of the patriarchal state, she has become as masculine as her sex, determined by her origin, permits."[25] Similarly, Adam and Eve are born without mothers, although Adam is created from the Adamah, the feminine earth, no less than Pelasgian man. As for Eve, Graves remarks that "the story of Eve's creation from Adam's rib is equalled in perversity by the post-Homeric Greek legend of Athene's birth from the head of Zeus, and Dionysius' birth from his thigh; according to all primitive myths, the female, not the male, gives life."[26] These myths of inverted origins find their real meaning in those analogous rites in patriarchal tribes where initiation involves the rebirth of the young men from their tribal fathers who may deliver them through tree trunks or coddle them like infants. The purpose of these rites, according to Wilhelm Schmidt, was a blatant attempt "to undo the harmonious state of equal privilege and mutual reliance of the two sexes that had originally prevailed in their simple society . . . and to establish . . . a cruel ascendancy of the males."[27]

Changing Female Status

Such mythological defamation of the female has been traced by numerous commentators to alterations in social organization which affected female roles. Humanity creates its gods in its own image, and as John Perry observes, a "prevailing view currently understands archaic myth to be the projection of human social forms into the divine world."[28] In the next two chapters I will argue that in *The Four Zoas* Blake attempts to deconstruct classical and biblical myths which were created to universalize the status quo in both his modern world and the ancient one. In doing so, he seeks to reconstruct those myths to reveal a history of social, sexual, cultural, and psychological evolution which they had served to cover up. One crucial event in his epic depicts Albion and the four Zoas casting off their female Emanations; consequently, sexual relations degenerate into archetypal battles of the sexes. Thus it seems valuable here, with our consideration of such mythic combat, to note some of the social conditions which other analysts have linked to such presumed deterioration.

The idea that social evolution resulted in a decline in female stauts, reflected in religion and myth, was made popular in the nineteenth century by such works as Morgan's *Ancient Society* and Bachofen's *Myth, Religion and Mother-Right*. Using such sources, Friedrich Engels offered the definitive synthesis of such a evolutionary view in *The Origin of the Family, Private Property and the State*, a work in many ways imaginatively anticipated by Blake's later prophecies. Challenging biblically based ideas of universal female subordination, Engels contended that "the world-historical defeat of the female sex" had been accomplished by "the overthrow of mother-right" and "the break up of the matrilineal clan." This theory was retained in the twentieth century by scholars such as Robert Briffault, Jane Ellen Harrison, and George Thomson, but later suffered the fate of evolutionary ideas generally.[29]

In recent years, under the impetus of a feminist challenge, a new generation of anthropologists and historians have reopened the debate about the causes of women's inferior social condition and are bringing new archaeological and ethnographic studies to bear on the question.[30] Many scholars would now argue that an evolution in woman's social role underlies changes in their religious significance, although Engels's assumption of a unilinear pattern of "general" evolution would probably be rejected for more historically concrete patterns of "specific" evolution. In fact, this new feminist anthropology insists upon a wide variation in female status from one culture to another, depending on ecological conditions and economic and kinship organization, even in "primitive" societies. Engels's focus upon the mode of production and how property is owned has often been supplemented by considerations of how the organization of producers affects the sexual division of labor. Finally, it is generally acknowledged that too little is known about pre-class societies, particularly in ancient history, to allow more than the formulation of better-informed, less culturally biased hypotheses. Contemporary ethnographical evidence can only suggest the conditions which may determine women's relative social status.

Within these limits, nevertheless, scholarly arguments are being made for a degeneration of women's status when more egalitarian hunting-and-gathering or horticultural (simple hoe-gardening) societies are transformed into hierarchic agricultural societies and urban civilizations. Moreover, just such a degeneration is said to be reflected, however distantly, in the iconography of the cultures of the Mediterranean and ancient Near East whose myths we are discussing. Similar arguments have been made as well for other peoples, ranging from Native Americans to African tribes, extending into the era of colonization. The factors identified as crucial to changes in gender relations are kinship forms, the level of communality and equality in access to economic resources and political power, the importance of women in relation to their reproductive role as bearers and nurturers of children, cultural attitudes toward sexual equality and autonomy, and the consequent treatment of these attitudes in cultural ideology. While they disavow claims for the existence of matriarchies (societies in which females dominate), and while they accept widespread differences in male and female roles, numerous scholars now argue that the different and frequently complementary functions given to men and women in early societies were still characterized by a relatively greater equality than has been the case in later more hierarchic societies.

Thus, for example, Jacquetta Hawkes summarizes the conclusions of historians in the UNESCO-sponsored volume *Pre-History and the Beginnings of Civilization* as suggesting that in the Neolithic (primitive horticultural) societies of the ancient Near East preceding the third millennium, "Mother Right and the clan system were still dominant, and indeed would have descended through the female line. Indeed, it is tempting to be convinced that the earliest Neolithic societies . . . gave woman the highest status she has ever known."[31] While admonishing us not to confuse this with matriarchy or to forget that such kinship structures have accompanied a wide variety of female situations, depending on other factors, Kathleen Gough writes: "In matrilineal societies where property, rank, office and group membership are inherited through the female line, it is true that women tend to have greater independence than in patrilineal societies. This is especially so in matrilineal tribal societies where the state has not yet developed, and especially in those tribal societies where reidence is matrilocal, that is, men come to live in the homes or villages of their wives." In such societies, Gough argues, "Women are less subordinated in certain crucial respects than they are in most, if not all, of the archaic states. . . . These respects include men's ability to deny women sexuality or to force it upon them; to command or exploit their labor to control their produce; to control or rob them of their children; to confine them physically and prevent their movement; to use them as objects in male transactions; or to withhold from them large areas of society's knowledge and cultural attainments."[32] In fact, in such societies, where a woman's children belong to her and are likely to be supported by her and her siblings, the word "father" may not even exist, or may refer to a group of maternal relatives but not the actual sire. One should not be surprised, as Jacquetta Hawkes and Merlin Stone point out, that in such cultures religious reverence is focused upon the figures of mother and child.

Gough also notes that "after the development of horticulture (which was probably invented and is mainly carried out by women), those tribes in which horticulture predominated over stock raising were most likely to be or to remain matrilocal and to develop matrilineal descent groups with a relatively high status of women."[33] Hawkes, V. Gordon Childe, and Fritz Heichelheim agree in crediting women with the discovery of cultivation, the greatest technological development of the late Stone Age.[34]

In hunting-and-gathering societies, men were invariably the hunters and women the foragers.[35] This often made woman the source of the clan's most reliable food supply, and her appearance as patron of the sacred fruit trees as grain goddess undoubtedly reflects these functions. For it was only a step from gathering to uprooting cuttings to planting them nearer home; and it is probably by some such process, as well as the woman's observation of seeds sprouting in her storage and cooking places, that she mastered this new skill. In hoe cultures throughout the world, simple gardening was the province of women, and this phenomenon was encouraged inevitably by magical beliefs about the innate association between women and all fertility. E. G. Payne reported that among some American Indians the males refused to interfere in agriculture, for, as one told him, "When women plant maize, the stalk produces two or three ears. . . . Why? Because women know how to produce children."[36] Thus, as childbearers and gardeners, women acquired the prestige that was manifested in the cult of earth as Mother.

It is within this context that assertions of male supremacy are likely to involve usurpations of the female function of procreation. In his *Oresteia* Aeschylus presents the transition from a female- to a male-dominated religion in relation to the overthrow of mother-right. The *Eumenides* turns upon the question of whether Orestes is guilty of matricide in killing Clytemnestra or whether his act is vindicated by her murder of his father, Agamemnon. According to the female Erinnyes (Furies), avengers of the old tribal justice, murder was only culpable within the clan and Orestes' only blood relationship was to his mother; the bonds between wife and husband, or father and son imposed no special duties. It is Athene, that creature of the patriarchal mind of Zeus, who revokes these ancient authorities in favor of a new male-dominated justice which vindicates Orestes and condemns Clytemnestra: "No mother gave me birth. Therefore the father's claim / And male supremacy in all things, save to give / Myself in marriage, wins my whole heart's loyalty." Apollo, son of Zeus and champion of the new patriarchal order of Olympus, goes even farther, denying not only the priority but also the existence of the maternal tie: "The mother is not the true parent of the child / Which is called hers. She is a nurse who tends the growth / Of young seed planted by its true parent, the male; . . . she keeps it, as one might / Keep for some friend a growing plant."[37] The Erinnyes, snake daimones of the earlier matrilineal culture, denounce this usurpation: "The old order is trampled by the new! / Curse on you younger gods who override / The ancient laws and rob me of my due." They threaten to dry up the powers of fertility which are thus being blasphemed: "A sterile blight shall creep on plant and child." But in the end they are beaten and disgraced, and concede, weeping, "O ancient Earth, see my disgrace."[38]

Athene is implicated in another story, an ancient legend retold by Varro, which describes the overthrow of mother-right. In this legend male supremacy and monogamy are dated from the reign of Cecrops and explained as a punishment inflicted by Poseidon on female citizens for having outvoted the men and deciding to name their city after Athene rather than after himself. The result is that the women are henceforth denied citizenship and it is declared that children shall from then on bear their fathers' names. As ancient Greek sources record, before the reign of Cecrops "there had been no marriage, intercourse was promiscuous, with the result that sons did not know their fathers or fathers their sons. The children were named after their mothers."[39]

Economic Change and the Condition of Women

Many commentators explain this alteration in female status as a consequence of economic transformations. Eleanor Leacock insists that the key to woman's status is the egalitarianism of a culture: "Societies that lived by gathering and by hunting (and fishing) were cooperative. People shared food, and thought of greed and selfishness as we might think of mentally ill or criminal behaviour. People made and valued fine possessions but as much to give away as to keep. People did not follow a single leader but participated in the making of decisions important to them."[40] In such societies as well as in the egalitarian horticultural ones which followed them, there was, according to Leacock, no sharp differentiation between a male "public" and female "private" and domestic sphere; roles were different but complementary and women were highly valued for their crucial contributions to the common life. Rohrlich-Leavitt thus summarizes the changes that occurred in the Goddess-worshiping culture of Sumer: "Essential to the consolidation of private property and the political state (institutions that first came into being in Sumer) was the breakup of the corporate kinship groups based on communal land tenure and the centrality and freedom of women. . . . As private ownership of land, political centralization and militarism gained momentum, the elites increasingly became male and male supremacy pervaded every social stratrum."[41] Eleanor Leacock identifies the transformation with the development of production for exchange:

> Networks of exchange were originally egalitarian in form, for profit was not involved. However, the production and holding of goods for future exchange created new positions and new vested interests that began to divide the commitments of some individuals from those of the group as a whole. . . . The seeds of class difference were sown as people began to lose direct control over the distribution and consumption of the goods they had produced. Simultaneously, the basis for the oppression of women was laid, as the communal kin group became undercut by conflicting political and economic ties. In its place, individual family units emerged in which the responsibility for raising future generations was placed on the shoulders of individual parents, and through which women's public role (and consequent public recognition) was transmuted into private service (and loss of public esteem).[42]

Others indicate that whereas the earliest cultures may not have even understood the male role in procreation, the accumulation of property and inheritance led to obsessions with paternity. Once property no longer passed from mother to child as a birthright in the common wealth of the clan, but individually through the father, a concern for the legitimacy of heirs led to an emphasis on female fidelity in patriarchal monogamy or polygamy. Demosthenes writes that marriage developed in ancient Greece so that "the heritage should not be left desolate and the name cut off."[43]

Where a woman possesed her own children and supported them

through her kin, she might enjoy personal independence, sexual freedom, and the special dignities afforded motherhood. No husband could rule over her. Once her main function became the production of heirs, she often became little more than a chattel.

Another factor which has been implicated in this process is the effect of the division of labor which had allocated foraging and later gardening to women, and hunting and then care of animals to men. Thus Kathleen Gough writes: "Where extensive hunting of large animals, or later the herding of large domesticates, predominated, patrilocal residence flourished and women were used to form alliances between male-centered groups. With the invention of metallurgy and agriculture as distinct from horticulture after 4000 BC, men came to control agriculture and many crafts and most of the great agrarian states had patrilocal residence with patriarchal, male-dominant families."[44] The domestication of animals also allows the replacement of female hoe-gardening—women working near their homes with their children often slung over their backs—by men tilling fields using ox-drawn ploughs. Robert Briffault believes the consequences were disastrous for women: "In the end no economic change established male supremacy more firmly. . . . Women, instead of being the chief producer, became economically unproductive, destitute and dependent. . . . One economic value alone was left to woman, her sex."[45]

The restriction of women to a narrow economic role, some argue, was accentuated by the fact that these new modes of production were more likely to be based upon private property and thus involved the dissolution of clan and the growth of patriarchal family structures. Cattle may have been among the earliest forms of capital, since cattle were a mobile, edible but relatively imperishable form of value and they could be accumulated and bartered as neither land nor produce could be. Interestingly, in Latin the words for cow (*pecus*) and money (*pecunia*) share the same root. Moreover, among agrarian tribes cattle owners could seize plots from once communal lands for cultivation by their oxen. The natural limits which allocated a group just so much land as they could tend by their own labor and whose produce they might consume for their own subsistence were transcended, as cattle promoted the accumulation and exchange of surplus products. Large landowners were motivated to acquire slaves through purchase or conquest for the cultivation of their enlarged holdings.

Internal processes of development, therefore, were undoubtedly intensified by the invasions of nomadic herders who swept through the Near East and the Mediterranean area, particularly in the second millennium B.C., contributing thereby to the downfall of Neolithic cultures already begun in the urban revolutions. Probably having originally split off from agrarian cultures in search of pasturage, now Indo-European pastoralists were forced by population pressures and land hunger to return to more developed areas in wave after wave of conquest during what historians have described as the "cult of frightfulness."

While it has been argued that nomadic cultures also show a range of sexual arrangements and might even have had matrilineal origins, these bellicose tribes are generally described as having become thoroughly patriarchal by the time they came to conquer and settle areas such as Greece and Palestine. Such nomadic patriarchs with their large herds and extensive households of subordinate kin and multiple wives were literally the baals (masters) of their communities. Thus Christopher Dawson describes them:

> The social organization of pastoral peoples was in almost every respect a complete contrast to that of the sedentary agriculturalist. Whereas the latter rested on the basis of a fixed territorial settlement and on common labour, the former was characterized by the development of property and kinship. The importance of a tribe or family depended on their wealth in flocks and herds, an ever varying factor which at once introduced an element of inequality, whereas the amount of land held by a primitive agriculturalist is strictly limited by his powers of cultivation; . . . it is not the land itself that is valuable but the labour which renders it fruitful. Thus the woman who cultivates the ground is . . . as important, or even more important than the man, and the primitive agricultural community often possesses a matrilinear or matriarchal organization. On the other hand, the pastoral tribe is patriarchal and aristocratic, and . . . produces types like Abraham, men rich in flocks and herds, with many wives and children, wise in counsel and resolute in war.[46]

The consequence of all these various historical factors, both of internal evolution and external conquest, was the reversal, in one social setting at least, of the position of women; Friedrich Engels sums it up:

> The man took command of the home; the woman was degraded and reduced to servitude; she became a slave of his lust and a mere instrument for producing children. . . . The original meaning of the word "family" (*familia*) is not that compound of sentimentality and domestic strife which forms the ideal of the present-day philistine. . . . *Famulus* means domestic slave, and *familia* is the total number of slaves belonging to one man. . . . The term was invented by the Romans to denote a new social organism whose head ruled over wife and children and a number of slaves.[47]

With this change, Engels adds, "Monogamous marriage comes on the scene as the subjugation of the one sex by the other; it announces a struggle between the sexes unknown throughout the whole previous historic period." Summarizing recent research, Elise Boulding, while challenging the universality of Engels's picture since "the role of accidental factors, whether of environment or of individual human personality, or the vagaries of social drift in patterning social organization could produce many variants of the transition," concludes that much of the evidence "seems to point in the same direction."[48] Moreover, Boulding's account supports Ruby Rohrlich-Leavitt's contention that this denigration of women "must have been accompanied by great resistance on their part and took a relatively long time to complete."[49]

Wars on Earth and in Heaven

We should not be surprised, therefore, to find that the myths which discredit the ancient goddesses also describe a conflict so total that it seems to embroil all the forces in the universe. Part of the significance underlying the warrior-gods who come to dominate ancient religion must be this strife between old clans and new classes, between women and patriarchs. In particular, they have been traced to the confrontation between settled peoples and their conquerors. In Dawson's words:

> With the advance of the pastoral culture . . . the Sky God tends to become personified as a celestial hero and chieftain. . . . The Sky God of the warrior peoples is . . . the god of the thunderbolt and the storm. These are incalculable and formidable powers . . . jealous and arbitrary rulers after the image of their own chieftains who must be feared and obeyed implicitly and blindly. . . . They are the guardians of the masculine tribal morality.[50]

We can recognize here the boisterous warring deities of Olympus. On one level, as Robert Graves points out, the myths of celestial combat reflect the exploits of the Indo-European conquerors who descended with their warrior gods to subdue the goddesses and peoples of Bronze Age cultures.[51]

The coincidence of these conquests with a transition from matrilineal to patriarchal society is reflected in the sexual associations of these cosmic wars. Thus we find that Zeus wars against three successive generations of the children of Gaia. His defeat of the Titans, the snake-tailed Giants and the serpent-headed and serpent-armed Typhon represents the new patriarchal deity's conquest of the life daimons of the old fertility cult. Moreover, the genealogy of the

Theogony, as Norman O. Brown indicates, mirrors an evolution from the primacy of the female to the primacy of the male. "This idea," he maintains, "is contained in the contrast between Mother Earth at the beginning who produces children without male partnership and mates with her own sons, and Zeus 'the father of gods and men' at the end."[52] Olympus, as Harrison notes, has by then been completely reorganized into a family group of the ordinary patriarchal type: "Zeus . . . is supreme; Hera, though in constant and significant revolt, occupies the subordinate place of a wife; Poseidon is a younger brother, and the rest of the Olympians are grouped around Zeus and Hera in relations of sons and daughters."[53]

The same story is told in the Babylonian *Enuma Elish*. A creation myth available since antiquity in the Berossus fragment summarized by various classical authors, it is believed to have exerted pervasive influence upon biblical and other mythology. It was partly available to Blake through Jacob Bryant and may have been known to Milton. In this story, creation proceeds from Tiamat, the Great Mother, a water monster identified with the ocean. She generates the other gods, first her husband, Apsu, and then the male trinity Ea, Anu, and Bel. When these sons murder their father (as Zeus did Cronus), Tiamat seeks to avenge him in battle against her sons. A war erupts in the heavens between the younger gods, who have chosen Ea's son, Marduk, as their leader and Tiamat with her brood of monsters. Assuming the powers of a storm god, armed with the wind, floods, and thunder, Marduk traps the goddess of the sea in a net which once symbolized her fecundity, pierces her heart, crushes her skull, and destroys her. Then, in a second creation, Marduk "split[s] her like a shellfish in two parts" and creates the universe out of her body which divided forms the earth and the sky. Marduk then emerges as the supreme god granted permanent kingship over the other deities in return for his victory. Again, the myth registers a genealogical evolution from a woman-dominated universe based on matrilineal kinship ties to a male order dominated by a warrior-god.

This myth of cosmic combat has numerous analogues: the battles of Baal against the dragons Yamm, Mot, and Lotan in Canaanite myth, the victories of Apollo over Python, Perseus over Medusa, and Heracles over Ladon. Biblical scholars suggest that a similar cosmic battle may have once introduced the Yahwist creation story but was removed by a priestly editor who sought to demythologize the Genesis account. A faint suggestion remains in the image of God moving over the watery chaos and the division of earth and sky. The mythic combat itself appears, however, in other parts of the Bible, particularly in the creation described in Psalms. There, Yahweh also establishes his supremacy as creator by defeating a water monster named Rahab or Leviathan (Psa. 74,89; Job 41:1–8; Isa. 51).

In all these myths the conquest of the gods of an older order by those of the new involves, at the same time, a distortion of the gods' original significance. As Joseph Campbell tells us, these stories dramatized "the conquest by a shining hero of the dark and . . . disparaged monster of an earlier order of Godhood."[54]

Yahweh and the Gods of Canaan

In another form, even more total, this mythological defamation is promulgated by the Old Testament. The Jewish people derived from nomadic tribes who entered areas where Goddess worship still prevailed, and an agrarian people still practiced the old fertility rites. At some point a number of such tribes merged into a nation by accepting a covenant binding them in a common cult of Yahweh, sky god of the desert. In *And They Took Themselves Wives: The Emergence of Patriarchy in Western Civilization*, David Bakan demonstrates that the Bible itself attests to a substratum of practices such as matrilineality and matrilocality barely glossed over by the patrilineal mythology of Abraham and his descendants.[55] These contrary legacies may point to prehistoric roots, to the absorbtion of matrilineally organized peoples, or to adaptations within Canaan. At any rate, we know that a long struggle was waged between patriarchal biblical religion and the surrounding nature cults; as late as 621 B.C., Josiah "discovered" the Law of Moses and prohibited the worship of false gods which had entered the temple itself. Only after a protracted conflict did Yahweh win out supreme.

As a product of post-exile Jerusalem whose priests had already been fully exposed during the Babylonian captivity to fertility cult and myth, Genesis can be understood as a polemic against the woman-centered religions of the Near East. The book elevates Yahweh as more than a tribal god among gods to sole creator of the universe and simultaneously defames the Mother of All Living with her luxuriant garden and attendant snake daimon. In the place of her procreation of the universe and her embodiment of eroticism and fecundity, we find a new version of creation which places the origin of all things in the political command of a supreme father god. Not surprisingly, this condemnation of the Goddess and her rites extends to the woman-centered society in which she arose. In the patriarchal Jewish Genesis, woman is the cause of all evil and mere afterthought of a supreme male mind, created for man's entertainment and for reproduction. Here, patriarchal monogamy is written into the very nature of the universe as a divine institution to which women shall universally be subjected: "Your desire shall be for your husband only and he shall rule over you" (Gen. 3:16). The uniqueness of the ingenious Hebrew tale does not lie with its affirmation of male domination, which was to triumph everywhere, but rather with its total obliteration of all prior or alternative realities. In Greek and Babylonian myth, the male gods are clearly usurpers, for the goddesses had existed too long to be ignored and at best could be reduced to subordinate places in the pantheon.

But the Jews had experienced no such gradual evolution towards patriarchal institutions. It is not exactly clear what process of tribal fusions, invasion, development, and accommodation to the con- quered people preceded what we know as the Hebrew nation. The Jews who entered Palestine did not, by and large, find agrarian tribes in Canaan but impenetrable fortified cities. They were forced to settle as simple herders in the hills surrounding this more advanced civilization. These conditions seemed to militate against their assim- ilation by that agrarian culture such as occurred when Zeus took over the shrines and symbols of pre-Dorian Greece. Rather, they clung all the more to the *mishpat* of Yahweh, the values of their tribal organi- zation, as a source of unity against the enemies around them. Their prophets proclaimed that only fidelity to Yahweh and the old clan values of mutual aid and solidarity would assure them victory over the baals, divine and human, of Canaan.[56]

This patriarchal primitivism was encouraged, furthermore, by the ways in which the fertility cult had degenerated when the old, egalitarian matrilineal clans were succeeded by urban civilizations. That worship, which had once inspired and united agrarian peoples, had been adapted to quite new purposes, until the Goddess came to give natural and supernatural justification to a new patriarchal and stratified civilization. Just as in Greece patriarchy altered the values of its goddesses, so too in Mesopotamia. With the transformation of woman from honored mother and co-worker into wife and mistress, the procreative cult turned into a decadent temple prostitution, as religion absorbed the energies of a newly frustrated and perverted sexuality. By the same token, the sacrificial sharing in the mana of the holy bull and holy fruits and wine was made into a priestly tribute and an offering of bloody gifts—often mass sacrifices of captive slaves—to inclement ruler gods. Hence, as the old agrarian com- munes were divided into an oppressed peasantry and a tyrannical elite dependent for their survival on continual military expansion, the magic of tribal solidarity became a superstitious dependency on the mumbo-jumbo of self-serving priests, while the pacific mothers of life, fecundity, and pleasure were metamorphosed into the warrior mistresses of bellicose baals. Thus not only in patriarchal prejudice, but also through a patriarchal rape of her heritage, the Great Mother yielded to the Whore of Babylon. It is no wonder in this context that prophets like Jeremiah and Isaiah, spokesmen of the Jewish masses, set the worship of Yahweh as a desert god of righteousness against the misery and idolatry of Canaan.

This issue, however, has still further complexities; for, as Blake never lets us forget, the Bible reflects the contending standpoints of prophet and priest. This duality pervades Genesis and the polemic against the Goddess cult as well. For while ⎽⎽ie prophets upheld a primitive *mishpat* of Yahweh against the crimes of civilization, a crafty temple priesthood, attracted to Canaanite religion, was already working to infuse the Yahweh cult itself with the values of an urbanized and aristocratic oriental culture.[57] Thus we will find Genesis an extremely ambiguous document and one torn by more than one contradiction, incorporating within itself both a nostalgia for and a denunciation of the world of the Goddess, and, consequently, both an opposition to and a rationalization of the society that rose on its ruins. These contradictions Blake hoped to resolve by rewriting the myth in such a way as to differentiate correctly between the prophetic and priestly stance, for, in his words, "These two classes of men . . . should be enemies; whoever tries to reconcile them seeks to destroy existence. Religion is an endeavour to reconcile the two" (*MHH* 16–17).

The real meaning of Genesis, apart from the moral values traditionally assigned to it, was perhaps revealed to Blake by Milton's depiction of Eve and Satan as deities of a primitive nature cult. We can now understand that Milton's uncovering of this mythic dimension required no modern critical analysis of Scripture, but was informed by the significance that Genesis's symbols inevitably took on in the context of the biblical polemic against paganism. Although Milton's logic in the face of comparative religion came to conclusions opposite to ours, he perceived the same connections. He saw the pagan deities as former devils, while Blake finds the devils to have been deities. In Book I, Milton offers a procession of these demons and a denunciation of their ancient cults. Blake must have been influenced by this condemnation of human sacrifice, the sexual religion of "wanton rites" and "lustful Orgies" (*PL* I.414,415), the seasonal cult of Thammuz, the adulation of female goddesses, superstitious magic, and the degrading veneration of idols—"brutish forms / Rather than human" (*PL* I.481–82). At the same time, Blake was inspired to formulate a critique which avoided Milton's puritanical repudiation of the moral laxity of Dionysian values.

The vehemence of Milton's attack on long-forgotten gods might at first seem to us incomprehensible but takes on significance in light of widely held seventeenth-century religious belief. Protestant reformers saw their own battles against Catholic idolatry as a continuation of the Old Testament's battle against paganism—as in a real sense, they were. For history is characterized by an uneven development in which stages accomplished in one area may not be reached in another for hundreds, even thousands of years. Thus, with the fall of the Roman Empire before the onslaught of maurauding tribes, very primitive aspects of culture were newly infused into civilization. As Milton himself notes, part of this amalgamation involved Christianity's accommodation to the customs of these tribes:

> In order to attract pagans to the Christian religion, and to make conversion easier, they retained the pagan rites with only a slight alteration of names or things. This practice proved very detrimental to religion and contravened the commandment contained in Deut. xii:30,31: *beware in case by following them you are snared . . . and do not inquire about their gods, and say, How did these pagans worship their gods, for I may do the same?*   (YP VI.667)

Saint Patrick's driving the snakes out of Ireland symbolized the conflict between Christianity and the old Celtic fertility cult. But it was equally common for the church to take over the traditional worship of wells and trees and simply canonize their pagan deities as Christian saints. In peasant culture, just below the surface of Catholic ceremonies, the old legacy of agrarian magic survived. The system of local patron saints, as Keith Thomas writes in *Religion and the Decline of Magic,* had "an almost totemic character."[58] The Virgin Mary, proclaimed "Mother of God" in the old Goddess-worshiping city of Ephesus, had, to a great extent, simply absorbed the attributes and titles of the Great Mother still revered by the agricultural peoples of Europe.

Thus the battles between Zeus and the Titans, between Apollo and Dionysius, between Jehovah and the Goddess continued, although now within Christianity itself. It was therefore appropriate for a Protestant enthusiast like Milton, entering the latest phase of that struggle and battling to replace a religion of magic with a religion of morality, to take up the old biblical polemics anew and to fashion his attack upon feudal Catholicism in terms of the myth of the conquest over tribal paganism. Moreover, as I have argued elsewhere, the naked conflict between Christianity and nature religion was being almost literally replayed by those of Milton's compatriots who confronted its "horrors" anew among the native peoples of the North American continent where they determined to establish their New Canaan.[59]

All these factors led Milton to try to reconstruct Genesis, and he did so in a way that managed to bring its long-hidden meanings into focus. When Milton assimilates the Christian war in heaven to the battles of Zeus and Eve to the goddesses of yore, he unveils the mythological foundations of Scripture. When he denounces Satan and Eve as remnants of a pagan idolatry complete with the cult of a mana-filled fruit tree, he uncovers their real identity as the disparaged deities of an alternative religion. In pursuit of this pagan analogy, Milton finally uncovers the profound bond between Eve and Satan which had ever remained hidden beneath their arbitrary biblical rendezvous. In his search for biblical types and poetic metaphors, Milton reforges the mythical links between the Mother Goddess in her primeval garden and her serpentine offspring, those Titans overthrown by a triumphant patriarchal god—links which had been so carefully obfuscated by Hebrew scribes many centuries before. Once such connections are made, the concomitant awareness, evident in the *Enuma Elish* and the *Theogony* but suppressed in *Genesis,* is inevitably called forth, the idea that those deities had preceded the Divine Father and were forcibly overthrown by him. In Milton's version of Genesis, this thesis can no longer be avoided; it appears as Satan's heretical self-justification, and a whole counter-reading of the Bible emerges from his allegation that Jehovah, like Jove "usurping reign'd" (*PL* I.514).

Historical contradictions are never buried only in the past; they survive in the very institutions constructed to resolve them. The ancient conflict between the matrilineal clan and the patriarchal family did not remain buried in myth awaiting discovery by historical scholarship. Rather, it persisted within that family structure in what Engels called "the antagonism between man and woman in monogamous marriage." So too, the political oppositions continued in new forms, for as Blake tells us "not one Moment / Of Time is lost" (*M* 22:18). As we will see in later chapters, it would be their attempts to apply the mythological legacy to continuing conflicts in society and the family that would lead Milton and Blake to their revelations of the myths' original meanings.

We began by insisting that *Paradise Lost* is characterized as much by conflicts as by unities and that those conflicts are real ones, arising from contradictions embedded in Milton's society and culture and are not—as Waldock and company would have it—the consequences of any failure of artistic control. Reading the poem today as a sympathizer of the devil's party, one recognizes how, having let so many enormous questions out of the bag, Milton has so artfully controlled the answers we are allowed to bring to them. As a student of rhetoric, he had mastered well the skill of turning his adversaries' arguments into grounds for his own position. If one argues that *Paradise Lost* is a polemic and Satan a weighty ideological opponent, one need not deny that within the constructs of his poem, Milton and his God win the debate. If Milton's materials backfire for a modern reader, the problem lies with what is buried in those materials. When Satan begins to formulate a critique of the Judeo-Christian God linking Genesis and the *Theogony*, and when he intimates an alliance between a deposed maternal goddess in an expropriated paradise and a generation of conquered divinities who turn out to be her *"Earth-born"* children (*PL* I.198), we encounter a stash of cultural dynamite of whose potency Milton was not sufficiently conscious even to try to control. If he had been, *Paradise Lost* would have been beyond the mastery of even his great genius. If he had known what history, anthropology, and comparative mythology were later to reveal, the magnificent tensions of his poem might have burst asunder with the explosion of its Genesis foundations. Had Milton possessed such a consciousness, we might have gotten instead that brilliant shower of fragments which occurred a century and a half later when, under the pressure of new historical knowledge and new social configurations, the blowup finally happened; we might have gotten *The Four Zoas*.

6

Blake's Genesis: Eden

*No man can have in his mind a conception of the future, for the future
is not yet. But of our conceptions of the past we make a future.*
                                                                    —Hobbes

"The Nature of my Work," Blake insists, "is Visionary or Imaginative it is an Endeavour to Restore what the Ancients calld the Golden
Age" (PB 545). Blake's idea of imagination has received such metaphysical treatment that it is important to be reminded here that for
him "vision" is an inherently political and historical concept and
seeks to create, not only art, but also the just society.

Visions of the future, as Hobbes tells us, are intimately entwined
with versions of the past. Thus we have noted that at the heart of the
revolutionary tradition, from the millenarians to Marx, had been a
welding of alpha and omega, Genesis and Revelation, theories of
origin and theories of apocalypse. For the same reason, George Thomson, the historian of antiquity, bemoans the specialization which has
kept contemporary anthropology and archaeology from formulating
a vision of human development; for, as he instructs us, "to tell the
whole story from beginning to end would not only reveal the present
as a continuation of the past—it would lift the veil on the future.
There's the rub."[1] This was precisely what Blake hoped to accomplish
in *The Four Zoas.*

Once we appreciate the political significance of Genesis and other
myths of the past, Blake's seemingly eccentric vision reveals itself as
the consummation of a long tradition of plebeian radicalism which
had seen Eden as a utopia, lost through social, rather than individual
moral degeneration. Drawing upon prophetic Judaism and apocalyptic primitive Christianity, radicals ranging from medieval peasant
chiliasts to left-wing Puritans and the English Jacobins of Blake's own

era had thus interpreted the story of the Fall to support their belief that they might restore Eden on earth by political means.

If this focus is clear, one can see that Blake's apparently eclectic and idiosyncratic assemblage of ideological allies and enemies possesses a fundamental consistency; he distinguishes the prophets of that tradition from the "priests" of a countertradition whose views of human origins and possibilities serve to legitimize the "fallen" world of the status quo. The sharp political character of his judgments of various views is evidenced by the fact that, almost invariably, Blake anticipates the assessments later shared by socialist thinkers. In this chapter, we will trace the confrontation between these two opposing traditions through history: the classical and apocalyptic views of the golden age and their rebuke by a developing orthodox insistence on original sin; the persistence of millenarianism up through the English Revolution in spokesmen from John Ball to Gerrard Winstanley and its refutation by new secular theories of the state of nature arising from bourgeois thinkers from John Locke to the Enlightenment and Rousseau; and the revival of radical views in Blake's time, drawing partly upon the inspiration of such peoples as the American Indians.

In reestablishing the links between human history and a primitive golden age, Blake had to overcome three perspectives which would leave humanity "rent from Eternity" (*FZ* 54:5). First, he rejected the priestly reading of the Fall as original sin, and a justification of existing oppression as either a punishment for or a consequence of the moral perversity of human nature. Blake was convinced that interpretations of Genesis ultimately distinguished revolutionary and counter-revolutionary tendencies in Christianity; he sought, therefore, to rewrite *Paradise Lost* in *The Four Zoas* in such a way as to separate those contrary traditions, so exasperatingly fused by the Puritan revolutionary.

In addition, Blake had to examine critically two approaches to the primitive which had come to dominate his own era. The first, typified by Locke, read bourgeois institutions, such as private property and monogamy, back into primal conditions as universals of human existence. The second, promoted by the Enlightenment, advanced an idea of progress which served to justify contemporary conditions as part of a long advance out of the horrors of original barbarism, or, in the nostalgic form advocated by Rousseau, saw a hopeless division between the animal innocence of savagery and the corruption of civilized, cultured life. In neither case could there be a return to the golden age for "civilized" humanity.

Blake opens *The Four Zoas* by dramatizing such nullifications of "the Universal Brotherhood of Eden" (*FZ* 3:5), as visions of history based upon amnesia, "Forgetfulness dumbness necessity in chains of the mind lockd up" (*FZ* 54:4). Such forgetfulness grants necessity, inevitability, to the institutions and psychology of fallen society; thus Blake portrays it as the work of Enion, in the role of the classical Fates, creating the circle of destiny by obliterating humanity's beginning and, hence, its end:

> Nine days she labourd at her work. & nine dark sleepless nights
> But on the tenth trembling morn the Circle of Destiny Complete
> Round rolld the Sea Englobing.   (*FZ* 5:23–25)

The circle suggests that the present human condition is inescapable. Enion, the female weaver of classical myth, has woven all the dangling, open threads of history into a closed warp and woof of human limitations in which it will henceforth remain fixed. The nine nights are the ages of humankind found in *The Four Zoas*. There, Blake will slash Enion's web of necessity, breaking open the chain of destiny at both ends simultaneously to reveal humanity's history from its original fall to the recovery of apocalyptic possibilities which he envisions beginning in his own revolutionary era. For it is within history itself that he expects to find new openings to Eternity, since

> Eno a daughter of Beulah took a Moment of Time
> And drew it out to Seven thousand years with much care & affliction
> And many tears & in Every year made windows into Eden. (*FZ* 9:9–11)

As has often been pointed out, Blake's Eden might ultimately exist beyond the "englobing" sea of time and space, but it is nevertheless to be approached through time, through the restoration in time of an earthly paradise of universal brotherhood which provides the only condition under which time and eternity are not rent asunder.

The Four Zoas, I will argue, offers a theory of historical stages similar to that proposed by nineteenth-century theorists—in particular, Marx and Engels—in which a primitive communist Eden characterized by egalitarian sexual relations is destroyed through the rise of hierarchic class civilizations based upon such institutions as private property, the family, and the state. According to this political theory, the tribal communism of nature-worshiping, mother-right clans gives way to stratified agricultural societies, and then either to slave empires or the "asiatic mode" with its theocratic bureaucracy. After the fall of these ancient civilizations, new developments would produce in turn feudalism, capitalism, and, presumably, socialism.

This theory, like others of its time, endorses a teleology of progress to be brought about by development of the forces of production. Blake's myth appears to be more nostalgic, but he too is ultimately more interested in the future than the past. Thus he must invent an Eden worthy and capable of being restored, a *new* Jerusalem possessed of every attribute of science and culture. Within his framework, he must therefore distinguish every negative aspect of early societies recorded in myth or history as pertaining to some later, already "fallen" era.

Here we will confront and examine Blake's argument against the primacy of the Goddess cult, for he aligns himself on this issue with Genesis, Milton, and the Hebrew prophets in denouncing "Canaanite idolatry," rather than with the romantic primitivism which later influenced Engels's view of mother-right and the celebrations of woman worship in the work of Robert Graves and contemporary feminism. In Blake, as in Graves, but with contrary allegiances, the millenarian traditions of a communal Eden completely diverge from the mythical ones of a maternal, natural paradise. They would be brought back together only in our own time in a new marriage accomplished by the cross-fertilization of radical—especially Third-World—and feminist primitivisms. Blake's vision of historical stages thus begins with a golden age characterized by a communal society, sexual equality and freedom, and mystical empowerment, but this golden age is catapulted first into a Beulah of matriarchal female domination, and only then into the Generation of patriarchal slave civilizations and later into the hell of atomized industrial society, hovering on the edge of a totally fascist Ulro. In the following discussion, we will trace the traditions endorsed and rejected in Blake's own vision of Eden.

Echoes of Eden: Golden Age, Garden Paradise, and Hebraic Primitivism

Blake derived his image of Eden from a Christian millenarianism with roots in classical ideas, myths of paradise, and the legacies of Hebrew tribalism, which we will consider in that order. The myth of the five ages of man first appears in Hesiod's *Works and Days*. There we find a decline from a golden age of peace and justice, without cares or labor, to a silver race dominated by mothers, a bronze age of warriors and Homeric heroes, and finally an iron race: degenerate, cruel, unjust, malicious, unfilial, libidinous, and treacherous.

As recorded by Ovid, this golden age of peace existed before Saturn (Cronus) was overthrown by Jupiter (Zeus):

> In the beginning was the Golden Age, when men of their own accord, without threat of punishment, without laws maintained good faith and did what was right. There were no penalties to be afraid of, no bronze

tablets were erected, carrying threats of legal action; no crowd of wrong doers anxious for mercy, trembled before the face of their judge: indeed there were no judges. . . . The earth itself, without compulsion, untouched by the hoe . . . produced all things spontaneously; . . . but modesty, truth and loyalty fled. Treachery and trickery took their place, deceit, violence and criminal greed. . . . The land, which had previously been common to all, like the sunlight and the breezes, was now divided up far and wide by boundaries, set by cautious surveyors.[2]

Virgil had written that once Saturn had been driven from Olympus, he had established that golden age in Italy where

> No fence dividing field from field was found;
> When to the common store all gains were brought
> And earth gave freely goods which none had sought.[3]

Ovid's contemporary, the historian Gnaeus Pompeius Trogus, traced to these conditions the source of the Saturnalia: "The first inhabitants of Italy were Aborigines. Their king, Saturn, is said to have been so just that under his rule nobody was a slave and nobody had any private property either; but all things were held by all in common and without division, as though there were one single inheritance for all men. In memory of that example it was decreed that during the Saturnalia all should be given equal rights."[4]

In the hands of the Stoics, such tales were elevated to the philosophic conception of an egalitarian state of nature, the belief that all men by nature were brothers and were free and equal which became the cornerstone of medieval political theory. Under Stoic influence, the Greek historian Diodorus Siculus composed the description of the Isles of the Blessed in his *Historical Library*, attributing to the primitive Heliopolitans (people of the sun) both sexual and economic communism. All land, tools, and livestock were there for common use, according to Diodorus, and all individuals worked for the good of all. Marriage, moreover, was unknown; rather, complete sexual promiscuity was allowed, and children were raised by the tribe.[5] Similar ideas about primitive sexuality appeared in Herodotus who described the Massagetas as having wives in common and the Scythians as having wives, children, and families in common. Aristotle attributes the same to African tribes; Plutarch says the Hyrcanians only began to marry under Alexander, and Varro, as we have seen, attributed the same change to Athens under the reign of the mythical Cecrops. The Roman Stoics, like the Greek, held that human beings had once lived by egalitarian communism which Seneca describes as follows:

> They enjoyed all Nature in common. She sufficed for them as mother and defender of all. Their defence was the secure possession of the common resources. Why, indeed, should I not call that the richest race

of mortals, since no poor man could be found among them? But Avarice broke in upon this best of all conditions and, seeking to possess something not shared by others and to claim it for her own, made all things the property of others, and thus passed from boundless wealth to meagerest poverty. It was greed that begot need, and, by craving much, lost all. . . . The stronger had not yet laid hands upon the weaker; not yet had the miser, by hiding his wealth away unused, deprived others of the very necessities of life. Each cared as much for his neighbor as himself, weapons were unknown.[6]

This idea of an egalitarian state of nature easily became linked with myths of a primitive paradise. In agrarian cults, the garden of the Goddess was a present reality, the eternal spring which she brought forth, or the island where she transported her lover for the barren season. As the conditions of primitive agriculture faded, it too became a lost paradise, the isle of Dilmun in ancient Sumerian poetry, a realm without war, sickness, or old age, or the isle of the blessed where Gilgamesh lost the flower of immortality to a serpent, as in Genesis. These myths of paradise, like Genesis, tended to locate it in the valley of the Tigris and Euphrates—that lush, naturally irrigated area where agriculture probably originated. As Jacquetta Hawkes describes it, "The many channels and lagoons teemed with fish; wild fowl and game swarmed in the reed brakes; date palms grew wild. . . . This natural paradise," she suggests, was "the original Eden."[7]

Paradise entered the Hebrew Bible long after urban civilization had developed (probably as a result of the direct influence of Babylonian culture during the exile) as a nostalgic longing for a past era free from alienating toil and sexual discord—both of which are attributed to the Fall. This social significance also is implicit in the prophetic use of the garden image, as in the postexilic Isaiah who transforms the agrarian paradise from a symbol of the past into a promise of future deliverance: "For the Lord will comfort Zion; he will comfort all her waste places, and will make her wilderness like Eden, her desert like the garden of the Lord; joy and gladness will be found in her, thanksgiving and the voice of song" (Isa. 51:3).

Agrarian primitivism, however, was less typical of Hebraic vision than was the nomadic ideal which, as we have noted, was an earlier inspiration of prophetic morality. Thus Hosea projects the redemption of Israel as a restoration to the desert: "I am Yahweh, your God; from the land of Egypt I will bring you, and again I will make you live in tents as in the days of old" (Hos. 12:9). The early Jews lived in extended families, patriarchal clans bound together by the exigencies of economic survival and mutual defense. The *mishpat* of Yahweh which became the touchstone of Jewish morality harkened back to the mores of a culture based upon kinship. There, God was their common father, and they are repeatedly referred to as the *banim* (children), the *bayith* (house or family) or even the *mishphachah* (clan) of Israel. The prophets saw the Hebrew nation as a literal group of blood relatives descended from a common ancestor, Abraham, and bound to treat each other as brothers. Thus Malachi writes, "Have we not all one father? hath not one God created us? why do we deal treacherously every man against his brother?" (Mal. 2:10). And Leviticus warns, "Over your brethren the children of Israel, ye shall not rule, one over another with rigor" (Lev. 25:46). Once the growth of landed estates threatened to divide the Israeli brotherhood into alien classes, religious radicals often sought a reversion to an egalitarian and ascetic desert life. Thus the leader of the Rechabites told his ninth-century (B.C.) followers: "You shall drink no wine neither you nor your sons for ever; and you shall build no houses, nor sow seed nor plant, nor own a vineyard; but you shall live in tents all your lives, so that you may live long in the land where you sojourn" (Jer. 35:6–7). This tradition was later carried on by the Essenes whose ascetic desert communism provided the immediate context of Christianity.[8]

Edenic Society in Early Christianity

These three traditions—the golden age, the primitive paradise, and the nomadic brotherhood—all merge in Christian interpretations of Genesis, arising within the syncretistic context of the Roman Empire. By the second century B.C., Hellenic Jews had linked to the pagan golden age their social ideals in the Jewish Sibylline oracles—apocalyptic writings modeled upon the alleged oracles of a Greek prophetess, Sibyl, which had had a strong impact on the apocalyptic thought of early Christianity.

At the same time, the church fathers were powerfully influenced by classical ideas and merged the notion of an egalitarian state of nature with the biblical myth of paradise. Thus Augustine interpreted Genesis: "[God] did not intend that His rational creature, who was made in His image, should have dominion over anything but irrational creation—not man over man, but man over the beasts. And hence the righteous men in primitive times were made shepherds of cattle rather than kings of men; . . . for it is with justice, we believe, that the condition of slavery is the result of sin."[9]

Cyprian argued that God's gifts were given to all; just as the sun and moon and rains were common property, God intended all humanity to share his gifts. Similarly, Ambrose writes: "Nature has poured forth all things for all men, to be held in common. For God commanded all things to be produced so that food should be common to all, and that the earth should be a common possession of all. Nature, therefore, created a common right, but use and habit created private right."[10] Ambrose synthesizes Genesis and the ideas of the Stoics, commenting elsewhere that "the Lord God specially wanted this earth to be the common possession of all and to provide fruits for all; but avarice produced the rights of property."[11]

A passage glorifying the communistic state of nature, including free love, even entered into Gratian's *Decretum*, the treatise which became the basic text of canon law. Gratian picked up a passage quoted by a French monk of the ninth century known as Pseudo-Isadore who had transmuted a quotation by Pope Clement I from pagan philosophy into an authoritative position of the pope himself. Clement had written:

> The use of all things that are in this world ought to have been common to all men, but through injustice one man says that is his, and another says that is his, and so division is created among mortals. In short, a very wise Greek, knowing these things to be so, says that all things should be in common amongst friends. And unquestionably amongst "all things" spouses are included. He also says, just as the air cannot be divided up, nor the splendour of the sun, so the other things which are given in this world to be held in common by all ought not to be divided up.[12]

Thus it became a medieval commonplace that primitive humanity in Eden had lived under communism.

Original Sin and Conservative History

This did not necessarily become a radical ideal, however. The priests who had finally put together the official Jewish version of the primitive past had hedged its tale of ancient bliss with ample explanation for the existence of an unjust and unequal fallen society. For God himself had banished Adam and Eve from that paradise and had imposed his curse of misery. Moreover, human beings had brought on that fate by their own disobedience, just as they were likely to corrupt any world in which they might find themselves. These implications were further developed in Augustine's concept of original sin which proposed that human desires had thereby suffered such a profound disturbance that human beings were, henceforth, no longer capable of peace and cooperation, but had an instinctual inclination toward violence, greed, and promiscuity.

It was no coincidence that it was Augustine who dealt the fatal theological blow to the millenarian expectations of early Christianity. According to his *City of God*, the Fall barred any restoration of Eden upon earth. Any suggestions to that effect in the Book of Revelation are only to be understood as an allegory of the spiritual Jerusalem already realized in the visible church, which might exert a reforming moral influence on society, but which sanctioned no revolutionary aspirations. The dominant Christian position, despite its affirmation of a communist Eden, was a conservative one. Christopher Hill summarizes it:

> If Adam's Fall had not brought sin into the world, men would have been equal, property would have been held in common. But since the Fall, covetousness, pride, anger and all the other sins have been transmitted to his posterity. . . . A coercive state is one consequence of the Fall, necessary to prevent sinful men from destroying one another. Private property is likewise a consequence of sin; but since it inevitably exists, it must be defended against the greedy lust of the unpropertied, who must be held in subordination.[13]

In this tradition, article 38 of the Elizabethan articles of faith defends property and the power of magistrates against radical Anabaptists. And William Perkins, the Puritan preacher, argued that even slavery was allowed, for "It is indeed against the law of nature as it was before the Fall; but against the law of corrupted nature . . . it is not."[14]

Such conclusions lay behind Blake's intense repugnance for Genesis morality and the doctrine of original sin. The Tree of Knowledge of Good and Evil, consequently, appears in his poetry as a tree of mystery whose fruit is fatalism and whose serpent is man himself fallen into passive submission to things-as-they-are. Thus in *The Four Zoas* Urizen calls on the doctrine to douse Orc's revolutionary fires:

> Then Orc cried Curse thy Cold hypocrisy. already round thy Tree
> In scales that shine with gold & rubies thou beginnest to weaken
> My divided Spirit   Like a worm I rise in peace unbound
> From wrath Now When I rage my fetters bind me more
> O torment O torment A Worm compelld.
> . . . .
>   therefore he made Orc
> In Serpent form compelld stretch out & up the mysterious tree
> He sufferd him to Climb that he might draw all human forms
> Into submission to his will.   (*FZ* 80:27–31; 81:3–6)

Milton, as we will see, uses ideas of the Fall in precisely this way in the political despair following the failure of the good old cause. He presents social tyranny in the later books of his epic as the inevitable, cyclic unwinding of the original Fall. Thus Blake is moved to rewrite *Paradise Lost* in *The Four Zoas* so as to purify Milton's apocalyptic and revolutionary legacy of this reactionary one and so perform that operation on Christian tradition as a whole.

That criticism of Milton and the Bible will be fully analyzed in later chapters. For now we must note that Blake's version of Genesis arises from an alternative tradition, which read the Fall more as a social than as a moral degeneration and which interpreted it, in the light of the prophets and Revelation, as the image of a social utopia to be reestablished upon earth. The millenarian sects argued that God still intended them to live in the egalitarian state he bequeathed to Adam and Eve, and that it was the arrogant upper classes who had imposed a fallen and miserable state upon the common people. John Ball, leader of the English peasant's revolt of 1381, was reported to have questioned whether when Adam delved and Eve span there had existed gentlemen. According to Froissart, Ball's sermon before the peasants urged a return to that primitive communist Eden: "My friends, the state of England cannot be right until everything is held communally and until there is no distinction between nobleman and serf, and we are all as one. . . . We are all descended from our first parents, Adam and Eve; how then can they say that they are better lords than us, except in making us toil and earn for them to spend?"[15]

During the turbulence of the late Middle Ages, such a doctrine could not have been more radical. Norman Cohn chronicles the effects of this merger of primitivism, chiliasm, and revolution in his *Pursuit of the Millennium* as a wave of uprisings which spread throughout England, Bohemia, and Germany from the fourteenth to the sixteenth centuries. These include the Taborite rising which, according to Cohn, seized the city of Prague and tried to impose an anarcho-communist paradise there, and the German Peasants' War inspired partly by the preaching of Thomas Muntzer. In its wake, Anabaptism survived as a lower-class movement of religious sects, many of whom professed to establish a kingdom characterized by community of goods and free love. The Anabaptists were frequently inspired by primitivist visions of Eden. Among their ranks the spurious Epistle of Pope Clement circulated widely; and the beliefs recorded by the humanist Sebastian Franck were prevalent: "Shortly after that [Fall] Nimrod began to rule and then whoever could manage it got the better of the other. And they started dividing the world up and squabbling about property. Then Mine and Thine began. . . . Yet God had made all things common."[16] Under the leadership of John of Leyden, these Anabaptists actually managed to impose their rule on the German city of Munster for three months; thereafter, the communism and promiscuity of these millenarians were to terrorize the ruling classes of Europe for over a century.

Cohn describes a radical fringe within these movements which became known as Adamites because of their explicit attempt to live according to what they believed was the life style of Eden. Throughout the later Middle Ages, there appeared a heresy associated with the Adepts of the Free Spirit who not only professed to live in an unfallen state, but also literally claimed to be God. An advocate of their radical incarnationalist doctrine asserts: "It is the same with me as with Christ in every way and without any exception. Just like him, I am eternal life and wisdom, born of the Father in my divine nature; just like him, too, I am born in time and after the way of human beings; and so I am one with him, God and man."[17]

The conclusion often drawn from this doctrine, notably by a group called the Spiritual Libertines, was that all the impulses of the godly, including sexual impulses, were necessarily holy. Hence, they often practiced a kind of mystical eroticism, calling the sexual act "the delight of Paradise." Such groups sometimes practiced an Adam cult based upon ritual nakedness. Thus Cohn describes the practices of a later sect, the Bohemian Adamites, who in addition to community of goods insisted upon complete immunity from law and from marriage, which they believed to be a sin: "The sect was much given to naked ritual dances held around a fire and accompanied by much hymn-singing. Indeed, these people seemed to have spent much of their time naked . . . claiming to be in the state of innocence enjoyed by Adam and Eve before the Fall."[18] Such doctrines passed into English experience through the radical sects of the English civil war, the Ranters and Diggers whom we will consider at greater length elsewhere. We cannot help but postulate some connection between these beliefs and Blake's when, for example, we recall the legend which depicts Blake and his wife naked in their garden reading *Paradise Lost*, calling out to a startled Thomas Butts, "Come in! It's only Adam and Eve, you know!"[19]

Blake shared, then, a radical interpretation of Genesis which, setting itself in direct opposition to the Augustinian notion of original sin, proclaimed the continuing innocence of human desire. By contrast, the patristic doctrine of a morally superior, but hopelessly irrecoverable, communist Eden provided an ambivalence exactly appropriate to a collectivist but drastically unequal feudal society. Private property was justified, but it was a clearly fallen institution which was continually to be modified by the higher values of Eden preserved in Christian charity and ideals of the common good. Property rights were to be exercised with a sense of social responsibility as a form of divine stewardship and hence were hemmed in by social obligations backed up by the authority of canon law.

Bourgeois Myths of Origin

If myths of origin arise "when a social or moral rule demands justification, warrant of antiquity," so too they can be expected to change with the development of new social institutions. Thus we should not be surprised to find that the rise of a middle class espousing a right to completely unrestricted individual accumulation of wealth was accompanied by a new version of the primitive which expunged the golden age from the historical record.[20] Blake's quarrel with Milton recognizes that he shared this tendency, for although he admitted in passing that marriage was the "sole proprietie, / In Paradise of all things common else" (*PL* IV.751–52), he offered a Genesis so replete with details from his own bourgeois milieu that Eden was virtually transformed into the private enterprise of an individualistic Puritan household.

Postponing this analysis, let us now consider the orientation brought to primitivism by the bourgeois philosophers, Locke and Rousseau. Locke set out deliberately to prove that despite the Scriptures' assertion that God gave the world to man in common, private ownership, rather than collective, characterizes the "state of nature": "Whether we consider natural Reason, which tells us, that Men, being once born, have a right to their Preservation . . . Or *Revelation*, which gives us an account of those Grants God made of the World to Adam . . . 'tis very clear, that God . . . has given the Earth to the Children of Men, given it to Mankind in common. . . . But I shall endeavour to shew how Men might come to have a property in several parts of that which God gave to Mankind in common."[21] Locke's logic is that, although man is given the earth in common, he can only appropriate it individually, thus making it his private property: "As much Land as a Man Tills, Plants, Improves, Cultivates, and can use the Product of, so much is his Property. He by his Labour does, as it were, inclose it from the Common."[22] Historically, the battle between common rights and individual rights was fought out over exactly this issue as the enclosures of the sixteenth to the nineteenth centuries evicted the English peasantry and transferred ownership of land to capitalist farmers. Locke simply reads these conditions back into the ancient world, turning the golden age into a laissez-faire kingdom of Robinson Crusoes, each eagerly carving the universe into his private turf.

Locke did the same for the patriarchal middle-class family, arguing that "the first Society was between Man and Wife, which gave beginning to that between Parents and Children."[23] "This Compact, where Procreation and Education are secured, and Inheritance taken care of," arose, he claimed, from the natural condition of a species which required protracted succour of its offspring. Similarly, "Rule . . . naturally falls to Man's share, as the abler and stronger."[24] "Nature" was thus rendered virtually synonymous with the bourgeois social order, so Blake's hostility to Vala must be seen as more pointedly political than is usually assumed by critics offering only metaphysical explications of his philosophy of mind.

Natural man, Locke assumed, was an untrammeled idividualist; so did Rousseau, whose vision in that respect also conflicted with Blake's. Nevertheless, Blake probably drew upon the French philosopher's radical theory of social evolution. Erdman points out that Blake's myth of history, like the *Discourse on the Origin and Foundation of the Inequality of Mankind*, assumes that private property was absent in the primitive state, for man "in the state of innocent equality is called Urthona, the Earth-owner." In Erdman's words: " 'Urthona was his name / In Eden' [*FZ* 3:11–4:1], and, according to Rousseau, as long as man owned all the earth and its plenty there was no ownership in private, no basis for one man's exploiting another, and nothing to fight over. The earth was man's dutiful mother, wife and daughter, providing him richly with all he desired—'food, a female, and sleep.' "[25] Erdman also remarks that "Blake casually substitutes the primal garden of Eden for [Rousseau's] state of nature.[26] These insights provide a fruitful basis for interpreting the poem Blake once called "Vala," but Blake's alterations are hardly casual; in fact, his poem might be seen as a partly friendly polemic against Rousseau's anarchistic state of nature.

Private property does not exist among Rousseau's primitives only because they are savages without possessions or production, ravaging for their sustenance like beasts. But Blake will depict this bestiality as the fallen, rather than the original state of humanity, the "houseless wanderer" of Enion's lamentations (*FZ* 35:19). In Rousseau, the absence of social conflict reflects a virtual absence of all social contact: "His fellow men were not for him what they are for us. . . . He scarcely had more intercourse with them than with other animals."[27] Man in this state remains totally egotistical, "self-preservation being almost his only care."[28] Man's complete freedom is that of a foraging nomad "wandering in the forests, without industry, without speech, without domicile, without war, without liaisons, with no need of his fellow men; . . . his intelligence made no more progress than his vanity. If by chance he made some discovery, he was the less able to communicate it. . . . Art perished with the inventor. There was neither education nor progress."[29]

Nothing could contrast more totally with Blake's vision in *The Four Zoas* which, as we shall see, is a polemic against the idea that equality is incompatible with the arts and sciences. There Blake completely rejects the bourgeois philosophers' portrayal of primitive man and recognizes that, instead, the "natural man" they so lauded was only a deformed creature of their own society. Thus in *Jerusalem* he castigates Rousseau as one who "teaches that Man is Righteous in his Vegetated Spectre" and advocates the "Worship of the God of this World by the means of what you call Natural Religion and Natural Philosophy, and of Natural Morality or Self-Righteousness, the Selfish Virtues of the Natural Heart" (*J* 52).

Blake's Eden and Radical Tradition

For Blake, the "eternal man" was neither Rousseau's propertyless scavenger nor, as Erdman would have it, an independent peasant proprietor. He took his vision neither from Rousseau nor from Thomas Jefferson, but challenged the Enlightenment with the ancient vision of a communist Eden. Where the bourgeois philosophers portrayed a fall from unrestricted individual rights into the restraints and limitations of a social contract, Blake saw precisely the reverse—a decline from the collective power and wisdom of a communal Eden into the atomization and barbarism of their state of nature.

The tradition behind Blake's vision was that presented by Gerrard Winstanley when, during the English civil war, the old plebeian dream first confronted the new middle-class assertions. In Winstanley's allegorical reading of Genesis, a race of people existing before the Fall once collectively enjoyed the world:

> In the beginning of Time, the great Creator Reason, made the Earth to be a Common Treasury to preserve Beasts, Birds, Fishes and Man, the lord that was to govern this creation; . . . not one word was spoken in the beginning, That one branch of mankind should rule over another. . . . So selfish imagination . . . did set up one man to teach and rule over another; and thereby . . . man was brought into bondage. . . . And hereupon The Earth . . . was hedged into In-closures . . . and the others were made . . . Servants and Slaves. And that Earth that is within this Creation, made a Common Store-house for all, is bought and sold, and kept in the hands of a few, whereby the great Creator is mightily

dishonored, as if he were a respecter of persons, delighting in the comfortable Livelihood of some and rejoycing in the miserable povertie and straits of others.[30]

Winstanley offers the most radical reading of Genesis, one in which property not only arises with the Fall but also is the direct cause of that catastrophe.

Moreover, this interpretation is uniquely close to Blake's through its identification of the Fall of Man with the creation of Adam. A literal interpretation of Genesis, such as Milton's, with Adam and Eve alone in paradise, had always posed an obstacle to a social analysis of that fall. Commentators had got around this barrier through allegorical readings, one of which held that human beings lived in Eden before Adam. Thus, in Winstanley's version, Adam is only the first *fallen* man, symbolizing in himself the covetousness that accompanied the rise of private property, the apple that he ate being an object of creation.[31] His name itself signifies "a damming" up of human sympathies. Blake's recreation of Genesis in *The Four Zoas* adopts a similar allegory. We begin with Albion, the eternal man, who in fact contains the unfallen society of the four Zoas; only with the breakdown of their unity do a series of Adam and Eve figures appear (Tharmas and Enion, Luvah and Vala, Los and Enitharmon) whose quarrels indicate the human condition in a conflict-ridden and atomized postlapsarian society.

Albion referred both to a heroic mythological ancestor of the English people and to England itself, where a race of giants supposedly founded a primitive society preceding the Fall; Blake associates it with fallen humanity and the lost city of Atlantis. As simultaneously a nation and a person, Albion expresses Blake's idea of the liberated humanity which was possible in a superior ancient civilization: "He is Albion, our Ancestor, patriarch of the Atlantic Continent, whose History Preceded that of the Hebrews & in whose Sleep or Chaos Creation began" (PB 548).

Christian doctrine had traditionally turned for an image of the perfect society to the godhead itself which was a miracle of three persons in one God, all united through love in a common life and essence. Blake humanizes this doctrine by applying it to the unfallen community of the four Zoas, who symbolize for unfallen humanity the unity within them and the unity between them:

> Four Mighty Ones are in every Man: a Perfect Unity
> Cannot Exist. but from the Universal Brotherhood of Eden
> The Universal Man. To Whom be Glory Evermore Amen.
>
> (FZ 3:4–7)

Blake's words here parody the doxology that traditionally climaxes liturgical prayer: "Glory be to the Father and to the Son and to the Holy Spirit, as it was in the beginning, is now, and ever shall be, world without end, Amen." In Blake's version, however, humanity is divine when united "as it was in the beginning" of Genesis and "as it ever shall be" when apocalyptically restored.

Nonetheless, the idea that mankind itself could become divine had support in a theological tradition which cited the same texts from the Gospel of John that Blake notes in his margins, "that they all may be one; even as thou Father art in me and I in thee, that they also may be one in us. . . . The glory which thou hast given me I have given to them, that they may be one even as we are one" (John 17:21–23). In radical Christianity, the idea that God had become man in Jesus was often reversed to suggest instead that man had become God. A variant of that belief, however, existed within orthodox doctrine in the idea that through love people come to share in the divine life.

This doctrine led to the other doctrine that all Christians had been redeemed from their individual selfhood and incorporated into the "mystical body of Christ," the "communion of saints" animated by a single divine spirit. This tenet lies behind Blake's vision of the human community as a single divine human being. As he expresses it in his *Laocoon,* "The Eternal Body of Man is the Imagination, that is God himself The Divine Body, Jesus we are his Members" (PB 271); but in his radical incarnationalist faith, God resides entirely in this loving body:

> I am not a God afar off, I am a brother and friend;
> Within your bosoms I reside, and you reside in me:
> Lo! we are One; forgiving all Evil; Not seeking recompense!
> Ye are my members.   (*J* 4:18–21)

Apparently this doctrine had come to have very radical connotations, for in the Westminster confession of faith, English Puritans found it necessary to argue that the communion of saints did not mean community of goods, "nor doth their communion one with another, as Saints, take away, or infringe the title or propriety which each man hath in his goods and possessions."[32]

Mysticism—The Highest Stage of Communism

Blake called this Christianity "The Everlasting Gospel," and as he articulates it in that poem, the affirmation of man's divinity implies a rejection of all inequality and authority:

This is the Race that Jesus ran
Humble to God Haughty to Man
Cursing the Rulers before the People
Even to the temples highest Steeple
. . . .
  If thou humblest thyself thou humblest me
Thou also dwellst in Eternity
Thou are a Man God is no more
Thy own humanity learn to adore.   (PB 511)

Blake's humanistic Christianity has been acknowledged by most critics. What must be understood, in addition, is that his use of the myth of Albion, trinitarian doctrine, and the idea of a "mystical body of Christ" demands that we read *The Four Zoas* as a myth which is simultaneously psychological and social. "*What* are the Natures of those Living Creatures," Blake tells us, "no Individual *Knoweth*" (*FZ* 3:7–8), for they evoke a social reality lost to fallen man.

In fact, Blake's mysticism is unique in its emphasis upon social incarnation. In his version of mythology, the Neoplatonist fall from the One into the Many signifies on one level a spiritual loss brought about by social fragmentation. Everywhere in his poetry Blake insists that entrance into that dimension in which the human spirit is one requires abandonment of all forms of individualism, domination, and ideological exclusion which cuts one off from extended divinity in the human community. For the "Divine Image" is found only in collective humanity:

And all must love the human form,
In heathen, turk or jew.
Where Mercy, Love & Pity dwell
There God is dwelling too.   (PB 13)

This is by no means a merely ethical vision. In Blake's dialectic, the "divine" powers of consciousness in spirit and body, energy and matter are dissipated when the flow of that energy is obstructed by social atomization and conflict, reducing humanity thereby to the passivity of inert individual bodies, the "worm of sixty winters" which he so deplored. In Blake's vision, one might say: mysticism is the highest stage of communism.

If Blake drew out most concretely the social implications of rooting mysticism in communism and vice versa, the tradition was as old as Christianity itself, and surfaced repeatedly throughout the Middle Ages. A. L. Morton points to the radical roots of Blake's faith when he reminds us that the "everlasting gospel" was the watchword of both the radical incarnationalist and the revolutionary,

millenarian traditions.[33] The phrase can be traced back to the apocalyptic spirituality of Joachim de Fiore, a twelfth-century abbot
from whom radical Christians drew their historical mythology.

Joachim preached that history fell into three ages, the age of the
father, or law; the age of the son, or the church; and the age of the
spirit, in which both those props would become unnecessary and
the *evangelium aeternum* would be directly revealed in the human heart. Joachim's vision posited immediate entry into this third
age, in which humanity, existing on a spiritual plane in contempla-
tive bliss, would require neither property, nor marriage, nor political
authority. His vision was barely articulated, however, before the idea
of the "new age" had been brought down to earth by others with
revolutionary aspirations. At first, the everlasting gospel inspired
Franciscan Spirituals to lives of voluntary poverty in proclamation
of the belief that Christian life was completely incompatible with
the accumulation of material wealth, views which soon threw them
into serious conflict with a worldly church. Eventually, a splinter
group under Fra Dolcino, called the Apostolic Brethren, were led to
pursue a third age socially identified with community of goods and
complete political liberty, an experiment which resulted in armed
conflict with existing authorities.[34]

Such ideas survive into Blake's era; as late as 1774 we find Shakers
leaving England to establish Utopian socialist communities in the
New World, having been, in their words, "commissioned of the
Almighty God to preach the everlasting Gospel to America."[35]
Blake's own communist vision emerges clearly when he parodies the
Lord's Prayer as follows, "Give us This Eternal Day our own right
Bread & take away Money or Debt or Tax . . . as we have all things
common among us" (PB 658). Consistently, Blake identifies true
Christianity with the just society, demanding in *Jerusalem*, "Are
not Religion & Politics the Same Thing? Brotherhood is Religion"
(J 57:10).

Underlying *The Four Zoas* is the central myth which pervades the
prophecies, the idea that this apocalyptic age would be a return to the
conditions of that primitive Eden where human beings had once lived
in love and cooperation.[36] "All had originally one language," Blake
writes, "and one religion, this was the religion of Jesus, the everlasting Gospel" (PB 534). The same myth appears in *Jerusalem* where the
sleep of Albion, equated with the flooding of Atlantis, signifies the
disintegration of the primitive community:

> Awake! awake O sleeper of the land of shadows, wake! expand!
> I am in you and you in me, mutual in love divine:
> Fibres of love from man to man thro Albions pleasant land.

In all the dark Atlantic vale down from the hills of Surrey
A black water accumulates, return Albion! return!
Thy brethren call thee, and thy fathers, and thy sons,
Thy nurses and thy mothers, thy sisters and thy daughters
Weep at thy souls disease, and the Divine Vision is darkend.

(*J* 4:6–13)

Similarly, in *The Four Zoas*, the fall is described as a fragmentation, a shattering of "the Universal Family" in which humanity lived as "One Man . . . & that one Man / They call Jesus the Christ & they in him & he in them / Live in Perfect harmony in Eden the land of life" (*FZ* 21:4–6). In this epic, Blake will sing of Albion's "fall into Division & his Resurrection to Unity" (*FZ* 4:4), of the breakdown of the good society and its ultimate reconstruction. The Eternal Man mourns the Zoas' divided state as "war within my members" (*FZ* 120:9), and cries, "Rent from Eternal Brotherhood we die & are no more" (*FZ* 41:10). The dissolution of the community means death to Albion, who, once his collective powers are asleep, survives only as a shrunken individual self, a shadow of his former life:

& he sunk down
From the Supporting arms of the Eternal Saviour; who disposed
The pale limbs of his Eternal Individuality
Upon The Rock of Ages.   (*FZ* 18:12–15)

The Golden Age Among American Natives

Blake's conception of "eternal brotherhood" has a concrete significance which should not be overlooked, for, in fact, primitive cultures were often literal brotherhoods, organized into clans whose members descended from a common ancestor. We are reminded in this regard by anthropologist Leslie White that "legends of the Golden Age might conceivably be ethnic memories of a time and a society when all men were brothers," when, E. B. Tylor tells us, "kinship" and "kindliness" went together.[37] Blake would have been familiar with this condition through all its traces remaining in the Old Testament whose prophets harkened back for their mores to the old tribal brotherhood of the desert.

But a more immediate inspiration was aso available, for among such American Indians as the Iroquois, a group of related clans was semantically defined as a brotherhood, or *phatry*. Blake tells us, moreover, that his ideas about the primal state were directly influenced by what he had gleaned about the Indians. Information was readily available in contemporary accounts by travelers and missionaries, which enabled as insightful an observer as Blake to leap to a kind of nascent comparative anthroplogy. Accounts of Native Americans and other newly discovered tribes could provide Blake with support for his contention that humanity's original condition involved egalitarian social relations, sexual liberty, and spiritual powers obliterated from the Genesis view of origins. In this sense, the new ethnographical information available at that time affected Blake as Lewis Henry Morgan's work on the Iroquois would later affect Engels and twentieth-century anthropology and archaeology would influence feminist theory, causing Blake to anticipate many of their judgments.

Commentators on Indian mores invariably remarked upon their egalitarianism. Indeed, the one aspect of Indian life most striking to outside observers was the savages' apparent disregard for private property. Hence a United States secretary of war would write in 1789 that all the Indian needed to join the march of progress was "a love for exclusive property."[38]

Nor would Blake have been the first to connect the collectivism of these peoples with Christian ideas of Eden and the Fall; it was a common observation of missionaries. In 1770 Father Jacob Baegert wrote admiringly of the California native that "envy, jealousy and slander embitter not his life, and he is not exposed to the fear of losing what he possesses, nor to the care of increasing it; . . . the Californians do not know the meaning of meum and teum, those two ideas which, according to St. Gregory, fill the days of our existence with bitterness and unaccountable evils."[39] Similarly, the eighteenth-century traveler Lahontan observed, "These savages know nothing of mine and thine, for it may be said that what belongs to one, belongs to another. . . . They think it strange that some should have more goods than others, and that those who have more should be more esteemed than those who have less."[40]

Blake shared this appreciation and lauded the liberty of primitive peoples in opposition to the increasingly dominant bourgeois myth of progress which saw all mankind rising from the horrors of barbarism to the crowning achievements of European empire. In his view, the worst barbarism resulted from the growth of inequality and conflict in advanced civilizations. Bristling at Bishop Watson's smug observation that "man, in a nearly savage state, approaches to brute creation," Blake retorts, "Read the Edda of Iceland, the Songs of Fingal the accounts of the North American Savages (as they are calld) Likewise Read Homer's Iliad, he was certainly a Savage . . . in the Bishops sense . . . & yet he was no fool" (PB 605).

Blake's admiration for the natives undoubtedly was inspired as well by their uninhibited sexuality, those "unnatural consanguinities and friendships" (J 28:7) described by horrified European observers:

The young men have licence to addict themselves to evil as soon as they are able, and the young girls prostitute themselves as soon as they are capable. Even fathers and mothers commonly act as pimps to their daughters. At night the young women and girls run from one hut to another, and the young men do the same and take their pleasure where they like, without, however, doing any violence, for they rely entirely on the will of the woman. The husband does the same with regard to his nearest neighbour and the wife with regard to the nearest male neighbour; nor does any jealousy appear amongst them on that account, and they incur no shame or dishonour.[41]

Such practices confirmed another aspect of the golden age myth, largely but not entirely suppressed under Christianity, the idea that it was a state characterized by a kind of sexual communism. We have already noted such accounts of primitive society in Aristotle, Varro, Diodorus Siculus, the spurious Epistle of Pope Clement, and Gratian. Herodotus, for example, described the Agathrysi as practicising promiscuity so that they all might be brothers and a single family so as to avoid suspicion and jealousy.[42] Ideas of a sexual Eden were revived, as we have seen, by the Adamite cults of the late Middle Ages, and, as we will discuss later, were prominent among the Ranters of Milton's England.

Blake's belief in an era before Adam led him to identify the institution of marriage described in Genesis as part of the Fall which characterized Adam's generation. Thus Henry Crabb Robinson reports: "He was as wild as ever . . . but he was led to day to make assertions more palpably mischievous, if capable of influencing other minds, & immoral . . . than anything he had said before. As for instance, that he had learned from the Bible that wives should be in common. And when I objected that marriage was a Divine institution, he referred to the Bible 'that from the beginning it was not so.' "[43] The first aspect of the Fall which Blake recounts in *The Four Zoas* is the establishment of monogamy. The sexuality of Eden is described as untrammeled self-expression: "in the Auricular Nerves of Human life / Which is the Earth of Eden, [Albion] his Emanations propagated" (*FZ* 4:1–2). This state is repeatedly evoked throughout the poem as a time of complete harmony between the individual and the community, man and woman, body and spirit. Hence the Spectre of Urthona yearns

> To reunite in those mild fields of happy Eternity
> Where thou [Enitharmon] & I in undivided Essence walkd about
> Imbodied. thou my garden of delight & I the spirit in the garden
> Mutual there we dwelt in one anothers joy revolving
> Days of Eternity with Tharmas mild & Luvah sweet melodious
> Upon our waters. This thou well rememberest listen I will tell

What thou forgettest. They in us & we in them alternate Livd
Drinking the joys of Universal Manhood.   (*FZ* 84:3–11)

Woman in a Tribal Eden

In this original state, according to Blake, the "Universal Manhood"
was androgynous; men and women were united in complete sexual
gratification, as he contends in *Jerusalem:*

> Humanity knows not of Sex: wherefore are Sexes in Beulah?
> In Beulah the Female lets down her beautiful Tabernacle;
> Which the male enters magnificent between her Cherubim.
>
> (*J* 44:33–35)

By contrast, the Fall involves the appearance of a separate female
personality, forced into conflict with man by the chaste demands of
monogamy. Blake interprets the myth of Eve's creation from the rib of
Adam to signify the separation from an androgynous manhood of a
contrary female being:

> One dread morn of goary blood
> The manhood was divided for the gentle passions making way
> Thro the infinite labyrinths of the heart & thro the nostrils issuing
> In odorous stupefaction stood before the Eyes of Man
> A female bright.   (*FZ* 84:12–16)

This disaster was followed immediately by the creation of the male:
"My masculine spirit scorning the frail body issud forth / From
Enions brain" (*FZ* 84:24–25).

The source of this split in Blake's narrative is the triumph of the
monogamous nuclear family: "Begin with Tharmas Parent power.
darkning in the West," he writes, and thereupon describes Tharmas
and Enion as our first parents, fallen from the sexual community of
Eden under the repressive regime of marital chastity. "Lost! Lost!
Lost! are my Emanations," Tharmas cries; "All Love is lost Terror
succeeds & Hatred instead of Love / And stern demands of Right &
Duty instead of Liberty" (*FZ* 4:5–6,17–18). The event is repeated in
the relations of the next generation, when Enitharmon accuses Los of
infidelity, "among the virgins / Of summer   I have seen thee sleep &
turn thy cheek delighted / Upon the rose or lilly pale. or on a bank
where sleep / The beamy daughters of the light starting they rise they
flee / From thy fierce love." (*FZ* 34:26–30).

The consequences of this catastrophe—the female passivity and
male aggressiveness, mystified romance, perverted desire, and patriarchal repression of succeeding generations—will be described in a

chapter on Blake's concept of the family. For now, let us focus upon Blake's identification of these realities with a breakdown of primitive society. We see the link in the resemblance between Blake's Eden and the life style of American Indians. In like manner, Engels would be provoked by Lewis Henry Morgan's study of the Iroquois to a similar analysis of the battle of the sexes. Engels saw the dissolution of the ancient clan leading to the creation of a separate and oppressed female, divorced from production, reduced to domestic slavery and to Blake's despised world of "generation," that is, to a purely sexual function, breeding heirs for a newly developed class of private owners.

Early commentators on American Indian culture agreed in abhorring the apparent servitude of the female who in many cases had primary responsibility for agriculture.[44] Eleanor Leacock argues that, to the contrary, it was precisely such responsibility that guaranteed many Indian women their uniquely elevated status; it introduced equality and dignity into relations between the sexes, "a quality of respectful ease, warmth, and assurance in personal relations" unlike "the tensions associated with conjugal relations in our society."[45] Robert Briffault, commenting on popular misconceptions about primitive life, makes a similar point:

> The contrast between the toiling primitive woman and the idle lady of civilization, which has been mistaken for an indication of the enslavement of the former and the freedom of the latter, marks the opposite relation. It is the primitive toiler who is independent and the unemployed woman who has lost her freedom and is destitute. . . . The woman who was no longer economically self-supporting became competitive in terms of the only value which remained to her, as an instrument of luxury and pleasure.[46]

Moreover, it is not without reason that visions of the golden age so often linked economic and sexual community. The sexual license of primitives is dependent, more than anything else, on the fact that legitimacy of offspring is not an issue since children are raised collectively by the clan, usually by the mother's siblings, and property is not inherited but reverts to the clan for periodic redistribution. The connection becomes clear in an exchange recorded between a seventeenth-century missionary and an American native. Rebuking the man for his wife's uninhibited sexuality, the priest warned him that now he would never be sure of the identity of his own children. But the Indian replied, unperturbed: "Thou hast no sense. You French people love only your own children; but we love all the children of our tribe."[47]

Significantly, when Blake envisioned his ideal primitives in his giant fresco "The Ancient Britons," those "naked civilized men" with "The flush of health in flesh, exposed to the open air, nourished by the spirits of forests and floods, in that ancient happy period" (PB 533,536), he seems to have pictured them as American Indians, for, we are told, "their naked forms are almost crimson."[48] Moreover, as Erdman points out, when in Oothoon of his *Visions of the Daughters of Albion* he depicted a liberated female free from monogamous restraints, he drew her as an American native, although in the narrative she appears also as a black slave.[49] One might conclude, though Erdman does not, that the "daughters of Albion" are England's colonized peoples, African and American, just recently robbed of the conditions of ancient liberty that civilized peoples had lost centuries ago. This reading makes sense of the echoes of a golden age myth throughout the poem, as when Theotormon asks:

> Tell me where dwell the joys of old! & where the ancient loves?
> And when will they renew again & the night of oblivion past?
> (*VDA* 4:4–5)

The story is that an innocent virgin, Oothoon, has been raped by the oppressive Bromion and then rejected as a harlot by her lover Theotormon:

> Till she who burns with youth. and knows no fixed lot; is bound
> In spells of law to one she loaths: and must she drag the chain
> Of life, in weary lust!   (*VDA* 5:21–23)

The theme is jealousy, but such sexual dominion is only part of a broader category of possession, "the self-love that envies all" (*VDA* 7:21). Blake links private acquisition in the fallen world to possessive monogamy and contrasts both to the generosity, sexual and economic, of the primitive Oothoon who offers Theotormon "girls of mild silver, or of furious gold" for "lovely copulation" (*VDA* 7:24,26); she promises that

> Oothoon shall view his dear delight, nor e'er with jealous cloud
> Come in the heaven of generous love; nor selfish blightings bring.
>
> Does the sun walk in glorious raiment. on the secret floor
> Where the cold miser spreads his gold?   (*VDA* 7:28–8:1)

These analogies are reinforced by the fact that Oothoon is not only female, but also "the soft soul of America" (VDA 1:3);[50] Bromion's rape of her is symbolically the rape of the American continent by a rapacious imperialism: "Thy soft American plains are mine, and mine thy north & south" (*VDA* 1:20). The genocidal attack on the

American Indians by Europeans greedy for land was, of course, justified to themselves by their superior civilization, invariably identified with private property and sexual prudery, "And Oothoon is the crafty slave of selfish holiness" (*VDA* 6:20). Ultimately, this questionable progress was triumphant; but Blake sees it as yet another stage of the Fall, leading Theotormon to ask, "in what gardens do joys grow? . . . and upon what mountains / Wave shadows of discontent? (*VDA* 3:24–4:1).

While this analysis expands upon Erdman's, it does not contradict his well-documented argument for the poem as an abolitionist polemic. Rather, this reading gives a historical unity to the analogous images noted by Erdman in which Oothoon is simultaneously an American Indian, an African slave, and a European woman.[51] In *Visions of the Daughters of Albion*, as in Blake's engraving, "Europe supported by Africa and America," we confront the irony that, in one sense, primitive women are free and the civilized enslaved. Or, rather, the recent subjugation of non-Western peoples reveals the hidden history of sexual and social exploitation underlying European civilization in which loss of liberty occurred so long ago that its fallen state has come to be viewed as natural. But in fact the pearls worn by the European woman symbolize a bondage to selfish possession much like that embodied in the slave bracelets of her darker sisters.

Recognizing, no doubt, the encouragement given his own faith in a golden age by contemporary representatives of what we now call the Third World, Blake assigned them a unique role in ushering in the apocalypse. As a consequence of their very recent exile from paradise, the colonized and enslaved peoples have kept alive into the modern world a memory of ancient times. Ironically, the overthrow of these last bowers of a tribal Eden by imperialism coincides in Blake with the restoration of its vision to the nations. Blake was perhaps the first to grasp the potential cultural impact that conquered and enslaved peoples would have upon the West when their tribal remembrances of brotherhood, closeness to nature, ecstatic worship, and uninhibited self-gratification were transmitted through music, dance, poetry, and religion to a redeemed Albion. In the apocalyptic ninth night of *The Four Zoas*, the triumphant "New Song" of Revelation is sung by a chorus of black slaves dreaming of the renewal of their tribal paradise:

Then All the Slaves from every Earth in the wide Universe
Sing a New Song drowning confusion in its happy notes
. . . .
So loud so clear in the wide heavens & the song that they sung was this
Composed by an African Black from the little Earth of Sotha

Aha Aha how came I here so soon in my sweet native land
How came I here Methinks I am as I was in my youth
When in my fathers house I sat & heard his chearing voice
Methinks I see his flocks & herds & feel my limbs renewd
And Lo my Brethren in their tents & their little ones around them.

(*FZ* 134:30–135:3)

An Eden of Ecstatic Common Labor

When Blake called the "Ancient Britons" of his engraving by that name "naked, *civilized* men," he distinguished his primitivism from all those who saw a fall from barbarism into culture as some inevitable tradeoff between innocence and cultivation. The archetypal expression of this view is the expulsion from the garden, but Blake's myth to the contrary envisions humanity first in the lost Atlantean civilization, also called Jerusalem, and only subsequently as "natural man" in a wilderness of vegetative existence.

Blake's view is thus directly opposed to that of Rousseau who had argued in his *Discourses on the Origins and Foundations of Inequality* that the development of agriculture and metallurgy had produced private property. Hence in his mind the possession of the arts and sciences inevitably led to greed, luxury, and the fall of a "noble savage" from anarchistic liberty into social bondage.[52] Blake, by contrast, anticipated Engels, for whom human beings create themselves through labor and skill, their very bodies, hands, brains, senses emerging over the millennia as the products of increasingly conscious labor. Just as Engels makes human beings congruent with their creativity, differentiating themselves from other species by their use of tools and speech, concomitants of collective labor, so Blake depicts a primal being whose essence is intelligent self-creation, for, he insists, "The Primeval State of Man was Wisdom, Art, and Science" (*J* 3).

In a direct affront to Rousseau, Blake declared that in the Bible "Cultivated Life. Existed First—Uncultivated Life. comes afterwards" (PB 626). Thus Urthona, the one Zoa presented in an unfallen state, is a metalworker, laboring with his sons at the forge to create the tools of agriculture; before the Fall he "stood before [his] anvil dark a mass / of iron glowed bright. prepard for spades & plowshares" (*FZ* 84:16–17). It is precisely as craftsman that humanity is Earth-Owner because actual creator of the world, propagator of his Emanations (*FZ* 3:11–4:1). In the writings of Plotinus and the Neoplatonists, the world is seen mystically as an emanation from the godhead, and in Blake's own ontology similar notions signify transformations of conscious energy into concrete material form. What is unique in Blake is the humanistic extension of such doctrine to describe the continual re-creation of the universe through the manifestation of human consciousness in creative labor, art, and "manufacture," practical material activity in the world. The creative powers of imagination and labor appear on a continuum and are spoken of interchangeably. Thus "to Labour in Knowledge is to Build Up Jerusalem," to create "the Divine Arts of Imagination" and "the labours of Art & Science" (PB 230–31).

Blake's mysticism lies in the claims he makes for the untrammeled power of imagination to transcend the limits of nature as ordinarily conceived. On this level, Eden signifies the unlimited creativity of the unfallen Urthona to propagate his Emanations as materializations of his consciousness, the "Auricular Nerves of Human Life" (*FZ* 3:10):

> For Los & Enitharmon walkd forth on the dewy Earth
> Contracting or expanding their all flexible senses
> At will to murmur in the flowers small as the honey bee
> At will to stretch across the heavens & step from star to star
> Or standing on the Earth erect, or on the stormy waves
> Driving the storms before them or delighting in sunny beams
> While round their heads the Elemental Gods kept harmony.
>
> (*FZ* 34:9–15)

The unity of Los and Enitharmon signifies a wedding of human consciousness and material nature, which may be directed to human ends "at will." Blake contends that mankind once lived in this Eden of potency in those "ages of imagination" when, worshiping their own "poetic genius," they found that "a firm perswasion removed mountains" (*MHH* 13).

But in Blake this faith in the miracles of consciousness is brought to the affirmation, rather than the disregard, of powers further over on the spectrum: the expression in art and ideology of genuine ends of human desire, as a motive behind historical action, and the practical efforts of conscious labor in molding the human environment to those desires. In Blake's dialectic, a peculiar co-determination between consciousness and material life arises from his perception of the mutual metamorphoses of spirit (or energy) and matter. Spirit can transform matter; energy can release the energies bound up in matter, but matter can also trap energy in particular forms, and material conditions can limit spiritual possibilities. Blake is a mystic to the extent that he emphasizes spirit as a direct power of consciousness, which he seems to portray as a transmitter and transformer of invisible energies. But he is a unique "mystical materialist" to the extent that he emphasizes the body, and, in particular, the embodiment of consciousness in the forms of human labor, and the dependency of spiritual development upon the social and ecological conditions of its expression or enslavement. Thus the unity of Los and Enitharmon also pertains to the impact of human activity in time (Los) upon the object world of space (Enitharmon), through which human beings exert mastery over their historical destiny.

The restoration of Eden depends, therefore, upon the revival of humanity as "Earth-Owner," liberated from relations of domination with its "ruinous walls" to "form the golden armour of Science" (*FZ* 139:8). Only then, through human activity, will the harmony of nature be achieved as the union of Tharmas (human sensuousness) with Enion (a benevolent, maternal environment) in a world completly adapted to human gratification. This paradise appears in "Night the Ninth" not as an unspoiled garden whose primitive harmony lies in the fact that humanity has not yet been differentiated from nature, but as the product of the ecstatic common labor dramatized throughout Blake's revolutionary climax in which "The noise of rural work resounded thro the heavens" (*FZ* 124:14).

Blake's original Eden, therefore, is not a garden of the Goddess, for he presents that garden of Venus as a lower paradise, presided over by the seductive Vala. Instead, his Eden is depicted as that lost continent of Atlantis referred to by Plato, a glorious urban civilization "Now barr'd out by the Atlantic sea: call'd Atlantean hills: / Because from their bright summits you may pass to the Golden world" (*A* 10:6–7). Blake's celebration of this garden city, in his assimilation of the Atlantis myth to the pastoral Eden, is one of the cases in which poetic inspiration may actually lift a veil on historical reality, for what Blake deciphers from myth in some ways anticipates later archaeological discoveries of the Bronze Age civilizations which arose on Neolithic social relations. The cultures uncovered by archaeologists like that of Minoan Crete of the third millennium B.C. seem to have been gracious, devoid of weapons, and characterized by sexual and social relations more egalitarian than any that would prevail once Iron Age patriarchs took over.[53] Moreover, Robert Graves argues that the splendid lost city "in the West" was not to be found in the Atlantic at all, but probably referred to pre-Mycenaen Crete as perceived by sailors from the ancient Near East.[54] Recently, Graves's speculation has received further support with the discovery of the Minoan city, Aphioteri, an island believed to have been sunk as a result of volcanic eruptions, just as Atlantis is described in mythology.

Blake turns to Atlantis for proof that man was not faced with a choice between egalitarian barbarism or exploitative civilization as Rousseau and others had suggested. He affirms its existence as a polemic against all those smug contemporaries who assumed that the absence of their own culture meant the absence of all culture. Where they could not find Christian marriage they saw only animal promiscuity; where there was no state, anarchic chaos; where their entrepreneurial genius had not yet penetrated, they presumed total ignorance and destitution. Blake may or may not be making a literal claim for an ancient unfallen civilization. What his myth definitely does allege is the anthropological wisdom that wherever there is man there is culture. In the symbol of the ancient gardened city of Atlantis, Blake depicts primitive humanity in a socially and culturally organized state, albeit along lines not likely to be appreciated by the Gradgrinds.

Rousseau pictured the growth of inequality and conflict as a consequence of the formation of society and the development of culture. Blake saw just the opposite, the loss of conscious mastery of the universe and a decline into barbarism as a result of the fragmentation of the human community into the individualistic anarchy of the state of nature. In *The Four Zoas* the harmony of man and nature, nostalgically celebrated in pastoral vision as an absence of disruptive technology, is presented instead as the cultural archievement of an egalitarian community, as "those sweet fields of bliss / Where liberty was justice & eternal science was mercy" (*FZ* 39:10–11). What a peculiarly Blakean touch is this inclusion of science in the fields of bliss!

Blake underlines these points by presenting the original union of Albion with his Emanation Jerusalem, the holy city, and by dramatizing the Fall as a product of their alienation. In depicting the human relationship to nature as Albion's sexual communion with a woman who is an extension of himself, Blake emphasizes again that the world is a humanized world, defined by our relations with it. Moreover, as we have noted, Jerusalem is repeatedly used to signify the environment most totally modified by the "labours of Art & Science." It is a city biblically identified with just social relations; as Blake tells us:

> JERUSALEM IS NAMED LIBERTY
> AMONG THE SONS OF ALBION   (*J* 26)

This image calls up both a human community and the civilized environment which expresses its collective life and work.

We might now comprehend in these terms Blake's idea of the Fall, for as Foster Damon summarizes the version of that myth in *Jerusa-*

lem, the Fall begins with the division of Albion's Emanation into Jerusalem and Vala, and his subsequent estrangement from Jerusalem and his liaison with Vala.[55] That story is alluded to in *The Four Zoas* and repeated in the divorces between each of the Zoas and their Emanations. We have already offered a sexual interpretation of this motif in which a state of Edenic consummation is overthrown by the subsequent imposition of monagamous fidelity. We may now suggest an interpretation of the social and ecological disaster which occurs when

> Among the Flowers of Beulah walked the Eternal Man & Saw
> Vala the lilly of the desert. melting in high noon
> Upon her bosom in sweet bliss he fainted.   (*FZ* 83:7–9)

The loss of both science and justice is symbolized in Blake's narrative by this suppression of Jerusalem and triumph of Vala. Vala does not really represent "nature"; she signifies a condition of scarcity, usually artificially imposed, in which human creativity is subjugated to the necessities of mere animal existence. Blake adamantly insists that "it is the same with Individuals as Nations works of Art can only be produced in Perfection where the Man is either in Affluence or Above the Care of it" (PB 551). When Blake titled the early version of this historical epic "Vala," he was suggesting that humanity had lived in this wretched condition ever since the loss of primitive cooperation. In doing so, he was challenging the mainstream of seventeenth- and eighteenth-century bourgeois philosophy which alleged than man in his original state was a proprietor (Locke, Pufendorf, Blackstone) or at least an anarchic individual (Hobbes, Rousseau) bent only upon self-preservation. From this "state of nature," these ahistorical rationalists projected their view of human nature and usually concluded that private property, inequality, and individualism were the inevitable human condition.[56]

In *The Four Zoas* Blake argues to the contrary that the primitive human state was cooperation and to that mankind shall eventually return. As we will see more concretely in the next chapter, he identifies the triumph of Vala with the development of social conflicts which prevent human mastery of nature and introduce scarcity and want. As we learned in *Visions of the Daughters of Albion*, the "jealousy" that divided Albion from his Emanations involved, in addition to sexual possessiveness, all other forms of covetousness. The fall of Urthona and the stifling of his furnaces of creativity we shall see as a consequnce of squabbles among the Zoas over possession. In Blake's analysis, only unity of will enables humanity to master nature. The fall of Urthona, as Frye points out, is a paralysis of will.[57] This paralysis does not occur, however, as criticism usually assumes, merely through demoralization or spiritual failure. The paralysis of will results from the conflict of wills; Vala and the alienated Emanations primarily signify the development of separate and egotistical wills set against the primeval community, that separate female will which Blake will develop in *Jerusalem*. Urizen mourns with regard to his Emanation that "Two wills they had two intellects & not as in times of old" (*FZ* 30:48). The separated female represents a conflict of egos and, at the same time, the alienation from nature that results from this paralysis, so different from the time when united in "universal manhood" the Zoas were free "to stretch across the heavens & step from star to star" (*FZ* 34:12). By linking this social division to sexual contention, Blake shows that by the same process man has been alienated from his own body and from all nature, both of which now appear as a coy mistress to tantalize him. Significantly, Vala's cruel seductiveness is directed at Luvah imprisoned in a furnace of both enslaved passions and literally enslaved labor:

> Luvah was cast into the Furnaces of affliction & sealed
> While Vala fed in cruel delight, the furnaces with fire.
>
> (*FZ* 25:40–41)

Numerous details of humanity's fallen state become comprehensible once they are recognized as elements of the bourgeois state of nature. The fallen Tharmas is particularly associated with this state in which man lives by his senses more than his intelligence. He and Enion and their offspring are continually portrayed as wanderers; they "wander in sweet solitude enraptured at every wind" (*FZ* 7:14) as with Rousseau's primeval nomads. Their world is one bounded by vegetative existence: Enion weaves for Tharmas a fallen body on her "loom of Vegetation" (*FZ* 6:1–2). When the Daughters of Beulah "closd the Gate of the Tongue" (*FZ* 5:43), this act signifies that the absence of speech, which Rousseau assigned to isolated primitive man, was in fact a breakdown of communication consequent upon the breakdown of community. That fall is presented as a flooding of Atlantis by the waters of Tharmas, the decline from a civilized to a barbaric condition:

> Albion gave his loud death groan The Atlantic Mountains trembled
> Aloft the Moon fled with a cry the Sun with streams of blood
> From Albions Loins fled all Peoples and Nations of the Earth
> Fled with the noise of Slaughter & the stars of heaven Fled
> Jerusalem came down in a dire ruin over all the Earth. (*FZ* 25:9–14)

By this image of floundering, Blake intensifies the theme that the dire change was primarily a loss of human control. Later he will present a second flood in which it is man who drowns, "Struggling to utter the voice of Man" (FZ 44:18). Then Vala truly replaces Jerusalem; Tharmas reigns over the fallen Zoas, and man is returned to a state of nature in which, devoid of social bonds, he is reduced to complete powerlessness before his environment, struggling against the waters of chaos for mere survival.

Given the communal basis of Blake's mysticism, this social catastrophe is a spiritual fall also. Blake seems to attribute to primitive cultures access to a higher state of consciousness, when "all had originally one religion . . . the Everlasting Gospel." In *The Marriage of Heaven and Hell* he identifies the sublime vision of Ezekiel with the shamanistic states achieved by Native Americans: "I then asked Ezekiel. why he eat dung, & lay so long on his right & left side? he answerd. the desire of raising other men into a perception of the infinite this the North American tribes practise" (MHH 13). But, as we have seen, the "everlasting gospel" is a doctrine of social community and sharing, which Blake proclaims to be the appropriate manifestation of the oneness of the human spirit:

> Then those in Great Eternity met in the Council of God
> . . . .
> As One Man all the Universal Family & that one Man
> They call Jesus the Christ & they in him & he in them
> Live in Perfect harmony in Eden the land of life.   (FZ 21:1,4–6)

The social unity of tribal society provided the basis for its spiritual unity and power; with social atomization and exploitation these powers were lost, then forgotten and denied: "Thus began Priesthood" when "men forgot that All deities reside in the human breast" (MHH 11). The ultimate spiritual consequence was what Blake called "Natural Religion," "the Worship of the God of this World" and "the Selfish Virtues of the Natural Heart" (J 52) in the accumulation of material objects, now an end rather than a means to the development of human potential.

Blake Against the Goddesses

This erroneous worshiping of the material world above human consciousness and creativity was, according to Blake, already evident in the ancient cult of the nature goddesses. Vala is a mother goddess and in describing humanity's fall under her domination, *The Four Zoas* is introduced as "The Song of the Aged Mother" (FZ 3:1). Thus we must now explore the reasons why, having derived from myth a historical vision which in so many ways anticipates that of later evolutionists, Blake is led by that mythology to rather different conclusions about the cult of woman and nature. For in the historical scenarios which we have found to be analogous to Blake's, the fundamental transformation lies in a passage from the egalitarian mother-right clans with their reverence for female and natural fertility to a hierarchical, patriarchal society and religion. In Blake, however, the goddesses of nature signify that a fall from the ancient brotherhood has already occurred, and a degenerate "matriarchy" with a mystified nature cult is paving the way to the fallen civilizations.

Blake's relationship to Genesis, therefore, turns out to be more ambivalent than may have appeared in our previous discussion. For while the millenarian poet rejects its validation of the institutions of property, law, the state, oppressed labor, and the monogamous patriarchal family, he adopts its attitude toward an alleged female domination identified with the Goddess and her fertility cult. On this, prophet and priest had not disagreed. Blake's treatment of these issues undoubtedly led him into a peculiar and inaccurate sense of historical development—the denial of the antiquity of mother-right, and the invention of an original urban Atlantis, antecedent to horticultural and pastoral cultures. Nevertheless, the problems Blake addresses, for example, the social and productive limitations implicit in organization based on physical kinship, and the ideological blindness arising from too-close identification with nature, when applied to the primitive clan itself are real ones to which we will eventually turn.

In *Paradise Lost* Milton had unveiled Genesis as just such a polemic against the fertility worship of matrilineal peoples, and, if anything, Blake pushes the critique further—assailing Milton and the Bible for having readmitted Goddess worship through the back door by modeling their Eden too closely on her orchard paradise. Blake's own comparative mythology led him to believe that a kind of Druid cult lay behind Genesis symbols; thus his remark, "Adam was a Druid, and Noah" (PB 533). As Frye points out, Blake derived this view from Milton, from Adam's fall "through adoration of Eve," her association with the " 'Druidic' symbols of the tree and the serpent," and the fact that "after Eve has eaten of the apple, she bows to the tree and does it homage."[58] In *The Four Zoas*, this motif informs a criticism of human decline under the Goddess-centered cultures. If we look once again at Enitharmon's recollection of the fall in which Albion abandons Jerusalem in submission to Vala, the passage implicitly abjures the nature cult of her pseudo-paradise:

Among the Flowers of Beulah walkd the Eternal Man & Saw
Vala the lilly of the desart. melting in high noon
Upon her bosom in sweet bliss he fainted   Wonder siezd
All heaven they saw him dark. they built a golden wall
Round Beulah   There he reveld in delight among the Flowers
Vala was pregnant & brought forth Urizen Prince of Light
First born of Generation.   (*FZ* 83:7–13)

The comparisons to Milton and Genesis, and the close identification
between their garden paradise and this Beulah (a connection strength-
ened, as we have seen, by Milton's own mythological analogies) leads
Blake to conclude that Adam represents humanity in an already
fallen state.

From mythology, Blake learned of an era when women had a far
superior status to that assigned them either in his own society or in
the patriarchal version of history offered by the Bible. From the
biblical polemic against paganism, particularly as exposed through
Milton's comparative mythology, Blake concluded that primitive
humanity had at some point lived under a matriarchy. In *The Four
Zoas*, the female Emanations disdain being sisters and friends and,
like the dreaming Eve, aspire to be goddesses. In this process, they
cease being co-laborers for eternity and are mystified as embodiments
of natural forces. Vala is a Venus in whom sexuality has become an
insatiable natural drive rather than an act of human communion.
Enion is Demeter weeping for her lost children and weaving all
existence into her vegetative web of destiny. Enitharmon repudiates
love for adoration and rises as a queen of heaven who has "the nine
Spheres rejoice beneath [her] powerful controll" (*FZ* 34:67). Ahania is
a moon goddess whose twelve sons are the signs of the zodiac and
who, like Asherah, has found her way into the Holy of Holies.

The triumph of these goddesses represents for Blake the subordination of man to nature in ancient agrarian cult. Their rites, as we have
seen, were based upon a system of natural analogies. At the heart was
nature's pattern of death and rebirth in the seasonal cycle of agriculture. The daimon of these processes was the sacred snake, whose
annual sloughing of his skin and whose visitations from the underground womb-tomb of nature mirrored the whole seasonal process.
This same pattern was seen in the movements of the zodiac and the
waxing and waning of the moon with its peculiarly "feminine" cycle,
and these came to symbolize the unchangeable laws by which nature
fixed the destiny of man.

Blake seems to envision a fall into the goddesses' garden as a
prelude to a subsequent decline into the slavery of ancient empires.
Thus he presents Milton's garden of bliss as Beulah, a "lower Para-

dise" (*FZ* 128:30) of erotic and sensuous gratification which lacks the more strenuous joys of creativity, as well as the specifically human pleasures of social solidarity. This realm of erotic pleasure, maternal nurturance, and natural delight is completely benevolent within Eden as a "rest before labour" and a park within a city, but tyrannical when it blocks strictly cultural achievements, as in fact was the case.

What Blake correctly perceived in the Goddess myths was an inability of primitive peoples to differentiate themselves fully from nature. This was the meaning, for example, of that totemism by which certain animals and plants were included within the kinship bonds of the clan, leading savages to speak quite literally of "brother bear" and "sister corn." As George Thomson explains, "The individuals who compose a clan are not conscious of their kinship with one another as an objective human relationship, but only as one aspect of a wider relationship, in which they identify themselves with a particular species or plant."[59] This kinship was the source of those half-animal gods who were traditionally born from the intercourse between the totem species and the ancestor who initiated the clan. These appear in Blake as those cherubim whose horrible wings hide from humanity the truth of its own nature. When Tharmas falls into the state of nature, he becomes such a being, "A shadowy human form winged" (*FZ* 6:6). As such, he makes love to Enion who is then metamorphosed: "high she soard / Shrieking above the ocean: a bright wonder that nature shudderd at / Half Woman & half beast" (*FZ* 7:2–4). Tharmas and Enion symbolize humanity's fall into the world of procreative nature symbolized by Eurynome and Tiamat and the generative ocean: "For Enion brooded groaning loud the rough seas vegetate" (*FZ* 7:10) and gives birth to Los and Enitharmon, the fallen Adam and Eve of Blake's myth.

Blake characterizes this state as idolatry: Tharmas "Reared up a form of gold" and Enion makes "Golden rocks rise from the [vortex] vast" (*FZ* 6:5,7:11). Blake takes his criticism of this ideology from Milton who denounced those who "seek / Thir wandring Gods disguis'd in brutish forms / Rather then human" (*PL* I.480–82), and those corrupted by the fallen angels

> to forsake
> God their Creator, and th' invisible
> Glory of him, that made them, to transform
> Oft to the Image of a Brute, adorn'd
> With gay Religions full of pomp and gold.   (*PL* I.368–72)

However, for Blake the idolatry lies in turning away from human creativity, rather than from a divine creator.

Anthropology suggests that implicit in the tribal rites was a failure to appreciate properly the human role in production. Men sought to magically master the natural forces of fertility because they did not yet understand what their own labor might accomplish. In attempting to tap the power in the thunder or the growing corn, or to absorb through sacred feasts the mana of the bull and the fruit trees, they showed that they had not yet grasped the infinitely greater power lying in human intelligence and skill.

This false consciousness was expressed particularly in their annual celebration of fertility rites based upon beliefs in magical correspondences between humanity and nature. The ritual intercourse between representatives of the Goddess and her consort were intended to promote the fertility of both the clan and the land. Unfortunately, as Blake would have known from Mallett's *Northern Antiquities*, the parallel was also drawn between human and natural death. Just as the seed had to die and be buried in the womb-tomb of Mother Earth, so also, it was believed, human sacrifices must fertilize the land. Thus the Goddess's ritual lover was slain in order that his blood might be sprinkled on the crops and his body planted in the fields. Blake's hostility towards the nature cult focused primarily upon this conjunction of sex and suffering in the subordination of human life to natural processes. Vala mourns for her consort Luvah whom she herself has slain:

> She rises from his throne and seeks the shadows of her garden
> Weeping for Luvah lost, in the bloody beams of your false morning
> Sickning lies the Fallen Man his head sick his heart faint
> Mighty atchievement of your power! Beware the punishment
> I see, invisible descend into the Gardens of Vala
> Luvah walking on the winds, I see the invisible knife
> I see the shower of blood.   (*FZ* 11:8–14)

Elsewhere, discussing the Druidism of ancient Britain, Blake ascribes it to a universal stage in human evolution: "Adam was a Druid, and Noah; also Abraham was called to succeed the Druidical age, which began to turn allegoric and mental signification into corporeal command, whereby human sacrifice would have depopulated the earth" (PB 533). The pursuit of metaphoric analogies between human life and nature led to the transformation of poetry into murder. Blake builds his own repudiation of the fertility cult upon the prophets' denunciation of Canaanite religion which, as we have said, had already degenerated into an expression of urban slave society. When Blake has Vala sacrifice Luvah to slavery, he is recognizing the role such rituals came to play as instruments of terror and social control involving wholesale slaughter of slaves and captives, casting a religious halo on the suffering of the oppressed.

He also acknowledges a devolution of the nature cult as historically Beulah turned into Generation:

> Hear ye the voice of Luvah from the furnaces of Urizen
>
> If I indeed am Valas King & ye O sons of Men
> The workmanship of Luvahs hands; in times of Everlasting
> When I calld forth the Earth-worm from the cold & dark obscure
> I nurturd her I fed her with my rains & dews, she grew
> A scaled Serpent, yet I fed her tho' she hated me
> Day after day she fed upon the mountains in Luvahs sight
> I brought her thro' the Wilderness, a dry & thirsty land
> And I commanded springs to rise for her in the black desert
> [Till] she became a Dragon winged bright & poisonous
> I opend all the floodgates of the heavens to quench her thirst
> And I commanded the Great deep to hide her in his hand
> Till she became a little weeping Infant a span long
> I carried her in my bosom as a man carries a lamb
> I loved her I gave her all my soul & my delight
> I hid her in soft gardens & in secret bowers of Summer
> Weaving mazes of delight along the sunny Paradise
> . . . .
> I blotted out
> That Human delusion to deliver all the sons of God
> From bondage of the Human form.   (*FZ* 26:4–27:6,16–18)

At first, it appears, man falls into a simple materialism, revering nature more than his own intelligence, seeing himself as a mere worm, a natural body subject to the cycle of life and death and completely absorbed in physical reproduction—feeding and propagating identified here with the phallic worm and its world of generation. Eventually, however, instead of feeding, nature begins to feed upon human emotions of desire and fear until, while humanity has become merely natural, nature has become more than human, "a scaled serpent" whose alien powers must be magically manipulated.

George Thomson describes this evolution of the nature cult.[60] The earliest rites, he contends, were materialist extensions of human productive activities; in them human beings dramatized the skills of the harvest and the hunt and mobilized their collective emotion for the exertions and dangers they faced. However, they did not distinguish between human productivity and nature's procreative powers; rather, they tried to enhance their own abilities by identifying with the unseen forces of natural growth. Thus we find the earliest artifacts of human culture to include stone female figures, often with exaggerated reproductive organs. As human beings became more dependent upon and aware of the natural cycles of the seasons, the stars, the rains, the floods, the moon, and the sun, they began in agricultural communities to try to tap these powers through full-scale magical systems. At first, according to Jane Ellen Harrison, there was only a ritual drama expressing reverence for the fructifying earth.[61] Through this dramatization, the earth became personified as Mother Earth attended by her serpent lover. From there it was only a step to abstract the dramatis personae from the human actors as persons in their own right, as fully supernaturalized gods and goddesses inhabiting a realm which is outside but precisely mirrors the human world.

Blake describes this process of abstraction as the alienation of human emotions and power: "Above him rose a Shadow from his wearied intellect" (*FZ* 40:2), and man became "Idolatrous to his own shadow" (*FZ* 40:11). With the nature cult, projection occurs through the elaboration of a fantasy world whose natural figures have become imbued with human qualities, as Blake explains in *The Marriage of Heaven and Hell:*

> The ancient Poets animated all sensible objects with Gods or Geniuses, calling them by the names and adorning them with the properties of woods, rivers, mountains, lakes . . . and whatever their enlarged & numerous senses could percieve. . . .
> Till a system was formed, which some took advantage of & enslav'd the vulgar by attempting to realize or abstract the mental deities from their objects; thus began Priesthood.
> Choosing forms of worship from poetic tales.
> And at length they pronounced that the Gods had orderd such things.
> Thus men forgot that All deities reside in the human breast.
>
> (*MHH* 11)

What began as a confusion of human creativity and nature's fecundity leads in the end to a disavowal of the human role altogether; the fantasy world loses all contact with human needs and activities out of which it emerged; all human life is absorbed by Vala. "I gave her all my soul," Luvah confesses. Nature is thereby completely mystified and becomes a "Dragon wingd bright & poisonous" which must be worshiped and served. Through his imagery of a passage through the wilderness, Blake identifies the process with the evolution of Hebrew religion in a Canaanite direction, which is the subject of the next chapter. The consequence was that man relinquished what could only have been a paradise of his own creation, allowing it to become the garden of an alien goddess with humanity locked outside its gates.

The Fall into the Family

Blake's multidimensional analysis of the Fall as a loss of conscious control over nature consequent upon the rise of private property and the family is summarized by the Eternals in Night IX when Eden is on the verge of recovery:

> Man is a Worm wearied with joy he seeks the caves of sleep
> Among the Flowers of Beulah in his Selfish cold repose
> Forsaking Brotherhood & Universal love is selfish clay
> Folding the pure wings of his mind seeking the places dark
> Abstracted from the roots of Science then inclosd around
> In walls of Gold we cast him like a Seed into the Earth
> Till times & spaces have passd over him duly every morn
> We visit him covering with a Veil the immortal seed
> With windows from the inclement sky we cover him & with walls
> And hearths protect the Selfish terror till divided all
> In families we see our shadows born. & thence we know
> That Man subsists by Brotherhood & Universal Love
> We fall on one anothers necks more closely we embrace
> Not for ourselves but for the Eternal family we live.   (*FZ* 133:11–24)

"Forsaking Brotherhood & Universal love in selfish clay," humanity has fallen through greed for material possession. Again, the walling-in of the garden evokes Locke's image of "natural man" whose way of establishing private property was to "enclose it from the common," an image which in Blake's day would evoke the devastation of an English peasantry, forcibly evicted from an English garden to become, like Adam and Eve, vagrants upon an earth which is no longer home to them. Ultimately, the materialism Blake dreads is the selfish materialism of a profit-oriented culture. Thus, the enclosed garden signifies humanity's imprisonment and burial in "walls of Gold," money, which evoked a system so horrifying to Blake that he said he grew pale if ever any were offered to him!

Given the contemporary significance of "family" and "birth," illustrated in the works of novelists like Jane Austen, where it is virtually synonymous with inheritance, it is no wonder that Blake makes these golden walls the "walls and hearths" of a family estate. Abandoning the "divine vision" of human community, the property-owning classes have retreated into the province of their private possessions, and humanity has disintegrated into those atomized, isolated, and actually impoverished individuals, a shadow of their former selves, for "life Eternal / Depends alone upon the Universal hand & not in us / Is aught but death In individual weakness sorrow & pain" (*FZ* 104:8–10). This process began, according to Blake, in that ancient Fall when Luvah and Urizen withdrew from the primitive brotherhood of Eden. Since then, the nuclear family had been retained as a minimal social bond, required by the dependency of the human infant to "protect the Selfish terror" (*FZ* 133:20) at the lowest limit to which individuality could be allowed to contract without threatening human survival itself.

The Fall into Matriarchy

Implicit here is a criticism of the maternal bond characteristic of tribal society as well, for Blake's emphasis on the "universal love" of the "eternal family" upholds a form of cooperation based upon a shared creation, rather than the narrow blood ties of a tribal kinship system in which the dominion of Vala, the ancient ancestress, meant that solidarity within groups was often accompanied by a complete hostility between them. Thus George Thomson instructs us that "the formation of a new habit, also peculiar to man, the habit of production, which supplemented and superseded the animal habit of simply appropriating the means of subsistence . . . necessitated the formation within the group of a new type of relations, neither sexual, nor parental, but social." David Aberle has argued that "matriliny is largely limited to a certain range of productivity and a certain range of centralization," leading Elise Boulding to pose the problem of women's declining status as a structural one. As productive roles become increasingly specialized, she contends, the egalitarian relations of kin-based society are inadequate to organize this new division of labor, or at least, the historical foresight was lacking to adapt matriliny to these new demands.[62] Blake, committed to maximizing human productivity and creativity, shows some insight into this problem when he insists that, unlike Vala, Jerusalem is not a mother but a city where men and women are joined in common action rather than by clan or tribe through the natural ties of birth.

This profound insight into the limitations of tribal communism creates a certain havoc in Blake's historical vision, forcing a distinction between his ideal Eden and its primitive realization. In his myth, Blake describes a fall from the "universal" brotherhood of Eden into the kinship ties of a Beulah dominated by the matriarchal Vala. Motherhood does not exist in Eden but begins with Enion's procreation of the fallen Los and Enitharmon: in actuality the ancient brotherhood was indistinguishable from a matrilineal clan in which human beings lived communally upon the earth because as their common mother she could not be possessed.

It is not clear whether Blake intended to suggest the literal existence of such an Atlantis; he might have developed his sequence from the experience of the Jews whose transformation from a nomadic to an agrarian people involved a uniquely late exposure to the Goddess. His denunciation of matriarchy may also be influenced by the patriarchal bias of the Bible and of myths in which patriarchal editors had already altered the image of the Mothers to one suggestive of Blake's tyrannical female Emanations. Thus the proud, uninhibited, and unmarried childbearers of ancient cult were turned into Hera, the jealous and bickering wife; Venus, the cruel seductress; and Athene, the cool virgin. Blake might have had greater sympathy for these female deities had he known that their aloofness and fury did not arise either from coy manipulation or squabbles over lovers, but that, before Hesiod got hold of them, their resistance was to marriage, not sex. Like the Erinnyes of the *Oresteia,* their rage was not jealousy but the revolt of matrilineal culture against patriarchal usurpations. Clytemnestra is indifferent to Agamemnon's infidelities, but outraged at the sacrifice of her daughter. Medea, reduced from queen to powerless wife, slaughters her sons rather than yield them to Jason. The pieties of mother-right rather than matrimony are at stake.

In fact, the idea of matriarchy was itself often the creation of rising patriarchs who hoped by describing such a precedent to justify their own abuses. Thus Father Wilhelm Schmidt reports that among the Onas of Tierra del Fuego, the males, having asserted their dominance in secret misogynist societies, allege the existence of an earlier female tyranny as a justification for their own patriarchal cruelties, leading Joseph Campbell to remark:

> The mythological apologia offered by the men of the Ona tribe for their outrageous lodge was magnificently close to that attributed to Adam by the patriarchal Hebrews . . . namely, that if he had sinned, it was the woman who had done so first. And the angry Lord of Israel—conceived in a purely masculine form—is supposed to have allowed a certain value to this excuse; for he then made the whole race of woman subject to the male.[63]

In sorting out Genesis, Blake thinks he discovers in the myth a denigration not of Eve or even the Goddess alone, but of a whole era of female tyranny, to which a yet earlier stage of egalitarian "brotherhood" had succumbed. A case has been made for the idea that among some horticulturalists an augmenting of women's status might have occurred at the same time that incipient social hierarchies had already begun to form. But Blake seems to be suffering from another erroneous assumption—that Goddess worship necessarily characterized matriarchal rather than egalitarian societies. He did not have access to scholarship based upon Lewis Henry Morgan's exploration of gentile (clan) societies or the archaeological excavations of the Goddess-centered cultures of Minoan Crete or early Canaan. Morgan showed the great dignity of women among the Iroquois where they could help select chiefs. This honor was far from a reign of Vala, since the Iroquois women's freedom from their husbands' domination was accompanied by close links with their brothers. The powers of the Mothers were circumscribed by the egalitarian processes of the clan.

Likewise in Crete, where goddesses and their priestesses prevailed, women were artistically depicted "mixing freely with the men, in the courts, in the bull ring—lovely, vivid and vivacious, gesticulating, chattering, even donning masculine athletic belts to go somersaulting dangerously over the backs of bulls." Although some social stratification existed here, as Campbell points out, this culture "represented a civilized refinement that has not often been equalled since. . . . There were no walled cities in Crete. . . . There is little evidence of weapons. . . . The tone is of general luxury and delight, a broad participation by all classes in a genial atmosphere of well being."[64] Had Blake sought a literal prototype for Atlantis, he would have found it nowhere as here under the smile of the Great Mother whose benevolence was erased from the records kept by the male-supremacist civilization by which it was overthrown.

Not usually a misogynist, Blake seems to have failed in this instance to distinguish between the life style of primitive people and the gender relations of his own society. In his own patriarchal culture, he observes women as the bulwark of marriage in that culture, defending it to his dismay with the stern demands of chastity.[65] Thus in *The Four Zoas* he sometimes seems to locate the motive force of history, at least partly, in the jealousies and fears of wives and mothers. In doing so, he is confusing effect and cause, a mistake which he does not make in *Visions of the Daughters of Albion* where he shows the creation of that jealous, fearful female role as arising from the destruction of the tribe. There, Bromion's arrogant male supremacy and Theotormon's jealous possessiveness, as reflections of a selfish society, bring about the imposition of female chastity. As a slave breeding children for Bromion to buy and sell, Oothoon reveals what would be the essence of her marriage to Theotormon as well, subordination to a system in which the bondage of women is a function of the reduction of all human relations to forms of property.

There are, finally, misogynist implications, if not intentions, in Blake's personifying the fallen state as Vala and in the "female will" of *Jerusalem* which are inherent in the myth of woman-as-nature. In separating Jerusalem and Vala, Blake is far ahead of his time in criticizing this female-nature association; but as bride, even Jerusalem remains primarily defined only by her sexuality—as creation rather than creator. So long as woman is seen as "born for the sport & amusement of Man" (*FZ* 10:25), she remains a lesser being. In *The Four Zoas* the primitive androgyne remains a vague suggestion, and we stay trapped in the sexual division of Zoa and Emanation.

Few questions have been more vexed of late than this one, for one of the primary debates provoked by feminist anthropology has been precisely over the question of whether the "woman-is-to-nature-as-man-is-to-culture" mythology reflects actual primitive conditions, or is merely a later rationalization.[66] Analysts who dispute this theory point to the wide variety of roles women have played throughout history—as hunters, artisans, farmers, priestesses, and even warriors—despite the sexual division of labor; they point also to the often androgynous and interchangeable characteristics of ancient gods and goddesses. But even defenders of primitive sexual equality acknowledge that in all societies the primary responsibility for the more biological functions associated with reproduction—giving birth, nursing, child-rearing, preparing food, and other nurturing activities—fall upon women. As societies became more stratified, these activities were relegated to a "domestic" sphere newly segregated from the "public" arena of craft and trade, and women became secluded in the monogamous, nuclear family. To the extent that women's role as breeders put them at a disadvantage under these new conditions, women would appear to be wed to nature; their Eden never fully existed in the primitive garden of the Goddess—(for that, women must await the development of birth control, labor-saving devices, mass production of food, clothing, and other goods). Women's Eden would only become possible, as Blake would have it, in a fully humanized Jerusalem.

The same problem pervaded Blake's treatment of the triumph of Vala in general, and the relationship between civilization and barbarism. In Night IX, he shows that along with the rise of property and the family there is a diminution of human science (*FZ* 133:11–24). Like a seed, mankind is buried in nature, suggesting the decline of technology and man's absorption in the agricultural cycle of seasonal recurrence where human consciousness is absorbed in the merely animal tasks of survival. Instead of achieving the highest form of existence, humanity undergoes a kind of reversed metamorphosis:

> a Worm wearied with joy he seeks the caves of sleep
> Among the Flowers of Beulah.
> . . . .

> Folding the pure wings of his mind seeking the places dark
> Abstracted from the roots of Science then inclosd around
> In walls of Gold we cast him like a Seed into the Earth.
>
> (*FZ* 133:11–16)

The imagery here of the male worm lying passive among female flowers is sexual, but the allusion is to a fall into fertility cult. Regressing to the gardens of Vala, Albion folds up the butterfly wings of his consciousness and, abdicating his mental powers for "caves of sleep," becomes "abstracted from the roots of Science" and degenerates into a worm totally absorbed in his environmental cocoon. In a similar reversal, instead of harvesting nature as a basis for his own development, he becomes a seed planted in labor for the flourishing of nature. If Blake means literally that the apex of science and culture was achieved in the primal societies, then he overestimates them as widely as Rousseau underestimates them.

More likely, Blake is suggesting that commentators like Rousseau ignore the knowledge that has been lost in the advances of technology. In stressing his belief that scientific advance can be compatible with social egalitarianism in an Eden of the future, Blake overlooks their real incompatibility in the past. In fact, as Eleanor Leacock points out, the development of new skills did help promote hierarchy in the ancient transition: "Specialization became common in the production of goods to be traded for luxury items and special tools and foods. The process enriched life and promoted skill. As an unforeseen result, it ultimately transformed the entire structure of human relations from the equality of communal groups to the exploitativeness of economically divided societies."[67]

Blake is on safer ground when he argues that it was such "selfish cold repose" that ultimately set new brakes on development. Moreover, he is correct that the rise of agriculture did bring about a reign of Vala, an intensification of magical obsession with the "places dark" and a religion of death and sacrifice. Even Jane Ellen Harrison, a foremost defender of primitive religion, recognizes that the worm within that flower was an eventually reactionary obsession with nature:

> As long as man is enaged in a hand to hand struggle for existence, his principal focus of attention must be on food. The magical inducement of the recurrent fertility of the earth is his first and well nigh his last religious duty. But, as civilization advances and he is freed from the more urgent necessities, his circle of need enlarges and the focus of his attention widens. . . . Moreover, a worship of the powers of fertility, which includes all plant and animal life is broad enough to be sound and healthy, but, as man's attention centers more and more intently on his own humanity, such worship is an obvious source of danger.[68]

Finally, that is why the benevolent Mother and her serpent lover had to be feared as the beast and whore whose garden of delights tempted human beings from the task of developing their own conscious powers and whose ocean of fecundity was an abyss of monsters, threatening them with the terrors that lie in an untamed nature. By contrast, the myth of their conquest survives today as a symbol of progress; for example, a Chinese peasant artist recently entitled a picture of the rural struggle for modernization, "Heroes Lock up the Dragon."[69]

Whatever problems one might have with chronology if Blake's Atlantis myth be taken literally, the historical vision in *The Four Zoas* remains an extraordinary achievement. The ultimate goal of his myth was not narrative accuracy, but a dialectical analysis that could disentangle the contradictory strands within Genesis and reveal the lines of the future under encrustations of the past. For, Blake says, "All these things are written in Eden. The artist is an inhabitant of that happy country; and if every thing goes on as it has begun, the world of vegetation and generation may expect to be opened again to Heaven, through Eden, as it was in the beginning" (PB 533). The poet has to project from history an alternative to its two dominant ideologies, worship of the Mother Goddess and of the Father God, both of which obscured the path through which history, Generation, might open again to heaven. He had to reassert the existence of a golden age preceding the Royal Father's ban on its gardens of delight. At the same time, he had to execute the precise incisions which might sever its vision of an egalitarian community, liberated sexuality, and un-alienated creativity from the mother-centered, kinship-based, nature-worshiping culture in which it had in fact been immersed. For as Marx wrote:

> Cooperation, such as we find it at the dawn of human development, among races that live by the chase, or, say, in the agriculture of Indian communities, is based, on the one hand, on the ownership in common of the means of production, and, on the other hand, on the fact that in those cases, each individual has no more torn himself off from the navel-string of his tribe or community than each bee has freed itself from connection with the hive.[70]

It was to cut this umbilical cord that Blake separated Vala from the Eden of cooperation, casting off all the mystery of backwardness in order to salvage from the past that which might be recovered in an apocalyptic future.

His difficulties are those of prophecy itself, for the prophet, Blake had insisted, was no omniscient god but just an honest, unselfish, undeluded interpreter of history, prognosticating, "If you go on So the result is So" (PB 607). The profundity and apparent originality of his own vision stemmed from his revival of the memories of an unacknowledged past and from the unique perspective on the present offered to one who was looking for the forces already moving to change it. But history could never entirely define the future, and there was an inherent difficulty in trying to project the apocalypse from a former golden age. Images of liberation remained nascent in technologies yet undiscovered and knowledge yet unachieved, and perhaps nowhere was this more true than in the case of women who awaited the development of birth control and domestic technology to lay the basis for shattering the myth of woman-as-nature once and for all.

No one was more aware of these problems than Blake, who espoused the golden age myth as a challenge to the rationalizers of the status quo, but always added to his belief a faith that the movement of mankind was finally forward rather than backward. Thus he had urged, "Reason or the ratio of all we have already known. is not the same that it shall be when we know more. . . . As none by travelling over known lands can find out the unknown. So from already acquired knowledge Man could not acquire more. therefore an universal Poetic Genius exists" (PB 2). Finally, Blake realized that history could tell one less about Eden than about the obstacles to it in a fallen world, the subject to which we must now turn our attention.

7

Blake's Genesis:
The Fall

*The demand that people give up illusions about their conditions is the
demand that they give up the conditions which require illusions.*

—Marx

In one of the more notorious statements in the history of Milton
criticism, William Empson once argued that the poet would ultimately be vindicated when others "adopted the manly and appreciative attitude of Blake and Shelley, who said that the reason why the
poem is so good is that it makes God so bad."[1] Empson followed this
seemingly perverse remark by calling attention to the impression
given by *Paradise Lost* that God has plotted the Fall of Man and
shifted the blame dishonestly onto his victims. His contention was
that this apparent inconsistency was, in fact, more a judgment on the
religious traditions that Milton expressed than on his own powers of
expression.

The Four Zoas takes its inspiration from Milton's exposure of the
contradictions in the Western God. In *The Book of Urizen*, Blake
dramatizes his belief that demonic revolt is the only appropriate
response to the abuses of a tyrannical deity, Urizen. The work turns
upon a contrast between diabolical and divine perspectives regarding
which came first, repression or revolt. The "demonic" rebels view the
Fall as provoked by divine oppression, Urizen's "hand / On the rock of
eternity unclasping / The Book of brass. Rage siez'd the strong" (*U*
4:42–44), while the "divine" Urizen exonerates himself, attributing
the subsequent chaos to "terrible monsters Sin-bred: / Which the
bosoms of all inhabit; / Seven deadly Sins of the soul" (*U* 4:28–30).
The Genesis account of original sin is revealed as a self-interested
Urizenic rationale, "When Eternals spurn'd back his religion" (*U* 2:2)
and a political allegory, justifying his "assum'd power" (*U* 2:1).

185

Contrary Mythologies: Cosmic War and Adam's Sin

The celestial war, I will suggest, always provided a more explicitly political analysis of the human condition than the story of Adam's sin. Where the former immediately called up associations with historical conflicts, the latter led to concern with individual moral failure. As we shall see in the next chapter, Milton had deliberately drawn such political parallels in *Paradise Lost*, enhancing the importance of the satanic battle by making it the direct cause of humanity's fall, displacing it to the center of his narrative, and elaborating it as never before. This rendition of the combat myth, explicitly linked by Milton to its classical analogues, fanned Blake's imagination, leading him to take the process even a step further. In *The Four Zoas* Adam and Eve's original sin is eliminated entirely in favor or a concrete historical rendering of Milton's war.

Pursuing the insight of its headnote (Eph. 6:12)—that the "principalities" and "powers" of heaven are the principalities and powers of "this world" in another guise—*The Four Zoas* attempts to trace the origins of Milton's God to a history of social conflict. Thus Blake's Urizen depicts the triumphs of that deity, from the development of inequality and injustice religiously mystified both in Babylonian and Egyptian theocracy and in Hebrew religion, through the development of Christianity and (in Blake's mind) its medieval perversion, to the rise of modern Puritanism as the concomitant of the new commercial order.

In this chapter we will follow the ancient dimension of Blake's mythic history. As Fred Whitehead has suggested, this history encompassed "the destruction of primeval psychological equality during the rise of urban societies in the ancient Near East about 4000 B.C. brought about by such dramatic and profound changes as the accumulation of an economic surplus, the use of metals such as bronze and later iron, division of society into ruling and working classes, establishment of the state, organized religion and legal systems."[2] Unlike Whitehead, who locates the entire plot in the ancient world, I will read *The Four Zoas* as a universal history, with its ancient chapter concentrated only in the first four nights, and I will emphasize its rendering of a history of consciousness through Blake's rereading of mythic and scriptural traditions. Thus the complex social and cultural history of the early nights can be seen to revolve around the presentation of the Fall as a mythic summary of Old Testament history, seen in Blake's topsy-turvy or "infernal manner," as recounting the creation of the biblical God. Clues for that reading had been provided by Milton's own conflations of biblical and pagan history with Christian and classical myth in *Paradise Lost*.

My method will be, in preface, to recognize contradictions historically inherent in the doctrine of the Fall, then to develop Blake's articulation of the theme in the various historical and ideological contexts which help illuminate it. First, we will consider his description of the rise of a ruler-god as monarchy evolves out of an age of conquest and exploitation. Second, we will consider Urizen's manifestation as "primeval priest" in the context of a consolidating temple religion. Third, we will analyze Blake's repudiation of a divine creator, linked to the building of urban civilization, and the dialectic he draws between ideas of creation and actualities of repression. Next, we will consider his allegations about the interdependencies between the usurpations of "reason" and the irrationalities of religion in a slave society. And finally, we will note the role Blake assigns to Christianity as the repository of both these legacies and the prophetic tradition which would be their adversary.

Controversies over Genesis were unavoidable, given the conflicting perspectives merged in the work itself. On the one hand, as modern scholars explain, it is "a straightforward aetiological myth, designed to explain why a man cleaves to his wife and why he is the senior partner in the union, why he has to labour in the fields and she in childbirth."[3] Yet hedged within this apologia lies a nostalgic image of primitive bliss that must have had behind it centuries of popular discontent with the very order it was intended to defend. In focusing on the question of which has priority—divine oppression or the human fall—Blake touches upon ambivalences in the document itself arising from the antagonistic traditions of a Jewish culture that alternately exalted and denounced the existing legal order. This conflict finds expression in Genesis itself which alternately locates marriage, male supremacy, law, and toil before and after the Fall, thus leaving their inevitability forever open to question.

An awareness of the problematic nature of this tale should serve as a caution to those who would find perversity in critical attempts to question the logic of Milton's narrative. Milton had not been the first believer who, feeling that the ways of God needed justifying, tried to fill in the gaps in Genesis's argument. As J. M. Evans demonstrates, Milton could call upon centuries of commentary that had been similarly inspired to tackle its inconsistencies. Two problems that had particularly perplexed its readers were how such great misery could stem from what seemed so trivial a fault, and how allegedly innocent beings could have ever sinned at all. Rather than shifting the crime, in

Blakean fashion, onto God himself, explicators have sought other agents; thus the identification of the serpent with Satan as a monstrous force of evil.[4]

Social Conflicts and Heavenly Wars

The idea of an evil spirit appealed to a miserable people's experience of the world, for them less the realm of a benevolent protector than a battleground invaded by destructive forces; such experience repeatedly produced visions of a universe divided between hostile cosmic powers. Such a conflict was evident in Zeus's war against the Titans and the battles of Marduk and Baal. This motif had probably once introduced the Genesis myth as well, but had been expunged by priests wishing to safeguard the absolute supremacy of their God.[5]

In fact, once it is told, the story of Adam and Eve is never mentioned again in the Old Testament, although the symbol of the garden reappears. Jewish commentators rarely used Genesis 1–3 to explain human fate, and when the Fall did receive attention it was in the apocryphal books, excluded from the official Scriptures. These more popular works tended to be apocalyptic, presenting a world characterized by cosmic, as well as by social discord. In these works the idea emerged that the present order had derived from a primal conflict and that God would lead his people in a subsequent battle which would reverse its verdicts and restore the Eden which had been destroyed. So, whether or not these corresponding myths—of human fall and heavenly war—were ever linked in Genesis, history would reunite them. According to N. P. Williams in *The Ideas of the Fall and of Original Sin*, the more common Jewish explanation of human misery was taken from the story in Genesis 6 where the "sons of God" (the "watcher angels" of the Apocrypha) seduce the daughters of men and propagate a fallen race.[6] *The Book of the Secrets of Enoch*, combining this tale of angelic seduction with apocalyptic themes, was the first to recombine the myth of combat and the myth of the garden, explaining,

> One from out the order of angels, having turned away with the order that was under him, conceived an impossible thought, to place his throne higher than the clouds above the earth, that he might become equal in rank to my power. And I threw him out from the height with his angels, and he was flying in the air continuously above the bottomless; . . . and the devil understood that I want [sic] to create another world, because Adam was lord on earth, to rule and control it. . . . And he understood his condemnation and the sin which he had sinned before, therefore he conceived thought against Adam, in such form he entered and seduced Eva.[7]

Virtually the same merger was achieved by Christian interpreters. Early Christianity developed in a Roman world characterized by the acutest oppression and, consequently, in an intellectual atmosphere permeated by images of a dualistic universe torn between divine and demonic powers. The Gnostics even went so far as to assign the creation of the material universe, with all its miseries, to a devil. The church fathers, seeking both to refute and accommodate this heresy, returned to scriptural accounts of cosmic battle. In the Book of Revelation, the revolutionary aspirations of first-century Jews had led to the vision of a final battle between the angels of God and the legions of Satan which would initiate a reign of peace and justice:

> Now war arose in heaven, Michael and his angels fighting against the dragon; and the dragon and his angels fought, but they were defeated and there was no longer any place for them in heaven. And the great dragon was thrown down, the ancient serpent, who is called the Devil and Satan, the deceiver of the whole earth. . . . And I heard a loud voice in heaven, saying, "Now the salvation and the power and the kingdom of our God and the authority of his Christ have come, for the accuser of our brethren has been thrown down."   (Rev. 12:7–10)

The dragon of course is our old nature daimon, easily identified with his close cousin the Genesis serpent, although by the first century transformed into an emblem of decadent empire. By reading this apocalyptic image back into Eden and thus the prehistoric context from which it originally emerged, the church fathers were able to incorporate into a Christian context a modified version of the Gnostic vision of a universe divided between antagonistic powers. This, as Evans explains, provided a more credible cause for the Fall, safeguarding Adam's and Eve's original innocence while heightening their sin as a virtual conspiracy with the enemy of God. At the same time, it appealed to the people's intuitive sense that they were at all times and everywhere beset by malicious foes.[8] In this form the story entered Christian tradition and was bequeathed to Milton whose encyclopedic knowledge and poetic genius were to bring its hidden sources into bold relief.

The Fall of Humanity and the Rise of the State: The Politics of the *Theogony*

Following Milton's lead, in *The Four Zoas* Blake goes even further in shifting the emphasis from Adam's and Eve's fault to the story of heavenly war, now rendered as a concrete historical phenomenon. In the crucial episode, modeled upon *Paradise Lost*, Urizen and Luvah reenact the contest between God and Satan: "the heavens were filld with blood" (*FZ* 12:35). To understand Blake's treatment of this motif, we must look at its sources in the *Theogony, Paradise Lost*, the Old Testament, and ancient history.

We have already discussed the classical analogues of this combat in terms of the triumph of the patriarchal god of civilization over the Mother Goddess of the primitive clan and her nature cult. Now we must note that this myth expresses a political as well as a sexual evolution. Gaia's forces, as Norman O. Brown points out, were drawn from her kin, while Zeus's were secured through political alliances. Moreover, the consequence of Zeus's triumph is being appointed king by the assembly of other gods. He gives Olympus its political structure, using his new powers to distribute rights and privileges among them. Consolidating his dominion, Zeus takes for his consorts Metis, representing a form of political wisdom, and Themis, the law. The latter bears him as children those civic attributes, Good Order, Justice, and Peace. Since his ascendance was by force, he must maintain it through his monopoly on violence. This achievement, Brown says, points to Zeus as the "founder of what Machiavelli calls 'civil society.' "[9] Law and order is achieved by the concentration of violence in the state. The other gods remain turbulent, and the wars in heaven never completely end, but Zeus now serves as the arbiter of these ongoing heavenly feuds.

We might find Zeus a crude kind of deity, embroiled in acts of outright vengeance, hurling other gods from their Olympian seats and throwing his thunderbolts at any who resist his will. But Gilbert Murray informs us that such behavior is completely consistent with the Olympians' social origins: "The gods of most nations claim to have created the world. The Olympians make no such claim. The most they ever did was to conquer it. Zeus and his *comitatus* conquered Cronos and his. . . . Zeus took the chief dominion and remained a permanent overlord, but he apportioned large kingdoms to his brothers Hades and Poseidon, and confirmed various of his children . . . in lesser fiefs." The Olympians promote neither agriculture nor trade: "They find it easier to live on the revenues and blast with thunderbolts the people who do not pay. They are conquering chieftains, royal buccaneers . . . cut loose from all local and tribal pieties intent on only personal gain and glory."[10]

George Thomson contends that Greece had passed through a tribal stage in which land was held in common and equally distributed by lot. Then, with the development of herds, came wars of plunder and the rise of a military elite. The first form of private property, Thomson explains, originated in the *temenos*, or cut-off portion of land, set aside as a reward for military heroes.[11] This practice is acknowledged in the *Iliad* where one of the chiefs asks, "Why have the people of

Lycia conferred on us the highest honors—pride of place and precedence in food and drink? They look on us as gods, and they have bestowed on us a temenos of rich ploughland. Therefore, we must be foremost in the fray that the people may say, these kings of ours who feed on fat herds and quaff our choicest wine, can fight."[12] Eventually these gifts turned into hereditary rights. The plunder of cattle led to the capture of slaves to cultivate the growing estates of the aristocracy, and enslavement of captives was followed by the enslavement and exploitation of former clansmen. The chief, who used to support the clan's artisans out of the surplus gathered from the clan, now claimed them as his private workmen to produce goods for him with which to barter with other chiefs, along with the equipment of war. Gradually an urban aristocracy separated itself off from the tribes who were forced to support it with tribute.

This process is reflected in the *Theogony;* in conjunction with the myth of cosmic war appears the story of Prometheus, son of a Titan, artisan, and representative of the subjugated clan. Several aspects of this tale reveal that the growing inequality between human beings and their gods described in it follows an inequality arising between classes in Greek society. Prometheus's conflict with Zeus began as a dispute over the division of the sacrificial animal. In fact, these sacrifices for "the gods" had become just another form of expropriation by the chiefs. Significantly, the quarrel also centered around the question of who controls fire and the arts of civilization. Moreover, Prometheus was identified with "men who earn their bread by work," and it is they who share his fate, part of which is oppressive labor, one of the evils released from Pandora's jar.[13] All men, however, had not been subject to these punishments. The intercourse of the gods with mortals produced an intermediary race of heroes, equals of the gods. The aristocracy, as it might be expected, claimed descent from these heroes whose cults they promoted. The war in heaven, then, is a highly political myth. Zeus's suzerainty over Olympus mirrors a period when wars of conquest led to the unification of several tribes for increased military effectiveness. Some gods were subordinated to others; wars between peoples were translated into wars between their deities in heaven, and the masses were reduced to a condition which they dared resist only at the risk of bringing down upon them the full violence of these divine beings.

Sources for Blake's Historicized Myth

In deriving his analysis of the Fall—particularly the war in heaven—as a reflection of power struggles on earth, Blake need not have been a scholar of ancient history: he could draw directly upon

Paradise Lost. In the historical panorama revealed by Michael in Books XI–XII, Blake could find notions of the Fall replicated in earthly conquests, and a later fall into social tyranny under Nimrod as an actual continuation of the cosmic strife between God and Satan. Blake needed only to turn Milton's account on its head to conclude that earthly battles were the actual sources, rather than the spiritual consequences, of heavenly war.

Michael allows Adam to view that other fall—so important, as we have seen, in Hebrew tradition—which occurred when liaisons between the "sons of God" and the daughters of Cain produced a corrupt race. Milton's passage describes a primarily social disaster, involving conquest, plunder, and tyranny, as settled peoples were ransacked by tribal invaders. Moreover, such a passage shows Milton himself integrating into the biblical story of impious dalliance Homeric material concerning that age of warring chieftains which we have just connected to the *Theogony*'s vision of conqueror gods:

> He lookd and saw wide Territorie spred
> Before him, Towns, and rural works between,
> Cities of Men with lofty Gates and Towrs,
> Concours in Arms, fierce Faces threatning Warr,
> Giants of mightie Bone, and bould emprise;
> Part wield thir Arms, part courb the foaming Steed,
> Single or in Array of Battel rang'd
> Both Horse and Foot, nor idely mustring stood;
> One way a Band select from forage drives
> A herd of Beeves, faire Oxen and faire Kine
> From a fat Meddow ground; or fleecy Flock,
> Ewes and thir bleating Lambs over the Plaine,
> Thir Bootie; scarce with Life the Shepherds flye,
> But call in aide, which tacks a bloody Fray;
> With cruel Tournament the Squadrons joine;
> Where Cattel pastur'd late, now scatterd lies
> With Carcasses and Arms th' ensanguind Field
> Deserted: Others to a Citie strong
> Lay Seige,
>   . . . .
>   so violence
> Proceeded, and Oppression, and Sword-Law.

(*PL* XI.638–56,671–72)

Our second point is that Milton himself suggested a connection among the Fall, the war in heaven, and social degeneration when he retold that biblical episode so favored by millenarians for its distinctly political and antityrannical character. This was of course that story of the rise of Nimrod, the oppressive "hunter of men" who brought about a virtual second fall from which humanity "as from a second stock" proceeded, supposedly new and purified, after the flood (*PL* XII.7). Milton offers a radical reading of this event when, associating it with more than just an aberrant act of vice, he uses it to explain the decline from a peaceful, patriarchal tribalism into an "Empire tyrannous" in which mankind has come to live by "Dominion" rather than the "Concord and law of Nature" which, for him, is liberty:

> Long time in peace by Families and Tribes
> Under paternal rule; till one shall rise
> Of proud ambitious heart, who not content
> With fair equalitie, fraternal state,
> Will arrogate Dominion undeserv'd
> Over his brethren, and quite dispossess
> Concord and law of Nature from the Earth;
> Hunting (and Men not Beasts shall be his game)
> With Warr and hostile snares such as refuse
> Subjection to his Empire tyrannous.   (*PL* XII.23–32)

Particularly provocative for Blake would have been Milton's presentation of this tale as an extension of the war in heaven, with Nimrod

> from Heav'n claming second Sovrantie;
> And from Rebellion shall derive his name,
> Though of Rebellion others he accuse.
> Hee with a crew, whom like Ambition joyns
> With him or under him to tyrannize.   (*PL* XII.35–39)

As we shall see in the next chapter, in his dismay at the failure of the revolution, Milton turned to ideas of the Fall and satanic influence to explain it; in his typological view of history all later catastrophes derived from that first spiritual disaster. Blake, in battle against a political defeatism supported by ideas of original sin, but perceiving the connections made in Milton's highly politicized epic, would invert its vision, deriving ideas of the Fall on earth and in heaven from the degeneration of society.

Blake might have made similar use of Jacob Bryant's *A New System or An Analysis of Ancient Mythology* (1776). Like Milton, Bryant pursued comparative mythology in order to argue the primacy of the Bible and its historical vision, which the degraded and plagiarized accounts of the pagans might be seen to substantiate. Blake knew and illustrated Bryant's work, drawing a different moral from it, namely, that "the antiquities of every Nation under Heaven, is no less sacred than that of the Jews. They are the same thing as Jacob Bryant, and all antiquaries have proved" (PB 516).

Bryant's attempt to give an account of the "first ages" could have provided Blake with the crucial sources and analogues for his own vision of history in *The Four Zoas*. In Bryant's view, the biblical account of Nimrod, the building of Babel, and the first wars between the descendants of Noah depict the same events as the Greek wars of the Titans. Moreover, he associates these Titans with the primitive inhabitants of Babylon (Babel), described in the Bible and in ancient Babylonian myth and history. Bryant would therefore have introduced to Blake the Babylonian cosmogony, for, although the ancient texts of the *Enuma Elish* (or Babylonian Genesis) had not yet been deciphered, Bryant devoted a lengthy discussion to a fragment supposedly preserved from Berossus, an ancient Babylonian priest, and passed on through the Greek author Alexander Polyhistor by Eusebius. In addition to providing Blake with this account of the wars of Bel (Marduk in the *Enuma Elish*) against an ancient goddess of chaos, Bryant also insinuated that Milton might have drawn upon the myth. More significantly, he identified all these ancient figures: Nimrod, the Titans, and the Babylonian gods with the invention of the arts of civilization, the building of the first city, the establishment of monarchy and the origin of war—events central to Blake's vision of the Fall in *The Four Zoas*, where the poet adopts Bryant's method of conflating pagan myth and biblical history for his own critical revisioning of the Bible.

Hebrew History Behind Blake's Version of the Fall

Thus both Milton and Bryant had offered Blake significant clues toward a reading of biblical history which might demonstrate an evolution of the Hebrews from an original "fraternal state" when they were still a nomadic people organized in tribes of extended kin.[14] We must note some factors in the biblical history that Blake was drawing upon so that we may recognize their transmutation in *The Four Zoas*. In fact, Hebrew tribal brotherhoods were ruled by assemblies of elders, male heads of households, and were quite egalitarian. While not necessarily involving common property, there was a strong ethos of mutual aid in which the community applied strict moral sanctions to insure that wealthier clansmen take care of their less fortunate kin. These comprised the values to which the prophets would later appeal as the *mishpat*, the justice of Yahweh. Since, for a long time, many Jews remained a semi-nomadic people inhabiting the hills of Palestine and were in a state of continual siege, both the pastoral life style of poor herders and the needs of mutual defense kept alive these democratic traditions for much of their history.

At some point a number of these tribes which entered Canaan formed a confederacy for greater military strength. They sealed their alliance by making a covenant with Yahweh whose common worship would henceforth cement their unity. The symbol of this league was its shrine at Shiloh where the ark of the covenant was kept until later captured by the Philistines. The leaders who emerged from this league were the military and charismatic heroes of the Book of Judges such as Samson and Gideon. Their authority remained strictly limited by the power of the tribal elders and their obligation to maintain traditional mores. As late as the end of this period, the prophet Samuel himself chose and judged kings, illustrating the power implicit in the tribal religious forms. War had by then produced a military aristocracy; in order to meet the Philistines' superior military might, Samuel elevated the charismatic warriors Saul and David into kings of a newly centralized nation. From David's reign dates a drastic transformation of Hebrew society; the old tribal structures broke down, and the people begin to divide into a ruling elite and an oppressed peasant and working class.

The Fall I: The Rise of Monarchy

Blake's myth, then, adopts a Miltonic conflation of the war in heaven story with the Greek war of the Titans, the Homeric age of conquests, and Nimrod's abrogation to himself of "Dominion undeserv'd." At the same time, Blake projects the Christian myth onto a vision of universal history, drawn from both biblical history and those classical analogues to it which he readily perceived. In *The Four Zoas* the celestial battle is literally identified with actual human wars for wealth and power when

> messengers from Beulah come in tears & darkning clouds
> Saying Shiloh is in ruins our brother is sick Albion He
> Whom thou lovest is sick he wanders from his house of Eternity
> The daughters of Beulah terrified have closd the Gate of the Tongue
> Luvah & Urizen contend in war around the holy tent.   (*FZ* 21:8–12)

The destruction of Shiloh symbolizes the fall of tribal culture, its "holy tent," the "tent of meeting," where Israel pledged its loyalty to the covenant and its holy leaders consulted oracles, now desecrated by the warring Zoas. The messengers from Beulah are subsequently identified with Conways Vale, the scene of Gray's "The Bard"; we may assume they are those prophets who, like the ancient Welsh poets, upheld the clan morality in judgment of a rising monarchy. Blake's assertion that they have "closd the Gate of the Tongue" may refer to the silencing of the voice of the tribe which, in the time of Samuel, spoke through ecstatic prophets; temporarily, at least, the oracles have ceased.

Blake symbolically associates the battles of Luvah and Urizen with Milton's heavenly war by identifying Luvah as Lucifer, "the first beam of the morning" (*FZ* 15:9) and Urizen as "the Mighty Father" (*FZ* 15:18), but concretely their conflict appears as a conspiracy to dominate their brother Zoas:

> Thou Luvah said the Prince of Light behold our sons & daughters
> Reposd on beds. let them sleep on. do thou alone depart
> Into thy wished Kingdom where in Majesty & Power
> We may erect a throne. deep in the North I place my lot
> Thou in the South listen attentive. In silent of this night
> I will infold the Eternal tent in clouds opake while thou
> Siezing the chariots of the morning. Go outfleeting ride
> Afar into the Zenith high bending thy furious course
> Southward with half the tents of men inclosd in clouds
> Of Tharmas & Urthona. I remaining in porches of the brain
> Will lay my scepter on Jerusalem the Emanation
> On all her sons & on thy sons O Luvah & on mine
> Till dawn was wont to wake them then my trumpet sounding loud
> Ravishd away in night my strong command shall be obeyd
> For I have placd my centinels in stations each tenth man
> Is bought & sold & in dim night my Word shall be their law.
>
> (*FZ* 21:20–35)

Numerous details here point to the history of the Jews, signified as a people living in tents. Specifically, the allusion to the seige of Jerusalem indicates the moment when David's accession to the throne in his captured Jebusite city put an end to the tribal order. David symbolized this change by moving the cult objects formerly kept at Shiloh into Jerusalem. The passage also evokes Milton's description of the process in which wars of plunder led to besieged cities whence "violence / Proceeded, and Oppression, and Sword-Law" (*PL* XI.671–72). The language clearly implies the establishment of a monarchy with tyrannical power, as the allusion to the division into a northern and southern kingdom recalls the consequence of that tyranny when Ephraim in the north revolted against the Davidic dynasty and separated from Judah.

Solomon ruled Israel like a veritable oriental potentate, building his palace upon the impoverishment of his people. After seizing power through a coup d'état, he set himself above all tribal authorities. The elders and prophets were deprived of power, and Palestine was divided into twelve districts under the rule of his royal officials. Jerusalem was transformed into a cosmopolitan center where this new elite lived in opulence. The city was built by forced labor, a practice flouting all Hebrew ethics, and supported by tributes exacted from the peasantry. There is even a story that Solomon exchanged his subjects for exotic metals and horses for his cavalry. After his death, the northern Ephraim rose in revolt, demanding that Solomon's son enter into the traditional covenant with their elders, saying: "Lighten the hard service of your father and his heavy yoke upon us and we will serve you" (I Kings 12:4). The king replied, "My father made your yoke heavy, but I will add to your yoke; my father chastised you with whips but I will chastise you with scorpions" (I Kings 12:14); thereupon the northern tribes seceded, protesting, "What portion have we in David? . . . To your tents O Israel" (I Kings 12:16). Alas, the northern kings soon degenerated into tyrannies of their own.

The Four Zoas records royal oppression through tax collectors and taskmasters; Urizen has placed "centinels in stations" and "each tenth man / Is bought & sold." Thus Blake describes the misery of the divided monarchy:

> Ephraim called out to Zion: Awake O Brother Mountain
> Let us refuse the Plow & Spade, the heavy Roller & spiked
> Harrow. burn all these Corn fields. throw down all these fences
> Fattend on human blood & drunk with wine of life is better far
>
> Than all these labours of the harvest & the vintage.
> . . . .
> The Villages Lament. they faint outstretchd upon the plain
> Wailing runs round the Valleys from the Mill & from the Barn
> But most the polishd Palaces dark silent bow with dread
> Hiding their books & pictures. underneath the dens of Earth
>
> The Cities send to one another saying My sons are Mad
> With wine of cruelty. Let us plat a scourge O Sister City
> Children are nourishd for the Slaughter; once the Child was fed
> With Milk; but wherefore now are Children fed with blood?
> (*FZ* 14:7–22)

Blake derives this picture from Samuel's prophecy of the destitution that monarchy will impose on Israel, forcing the peasantry to serve the military interests of their rulers, turning ploughshares into swords in a reversal of prophetic vision, and reducing the people almost to the condition of slaves:

> So Samuel told all the words of the Lord to the people who were asking a king from him. He said, "These will be the ways of the king who will reign over you: he will take your sons and appoint them to his chariots and to be his horsemen, and to run before his chariots; and he will

appoint for himself commanders of thousands and commanders of fifties, and some to plow his ground and to reap his harvest, and to make his implements of war and the equipment of his chariots. . . . He will take the best of your fields and vineyards and olive orchards and give them to his servants. He will take the tenth of your grain and of your vineyards and give it to his officers and to his servants. He will take your menservants and your maidservants, and the best of your cattle and your asses and put them to his work. He will take the tenth of your flocks, and you shall be his slaves."   (I Sam. 8:10–17)

The emphasis here on theft should remind us that the Zoas' wars began with an act of robbery, when "Luvah siez'd the Horses of Light, & rose into the Chariot of Day" (*FZ* 10:13). We might also remember that the lust for Vala has been shown to signify the greed of the natural man, who seeks nature as a possession rather than as an emanation of humanity's common creativity.[15] Thus Luvah's desire for Vala is identified with the enclosure of the land and the destruction of the community of Albion:

And Luvah strove to gain dominion over the mighty Albion
They strove together above the Body where Vala was inclos'd
And the dark Body of Albion left prostrate upon the crystal pavement.
                    (*FZ* 41:13–15)

Among the squabbling chieftains of the period to which Blake alludes, theft of horses was integral to plans for military domination. The Israelites had never possessed chariots or horses, but they had survived because this equipment was useless in the hill country they inhabited. However, when David passed from defensive to offensive wars, he seized the chariots of Syrian troops, an event which may lie behind Luvah's action. The chariot symbol has complexities in Blake's work which we will postpone discussing for the time being, but as the Book of Samuel indicates, horses appear in the Bible consistently as a symbol of war: "Everywhere the horse was used for the war chariot alone, not for ordinary draught purposes or for riding. . . . Chariot owners formed the highest social class. When, as in Egypt, the charioteer provided his own equipment—which only the rich could afford to do—the development of the arm also increased the position of the aristocracy in the state."[16] This change occurred in Israel when Solomon built an army of charioteers, constructing chariot cities along the borders and even stabling horses in the temple. This professional army replaced the old people's militia, their last source of popular power, and created a military nobility. When Solomon also traded Israeli labor for horses, then indeed, as Blake protests, "the Horse is of more value than the Man" (*FZ* 15:1).

Thus chariots and horses become emblems of despotism in the Bible. Isaiah castigates the aristocracy because "their land is full of silver and gold . . . their land is full of horses; neither is there any end of chariots" (Isa. 2:7). Zechariah prophesies that eventually God "will cut off the chariot from Ephraim / and the war horse from Jerusalem" (Zech. 9:10) and will send a messianic deliverer, "humble and riding on an ass" (Zech. 9:9), to show that he is no arrogant military conqueror. Deuteronomy warns that a king "must not multiply horses for himself or cause the people to return to Egypt in order to multiply horses" (Deut. 17:16).

"To return to Egypt" means to return to slavery, and, in Blake's myth as in the Bible, this is the precise consequence of these disastrous conflicts. The ruler's conquests do not lead to power and wealth for most of the people, but to "the woes of Luvah" which Vala bemoans as an Egyptian captivity:

> O Lord wilt thou not look upon our sore afflictions
> Among these flames incessant labouring, our hard masters laugh
> At all our sorrow. We are made to turn the wheel for water
> To carry the heavy basket on our scorched shoulders, to sift
> The sand and ashes, & to mix the clay with tears and repentance.
>
> (FZ 31:4–8)

Blake's analysis here is very penetrating. Israel's problem (as that of ancient society generally) was the inability of warring tribes to achieve the unity essential for prosperity. Unfortunately, when unity was achieved under the monarchy, it is through a domination which led to an internal split between chiefs and slaves. This fact might explain the confusion in *The Four Zoas* which within a few verses represents Luvah as first a conquering chief, then an oppressed slave. As in the unfallen world, this Prince of Love embodies the solidarity of the clan; he may also represent its simultaneous segmentation into oppressor and oppressed classes. On the other hand, Blake may be dramatizing a point often underlined by the prophets: whenever the people as a whole engaged in military expansion, they were punished by being conquered by larger empires and reduced to captivity.

The Fall II: The Rise of Priesthood

While on one level Luvah dramatizes heroic conquest, on another he symbolizes a second route to popular tyranny through the rise of priestly religion. Again, an investigation of ancient mythology—in this case the Babylonian Genesis and its biblical parallels—can illuminate the idea of religious history illustrated in *The Four Zoas*.

In the rise of Urizen as king, god, and primeval priest portrayed in such incidents as the building of the temple, Blake offers an analysis of the role played by religion in the evolution of the tribal chieftaincy, and then of the dynastic monarchy of an oppressive society.

Luvah, as we have already seen, appears as a sacrificial victim in the Goddess's fertility cult, a Blakean version of the Thammuz-Adonis-Dionysius-Orpheus gods of death and resurrection: "Luvah was cast into the Furnaces of affliction & sealed / And Vala fed in cruel delight, the furnaces with fire" (FZ 25:40–41). We have argued that behind the rites of Thammuz-Dionysius there was originally a communal initiation rite, a sexual cult which literally integrated the procreation of the clan with its participation, through agriculture, in the cycle of nature.[17] Later, the ritual became symbolic, and the sacred marriage was enacted by a tribe's representatives. Originally this symbolic king and queen might have been selected in an athletic contest, but eventually the rites became the province of special magical fraternities. Also, whereas once the "corn king" was only a ritual leader and was sacrificed after a year's reign to be replaced by a youth representing the new year (sometimes the cycle was longer), ultimately the ritual chief managed to eliminate this unfortunate custom and proclaim himself a permanent king on the basis of his magical role.[18] Magic provided a real basis of power, justifying Blake's repeated association of such cults with the development of tyranny. Magicians represented one of the first divisions of labor, and magical manipulation of nature rose in combination with its scientific domination. The priests who performed the seasonal rites also acquired the astronomy and mathematics necessary to predict seasonal changes and, through their monopoly of knowledge, came to manage agriculture. This administration arose, in particular, in areas where labor had to be organized for large public projects, such as irrigation, deriving from times when communities still led by elders engaged in collective labor under the symbolic leadership of a priest-chief. Often these developments coincided with class differentiation brought about by other new divisions of labor:

> Private property, social stratification, political subjugation and institutionalized warfare with standing armies are all social inventions that evolved through the course of human history. . . . The dominance hierarchies . . . first arose in the fourth millennium B.C. during what has been called the urban revolution. In the long course of human history, various egalitarian gathering, hunting and later horticultural societies elaborated ritually on various forms of social and ceremonial rank, but still maintained . . . the equal right of all to basic sources of livelihood. Then, as a result of human ingenuity and inventiveness,

specialization of work gradually developed and removed part of the population from basic food production. Barter became transformed into commerce and traders into merchant intermediaries. Priest-chiefs increasingly manipulated the goods that were stored with them for redistribution and what had been ritual rank was transformed into exploitative elitism. Equal access to land became restricted as free lands were turned into privately controlled terraced, irrigated, fertilized, or otherwise worked fields. In short, class systems were created. . . . Fully stratified societies emerged first in Southwest Asia and northeast Africa, in Mesopotamia, Egypt, Jerusalem, Persia.[19]

As the new priestly class removed to the cities and took power over both lands and crafts, they claimed this rule, of course, not for themselves, but for the gods. They built their deities elaborate temple sanctuaries where they resided with them, shared their sacrificial meals, collected their tributes and managed their property. From these temples, which came to dominate the entire economy, the priestly aristocracy conscripted labor, managed artisan production, and expropriated the harvests of temple lands, worked by slave or forced labor. In time of war, this elite would select a leader from among its ranks, and inevitably this elected "king" would use his military power to pursue permanent rule. Finally, a king would declare himself "chief tenant of the god," chosen to live enthroned in his temple.

Blake conceived of religion as arising on two foundations. On the one hand, there was the passage from a reverence of natural forces to their abstraction as deities. Thus he indicates the derivation of Western religion's father-king from earlier fertility cult: "Vala was pregnant & brought forth Urizen Prince of Light / First born of Generation" (*FZ* 83:12–13). On the other hand, he insists that it was human exploitation and not just an error of consciousness that provoked this development: "some took advantage of & enslav'd the vulgar by attempting to realize or abstract mental deities from their objects; thus began Priesthood" (*MHH* 11). Elsewhere Blake presents the idea of God as a projection of the social realities of monarchy and priesthood, parodying the Lord's Prayer thus:

> For thine is the Kingship or Allegoric Godship & the Power or War & the Glory or Law Ages after Ages in thy Desendents for God is only an Allegory of Kings & nothing Else Amen
>   I swear that Basileia βασιλεια is not Kingdom but Kingship . . . & God is The Ghost of the Priest & King who Exist whereas God exists not except from their Effluvia.   (PB 659)

Blake anticipated by a century the researches which have flowed from Sir James Frazer's observations in *The Golden Bough* on the interrelationship between kingship and the gods. In this regard, for example, George Thomson has pointed out that in Australian tribes, where there is still no chief, there is no god, while Jane Ellen Harrison calls attention to Tzetzes' statement that "Zeuses the ancients used to call their kings,"[20] a remark substantiated by the fact that names of many deities (the Canaanite Moloch, the Tyrian Melquart) literally meant king. Blake would have confronted this reality in the Bible's Canaanite Melchizedek (king-priest) whose meeting with Abraham to offer sacrifices provided the justification for a Jewish preisthood. When Blake rewrites Genesis to show how "the primeval Priests assum'd power" (*U* 2:1) through the invention of God, he expresses a conception of religious origins much like that of anthropologist Paul Radin: "As we proceed from the food gathering to the fishing and hunting and then to agricultural tribes, the figure of the Supreme Deity assumes more and more the character of a priestly construct, bears more and more the earmark of a special and privileged group and class. Where the latter [the medicine men] have elaborated the concept of an original Supreme Power . . . it is only the shamans who share it and enjoy any close relation to him."[21]

The Babylonian Genesis

Scholars like Thorkild Jacobsen have analyzed the link between kingship and the gods in a Mesopotamian world view which linked society and cosmos—the throne in the palace and the god enthroned above the flood. The Babylonian creation epic, the *Enuma Elish*, has been a primary text for such analysis. Although it was discovered and deciphered after Blake's time, a partial description of Berossus's account was available, as we have seen, to mythographers like Jacob Bryant.[22] More significantly, the myth had numerous analogues and many of its symbols, according to scholars like S. H. Hooke, had come to form the basis of much biblical rite and imagery.[23] For our purposes it is important, not as a source for Blake, but for the insight it provides into an ancient theocratic world view which, whatever his sources, Blake manages to delineate so perceptively in *The Four Zoas* as to anticipate much of this modern scholarly view.

In the Babylonian epic, Marduk, like Zeus, emerges from his heavenly battles as king of the gods. In enlisting his leadership in battle against the monstrous female dragon Tiamat, the other gods had conceded him royal power:

> They erected for him a princely throne
> Facing his fathers he sat down presiding
> Thou art the most honored of the great gods

Thy decree is unrivalled. . . .
From this day unchangeable shall be thy pronouncements
To raise or bring low.[24]

Jacobsen explains that Babylonians saw the cosmos ordered like the political state whose creation is recounted in the *Enuma Elish*. Here the assembly of the gods yields temporary rule to Marduk, just as the assembly of elders in aristocratic society chose one of their number as a military leader in times of crisis. By the end of the epic, Marduk has achieved complete autocracy. He establishes his claim to ownership of the universe when he creates heaven and earth out of the severed body of Tiamat. He confirms his dominion over the other gods, adopting their titles as his own and absorbing the powers of the assembly. The elective kingship has passed into an absolute monarchy as the result of Marduk's wars. "The transition," Jacobsen proposes, "mirrors a historical development from primitive social organization, in which only custom and authority unbacked by force are available to insure concerted action by the community, to the organization of a real state, in which the ruler commands both authority and force."[25]

The triumphant Marduk also consolidates religious authority. Marduk was the patron god of Babylon; his ascendancy paralleled the rise of that city as an imperial center. This development was accompanied by the rise to absolute power of the king who was Marduk's high priest, ruling from the temple around which the city was organized. The epic culminates with the gods joining Marduk in establishing that temple, the towering ziggurat which will link heaven and earth; they say to each other, "Let us make [something] whose name shall be called 'Sanctuary.' . . . There let us erect a throne."[26] Thus the kings of Babylon claimed sacred origin and sat on the throne as a living embodiment of that link between heaven and earth. Hammurabi, in his famous code, claimed himself to be chosen from the time of creation enshrined in myth, a literal participant in the divine attributes of its sun-god, Marduk:

> When exalted Anu . . . and Bel . . . committed the sovereignty over all people to Marduk; . . . when they made Marduk great among the great gods; when they proclaimed his exalted name to Babylon, made Babylon unsurpassable in the regions of the world, and established for him in its midst an everlasting kingdom whose foundations are as firm as heaven and earth: At that time Anu and Bel called to me, Hammurabi, the pious prince, worshiper of the gods, summoning me by name, to bring about the rule of righteousness in the land . . . to go forth like the sun over the human race, to illuminate the land, and to further the welfare of mankind.[27]

The Four Zoas *and the Jewish Temple*

We will return to the import of Marduk's role as builder and sanctifier of urban civilization, but first we must consider that nothing could appear to be more antagonistic to a theological defense of autocracy than the religion of the Hebrew brotherhood, where the *mishpat* of Yahweh sanctified the equality of all his children. Thus the position has been advanced that the Bible should be read as a record of the struggle betwen Yahweh and his tribal ethos and Baal (a Canaanite Marduk) with his rationalization of social hierarchy and tyrannical rule. In such a reading the struggle against paganism appears as a manifestation of a deeper confrontation between social systems as the Jewish peasants and herders upheld their tribal values in resistance to the gods of a degenerate Asiatic despotism.[28]

Thus we find in *The Four Zoas* the same connections Florence Sandler has shown Blake to be making in *Milton*, between a political degeneration of Israel into monarchy and its religious parallel, the development of a temple cult based on Canaanite ideology.[29] With David's seizure of Jerusalem, the Jewish and Amorite peoples, who had coexisted without being assimilated for centuries, were united in a single Palestinian nation. As the Jewish upper classes began to intermarry with and to imitate the cosmopolitan Amorite nobility, Israel underwent a process of wholesale accommodation to the more advanced urban culture. The removal of the ark of the covenant to Jerusalem from Shiloh signified the transfer of religious loyalties from the tribal league to the nation. The pagan basis of the Jerusalem cult would inspire Ezekiel's charge against the city: "Your origin and your birth are of the land of the Canaanites; your father was an Amorite, and your mother a Hittite" (Ez. 16:3). While David paid some respect to the tribal heritage, becoming king through a covenant with its elders, Solomon ignored such tribal proscriptions and modeled his kingdom upon the pagan empires. Hence Israel was transformed into a status-ridden society, ruled by a royal bureaucracy, a mercenary army, and a king ensconced amid a pagan harem with all the opulence of an eastern tyrant. These abuses, as we have seen, provoked immediate resistance. The books of Samuel and Kings record a Deuteronomic polemic against the monarchy's Canaanite innovations; thenceforth, the kingship existed in tension with a tribal legacy upheld by the rude and righteous prophets of Yahweh.

Therefore Solomon undertook the creation of a priestly cult which would sanctify his rule by revising the image of Yahweh to conform to Mesopotamian concepts of divine kingship. Hebrew worship adopted the rituals of the Jebusite city, and Yahweh followed David in being

transformed from a tribal leader into a cosmic king. As John Weir
Perry explains: "The real divine king of Israel was Yahweh himself,
who at the time of the people's urbanization and altered way of life,
was transformed from a desert God into a 'King of Kings' and 'God
Most High' with attributes of the Canaanite city's deity, enthroned at
the center of the world."[30] The most drastic innovation of all was the
adoption of Mesopotamian notions of sacral kingship which elevated
the ruler ontologically above his people. A special set of "royal
psalms" announced that Yahweh had transformed his covenant with
the whole people into a covenant with the house of David through
which it would henceforth be mediated:[31]

> I have made a covenant with my chosen one;
>> I have sworn to David my Servant.
> I will establish thy seed forever;
>> Yea, I will maintain thy throne through all generations.
>
> (Psa. 89:3–4)

Here, as in the *Enuma Elish,* we pass from the elective kingship of a
military chief to dynastic monarchy, freed, moreover, from the ethical constraints that previously hedged rule in Israel. While there can
be no question in monotheistic Judaism of literally identifying the
king with God, or as a descendant of God, the king could be elevated
to a kind of semidivinity through divine adoption. Thus the status of
all Jews as children of God was superseded by the establishment of a
direct lineage between God and his king:

> But I, as you see, have set up My King
> Upon Zion, My sacred mountain
> Let me tell of Yahweh's decree:
> He hath said to me, "Thou art My Son;
> This day have I begotten thee,
> Ask of Me and I will make
> The nations thine inheritance
> The ends of the earth thy possession."   (Psa. 2:6–8)

Returning to *The Four Zoas,* we find all these images converging in
the figure of Urizen, Blake's poetic realization of the ancient theocracy. As priest, king, lawgiver, and creator, he signifies that elevation of social authority to cosmic status which characterized the
religion of the "royal father," triumphant in Israel as in Egypt and
Babylon. Just as Luvah represented the appearance of oppression in
military chiefs that arose at a certain stage of tribal society, Urizen
embodies the full consolidation of a ruling class in the state. He
justifies his rise to power as necessary to terminate the chaotic age of
conquests when, like David in the Book of Samuel, any bold warrior

could make the whole land his spoils. Enitharmon recalls how Albion, weakened by fratricidal wars, abdicated power, yielding his scepter to Urizen. As was typical in these theocracies, Urizen took power as a god as well as a king, professing: "Now I am God from Eternity to Eternity" (*FZ* 12:8), usurping the divinity which once resided in Albion, the community itself.

Lest we have any doubts about his identity, Blake casts Urizen specifically in the role of Solomon by whom this transformation of Jewish society and religion was consummated. Solomon is traditionally remembered for his wisdom, so Blake establishes Urizen's identification with him by having the mythic king walk in the "gardens of wisdom" (*FZ* 63:30) of Solomon's Song of Songs. Moreover, in the biblical literature attributed to Solomon, wisdom is sometimes personified as a female, much like Urizen's Emanation, the bright Ahania, who splits off from his consciousness much as Athene, the Greek goddess of wisdom, is born from the head of Zeus. Furthermore, like Solomon, Urizen is a temple builder:

> Then rose the Builders; First the Architect divine his plan
> Unfolds, The wondrous scaffold reard all round the infinite
> Quadrangular the building rose the heavens squared by a line.
>   . . . .
> Multitudes without number work incessant: the hewn stone
> Is placed in beds of mortar mingled with the ashes of Vala
> Severe the labour, female slaves the mortar trod oppressed
>   . . . .
> His Shadowy Feminine Semblance here reposd on a White Couch
>   . . . .
>   Urizen formd
> A recess in the wall for fires to glow upon the pale
> Females limbs in his absence & her Daughters oft upon
> A Golden Altar burnt perfumes with Art Celestial formd
>   . . . .
>   Also her sons
> With lives of Victims sacrificed upon an altar of brass
> On the East side. Revivd her Soul with lives of beasts & birds
> Slain on the Altar up ascending into her cloudy bosom
> Of terrible workmanship the Altar labour of ten thousand Slaves
> One thousand Men of wondrous power spent their lives in its formation
> It stood on twelve steps namd after the names of her twelve sons.
>   (*FZ* 30:8–41)

Ahania is ensconced in Urizen's temple just as Ashtoreth, the goddess of the Sidonians, was placed in the Jerusalem sanctuary by Solomon; her couch represents the bed on which the king in the mystery cult achieved divinity through intercourse with the Goddess. As the "primeval priest," Urizen imitates Solomon in replacing a religion of righteousness with a religion of sexual and sacrificial magic whose propitiations are simply the cosmic bribes which a greedy temple aristocracy is able to extract from a people seeking divine relief from their misery. Ironically, the misery arises from the temple itself, whose construction required the introduction into Israel of forced labor, the ultimate blasphemy against tribal equality. As offerings are sacrificed to Ahania, so the people are sacrificed to royal extravagance: "Men of wondrous power spent their lives in its formation." It is a structure of oppression which rests upon "twelve steps namd after her twelve sons," just as the monarchy bore down upon the tribes of Israel, whose authority is eliminated in this period when Solomon carves them up into districts under his royal bureaucracy.

The Fall III: Cosmocreator and Culture Creation

The wedding of Urizen to the Goddess and her secret enthronement in the Hebrew temple is one of a number of details through which Blake proposes that the new royal religion, in Israel more covertly than in Babylon, had incorporated the old fertility cult. Elsewhere he presents to the same end the cherubim guarding the ark of the covenant and the secret sexual rites behind the Holy of Holies. Indeed, this allegation must be understood within Blake's recognition of the complex relations between the God of power and authority, creator of nature, and the rise of urban cultures in antiquity. To comprehend this relationship, let us first consider the historic absorption of the nature cult, then the emergence of Marduk as both creator and culture builder, and finally the ways in which *The Four Zoas* parodies a theocratic world view which joins the creation of the cosmos, the city, and human society.

In the *Enuma Elish* Marduk assumes the dual role of creator of the universe and builder of urban civilization. The epic has, in fact, two accounts of creation. First the universe is born from the watery goddess Tiamat; then creation is inexplicably repeated by Marduk in a manner than accomplishes her destruction. On the one hand, this revision signifies the triumph of a patriarchal order over the matrilineal clan. But the passage from the *procreation* of the universe to its *construction* also points to the triumph of a more technological culture. Moreover, the emphasis is on taming the watery chaos, as Ea measured and divided the waters to build his abode, the earth, as a canopy above the Apsu, or sweet waters. This process points to the construction of the great irrigation works through which the new ruling class arose. Moreover, Marduk is credited with having overseen the construction of Babylon itself, thus giving divine sanction to this new urban order: "So shall Babylon be, whose construction ye have desired. . . . Let its brickwork be fashioned."[32] Such remarkable feats of creation easily displaced the old reverence for fertility as a focus for religious emotion.

The idea of God as creator, for Jehovah as well as Marduk, arose in close connection with the monarchy and its celebration in enthronement rites linking creation of the cosmos and the origins of royal authority. Thus not until the reign of Solomon did the Hebrew God assume such attributes as the "God Most High" who created the entire universe.[33] The composition of the Yahwist account of Genesis at that time played a role in this transformation.[34]

The royal psalms are believed to have been originally sung at such Jewish rites as the annual harvest festival, the Feast of Tabernacles, modeled closely upon the Babylonian new year celebration.[35] In this festival the monarchy no longer appears as a development of the historical circumstances recorded in the Book of Samuel, but as a divine institution established with the foundation of the universe. At the center of the king-cult was the Jerusalem temple built by Solomon on Mount Zion in imitation of the Babylonian ziggurat, believed to link heaven and earth. In this sanctuary, simultaneously a house of God and a royal palace where he performed the role of chief priest, Solomon became the mediator between the people and their God. The new year festival celebrated Yahweh's ascension to his throne, but since the king probably played the role of Yahweh in the cult, it was also a re-enthronement rite, commemorating the annual "renewal of the kingdom" (I Sam. 11:14)—that is, God's covenant with his king. Thus, in a coronation ceremony complete with the full monarchic rigamarole of scepters and thrones, the people were led to accept as unquestionable and divine the legitimacy of their rulers.

Fertility elements in this ceremony linked the king and his God to creation. Thus the Jewish temple was built along the axis of the rising sun, and on the Feast of Tabernacles, the king would open its eastern doors so that the dawn would flood his sanctuary with glory, striking the huge bronze image of the primeval ocean, just as the divine light of creation once moved upon the waters. The integration of fertility symbols in the Holy of Holies follows this pattern of integrating the life of nature and the power of the monarch.[36] These ceremonies were believed to have magical significance for the flourishing of the crops, as evidenced in Zechariah's proclamation that everyone "shall go up from year to year to worship the King, Yahweh of Hosts, and to celebrate the Feast of Tabernacles; . . . who so . . . goeth not up to Jerusalem . . . upon them the rain shall not come" (Zech. 14:16–17). Thus the monarchy was elevated above human institutions and became both an extension of God and the foundation of nature. Like their pagan neighbors, the Jews came to believe that only the king could insure the well-being of the whole community, the fertility of the land, livestock, and the people.[37]

Blake's presentation of Urizen both as creator and builder of a whole civilization, the "Mundane Shell around the Rock of Albion" (*FZ* 24:8) expresses such interconnections. Albion lies asleep and imprisoned on his rock as an image of the lost brotherhood. Earlier I maintained that Blake may have taken his vision of this evolution from a "fraternal state" to a tyranny from Milton's Nimrod. It is significan in this regard that this original lord was also the architect of the tov er of Babel, "A Citie & Towre, whose top may reach to Heav'n" (*PL* XII.44). The "mundane shell" consequently turns out to be the ancient world of Babylon and Egypt:

> The Bands of Heaven flew thro the air singing & shouting to Urizen
> Some fix'd the anvil, some the looms erected, some the plow
> And harrow formd & framd the harness of silver & ivory
> The golden compasses, the quadrant & the rule & balance
> They erected the furnaces, they formd the anvils of gold beaten in mills.
>
> (*FZ* 24:9–13)

The identity of this civilization is revealed by its associations: "many a pyramid / Is form'd & thrown down thund'ring into the Deeps of Non Entity" (*FZ* 28:26–27). Luvah and Vala, "mourning among the Brick kilns" (*FZ* 31:1), connect Urizen's world with ancient civilization, with Egypt. The tyranny of Urizen, "Binding Jerusalems children in the dungeons of Babylon" (*FZ* 25:31) evokes the ancient Mesopotamian empire, while the brick kilns and dungeons recall a world of slavery.

A similar development may be seen in Babylonian myth. When he created the city of Babylon, Marduk also invented its social classes. From the blood and gore of Tiamat's defeated monster child, Kingu, the gods created a race of servants for the gods: "After Ea, the wise had created mankind / (And) they had imposed the service of the gods upon them / That work was not suited to (human) understanding."[38] The work of slaves, the corvees of serfs (forced public labor), the tithes and mandatory "sacrifices" which supported the theocratic elite were all "for the gods." The common people became the slaves of monarchs whose power was safeguarded by control over a religion which based all order on their reign.

Urizen's "mundane shell" recalls Jacobsen's description of the Mesopotamian universe as simultaneously a cosmic and a social order. That social order, according to George Thomson, was also embedded in the structure of its temple cities with the king enthroned at its center:

> The rigid stratification of society is seen in the city's lay out. In the centre towering over everything stood the temple, large, luxurious, exquisitely furnished, surrounded by offices, treasuries, granaries, warehouses, and workshops for the accommodation of officials, craftsmen and manual workers of all kinds . . . dependent on the priests, their masters, the largest employers in the city. Outside lay the arable land. A portion was let out to tenant farmers or worked directly for the temple under some form of labour service. The rest was divided into family holdings . . . subject to the moral exactions with which a powerful priesthood always exploits the faith of the masses. Only the pastures remained common.[39]

Significantly, Urizen's creation is a temple-city, a cosmic order and also a social structure:

> But infinitely beautiful the wondrous work arose
> In sorrow & care. a Golden World whose porches round the heavens
> And pillard halls & rooms recievd the eternal wandering stars
> A wondrous golden Building; many a window many a door
> And many a division let in & out into the vast unknown
> [Cubed] in [window square] immoveable, within its walls & cielings
> The heavens were closd and spirits mournd their bondage night and day.
>   (FZ 32:7–13)

Under the direction of Urizen as priest-king, the irrigation works and towers are erected which reveal his "mundane shell" as another Babylon:

> Sorrowing went the Planters forth to plant, the Sowers to sow
> They dug the channels for the rivers & they pourd abroad
> The seas & lakes, they reard the mountains & the rocks & hills
> On broad pavilions, on pillard roofs & porches & high towers
> In beauteous order.   (FZ 32:16–33:3)

The language is Blake's contemporary language of class, of "divisions," "degrees," and "stations." Urizen's golden city copies the social stratifications of the new "divisions" of labor in which Urizen directs the mindless, servile drudgery of his slaves.

But the "mundane shell" is also the universe and Urizen the cosmocreator, measuring the immense with Miltonic compasses and erecting his universe above the waters of Tharmas: "Am I not God   said Urizen. Who is Equal to me / Do I not stretch the heavens abroad or fold them up like a garment?" (*FZ* 42:21–22). As in Mesopotamian myth, civilization and cosmos mirror each other:

> the golden Looms erected
> First spun, then wove the Atmospheres,
>   . . . .
> They bear the woven draperies; on golden hooks they hang abroad
> The universal curtains & spread out from Sun to Sun
> The vehicles of light.   (*FZ* 29:3–4,10–12)

Urizen creates a "golden world" in the image of a temple "whose porches round the heavens / And pillard halls & rooms recievd the eternal wandering stars."

The idea of a God who is both creator of the universe and builder of civilization goes back to Marduk. Blake takes it from Milton whose God was also a "great Work-Maister" (*PL* III.696; *FZ* 24:5) and a "sov'ran Architect" (*PL* V.256; *FZ* 49:1). His hostility to the idea of the creator becomes comprehensible when we observe that it rose precisely, as Blake shows, out of the theocratic empires.

Finally, such correspondences yield a complete rationale for the status quo; they install social relationships right into the structure of the cosmos. In Urizen's creation, even the stars obey his hierarchies:

> Thus were the stars of heaven created like a golden chain
> To bind the Body of Man to heaven from falling into the Abyss
> Each took his station, & his course began with sorrow & care
>
> In sevens & tens & fifties, hundreds, thousands, numberd all
> According to their various powers. Subordinate to Urizen
> And to his sons in their degrees & to his beauteous daughters.
>   (*FZ* 33:16–21)

The Fall IV: Repression and the Rise of Law

The hostility to the creator found in *The Book of Urizen* and *The Four Zoas* derives from Blake's view of the social origins of the Genesis myth and its uses in justifying a social order based upon exploitation and repression. He insists that Urizen only creates *his* universe, a deformed world, modeled upon his tyrannical social assumptions. Blake was inspired to this position by Milton's insistence that creation was a by-product of the war in heaven:

> For he strove in battles dire
> In unseen conflictions with shapes
> Bred from his forsaken wilderness,
> Of beast, bird, fish, serpent & element
> Combustion, blast, vapour and cloud.   (*U* 3:13–17)

The Newtonian echoes here signified the middle class's reconstruction of the cosmos to suit its own aspirations to technological dominance; however, the principle, from Hammurabi to Newton, is the same. The myth of course derived from a theocratic context in which no one hid the fact that Yahweh's power over creation was won through conquest, and it echoes those great solar myths in which a hero associated with sun and sky overthrows the forces of darkness and chaos identified with the primordial ocean. In fact, the dramatization of this combat was at the center of the enthronement rites, celebrated in the royal psalms which inextricably linked creation and power:

> Thou dost rule the raging of the sea; when the waves rise thou stillest them.
> Thou didst crush Rahab like a carcass, thou didst scatter thy enemies with thy mighty arm.
> The heavens are thine; the earth is also thine; the world and all that is in it, thou hast founded them.
> . . . .
> Righteousness and justice are the foundation of thy throne.
>
> (Psa. 89:9–14)

In Blake's interpretation of this motif, the idea of creation sanctions the claim of an allegedly divinely appointed ruler to possession of the universe and brands his political opponents as the very enemies of God. Thus Urizen's creation is repression: his universe "arose on the waters / A wide world of solid obstruction (*U* 4:23); he maintains his order only by violence: "his ten thousands of thunders / Rang'd in gloom'd array stretch out across / The dread world" (*U* 3:28–30). The chaos which Urizen must suppress is merely human resistance to his tyrannical impositions.

Hammurabi's supernatural claims appear in the preamble to his famous legal code, which gives divine sanction to his political system. By the same logic, the Hebrew Torah was said to have been delivered by God himself to Moses on Sinai; in fact, however, the Hebrew laws were probably first codified by officials in Solomon's court, and Deuteronomy reflects a compromise between a popular ethos and a priestly one in post-exile Jerusalem.[40] In *The Book of Urizen*, Blake's tyrant is given explicitly Mosaic overtones:

> Lo! I unfold my darkness: and on
> This rock, place with strong hand the Book
> Of eternal brass, written in my solitude.
>
> Laws of peace, of love, of unity:
> Of pity, compassion, forgiveness.

Let each chuse one habitation:
His ancient infinite mansion:
One command, one joy, one desire,
One curse, one weight, one measure
One King, one God, one Law. (*U* 4:31–40)

Similarly, in *The Four Zoas*, Urizen demands that the Zoas "obey [his] awful Law" (*FZ* 12:17), ordering Los: "Obey my voice young Demon I am God from Eternity to Eternity" (*FZ* 12:23). The emphasis makes clear that Urizen's laws are intended to preserve the existing social structure, limiting each to his "station." "His ancient infinite mansion" is an oppressive "curse" and "weight" disguised as an ethical ideal. When Urizen hands down his book of brass, a variation of Moses' stone tablets, it is to "Compell the poor to live upon a Crust of bread by soft mild arts" (*FZ* 80:9).

The Fall V: The Rise of Reason and Unreason

Bearing in mind these correspondences between god and king, conqueror and creator, the natural laws of Vala and the social edicts of Moses, creation and production, Jerusalem and Babylon—we may now approach a fuller analysis of the chariot incident around which the narrative of *The Four Zoas* turns. At the same time, we might bring our historical framework back in touch with more customary readings of the epic which have tended to read it as a dramatization of a fallen humanity's warring faculties, of the conflict between human intellect, manifested in Urizen, and the desires embodied in Luvah.[41]

The chariot symbol appears in two different ways in Blake's epic: as the archetypal image of the unfallen Zoas, and as an object of contention between Luvah and Urizen, the central conflict of the narrative. These two dimensions must be seen to be related, illuminating Blake's sense of the fate of intellect in antiquity. Never fully described, the chariot incident is alluded to several times as various characters recall the Fall. "Luvah," we are told, "siez'd the Horses of Light, & rose into the Chariot of Day" (*FZ* 10:13), an incident which is later related to a conspiracy between Luvah and Urizen; the latter clouded the "Eternal Tent" while Luvah seized "the chariots of the morning" (*FZ* 21:25–26). Elsewhere Tharmas tells us that Urizen gave the "horses of Light" to Luvah (*FZ* 50:30), and Urizen himself admits having withheld his "chariot of mercies" from Albion by trading the "steeds of Light" to Luvah for the "wine of the Almighty" that provoked his drunken fall (*FZ* 65:5–8). Orc adds that by stealing the light Luvah turned it into a consuming fire (*FZ* 80:39–40), and Urizen relates that when he gave up the horses he left Albion dying on a "rock far in the South" (*FZ* 119:26–29). Thus an intrigue of greed and ambition provoked the Fall through the loss of the horses of light which pulled Urizen's sun-chariot. Henceforth, those horses became wild and disobedient in the rage of Orc, and the sun-chariot became implicated in the perverted rites of secret religion. Only when Urizen reclaims his horses in "Night the Ninth" can they once again be harnessed to the "instruments of harmony" to perform the labors of imagination.

The relationship between Urizen as a psychic and a social tyrant which lies behind these events has been noted by Frye, Bloom, and Beer, but for them it is a purely analogical relationship. In fact, we can find a far more integral connection if we direct our attention to the social functions of intellect in the theocracies which are his context. After the collapse of his empire, Urizen nostalgically recalls his former life in language evoking Solomon's wisdom and the gardens of his Song of Songs:

> Once how I walked from my palace in gardens of delight
> The sons of wisdom stood around the harpers followd with harps
> Nine virgins clothd in light composd the song to their immortal voices
> And at my banquets of new wine my head was crownd with joy
>
> Then in my ivory pavilions I slumberd in the noon
> And walked in the silent night among sweet smelling flowers
> Till on my silver bed I slept & sweet dreams round me hoverd
> But now my land is darkend & my wise men are departed. (*FZ* 64:1–8)

Solomon, like other Asiatic despots, consolidated all knowledge and skill in the hands of his temple aristocracy. The crude tribal patriarchs who had led Israel in its more primitive state gave way to an urbane, educated administration composed of scholars and technocrats who directed the skill of artisans recruited from all over the ancient world. In an era when literacy itself was centered in a class of scribes, this priestly aristocracy asserted a monopoly over knowledge and science and began to codify Hebrew oral traditions (closing the gate of the tongue), to assimilate the "wisdom" of neighboring kingdoms, and to transform Jerusalem into a center of cosmopolitan sophistication. Blake's critique of "reason" proceeds from his insight that its character throughout history has remained what it became in these ancient theocracies—the province of an elite in pursuit of profit and power. He must have raged at the sycophantic adulation of Solomon's "wisdom," sneering at the tyrant: it was only "your reason," not our reason.

In Blake's narrative, Urizen, mourning the fall of his empire, confesses his role in the chariot incident, thereby illuminating the social significance of Blake's symbols. The material basis of this mythology is the revolutionary significance of the wheel. The appearance of ox-drawn carts and wagons and, eventually, horse-drawn chariots radically altered transportation and trade, enabling the first development of cities. Thus the wheeled chariot exerted a compelling power over the human imagination, presenting humanity for the first time with an image of its own power, as intellect conquered nature in the achievements of civilization.

An equally important breakthrough in the third millennium B.C. was the replacement of the old monthly lunar calendar with the solar calendar, which V. Gordon Childe calls "the first triumph of mathematical astronomy and the first vindication of the claim of science to predict."[42] These calculations enhanced control of agriculture, enabling human beings to synchronize their productive activities with the cycles of sun and rain. Consequently, the sun traversing the heavens like a flaming chariot came to symbolize the conquests of human intelligence. We are familiar with this motif through the stories in which Marduk routed Tiamat and Zeus defeated Typhon from horse-drawn chariots, as well as from the exploits of such solar deities as Apollo and Baal. As the earth daimons in their underground habitations had been the focus of an earlier age's reverence for dark, uncomprehended natural forces, now humanity hailed the combats of these anthropomorphic heroes as the victory of shining human reason over the superstitions of the past. Hence Apollo was above all a god of civilization, a patron of music, poetry, philosophy, astronomy, mathematics, medicine, and science.

In a related mythic development, the animal forms in which the divinity had previously been submerged were now, like nature itself, tamed and subordinated, becoming the steeds who drew the sun-chariot.[43] The pre-Socratic philosophers transferred their attention from the chariot to the charioteer, using this *typos* to express the role of the Logos in steering the vehicle of the universe. Plato elaborated the psychological meaning of the fable in the allegory of the *Phaedrus*, where reason is shown controlling the horses of the lower impulses. Writing in Babylonian captivity, Ezekiel adapted the myth to his glorious vision of God as a chariot surrounded by four living creatures emblazoned with light and vibrant with furious winged imagery, thundering like a storm and supporting the firmament above their heads. Its wheels full of eyes and its propulsion by spiritual force revealed it to be a celebration of intelligence, as was also the creator of Genesis who made the universe by his almighty word. Blake must have been especially inspired by the prophet's report that the creatures had the likeness of men, for he adopts the symbol in *The*

Four Zoas as the luminous emblem of divine humanity's collective creativity. This magnificent symbol reverses the values which led the fertility cult to merge humanity with nature in a worship of chthonic gods of flora and fauna; here, instead, man has made nature and technology his "Vehicular Form" (*J* 53:1), the extension of his own creative powers.[44]

Urizen's crime lies in retaining this power for his own aggrandizement instead of using it to guide the Eternal Man:

> My songs are turned to cries of Lamentation
> Heard on my Mountains & deep sighs under my palace roofs
> Because the Steeds of Urizen once swifter than the light
> Were kept back from my Lord & from his chariot of mercies
>
> O did I keep the horses of day in silver pastures
> O I refusd the Lord of day the horses of his prince
> O did I close my treasuries with roofs of solid stone
> And darken all my Palace walls with envyings & hate
>
> O Fool to think that I could hide from his all piercing eyes
> The gold & silver & costly stones his holy workmanship
> O Fool could I forget the light that filled my bright spheres
> Was a reflection of his face who calld me from the deep
> . . . .
> I went not forth. I hid myself in black clouds of my wrath
> I calld the stars around my feet in the night of councils dark
> The stars threw down their spears & fled naked away
> We fell. I seizd thee dark Urthona In my left hand falling.
>
> (*FZ* 64:9–28)

The images here speak of a hoarding, enclosing one's treasury, hiding the gold and silver and costly stones, retreating to the selfish pleasures of one's palace "with envyings & hate." Like Solomon and the ancient theocracies, Urizen refuses to use his knowledge, the "horses of instruction" (*FZ* 25:3), for all mankind by harnessing them to a "chariot of mercies" (*FZ* 64:12). He ignores the divinity of Albion, the community, and, taking a scepter and crown for himself, retreats into the mystifications of Miltonic heavens to begin wars of repression against those who presumably object to his possessiveness.

These events culminate in the fall of Urthona who, as a craftsman, embodies the universal creativity of the unfallen world, a disaster reported elsewhere as a consequence of the wars between Urizen and Luvah:

> Beside his anvil stood Urthona dark. a mass of iron
> Glowd furious on the anvil prepard for spades & coulters   All
> His sons fled from his side to join the conflict pale he heard

The Eternal voice he stood the sweat chilld on his mighty limbs
He dropd his hammer.   (*FZ* 22:16–20)

Man's capacity for constructive labor has been undermined; from forging the implements of agriculture, he has turned to making the equipment of war. Here lies the contradiction in the chariot itself, which, as we have noted, came to be used primarily for combat. Thus Blake alleges that Urizen, in addition to hoarding knowledge, has perverted it, turning it over to the ambitious and combative Luvah:

Because thou gavest Urizen the wine of the Almighty
For steeds of Light that they might run in thy golden chariot of pride
I gave to thee the Steeds   I pourd the stolen wine
And drunken with the immortal draught fell from my throne sublime.
                                                        (*FZ* 65:5–8)

Luvah, like Marduk and Zeus, not only conquers nature with his chariot, but also overthrows the egalitarian tribal society. Thus Urizen, like the theocratic elite, turned the advances of civilization into new forms of barbarism, constructing sophisticated cultures on the corrupt foundations of slavery and war.

Eventually Urizen's "mundane shell" falls under the weight of its own contradictions. His quarrel with Ahania symbolizes his growing resistance to her "wisdom," which now begins to reveal the truth about his repressive order as defensive, reactionary, and threatened by any change:

O Prince the Eternal One hath set thee leader of his hosts
Leave all futurity to him Resume thy fields of Light
Why didst thou listen to the voice of Luvah that dread morn
To give the immortal steeds of light to his deceitful hands
No longer now obedient to thy will thou art compell'd
To forge the curbs of iron & brass to build the iron mangers
To feed them with intoxication from the wine presses of Luvah
Till the Divine Vision & Fruition is quite obliterated.
                                                    (*FZ* 38:15–39:7)

The "divine fruition" of human culture is incompatible with Urizen's static hierarchies. The fully humanized environment of Albion could only be achieved by the democratic realization of the skill and consciousness of all people. The building of Jerusalem, the enhancement of both physical and human nature, is antagonistic to the maintainance of an elite whose luxury rests upon others' debased labor and whose power depends upon the ignorance of their slaves. In the collapse of Urizen's world, Blake points to the social contradictions that finally produced the fall of all ancient civilizations from Babylon to Rome.

Religion as a Fable for Slaves

When Ahania reminds Urizen that he has been compelled to feed his immortal steeds with "intoxication from the wine presses of Luvah," she exposes the corrupt intellectual foundations of empire. The winepresses signify the barbaric magic and military vengeance upon which rose Luvah's tribal chieftaincy. Now we are told that Urizen, despite his fine cities and urban scholars, must ultimately rest his throne on those same props. He must relinquish his steeds of science to drink the "wine of the Almighty," because, like Solomon, he is forced to clothe his despotism in divinity. Thus, in addition to cosmopolitan erudition, backward Canaanite fetishism comes to characterize Urizen's temple. Theocratic civilization enters into a pact with Luvah and into secret intercourse with Vala, the goddess of primeval darkness who had "now become Urizens harlot / And the Harlot of Los & the deluded harlot of the Kings of Earth" (FZ 91:14–15). Eternal science, as Ahania reminds him, is mercy, but his regime cannot stand its light. The cults of ignorance must be sustained to provide illusions for power, the worship of alien nature transformed into a homage to alien rulers for whom the temple has become a gigantic coverup operation:

And in the inner part of the Temple wondrous workmanship
They formd the Secret place reversing all the order of delight
That whosoever enterd into the temple might not behold
The hidden wonders allegoric of the Generations
Of secret lust when hid in chambers dark the nightly harlot
Plays in Disguise in whisperd hymn & mumbling prayer The priests
He ordaind & Priestesses clothd in disguises beastial
Inspiring secrecy & lamps they bore intoxicating fumes. (FZ 96:1–8)

The diversion of the chariot of intellect to these ignoble ends might have been suggested to Blake by biblical descriptions of royalty using the chariot as a symbol of their elevation above the ordinary pedestrian masses; both Absalom and Adonijah had used chariots to assert their regal pretensions (2 Sam. 15:1; I Kings 1:5). Moreover, as part of the sun cult, the chariot had entered the enthronement rites. Thus, when Josiah reformed the temple cult, he "removed the horses which the kings of Judah had dedicated to the sun, at the entrance of the house of the Lord . . . and he burned the chariots of the sun with fire" (I Kings 23:11). Consequently, Blake explains, what is ultimately involved in Urizen's diversion of the chariot from its role in guiding man is a royal arrogance which seeks instead to subordinate both the cosmic power of the sun, and the human invention manifest in the chariot, to its own glorification:

& they took the Sun that glowd oer Los
And with immense machines down rolling. the terrific orb
Compell'd. The Sun reddning like a fierce lion in his chains
Descended to the sound of instruments that drownd the noise
Of the hoarse wheels & the terrific howlings of wild beasts
That dragd the wheels of the Suns chariot & they put the Sun
Into the temple of Urizen to give light to the Abyss
To light the War by day to hide his secret beams by night
For he divided day & night in different orderd portions
The day for war the night for secret religion in his temple.

(*FZ* 96:9–18)

This cultural catastrophe, the waste of human intelligence in slavery and war, is depicted in Urizen, who thus represents far more than the overly cerebral psyche of civilized man. From ancient theocracy, to Plato, to the feudal chain of being, hierarchical philosophies have established correspondences between the domination of king over subjects, God over humanity, mind over body, and reason over desire. Reason has been invariably identified with the educated and leisured elite who produced culture, and desire with the vulgar masses who, for some inexplicable reason, lacked an appreciation for such intellectual pursuits and preferred the world of matter, laboring to satisfy their gluttonous bellies. Hence the praise of reason is the elite's self-congratulation and the denigration of desire, a justification for an asceticism imposed upon the people by their masters' parasitism. To give this state of affairs even greater legitimacy, the exploiters invariably claim that it derives from God himself. Blake called such systems "State Religion which is the Source of all Cruelty" (PB 607) and saw Genesis as its primary document.

Thus in Blake's myth Adam and Eve are the creation, not the creators of fallen society; formed when Los "found the Limit of Contraction & namd it Adam / While yet those beings were not born nor knew good or Evil," they represent the lowest state into which "Enslavd humanity" (*FZ* 55:22) can fall without ceasing to be human altogether. For, if the four Zoas in Ezekiel's flaming chariot offer an image of unfallen humanity as a harmonious and self-determining collective empowered by its own incarnate energies, then Genesis presents man in a precisely opposite light—as a child, a dependent, a kind of tenant farmer, and a subject dominated and terrorized by an external lord, like that "wheel without wheel, with cogs tyrannic / Moving by compulsion each other: not as those in Eden: which / Wheel within Wheel in freedom revolve in harmony & peace" (*J* 15:18–20).

For Blake, Genesis is a fable for slaves; it denies human beings self-determination with regard to their own desires, their thoughts, their means of subsistence, their morality, and finally even their lives, all of which they must acknowledge as falling within the domain of a God who, as creator, claims complete authority over human existence. Eve's fundamental challenge, in aspiring to be like God, is, of course, to this principle of hierarchy itself and the stratified society which it implies. The tale revolves around the right of this God to impose his will through arbitrary laws; hence Blake's association of Eden's tree of mystery with the Mosaic law, Urizen's book of iron, and the repression of Orc, the spirit of social revolt:

> For Urizen fixd in Envy sat brooding & coverd with snow
> His book of iron on his knees he tracd the dreadful letters
> While his snows fell & his storms beat to cool the flames of Orc
> Age after Age till underneath his heel a deadly root
> Struck thro the rock the root of Mystery accursd shooting up.
>
> (*FZ* 78:1–5)

The source of his imposition is "envy"; so in *Jerusalem* Albion will fall through selfish possession, claiming, "My mountains are my own, and I will keep them to myself." He immediately justifies his claim with inducements to asceticism: "here will I build my Laws of Moral Virtue!" (*J* 4:29,31). Likewise, the God of Genesis seems more like a harsh landlord than an benevolent father, and his power to deny human appetites not surprisingly serves as the basis for all hypocritical denunciations of human desire; for, as Blake writes, "God made Man happy & Rich but the Subtil made the innocent Poor" (PB 601). Only ignorance could protect such injustice, and Genesis defends it, creating the concept of forbidden knowledge which brands as heretics any who follow Eve in challenging the existing authorities. Finally, however, that order finds its best defense in violence; and Genesis, by imposing capital punishment on Adam and Eve, mirrors the *Theogony* in celebrating a state which rests upon power over its subjects' lives. Lest we still have any doubts, Adam's and Eve's punishment makes it quite clear that Genesis 1–3 is merely a rationale for existing social arrangements, linking the patriarchal family and oppressive labor to the will of God himself so that any revolt against them becomes both futile and blasphemous.

Blake sensed the irony by which a creation myth culminates in a complete denigration of the creativity of man who is henceforth reduced to eking out a living by the sweat of his brow. He expressed that reversal by showing that in fallen society, instead of finding man as Earth-owner, using his furnaces to forge his world, we find Luvah and Vala inside the ovens, reduced to mere elements of production:

They melt the bones of Vala & the bones of Luvah into wedges
The innumerable sons & daughters of Luvah closd in furnaces
Melt into furrows.   (*FZ* 16:1–3)

Similarly, in place of the Zoas triumphantly directing the chariot of creation, we find men yoked like oxen, "the bulls of Luvah," bound to the labors of Urizen:

But Urizen silent descended to the Caves of Orc & saw
A Cavernd Universe of flaming fire the horses of Urizen
Here bound to fiery mangers furious dash their golden hoofs
Striking fierce sparkles from their brazen fetters. fierce his loins
Howl in the burning dens his tygers roam in the redounding smoke
In forests of affliction. the adamantine scales of justice
Consuming in the raging lamps of mercy pourd in rivers
. . . .
The plow of ages & the golden harrow wade thro fields
Of goary blood the immortal seed is nourishd for the slaughter
The bulls of Luvah breathing fire on burning pastures. (*FZ* 77:5–16)

For Urizen to feed the steeds with intoxication from the winepresses of Luvah is ultimately to provide religion as the opium of a people reduced to beasts of burden; in now another sense, "The Horse is of more value than the Man."

The Fall VI: Decline of the Ancient Empires

In the end, as V. Gordon Childe explains, this diversion of intellect meant the end of ancient civilization, whose vast capabilities were thwarted and retarded by an elite fearful for its own power:

Magic and religion constituted the scaffolding to support the rising structure of social organization and of science. Unhappily the scaffolding repeatedly cramped the execution of the design and impeded the progress of the permanent building. It even served to support a sham facade behind which the substantial structure was threatened with decay. The urban revolution, made possible by science, was exploited by superstition. The principal beneficiaries from the achievements of farmers and artisans were priests and kings. Magic rather than science was thereby enthroned and invested with the authority of temporal power.[45]

Urizen's creation is undermined by its dependence upon an unrelenting subjugation of his children; rationality breeds irrationality; wealth yields poverty; and progress turns out in the end to be only a greater retrogression:

Terrific ragd the Eternal Wheels of intellect terrific ragd
The living creatures of the wheels in the Wars of Eternal life
But perverse rolld the wheels of Urizen & Luvah back reversd
Downwards & outwards consuming in the wars of Eternal Death.

(FZ 20:12–15)

Finally, Urizen's "mundane shell" collapses altogether in a second flood that overwhelms all the cultures of the ancient world:

Now all comes into the power of Tharmas. Urizen is falln
And Luvah hidden in the Elemental forms of Life & Death
Urthona is My Son   O Los thou art Urthona & Tharmas
Is God. The Eternal Man is seald never to be deliverd
I roll my floods over his body my billows & waves pass over him
The Sea encompasses him & monsters of the deep are his companions
Dreamer of furious oceans cold sleeper of weeds & shells. *(FZ 51:12–18)*

At this point we have reached those "dark ages" in which man retreats into barbarism, reduced like a dumb brute to struggling for survival in the hostile wilderness of nature. When Urizen re-emerges in Night VI to rebuild civilization in the Industrial Revolution, he realizes the disaster he has been suffering since that fall: "I lose my powers weakend every revolution till a death / Shuts up my powers then a seed in the vast womb of darkness" *(FZ 73:8–9)*. Urizen's plight suggests the decline of science in those eras when human activity is so totally swallowed up in agricultural drudgery that no one can produce artifacts of intelligence. Blake's reliance on biblical history, his comparative ignorance of the Middle Ages, and his view of the medieval period as devoid of progress lead to a waning of concrete historical reference in these books; finally, in Night VI the frequency of Miltonic and contemporary allusions indicates that we have finally reached modern Europe.

What is addressed here is a theory of history, the chain of generations which Frye has termed the "Orc cycle," as a struggle of human labor against nature, repression, and intellectual delusion. The material situation could not be worse. Enion, once a benevolent mother earth nurturing her offspring, now wanders "in the dismal air / Only a voice eternal wailing in the Elements" *(FZ 46:6–7)*. Her abandoned offspring, Los and Enitharmon, wander in the world of experience without culture or technology, shelter or nourishment, competing with the beasts for mere physical subsistence:

Why does the Raven cry aloud and no eye pities her?
Why fall the Sparrow & the Robin in the foodless winter?
Faint! shivering they sit on leafless bush, or frozen stone
Wearied with seeking food across the snowy waste. *(FZ 17:2–5)*

Man acquires a fallen body, characterized not only by the restricted perception often remarked upon by the critics, but also by the pain, disease, extremities of cold and heat, and starvation typical of such improverishment: "In ghastly torment sick. within his ribs bloated round / A craving hungry cavern . . . a tongue of hunger / And thirst" (*FZ* 55:1–4).

There is no alternative for humanity in such circumstances but painfully to restore production, so Tharmas calls upon the fallen Urthona to revive his labors:

> I will compell thee to rebuild by these my furious waves
> Death choose or life thou strugglest in my waters, now choose life
> And all the Elements shall serve thee to their soothing flutes
> Their sweet inspiriting lyres thy labours shall administer. (*FZ* 52:1–4)

The conditions are not auspicious: Urthona's tools are gone and the furnaces in ruins; labor has been disorganized and scattered, and poverty saps his powers. Blake understood the limits placed by material circumstances upon human creativity, having urged those who ignored them to reflect upon "the State of Nations under Poverty and their incapability of Art" (PB 551), so he empathizes with Los's fears here as he begins the terrible tasks of reconstruction:

> Then Los with terrible hands seizd on the Ruind Furnaces
> Of Urizen. Enormous work: he builded them anew
> Labour of Ages in the Darkness & the war of Tharmas.
> (*FZ* 52:15–17)

The emphasis here, as in no poetry but Blake's, is on the "enormous work" which is the unacknowledged prerequisite of all higher culture. Here Los is tending diligently the furnaces, forming the anvils, mills, and works of many wheels, pouring the molten iron, hammering the metals, and beating out the material links of which history itself is composed:

> in his hand the thundering
> Hammer of Urthona. forming under his heavy hand the hours
> The days & years. in chains of iron round the limbs of Urizen
> Linkd hour to hour & day to night & night to day & year to year.
> (*FZ* 52:28–53:3)

In assuming this arduous task, Los must also forge a vision of history so that present exertions might be directed towards that future when mankind will have built more than "a bower in the midst of all [Tharmas's] dashing waves" (*FZ* 49:19)—rather, a new Atlantis in which a people no longer worried about mere survival can strike sparks of genius off golden anvils, engaging wholly in the "Labours of Art & Science."

Christianity as Mystery Cult

The story of Los's failure in his mission and of history's subsequent decline into centuries of futility is told in Nights IV and V as the degeneration of prophetic Christianity. With the promise of liberation denied at every turn, Los cannot illuminate a path beyond the immediate facts of experience, succumbing to the prime heresy in Blake's canon—fatality:

> The Prophet of Eternity beat on his iron links & links of brass
> And as he beat round the hurtling Demon. terrified at the Shapes
> Enslavd humanity put on he became what he beheld
> Raging against Tharmas his God & uttering
> Ambiguous words blasphemous filld with envy firm resolvd
> On hate Eternal in his vast disdain he labourd beating
> The links of fate link after link in an endless chain of sorrows.
>
> (*FZ* 53:22–28)

His subsequent lapse into a frenzied medieval dance of death signifies the transformation of apocalyptic Christianity into a religion of despair, courting death to the ethereal polyphony of cathedral choirs: "the sweet sound of silver voices calm the weary couch / Of Enitharmon but her groans drown the immortal harps" (*FZ* 58:4–5):

> Infected Mad he dancd on his mountains high & dark as heaven
> Now fixd into one stedfast bulk his features stonify
> From his mouth curses & from his eyes sparks of blighting
> Beside the anvil cold he dancd with the hammer of Urthona.
>
> (*FZ* 57:1–4)

The "anvil cold" denotes an ideology that has abandoned all connection with the human project of building Jerusalem, preferring the heights and obscurity of heaven, while the fact that Los begins to "stonify" like Urizen suggests that the prophet has succumbed to the hardness of heart of a new state religion.

This potential for inversion, Blake grasped, arose from the contradictory traditions that merged in Christianity in the first place. The distinction of these two weltanschauungs—mystery and prophecy—will be crucial for understanding his analysis of Milton. We have already described the appropriation of the tribal fertility cult by the monarchy. Even more insidious, perhaps, was the manner in which it permeated the culture of the oppressed in the ancient mystery religions which intoxicated urban populations, especially when incorporated into Christianity. Blake elaborates these relationships in Luvah who is the old Adonis of natural religion, Jesus, and the enslaved masses. As the dying and rising god, we find Luvah associated with the reincarnating snake, with sacrifice, with the bread and wine of the divine meal (the *omphagia*), and with its promised communion with divinity. Because he is a slave, his sacrifice has become a symbol of suffering humanity while his preservation of tribal rites of solidarity signifies its actual survival in the shared misery and labor of the oppressed:[46]

> the Divine Lamb Even Jesus who is the Divine Vision
> Permitted all lest Man should fall into Eternal Death
> For when Luvah sunk down himself put on the robes of blood
> Lest the state calld Luvah should cease. & the Divine Vision
> Walked in robes of blood till he who slept should awake.
>
> (FZ 33:11–15)

Once sacrificed that the crops might live, now a victim of human cruelty, Luvah becomes the Lamb whose offering, it is hoped, will appease cosmic enemies and the model of a death, which again it is hoped, will lead to a life everlasting. Once a figure of tribal brotherhood, now Luvah expresses the love and community which survives in a humanity that now has in common only its terrible misery:

> Eternity appeard above them as One Man infolded
> In Luvah[s] robes of blood & bearing all his afflictions.
>
> (FZ 13:8–9)

George Thomson's researches indicate that Blake's metaphoric associations carry a profound historical insight. He argues that the mystery cults, which appeared in Greece and spread throughout the Roman Empire, had their origins in an agrarian magic kept alive by dispossessed peasants, nostalgic for a lost tribal unity. As these people fell into debt and slavery, the old rites, which once initiated a candidate into full tribal status through a symbolic death and rebirth, came to mean the passage into a better life after death. As Thomson explains, "Robbed of their birthright, the exploited and dispossessed turn away in despair from the real world towards the hope of recovering their lost heritage in an illusory world to come."[47] With this alteration, all the old symbols and ceremonies are transformed. The old communal meal, where a whole society once shared the fruits and the energies of its common harvest, in a fragmented society becomes a ritual through which a band of believers, turning to each other for mutual solace, seek relief in a mystical community and absorption into the divine. They yearn for a redeemer (which once literally meant a man who bought slaves their freedom), but since it is now life itself from which they seek deliverance, they seek a redeemer who can show them the way through the grave.

Thomson shows how the mystical and dualistic vision of reality found in such mystery cults as Orphism ultimately originated in the lives of slaves who experienced their bodies as organs of pain, not instruments of delight:

> According to Orphic doctrine, life is a penance by which man atones for the sin of the Titans. The immortal part of him is encased in the mortal; the soul is imprisoned in the body. The body is the tomb of the soul. We are the chattels of the gods, who will release us when they choose to do so, from the prison house of life. All life is a rehearsal for death. Only through death can the soul hope to escape from its imprisonment and find deliverance from the evils of the body.[48]

This exact process is dramatized in *The Four Zoas* when Albion falls under Luvah's cloud and in complete self-abnegation projects an alienated aspect of his own consciousness into a spirit-world which he then worships as divine:

> Then Man ascended mourning into the splendors of his palace
> Above him rose a Shadow from his wearied intellect
> Of living gold, pure, perfect, holy; in white linen pure he hover'd
> A sweet entrancing self delusion, a watry vision of Man
> Soft exulting in existence all the Man absorbing
>
> Man fell upon his face prostrate before the watry shadow
> Saying O Lord whence is this change thou knowest I am nothing
> . . . .
> Idolatrous to his own Shadow words of Eternity uttering
> O I am nothing when I enter into judgment with thee
> If thou withdraw thy breath I die & vanish into Hades
> . . . .
> O I am nothing & to nothing must return again.   (*FZ* 40:1–16)

Why such mental perversity? Is the whole history of mankind, then, to be traced back to a penchant for self-delusion? Blake implies a more satisfactory explanation when he associates this mystification in Luvah with the phenomenon of slavery. Likewise, the posture that Albion adopts here as a subject before his lord hints that a cosmos divided between human and supernatural dimensions mirrors a society that divides masters from slaves. For the same reason, Urizen's assertion of his monarchy has simultaneously involved his ascension as both a split-off part of human consciousness and as a god. Blake suggests here that it is because the master actually takes over the mind and the will of the toiler, leaving the slave to feel like the puppet of another's consciousness and will, that religion can develop as a projection of this split. That state religion then presents the image of humanity worshiping a divinity outside itself, which, Blake insists, is really the reflection of its own lost mental powers.

The situation inevitably involves a second split as well, for the subjugated now experience the material world as an antagonistic reality, completely out of human control. This deranged relationship occurs when Albion loses Jerusalem and falls under the spell of Vala. The romantic agonies of Luvah and Vala, while on one level dramatizing a perverted sexuality, also depict the torments of an enslaved humanity facing nature as a temptress who frustrates human desires and as a tyrant who drains human powers.

Under such circumstances, says Blake, the separation of the worker from consciousness and the thinker from material activity has produced the dualistic conception of a world divided into matter and spirit.[49] We have seen how the theocracy elevated its intellectual control into a supernatural realm; in the mystery cults, a complementary vision emerged from the experience of the oppressed. Deprived of both pleasure and conscious will, struggling under the command of external lords, enthralled to a bodily life which they cannot control, human beings fall into the error of rejecting the body instead of the master. The miserable wretch, attempting to withdraw his consciousness as far as possible from his immediate pain, invents for distraction a daydream world where he is free and happy. With his real energies fallen, Albion wanders in a land of dreams. In this schizophrenic state, the dreamworld into which one pours all one's stifled affections and creativity begins to seem like a separate and more vivid self. Hence the error develops "That Man has two real existing principles Viz: a Body & a Soul" (*MHH* 4). Blake's analysis here resembles Hegel's in *The Phenomenology of Spirit*, a spiritual history of mankind written at the same time as *The Four Zoas*. There, Hegel analyzes the psyche's division between two separate beings, lord and bondsman, and its subsequent reintegration in a divided form as the "unhappy consciousness" of medieval religion: "The Alienated Soul which is the consciousness of self as a divided nature, a doubled and merely contradictory being."[50] In religion, the oppressed conceive the fantastic project of releasing the dreaming self entirely from its painful bodily experience. Unlike those religions that merely urge submission to the ruler-god, the mystery cults offer a vision of liberation through reunion with this being who has all those qualities denied the self, who can make the imaginary world real and lead one from the hell of thralldom into the loving community and complete gratification of a spiritual kingdom. These dialectics form the internal structure of *The Four Zoas* in which a "Division" (*FZ* 4:4) identified with the fragmentation and stratification of the community and the fall of Urthona, the free craftsman, produces both an alienation of nature, the Emanation, and an estranged self-consciousness, the Spectre.

Christianity as Prophecy

Nevertheless, out of oppression there also arose an alternative vision, one that demanded the realization of human hopes in an actual future rather than in a fantasy world. The basis for this perspective may be found in the Jewish prophets who led people to seek their liberation neither in transcendence of the body, nor in a life after death, but rather in the entire community's movement towards a restoration of Eden in history. Rooted in a community that had not yet experienced the atomization which produced yearnings for individual salvation in the classical world, the prophets were less interested in encouraging passage into a spiritual realm than in pointing the way from slavery to freedom, war to peace, discord to community, and destitution to abundance in a reconstructed nation.

As in the mystery cults, these visions echoed the lost tribal order, for it has been noted that the prophets were "the inheritors and the guardians of that democratic principle which Israel had preserved from nomad days."[51] Here, however, where Yahweh had long since been transformed from a sky god to an ancestral "God of the fathers" and eventually the nation's leader through its historical vicissitudes, the social ethos had been preserved independent of primitive nature cult.[52] While Yahweh's voice in the storm becomes increasingly metaphoric, his role as a guarantor of justice continually deepens.

What uniquely characterized Israel was its postion at the crossroads of civilization at a time when the continual confrontation between invading tribes and advanced states made it into a crucible for the development of its historical self-consciousness.[53] Even more unique was the influence wielded by so democratic a social vision. We can understand it if we realize that the prophets were the leaders of popular elements of a national liberation struggle. In such cases the need for consolidation against a common enemy may lead an elite to tolerate or even temporarily to embrace the egalitarian traditions of the people, raising the national flag as a banner of freedom against the autocratic institutions of its enemies. Thus the prophets, despite the subversive implications of their ideas, by merging the issue of justice with that of national destiny, found their way into that great national epic, the Bible.

We need not recount here the stories of those righteous men who, like Amos, came down from the hills to raise the complaints of poor peasants and herdsmen against aristocratic arrogance. Arising in direct oppostion to the monarchy, the prophets turned the events of Jewish history into symbols of the people's democratic aspirations. For example, when the exiled nation longed for Jerusalem as a symbol of restoration, the prophets expressed the hopes of the masses for a "New Jerusalem" based upon prosperity and justice. In like manner, Isaiah transformed the Davidic covenant from a rationale for absolute monarchy into the promise of a deliverer, a just king who would lead the poor back into the paradise from which they had been banished.

In the syncretistic environment of the Roman Empire, Christianity arose out of a matrix in which the ideas of mystery and prophecy mingled among the masses, producing for example in the contemporary Essenes a combination of Gnostic asceticism and Jewish egalitarianism. In a Jerusalem characterized by peasant discontent, labor strife, and national resistance, Jesus's revival of the prophetic promise made him the center of tumultuous popular agitation.[54] His message ran directly counter to the validation of the status quo fround in Genesis: God is not the sanctifier of hierarchy, but the guarantor of equality, having become incarnate in Jesus and in all his followers. Paradise has not been lost, nor does sin justify the people's misery; all sins are forgiven, and the kingdom of God is at hand. Entering Jerusalem on an ass, Jesus was hailed as the Messiah by crowds who surely expected actual liberation. His message to them was provocative: the law is done away with, the wisdom of the simple is superior to the erudition of the rabbis, human beings owe allegiance to none but God, the wealthy are barred from the kingdom of heaven, but the poor will inherit the earth. Despising the morality of the respectable, Jesus taught one commandment, admonishing the oppressed to "love one another," an injunction which under these circumstances was a celebration of their intuitive solidarity and a call to get themselves together. And they did, in congregations which the Acts of the Apostles tell us abolished social distinctions, established communal ownership of goods, and cared for the poor, leading Ernest Renan to comment, "If I wanted to give you an idea of the early Christian communities, I would tell you to look at a section of the International Working Men's Association."[55]

Jesus apparently had no intention of leading an uprising, but his claim to be the deliverer, arousing the people as it did, was sufficient to get him executed, not for blasphemy but for sedition. Blake, at any rate, seemed to think of him as revolutionary, remarking to Henry Crabb Robinson, "He should not have attacked the government" or "sufferd himself to be crucified."[56] Whether the poet is being ironic here, or whether he is arguing that Jesus, like Milton, should have stuck to his mission of creating a revolutionary consciousness and left the politicking to others, is not clear. But in *The Everlasting Gospel* Blake clearly identifies Jesus's greatness with his courageous advocacy of a radical vision, abjuring the "Sneaking submission" that "can always live" and "Cursing the Rulers before the People" (PB 511) in complete disregard for his own safety.

As Joseph Wittreich has conclusively demonstrated, the most important book of the Bible for Blake was the Apocalypse. It was there that he found Christ presented entirely as a liberator who would lead his people in an assault on the powers of "this world." Written twenty years after the siege of Jerusalem, that book draws upon prophecies circulating during the brave, if hopeless, insurrection of Jewish nationalists against the Roman Empire in 70 A.D. in a moment when a people, tantalized by centuries of promises, sought to turn them into fact. There also we find the transformation of that prophetic tradition as it was wrested from a defeated and dispersed Israel by plebeian Christians who claimed the vision of democratic Jewish nationalism for all oppressed people, making the liberated Jerusalem a symbol for a completely reconstructed world order where there will be neither mourning nor pain.

Nights IV and V describe the emergence of this radical, egalitarian outlook and its subsequent absorption back into the reactionary errors of mystery and state religion. At the end of Night IV, we meet the daughters of Beulah mourning over "the Body / Of Man clothd in Luvahs robes of blood" (*FZ* 55:10–11). The allusions here to the emtombed Christ, the dead Lazarus, and the lamentations for Adonis mean that Christianity is in one aspect another mystery cult, worshiping, as Frye puts it, the "death principle."[57] The passage recalls that Easter morning when the women are still looking for Jesus in the grave, while he has already risen and gone to join his disciples. Fixed in pious paralysis at the entrance to a tomb, which for mystery is the gateway to another life, they are seeking refuge and dreamy repose in which they "may be hidden under the Shadow of wings" (*FZ* 56:8), rather than liberation.

The Saviour's response, "If ye will Believe your Brother shall rise again" (*FZ* 56:18), promises on the contrary a resurrection of Albion which in Blake's system is the restoration of the shattered community. Thus immediately upon pronouncement of this vision "wondrously the Starry Wheels felt the divine hand" (*FZ* 56:23). Given Blake's humanism, this assertion of providence can only mean that history is once again being claimed by the human hands which alone can abolish the tyranny of astronomical cycles of destiny. The appearance of Luvah as both victim and redeemer, which interpreted by mystery proclaims suffering as the path to salvation, for prophetic Christianity is an affirmation of the power of the "weak things of this world" to deliver all creation into the glorious liberty of the children of God—once, that is, they have learned the age-old wisdom which distinguishes these opposing visions: "Don't mourn, organize!"

In these passages, Blake is turning an orthodox theological confla- tion of three biblical events—the birth, resurrection, and second coming of Christ—to a radical conclusion. By switching the focus from a transcendent deity and Jesus as his individual manifestation to an identification of Jesus as Luvah with the enslaved Albion, the lost brotherhood and the divinity incarnate in the overburdened masses, Blake gives this analogy a profound historical meaning. The birth of Jesus comes to signify the first stirrings of Albion, when Luvah is reborn in Orc and the dormant people have revealed to them for the first time their own potential power. What theologians call "salvation history" becomes precisely that, but with one alteration: now it is the history of the people's struggles to liberate themselves. And the birth of Jesus retains its central position in that history because for Blake the gospel of Jesus was the first appearance of a universal ideology of the oppressed.

These implications pervade Blake's treatments of Jesus, particu- larly the association of his birth with that of the rebellious Orc:

> The Wheels of turning darkness
> Began in solemn revolutions. Earth convulsd with rending pangs
> . . . .
> The winter spread his wide black wings across from pole to pole
> . . . .
> The groans of Enitharmon shake the skies the labring Earth
> Till from her heart rending his way a terrible Child sprang forth
> In thunder smoke & sullen flames & howlings & fury & blood.
> (*FZ* 58:7–18)

Like Jesus, Orc is born, as Northrop Frye has so marvelously put it, "in the dark frozen terror of the winter solstice, when all things seem to be gathering together for a plunge into an abyss of annihilation."[58] We recognize it as the "Darkness & the war of Tharmas" (*FZ* 52:17) when the accelerating decay of ancient civilization is bringing human history to its nadir. The appearance of Christianity at this time reveals to Blake the dialectical principle by which an oppressive society produces not only its own gravedigger, but also the foundations of a totally new order. Thus the appearance of Jesus-Orc, foretold by the prophets, had been feared by Urizen, as by a troubled Herod, as the coming of that deliverer who would overthrow their rule:

> O bright *[Ahania]* a Boy is born of the dark Ocean
> Whom Urizen doth serve, with Light replenishing his darkness
> I am set here a King of trouble commanded here to serve
> And do my ministry to those who eat of my wide table
> All this is mine yet I must serve & that Prophetic boy
> Must grow up to command his prince but hear my determind Decree
> Vala shall become a worm in Enitharmons Womb
> Laying her seed upon the fibres soon to issue forth
> And Luvah in the loins of Los a dark & furious death
> Alas for me! what will become of me at that dread time? (*FZ* 38:2–11)

Here the prophecy of a messiah who will replace the tyrant on his throne becomes Blake's vision of the social force which will topple all thrones. As a reincarnation of Luvah, Orc represents the arousal of a passively enthralled populace into a fiery, rebellious host. It was this revolt that Ahania had warned Urizen was inevitable unless he released his subjects from their "iron mangers" and abdicated his control over history and "all futurity" in favor of collective humanity, the "Eternal One" (*FZ* 39:5,39:1,38:15).

Orc's social character is also revealed by his Promethean nature, bound to the rock of repression where he rages unrepentant: "Crackling the flames went up with fury from the immortal demon" (*FZ* 61:5). As a recalcitrant craftsman, Prometheus is identified with those "who earn their bread by work" and suffer the curses of labor and hardship. His brother Atlas is Blake's Albion, once "Patriarch of the Atlantic" (PB 534), who now, like the weary multitude, must carry the whole burden of the world on his shoulders. Similarly, Prometheus, the last of the Titans, is a rebel like Orc who struggles with the powers that be over the arts of civilization. Hence this Titan's endurance beyond a tribal era, defeated but unyielding, signifies the way in which the conquered clans, turn into the oppressed strata of a new hierarchic society, and continue the struggle for their birthright under new conditions.

Christianity itself embodies this continuity, representing the reemergence of the everlasting gospel of brotherhood which had been the religion of antiquity. Thus Orc, the descendant of Luvah and Vala, like Jesus and the prophets transmits the ethos of a lost tribal solidarity into the historical world of Enitharmon and Los. As their child

he is also the outgrowth of conditions which bring about his metamorphosis into an angry insurgent. Hence the Titans—devils, rather
than angelic choirs—attend his terrible birth:

> The horrid trumpets of the deep bellowd with bitter blasts
> The Enormous Demons woke & howld around the new born king
> Crying Luvah King of Love thou art the King of rage & death.
> (*FZ* 58:20–22)

The immediate consequence of his appearance is not peace but war in
heaven:

> Urizen cast deep darkness round him raging Luvah pourd
> The spears of Urizen from Chariots round the Eternal tent
> Discord began then yells & cries shook the wide firma[m]ent
> (*FZ* 58:23–25)

These continuities also underlie Blake's iconography in the *Paradise
Lost* engravings where, as Jean Hagstrum notes, "the four Zoas, who
appear broodingly in the sky at the time of the expulsion . . . are fallen
gods yearning for the day that will restore their primal unity." However, as Wittreich adds, they are also the four horsemen of the Apocalypse by which Blake "accomplishes the contrast of beginning and
end, of defeat and triumph."[59] In *The Four Zoas*, these symbols
characterize the forces which move history as well, for the previous
war of the Titans, the present struggle of Orc, and the future victory of
the apocalyptic Christ (the resurrected Albion) are all manifestations
of the same social forces at different stages of history, the collective
multitude which was overthrown with the tribal clan, reasserted
itself throughout the whole history of class struggle, and would
finally reconstruct its unity and freedom in a future liberation.

For this reason, the "divine vision" emerges out of the very sufferings of Orc, the crucified savior whose rage against repression fuels
his imagination, intensifies his aspiration to full human realization:

> His limbs bound down mock at his chains for over them a flame
> Of circling fire unceasing plays to feed them with life & bring
> The virtues of the Eternal worlds ten thousand thousand spirits
> · · · · · · · ·
> To bring the thrilling joys of sense to quell his ceaseless rage
> His eyes the lights of his large soul contract or else expand
> Contracted they behold the secrets of the infinite mountains
> · · · · · · · ·
> Expanded they behold the terrors of the Sun & Moon
> · · · · · · · ·
> His bosom is like the starry heaven expanded all the stars
> Sing round. there waves the harvest & the vintage rejoices. the Springs
> Flow into rivers of delight. (*FZ* 61:11–29)

Nevertheless, the binding of Orc in the cycle of Generations shows the failure of the ancient poor and their successors to throw off their shackles even up to Blake's own era. His binding by Los, a renegade prophet, demonstrates the role played by a perverted Christianity in forming the "mind forg'd manacles" which forestall victory. Blake is concerned here with the import of Jesus's crucifixion which—Frye to the contrary notwithstanding—is also the chaining of Orc and the consolidation of both actual terror and ideological delusion. Thus Blake jotted in the manuscript his fear that "Christs crucifix shall be made an excuse for Executing criminals" (PB 753). However, physical repression alone was inadequate to stifle the apocalyptic expectations of the suffering Orc. Unless the everlasting gospel be effaced from people's consciousness, an ever present threat remained. So it was necessary for Urizen to seek an ally in Los who would crucify mankind when he "piercd the Lamb of God in pride & wrath" (FZ 113:52) by preaching submission to natural limitation and social tyranny and salvation through martyrdom.

Christianity, as an eclectic religion, merging prophetic radicalism with legacies from both mystery cult and theocratic traditions, could easily be given such a conservative cast. With the destruction of Jewish messianism and the radical church of Jerusalem, what remained dominant was Paul's integration of Jesus, the executed revolutionary, into the mysteries of death and rebirth. The cross, which might have symbolized a hated tyranny and repression, thus became an emblem of purification through suffering and sacrifice of life to afterlife. The idea that "the kingdom of God is among you" loses its sense as an affirmation of community and a democratic affirmation of the equality of all people and becomes translated only as a kingdom of God which is "within you," advocating psychological retreat from sensuous reality.[60] Eventually a new Christian elite would resurrect the Jewish state religion, against which Jesus had railed, into a defense of feudal hierarchy. So the kingdom of righteousness reverts to the kingdoms of David and Solomon, and the prophet's inverted vision is turned right side up again as Jesus himself is elevated into another king-god enthroned in metaphysical heavens.

Later, as all this sorry history draws to its climax in Blake's own era, he shows Los, the misguided visionary, acknowledging these crimes against humanity:

> I am that shadowy Prophet who six thousand years ago
> Fell from my station in the Eternal Bosom. I divided
> To multitude & my multitudes are children of Care & Labour.
> . . . .

Hear me repeat my Generations that thou mayst also repent.
                                                        (*FZ* 113:48–53)

His generations include those of David, Solomon, Paul, Constantine, Charlemagne, Luther, and Milton (*FZ* 115:5–6). But, we might ask, what is Milton, the scourge of monarchy, doing in the company of these kings and defenders of kings? For the answer, we now turn to a Blakean analysis of *Paradise Lost* where all these traditions culminate in a political vision which renders Blake's precursor as both the greatest and most problematic of prophets.

PART III

Paradise Lost: A Blakean Reading

8

The Politics of Paradise Lost and The Four Zoas

Hegel remarks somewhere that all facts and personages of great importance in world history occur, as it were, twice. He forgot to add: the first time as tragedy, the second time as farce. —Marx

*A*s we pass from *Paradise Lost* to *The Four Zoas*, from the combats of God and Satan to those of Urizen and Luvah-Orc, we seem to have entered one of those vortexes in which the world is suddenly turned upside down. The "Omnipotent, / Immutable, Immortal, Infinite / Eternal King" (*PL* III.372–74) who reigned in calm dignity enthroned in a masterpiece of ideological architecture has been reduced to a mad, impotent despot roaming helplessly in an abyss of intellectual and social chaos. Yet even more remarkable is how much of this parody could be drawn from Milton himself; as Malcolm Ross comments: "In *Paradise Lost* God is Caesar. The order of the universe is no longer a mathematical harmony drenched in light, but a mighty tyranny. . . . God is the utter and absolute despot ruling by decree, crushing revolt and dissension by military force."[1] Similarly, Blake's transmutation of Satan into the terrible fiery demon whose revolt challenges that dominion has its roots in the dense political allusions of Milton's poem. There, we are immediately thrust into the "fowl revolt" of "Rebel Angels" who "trusted to have equal'd the most High" and "with ambitious aim / Against the Throne and Monarchy of God / Rais'd impious War in Heav'n" and "durst defie th' / Omnipotent to Arms" (*PL* I.33–49).

Thus, one's immediate impression is that the poem seems more likely to have been written by Archbishop Laud than the republican Milton. In the eighteenth century, this sense produced the argument, quoted earlier, that the epic was Milton's political recantation.[2] On the other hand, Blake's observation that Milton "wrote in fetters when he wrote of Angels & God, and at liberty when of Devils & Hell" because he was "of the Devils party without knowing it" (*MHH* 6) initiated a long debate over the real allegiances of his poem. At this stage, the critical consensus seems to be that Milton remained decidedly in the camp of the angels, using all his philosophic and poetic weapons to deflate the pretensions of his aspiring demons. From this verdict Blake would not demur; for it was, after all, to reverse his precursor's judgments that he had offered his own truly diabolical version of the epic in *The Four Zoas*. Nevertheless, I must agree with A. S. P. Woodhouse that the feeling of "innumerable readers . . . that somehow at bottom the antagonist has the poet's sympathy . . . is far too widespread to be simply dismissed."[3]

In this chapter I hope to show that Milton's contradictions arose from ambiguities at the heart of the "Devils party" itself. The progress of the English civil war had been from revolution to repression, from the tyranny of Charles I to Cromwell's revolutionary dictatorship and back to a monarchy overwhelmingly embraced by the same parliament that had instigated its demise. In Blake's day, France seemed hopelessly to be repeating the same weary round, as the insurgency of the early 1790s gave way to Napoleonic empire and eventually the bourgeois monarchy of Louis Phillipe. It is no wonder that, in the midst of this apparent historical replay, Blake was moved to reconsider the forces dramatized in Milton's epic. A century of parliamentary rule and religious toleration, the cornerstones of Milton's program, had so little vindicated his prophetic hopes that Blake might well ask: if Milton were to awaken in a world where his vision of liberty was supposedly realized, might not he too protest: "Whether this is Jerusalem or Babylon we know not" (*FZ* 42:18), and proceed to further revolutions?

This of course was the fantasy realized in Blake's *Milton*. In *The Four Zoas*, the same contradictions would lead Blake to develop Urizen as a monstrous caricature of Milton's God and an expression of his bourgeois society, a system of individual ownership, constitutional oligarchy, and patriarchal monogamy which Blake found very little different from the tyranny it replaced. As he ponders these ironies, his satanic characters begin to change, until the fiery spirit of America and France acquires, by the later epics, an alter ego modeled upon Milton's devious demon. This ambiguity, I will argue, does not represent, as is sometimes thought, a retreat from political radicalism. Rather, by Night IX of *The Four Zoas*, Blake is demanding a transformation of society and culture so total that it constitutes a critique even of those revolutions which have gone before. Hence, this breakthrough demands the reevaluation of Milton's struggle which inspires *The Four Zoas* and the bard's song in *Milton*.

In recognizing this analysis as a call for ongoing revolution, we should not expect to find in Blake the same assessment that a historian would make of Milton's role as he faced the strategic challenges of his own time. It is far easier to criticize revolutions than to make them, especially with hindsight, and far different to imagine Utopias than to achieve them. While it is true that Blake's objections had seventeenth-century precedents in Milton's leftist opposition, it is also true that their program, however prophetic, was not on the historical agenda in that era. Milton's revolution may have revealed its inadequacies by Blake's time; but when the Puritan endorsed it, it was the task of the hour, and one that found few such committed defenders. The leftists' vision of a Jerusalem liberated from all entanglements of privilege would remain, as Milton called it, "fanatick dreams" (YP II.278), awaiting developments which only began in Blake's era and have flowered in ours. Time would vindicate those dreamers as something more than irrational extremists, while leading Milton's own party to the bar of historical judgment. This course of events would inspire Blake's inversion of his forerunner's myth. It cannot, however, be raised ex post facto as an estimation of the Puritan poet himself. Surely, Blake himself never intended this; he compared Milton, even as he repudiated his doctrines, to the great star of Revelation, the undaunted iconoclast, the angel of apocalypse.[4] His respect never faltered for his prophetic precursor, who wedded poetry more totally to humanity's struggle for liberation than anyone before him and very few after. Blake's exposure of Milton's contradictions was primarily intended to clear away ideological clouds from future horizons, for the consciousness he really must purge is that of his own contemporaries. From a new vantage point, they must see beyond the rim of Milton's universe. Arising from a rebirth of Orc representing far broader social forces than those activated in the civil war, Blake's vision is unquestionably more radical. However, Milton was ultimately more of a revolutionary than Blake. For it was Milton who laid aside poetry for polemics, who adapted his utterances to the tortuous shifts of political possibility, and who proclaimed paradise to be lost only after having strained, under the veritable shadow of the executioner, to stave off the growing reaction. It is because Milton saw so far that his own exalted hopes provoke us to question their ambiguous realization. When Blake challenges his limitations in the service of a new insurgency, it is with confidence that he could render no greater honor to his nation's most critical intellectual.

The more one compares the two poets, the more one realizes also how much of Blake's assessment of the politics of religion is offered in Milton's own rhetoric. The traditions we have been exploring were at the very center of Milton's reading of the Bible. In *The Tenure of Kings and Magistrates*, Blake could find Milton describing an egalitarian and communist Eden and attributing both property and magistracy to the Fall. He might note that his predecessor associated Canaan, Babylon, and Egypt with slavery, denounced state religion, traced the history of Israel's fall from a republic into a monarchy, and celebrated subsequent resistance as biblical authority for revolution. From Milton, Blake might also have heard of Christ as a revolutionary who "never failed to preserve the heart of a liberator" (YP IV.375), whose cross was no sign of submission but who rather had come to lift the bondage of the law and initiate a new era of liberty. Finally, in Milton's works Blake would have encountered the great conflict between that Christ and demonic tyranny, foretold in Revelation as an image of the political struggle to be waged on England's own soil.

Inheriting this radical Christian tradition, Blake would bring it to conclusions which redound on Milton himself. The central premises of Blake's analysis are foreshadowed in *The Marriage of Heaven and Hell* where he challenges his precursor's version of that conflict:

> The history of this is written in Paradise Lost. & the Governor or Reason is call'd Messiah.
> And the original Archangel or possessor of the command of the heavenly host, is calld the Devil or Satan and his children are call'd Sin & Death
> But in the Book of Job Miltons Messiah is call'd Satan.
> For this history has been adopted by both parties
> It indeed appear'd to Reason as if Desire was cast out, but the Devils account is, that the Messiah fell and formed a heaven out of what he stole from the Abyss. (*MHH* 5–6)

Three themes emerge here which characterize Blake's re-creation of *Paradise Lost:* (1) in the confrontation between Milton's Messiah and his Satan, Blake suggests, the roles of the liberator and the accuser of Revelation have been reversed; (2) Christ's claim to be a creator is also a ruse, masking his theft from the truly productive demons; (3) behind these reversals lies Milton's hierarchic subordination of a desire, identified by Blake with plebeian imagination and revolt, to a reason embodying bourgeois repression. In the following pages, I hope to show that through his mythic inversions of these contending forces Blake offers, within a study of Milton, an analysis of the entire bourgeois order as a system based upon theft and sustained by political and cultural repression.

Miltonic Liberty and Satanic Despotism

While the revolution's progress caused Milton increasingly to demarcate his position from more radical ones, he never regretted his own libertarian beliefs. On the contrary, he enshrined them, as he promised, in "something so written to aftertimes, as they should not willingly let it die" (YP I.810). To perceive its political bias, we need only set his epic against *The Faerie Queene* in which Spenser proposes to "sing of Knights and Ladies gentle deeds; . . . to blazon broad amongst her learned throng: / Fierce warres and faithful loves." Milton's poem is an explicit rejection of the heroic feudal epic:

> Warrs, hitherto the onely Argument
> Heroic deem'd, chief maistrie to dissect
> With long and tedious havoc fabl'd Knights
> In Battels feign'd; the better fortitude
> Of Patience and Heroic Martyrdom
> Unsung.   *(PL* IX.28–34)

The poet disdains to describe "Races and Games, / Or tilting Furniture, emblazon'd Shields, / Impreses quaint, Caparisons and Steeds . . . gorgious Knights" or any other "tinsel Trappings" *(PL* IX.33–36) of that tradition.

"Chivalry" is derived from the French *chevalerie,* or mounted soldiers; the term came to signify the idealized values of a medieval warrior class. In feudal society rank had allegedly followed function. In the world view outlined in E. M. W. Tillyard's *Elizabethan World Picture,* the medieval social order, like the cosmic, was believed to be organized as a hierarchy of functions, stretching from God and his angels down to inanimate objects, from the king and the nobility down the scale to the gentry and the common people.[5] While the lower classes did all the work, the lords looked after government and war. In fact, they were a military aristocracy whose power ultimately rested upon their monopoly over horses and arms and their private armies of vassals. Milton's polemic against his Homeric models, with their celebration of ancient conquistadors (in many ways like the conquering chiefs who inherited the collapsing Roman Empire), is an attack on this class which had been ruling Europe for so many centuries. A contemporary point might be seen, therefore, in Michael's revelation of the inner decadence behind the apparent grandeur of those ancient realms:

> For in those dayes Might onely shall be admir'd,
> And Valour and Heroic Vertu call'd;
> To overcome in Battel, and subdue

Nations, and bring home spoils with infinite
Man-slaughter, shall be held the highest pitch
Of human Glorie, and for Glorie done
Of triumph, to be styl'd great Conquerours,
Patrons of Mankind, Gods, and Sons of Gods,
Destroyers rightlier call'd and Plagues of men.

(*PL* XI.689–97)

The frequency with which the accusation of "conqueror" appears
(*PL* I.143,323; II.208,338,695) may indicate Milton's acceptance of the
contemporary myth which traced the English ruling class back to
the Norman conquerors who had allegedly abrogated former Saxon
liberty. Milton decried this "Norman villenage" in *Eikonoclastes*
(YP III.581) and, probably also in Samson's protest: "My Nation was
subjected to your Lords. / It was the force of Conquest; force with
force / Is well ejected when the Conquer'd can" (*SA* 1205–07).[6]

To be accurate, Spenser had already gone a long way towards internalizing and moralizing the chivalric epic which had glorified that
class. Spenser was a middle-class Protestant in the service of various
Elizabethan courtiers. In an era when the rising bourgeoisie was
allied with the monarchy to strengthen the nation and undermine
baronial power, the point was to elevate "true" nobility to equality
with merely external status. An ambiguity would long cling to the
concept of a "gentleman" as denoting both social position and ethical
standards. However, with the passage from such alliances to the open
class warfare of the Interregnum, we find Milton torn between co-
opting and utterly rejecting those images, as he does when he makes
his devils the exemplum of knightly glory:

Ten thousand Banners rise into the Air
With Orient Colours waving: with them rose
A Forrest huge of Spears: and thronging Helms
. . . .
Anon they move
In perfect *Phalanx* to the *Dorian* mood
Of Flutes and soft Recorders; such as rais'd
To highth of noblest temper Hero's old
Arming to Battel.   (*PL* I.545–53)

By thus assigning the nobility's crests to Satan's forces (as by contrast-
ing an extravagantly armed Harapha to the pious Samson) Milton
seeks to undermine the claims of a feudal aristocracy. Much of his
ambivalence towards military exploits throughout his epic arises
from the necessity to distinguish the combats of these conquerors

from the divinely inspired battles fought by his own Puritan saints, for whom "force with force / Is well ejected when the Conquer'd can."

At the apex of the social pyramid stood the king, providing in feudal, as in ancient Mesopotamian ideology a virtual link between the heavenly and earthly chain, merging natural and moral superiority. With the strengthening of the central state against noble fiefdoms, this aspect of medieval ideology was intensified, producing the notorious doctrine of "divine right of kings," accurately perceived by Milton as a Canaanitish regression. Thus the king claimed direct supernatural sanction, making him independent of both the general populace and his feudal peers. Milton considered this presumption the supreme heresy in which "the People . . . are prone ofttimes not to a religious onely, but to a civil kinde of Idolatry in idolizing thir Kings; though never more mistak'n in the object of thir worship" (YP III.343). His outrage at the displacement of spiritual values onto material objects, and divine virtues onto human ones, was never more inflamed than when *Eikon Basilike* had aroused "the worthless approbation of an inconstant, irrational, and Image-doting rabble . . . with a new device of the Kings Picture at his praiers" (YP III.601).[7] In defending the execution of Charles I, a step essential in his mind to thwarting counter-revolution, Milton had to face the resiliency of feudal notions that endowed the royal person with a special sacredness: "that the Anointment of God, should be as it were a charme against Law" (YP III.586). And when such fancies were triumphant after 1660 over sober republican virtues, he had to endure the spectacle of Charles II gracing upwards of 92,000 subjects with the laying-on of royal hands.

Milton's contempt for such feudal anachronisms as a kind of papist superstition and pagan throwback suffuses his picture of Satan as a royal despot, claiming the excessive honors of ancient oriental theocracy. Satan appears in Book II "High on a Throne of Royal State, which far / Outshon the wealth of *Ormus* and of *Ind*" like "Kings Barbaric" (*PL* II.1–4). He is "Hells dread Emperour with pomp Supream" (*PL* II.510) who resumes his throne in Book X like a Muscovian potentate or a Turkish sultan mounting his canopied royal divan. The fact that he does so with "God-like imitated State" (*PL* II.511) implies Milton's belief that monarchy seeks to usurp the throne of the Almighty himself. Satan had appeared for heavenly battle, "High in the midst exalted as a God / Th' Apostat in his Sun-bright Chariot sate / Idol of Majestie Divine" (*PL* VI.99–101). And before him, his fellow demons "bend / With awful reverence prone; and as a God / Extoll him" (*PL* II.477–79).

When we meet this pretender again in another sun-god, Urizen, Blake will be developing Milton's even more radical belief that monarchy was idolatrous to man. For he held that the elevation of a single person to godlike state showed disrespect for the image of God that shone forth in all Christian saints. Such dignity belonged preeminently to unfallen man, so Milton depicts Adam and Eve as imbued with an inner nobility surpassing all the superficial trappings of rank or title:

> Godlike erect, with native Honour clad
> In naked Majestie seemd Lords of all,
> And worthie seemd, for in thir looks Divine
> The image of thir glorious Maker shon,
> Truth, Wisdome, Sanctitude severe and pure,
> Severe, but in true filial freedom plac't;
> Whence true autoritie in men.   (*PL* IV.289–95)

Likewise, when these children of God first meet his angelic emissary, Milton dismisses external ceremony and cosmic hierarchy to laud the worth of human beings who can thus converse with angels:

> Meanwhile our Primitive great Sire, to meet
> His god-like Guest, walks forth, without more train
> Accompani'd then with his own compleat
> Perfections, in himself was all his state,
> More solemn then the tedious pomp that waits
> On Princes, when thir rich Retinue long
> Of Horses led, and Grooms besmeard with Gold
> Dazzles the croud.   (*PL* V.350–57)

Milton, who believed that even after the Fall reason was the image of God in us yet remaining, wrote *Paradise Lost* as a paean to the human conscience which existed in Adam and Eve completely untrammeled. As Eve tells the serpent, "we live / Law to our selves, our Reason is our Law" (*PL* IX.653–54). Elsewhere Milton would remark that reason was but choosing, and his intent in portraying man in his native state, prior to all inhibiting circumstances of custom and authority, was to affirm his rightful freedom of conscience. For God had granted man such power for discerning his own morality that all laws, God's included, remain subordinate to his "right reason" so "no ordinance human or from heav'n can binde against the good of man" (YP II.588). Indeed, the consummate purpose of *Paradise Lost* is to impress upon us Milton's conviction that all human destiny rests upon individual moral choices. Although clouded by the Fall, this rational conscience is illuminated by redemption which liberates the Christian "From imposition of strict

Laws, to free / Acceptance of large Grace, from servil fear / To filial" (*PL* XII.304–06).

Satan as Republican Hero

Such ethical self-mastery, according to Milton, implies political self-governance as well.[8] Man reflects the divine image in rule as in reason, having "so many signes of power and rule / Conferrd upon us, and Dominion giv'n / Over all other Creatures" (*PL* IV.429–30). A radical affirmation of the right of wise and pious men to govern themselves is the foundation of Milton's political philosophy. Monarchy is veritable "treason against the dignitie of mankind" (YP III.204), negating that "pious and just honouring of our selves" (YP I.841) which is appropriate to the virtuous man. For, as Raphael admonishes Adam, "Oft times nothing profits more / Then self-esteem, grounded on just and right / Well manag'd" (*PL* VIII.571–73).

All Milton's politics, he tells us, derived from two principles, "This liberty of conscience which above all other things ought to be to all men dearest and most precious, no government more inclinable . . . to protect, then a free Commonwealth" (YP VII.456) and the "other part of our freedom" which "consists in the civil rights and advancements of every person according to his merit" (YP VII.458). These premises led him along an increasingly radical path in those civil war years. In the antiprelatical tracts he upheld the rights of conscience against episcopal intrusions which threatened to bind those of highest moral principle to their inferiors' carnal understandings imposed through civil force. Supporting Parliament against church and court, Milton's own enlightened conscience soon led him to conclusions about divorce which placed him in opposition even to that august body. Finding himself denounced alongside radicals and heretics of every stripe, he pleaded in *Areopagitica* for freedom of speech for all Christian revolutionaries. The unwillingness of a Presbyterian Parliament, determined to impose its own doctrine and discipline, to concede such liberty led him into the camp of Independency and toleration. Eventually, he renounced all established religion and the tithes that supported it.

Meanwhile, the desperate efforts of the king to shore up his waning power convinced Milton that monarchy was incompatible with individual freedom. The Royalists' inclination to set the king above the law, to allow his personal whim to override his subjects' rights, would leave the people bereft of their native right to self-government. Milton believed that citizens should yield authority only to true moral superiority, which the kings of England with their extravagance and sloth had scarcely shown themelves to possess. All other deference must call upon ignorant custom; but if the "dim reflexion of hollow antiquities" (YP I.822) was to be arbiter of human affairs, what then was to become of the whole effort of the Reformation to remove the historical encrustations of falsehood by the beam of enlightened conscience? Thus by a zealous fidelity to believers' rights to order their own private lives Milton followed the logic of revolution from a denunciation of the bishops to the execution of Charles I. By 1649, he was championing the English people's right to sweep away all established forms of power and to devise for themselves a new government by the light of faith and reason.[9]

Having established this history, we must face the seeming contradiction that no voice in *Paradise Lost* appears to speak more clearly in the tones of Milton's prose than that of his arch-villain Satan. Milton's occasional reference to Satan as a monarch appears as mere surface embellishment compared to the fact that he stands at the center of the drama as the incarnation of revolution, echoing the arguments, indeed the very words, of his own defense of the good old cause. Before we proceed to the qualifications that will distinguish Milton's revolution from Satan's, let us observe these parallels. Consider, for example, Milton's plea in 1659 against returning to monarchy:

> It may be well wonderd that any Nation styling themselves free, can suffer any man to pretend hereditarie right over them as thir lord; when as by acknowledging that right, they conclude themselves his servants and his vassals, and so renounce thir own freedom . . . into the base necessitie of court flatteries and prostrations, is not only strange . . . but lamentable to think on; . . . basely and besottedly to run their necks again into the yoke which they have broken, and prostrate all the fruits of thir victorie for naught at the feet of the vanquishd, besides our loss of glorie, and such an example as kings or tyrants never yet had the like to boast of, will be an ignominie if it befall us, that never yet befell any nation possesd of thir libertie; worthie indeed themselves . . . to be for ever slaves.   (YP VII.427–28)

What greater shame, Milton asks, than "to creep back so poorly as it seems the multitude would to thir once abjur'd and detested thraldom of Kingship" (YP VII.422), bound again to the "perpetual bowings and cringings of an abject people, on either side deifying and adoring him for nothing don that can deserve it?" (YP VII.426).

Turning to *Paradise Lost*, we find the very ring of Milton's "injur'd merit" (*PL* I.98) in Satan's proud self-assertions. He too disdains to "bow and sue for grace / With suppliant knee, and deifie his power" (*PL* I.111–12) or in an "abject posture . . . To adore the Conquerour"

(*PL* I.322–23), to "cringe, not fight" (*PL* IV.945). Milton's denunciations of custom are turned against heaven's king who has always "Sat
on his Throne, upheld by old repute, / Consent or custome"
(*PL* I.639–40). "Whom reason hath equald," Satan contends, only
"force hath made supream" (*PL* I.248). Mammon, sharing Milton's
distaste for humiliating courtly protocol, also shares his proud
refusal of reconciliation:

> Suppose he should relent
> And publish Grace to all, on promise made
> Of new Subjection; with what eyes could we
> Stand in his presence humble, and receive
> Strict Laws impos'd, to celebrate his Throne
>   . . . .
>   while he Lordly sits
> Our envied Sovran, and his Altar breathes
> Ambrosial Odours and Ambrosial Flowers,
> Our servile offerings.   (*PL* II.237–46)

Rejecting this state of "splendid vassalage," Mammon, like Milton
(and Samson), urges his comrades to reject all easy compromise
which would prefer "Bondage with ease" to "strenuous liberty"
(*SA* 271). Mammon addresses them:

> [Let us] rather seek
> Our own good from our selves, and from our own
> Live to our selves, though in this vast recess,
> Free, and to none accountable, preferring
> Hard liberty before the easie yoke
> Of servile Pomp.   (*PL* II.252–57)

Moreover, what Satan revolts against is the extremely authoritarian monarchy in heaven. Blake called its God "Our Father
Augustus Caesar" (*PB* 658); and indeed what literary character anywhere has been so obsessed with his own power as Milton's God?
Heaven is an elaborate feudal court where

> th' Empyreal Host
> Of Angels by Imperial summons call'd,
> Innumerable before th' Almighties Throne
> Forthwith from all the ends of Heav'n appeerd
> Under thir Hierarchs in orders bright
> Ten thousand thousand Ensignes high advanc'd,
> Standards, and Gonfalons twixt Van and Reare
> Streame in the Aire, and for distinction serve
> Of Hierarchies, of Orders, and Degrees.   (*PL* V.583–91)

When Blake merged *Paradise Lost*, the Old Testament, and ancient

npire in *The Four Zoas*, he was only mimicking Milton who
esigned heaven as a full-fledged theocracy, rivaling Babylon itself as
an image of grandeur and autocracy. Urizen, "the King of Light on
high upon his starry throne" (*FZ* 37:1)—promulgating arbitrary edicts, issuing defensive demands for obedience, and punishing his own
children with "cords of twisted self conceit / And whips of stern
repentance" (*FZ* 68:22–23)—is scarcely an exaggeration of this deity.
Milton's God has long puzzled critics, but Blake recognized him
immediately as the ruler of a civilization based upon political tyranny, economic slavery, and patriarchal repression. In *Paradise Lost,*
centuries of embellishment with metaphysical wisdom and light fail
to obscure a political significance which stands exposed as never
before. Above all, God is a symbol of power, "almighty" and "omnipotent." Indeed, taking the words "power" and "powers" as one, "power"
is the fifth most frequent noun in the poem. Like Urizen, Milton's
God is that lawgiver, judge, warrior, and king through whom all the
powers of the state had been both symbolized and legitimized. It
appeared to Blake that Milton, no less than his despised prelates, had
worshiped a Canaanite amalgamation of divinity and dominion.

This impression is heightened by the fact that Satan's rebellion is
provoked when God exalts his son as "Victorious King, / Son, Heire,
and Lord, to him Dominion giv'n" (*PL* VI.886–87). The act is celebrated with all the luxury and solemnity of an earthly coronation and
with such regaling as Milton had once denounced as the extravagant
and decadent concomitant of royalty: "a king must be ador'd like a
Demigod, with a dissolute and haughtie court about him, of vast
expence and luxurie . . . who for any thing wherin the public really
needs him, will have little els to do, but to bestow the eating and
drinking of excessive dainties . . . to pageant himself up and down in
progress among the perpetual bowings and cringings of an abject
people" (YP VII.425–26). How contrary this heavenly court with
angels bowing and suing for grace and feasting themselves on "sur-
feit" and "excess" (*PL* V.639–40) to Milton's own ideal, "wherin they
who are greatest, are perpetual servants and drudges to the public . . .
yet are not elevated above thir brethren; live soberly in thir families,
walk the streets as other men, may be spoken to freely, familiarly,
friendly, without adoration" (YP VII.425).

Satan's arguments against the Son's investiture are, as Balachandra
Rajan comments, "a perfectly orthodox version of the claim that
Monarchy is not grounded on the law of Nature."[10] Protesting that
"by Decree / Another now hath to himself ingross't / All Power, and us
eclipst under the name / Of King anointed . . . coming to receive from
us / Knee-tribute yet unpaid, prostration vile" (*PL* V.774–77, 781–82),
Satan appeals to his comrades:

> Will ye submit your necks, and chuse to bend
> The supple knee? ye will not, if I trust
> To know ye right, or if ye know your selves
> Natives and Sons of Heav'n possest before
> By none, and if not equal all, yet free,
> Equally free; for Orders and Degrees
> Jarr not with liberty, but well consist.
> Who can in reason then or right assume
> Monarchie over such as live by right
> His equals, if in power and splendor less,
> In freedome equal? or can introduce
> Law and Edict on us, who without law
> Erre not, much less for this to be our Lord,
> And look for adoration to th' abuse
> Of those Imperial Titles which assert
> Our being ordain'd to govern, not to serve? (*PL* V.788–802)

Truly this is the very breath and spirit of Milton's prose: the assertion of natural rights, the distinction between liberty and equality, the right of those by nature free to govern themselves, and the rejection of monarchy as a form of slothful abdication of that responsibility. If Satan appears heroic in *Paradise Lost*, it is because Milton has poured into him the most passionate of his own sentiments in defense of that "diabolical" party which for twenty years had been turning English society upside down. In this defiant self-assertiveness, flaunted in the face of every threat and punishment, we are reminded of Henry Burton's proclamation that the pillory where he had been dragged to have his ears chopped off for sedition was "the happiest pulpitt hee had ever preached in."[11] In Satan's proud refusal to bow before the Son, we see a Lilburne refusing to remove his hat before the Star Chamber and distributing treasonous tracts from the very stocks in which they tried to silence him. In *Paradise Lost*, on the other hand, the good angels are a pack of yea-saying lackeys. Satan evokes men like George Fox rising from their pews to take issue with the official minister, or Milton himself successively defying bishops, king, and Parliament in a refusal to acknowledge any authority higher than his own conscience. If Satan, despite all the author's efforts to denigrate his motives and expose his malice, threatens to become the hero of Milton's epic, it is for a reason Blake uniquely understood. Epic characters such as Satan embody such profound social forces that the conscious artistry of a poet can only partially circumscribe them. In making Satan a rebel, the rebellious Milton could not help but evoke the literally thousands of episodes of struggle which characterized those years of teeming liberty.

Freedom or Providence—A Puritan Dilemma

We are thus faced with the contradiction that, in identifying Satan with the English Revolution, Milton would seem to be either renouncing that struggle or supporting Satan's attack on God. Rather, I would suggest that Milton knew exactly what he was doing in making Satan a revolutionary. The only plausible explanation for his denigration is that, through him, Milton wishes to criticize not only the old order but also those aspects of the revolution which he believed responsible for its failure and from which he wished to separate himself. In *Paradise Lost,* Milton remains the engaged polemicist still hoping to prepare his countrymen for the next round of battle.

When we turn to Milton's own conceptions of revolution, we find them, in Arthur Barker's words, "flatly contradictory."[12] The ambiguities of *Paradise Lost* also exist in the prose. On the intellectual level that Barker analyzes, Milton shares a "Puritan dilemma" inherent in the conflicting demands of liberty and reformation, civil freedom and Christian discipline. While Milton declined to see these values reconciled in an institutionalized state church, his belief that the goal of freedom was a godly commonwealth left a theocratic cast to his thought.

We should not be surprised then that Christ's exaltation in Book V invokes Psalm 2, the arch-document of Jewish theocracy:

> Hear my Decree, which unrevok't shall stand.
> This day I have begot whom I declare
> My onely Son, and on this holy Hill
> Him have anointed, whom ye now behold
> At my right hand; your Head I him appoint;
> And by my Self have sworn to him shall bow
> All knees in Heav'n, and shall confess him Lord.
>
> (*PL* V.602–08)

When Satan indicts this promotion as abrogating a heavenly assembly of angelic equals, he unwittingly discloses the real historical significance of this text. For it was this coronation rite which had justified Israel's transformation from a tribal democracy to a dynastic monarchy. As we have seen, it was by claiming to be adopted sons of God that the sons of David had rationalized their break with traditions of popular power. In fact, Milton himself had repeatedly evoked that charge disapprovingly against Royalists who traced back to David the divine right of kings. David, a providential figure, was a problematic one for Milton. He stressed David's covenant with the elders at Hebron and interpreted the monarchy as the concession of an angry God to a people straying into the ways of Canaan. He saw the kingship as a degeneration from the desert republic when the Jews founded "Thir government, and thir great Senate [chose] / Through the twelve Tribes, to rule by Laws ordaind" (*PL* XII.225–26).[13]

This is the radical tradition, and it is Blake's. What then are we to make of the fact that the revolt against the monarchy, applauded by Milton as a time when "ten tribes drove out Solomon's son" and "soon showed in word and deed what their rights were" (YP IV.373), seems to have become the type of Satan's rebellion? The Hebrew insurgents' cry, "What portion have we in David . . . To your tents O Israel!" (I Kings 12:16), had become a rallying cry for Puritan rebels.[14] Yet in *Paradise Lost* it is Satan who departs for "Quarters of the North" and erects his "wicked Tents" "to cast off this Yoke" of monarchy, once protested by the northern tribes (*PL* V.689,890,786).

In the figure of David the conflicts between Milton's ideas of freedom and providence begin to emerge. However, we should realize that Psalm 2 had come to be interpreted by other traditions. The prophets had turned it into the vision of a divinely appointed leader whom God would raise from the line of David to deliver his people from all injustice, his Messiah or Christ. After Jesus's brief sojourn in Jerusalem had left the thrones of tyrants intact, and the hopes for a Jewish kingdom had been crushed with the insurrection in 70 A.D., this prophecy came, as we have seen, to refer to a Second Coming in which Christ would establish a New Jerusalem on earth. During the civil war years there was a widespread expectation, shared at times by Milton, that the "shortly-expected King" (YP I.616) would soon ascend an English throne and begin his thousand-year reign. Milton's warrior Christ is this "*Messiah* his annointed King" (*PL* VI.718), and his primal battle with Satan a foreshadowing of the final triumph in which he will overthrow all oppressors and establish his own just kingdom.

The radical implication which Milton drew from Christ's kingship was that it proved all earthly monarchy to be an idolatrous usurpation of the throne of him who is "our true and rightfull and only to be expected King, only worthy as he is our only Saviour, the Messiah, the Christ, the only heir of his eternal father, the only by him anointed and ordaind" (YP VII.374). An omnipotent God provided a power in whose name one might challenge all earthy authorities. Puritans could castigate the Royalists for being (somewhat like Milton's devils) loyal to their king, "Rebels in the mean time to God" (YP III.346) and could justify themselves, conversely, as loyal to God though rebels to their king.

In subtle ways the centralization of power in heaven mirrored and aided shifts of influence on earth. The rise of the middle class saw a consolidation of the nation-state, beginning in sixteenth-century England when the bourgeoisie turned to the Tudor monarchy as an ally against the independent powers of the aristocracy and the church. Nobles lost their private armies of retainers, and a monopoly of force was centered in the court. The increasingly transcendent and omnipotent image of God may have reflected this experience, for, as Michael Walzer writes,

> Despotism often plays an important part in clearing the way for democracy. A despot destroys the structure of intermediate powers and makes possible a politics based on individual interests. He overcomes the feudal baronage, breaks down . . . clan and tribal loyalties . . . imposes uniformity, a kind of rough equality; he levels the political universe. Something of the same role is played by the Calvinist God; his very existence endangers the medieval hierarchy of orders and powers. He establishes his own omnipotence by levelling the cosmos, by destroying the intermediate power of the angels, of the Blessed Virgin and the saints, of the pope, the bishops, and finally even the king.[15]

One outcome of this process is Milton's own heaven. There God has become an autocrat and, as Walzer notes, all real significance has been eliminated from the angelic hierarchy who once served as mediators of divine power, semi-autonomous intellectual beings, maintaining the celestial spheres. Milton scrambles their ranks and reduces them to errand boys.[16]

This concentration of a plurality of powers in God himself has of course one exception—the exaltation of Christ; and it is crucial to Milton's political vision. What had happened by the seventeenth century is that the erstwhile alliance between the monarchy and the middle class had reverted to antagonism again. The Stuarts realized that the leveling of the nobility could go no further without sweeping out from under the monarchy the whole social pyramid on which it rested. The tradespeople were finding the king as great an obstruction to progress as the barons. What the middle class wanted was to continue strengthening the state and at the same time to broaden its base, and this is what happened after 1640 as Parliament seized power, swept away local justices and appointed bodies accountable to itself to administer the nation. Now divine omnipotence could be seen as both the negation of royal pretensions to single rule and at the same time the guarantor of oligarchic parliamentary authority. But the issue soon became whether divine power was delegated at all—and if so, how. While Milton argued against the Royalists that since "Christ in his church hath left no vicegerent of his power . . . how then can any Christian man derive his kingship from Christ?" (YP VII.429), he also sought to avoid the drastic anarchistic or democratic conclusion which might be drawn from the idea that all magistracy resided in God alone and had been delegated to no identifiable representatives.[17] Radicals did hold this view and were accused by one detractor as a "lawless generation which is crying out, 'Let Christ rule' because they would have no rule."[18]

Against such anarchism stood the conviction of bourgeois saints that they themselves had been singled out by the Almighty to carry on his great work of reformation in civil as well as in ecclesiastical affairs. Milton's heavenly polis substantiated their faith that God had not led them from the anxieties of despotism to the terrors of what they considered mob rule, but toward the godly reign of liberty and virtue. Regarding that alliance, the parallels of belief between Milton and Blake break down. The romantic poet had seen enough of the rule of the righteous middle class to conclude that there was no tryst more sinister, and to propose as an alternative a revolutionary pact with hell. We must proceed, therefore, to a consideration of the political implications of their divergent attitudes toward sin.

The Fall into Inequality

In Blake's opinion, the Puritans had built a new system of privilege and repression, weaving "a New Religion from new Jealousy of Theotormon!" (*M* 38), the champion of material greed and moral righteousness in *Visions of the Daughters of Albion.* Spurning the ideas of election and damnation, virtue, and sin which inform Milton's depiction of heaven and hell, Blake charges:

> Miltons Religion is the cause: there is no end to destruction!
> . . . .
>
> Asserting the Self-righteousness against the Universal Saviour,
> Mocking the Confessors & Martyrs, claiming Self-righteousness;
> With cruel Virtue: making War upon the Lambs Redeemed;
> To perpetuate War & Glory. to perpetuate the Laws of Sin:
> . . . .
>
> To destroy Jerusalem as a Harlot & her Sons as Reprobates;
> . . . .
>
> Shewing the Transgresors in Hell, the proud Warriors in Heaven:
> Heaven as a Punisher & Hell as One under Punishment. (*M* 22:39–52)

When Blake wrote *The Four Zoas* as a revision of traditional concepts of the Fall, he understood the political significance of that doctrine. So did Milton, for interpretations of Genesis were hotly contested by his contemporaries. A flourishing "political primitiv-ism"[19] characterized the era in which partisans of all political stripes sought to provide their various institutions with legitimizing founda-tions. Milton shared this tendency to treat Genesis as a political myth.[20] When he abandoned the Arthurian theme for the biblical, it was under the same inspiration that would send secular philoso-phers harkening to an imagined state of nature for their first princi-ples. As we have seen, Milton portrays human beings in Eden as self-governing creatures, subordinate only to God, until the Fall led to the rise of tyrants like Nimrod, to themselves assuming

> Authoritie usurpt, from God not giv'n:
> He gave us onely over Beast, Fish, Fowl
> Dominion absolute; that right we hold
> By his donation; but Man over men
> He made not Lord; such title to himself
> Reserving, human left from human free. (*PL* XII.66–71)

This benevolent Edenic democracy had, however, been forfeited, with postlapsarian chaos requiring the establishment of magistrates:

> No man who knows ought, can be so stupid to deny that all men naturally were borne free, being the image and resemblance of God himself, and were by privilege above all the creatures, born to command and not to obey: and that they liv'd so. Till from the root of *Adams* transgression, falling among themselves to doe wrong and violence, and foreseeing that such courses must needs tend to the destruction of them all, they agreed by common league to bind each other from mutual injury. . . . Hence came Citties, Townes and Common-wealths.
> (YP III.198–99)

So, Milton argues, some men came to rule over others through their greater merit or their greater force.

Milton's intent here is to argue for liberty under the conditions of inequality outside Eden. As Michael Walzer shows, the strict Cal-vinist view was more bluntly authoritarian. Calvin thought the Fall to have been such a political disaster that society was forever after teetering on the edge of chaos.[21] He wrote, "The nature of man is such that every man would be lord and master over his neighbors and no man by his good will would be a subject," for "we know that men are of so perverse and crooked a nature that everyone would scratch his neighbor's eyes out if their were no bridle to hold them in."[22] In the fallen world man was by nature an outlaw, a rebel, and a traitor; ambition and greed were universal and inequities of wealth and power the norm.[23]

Christian redemption offered the only alternative to this world of total lawlessness. God had chosen to save not humanity, but only a small minority of it. These he had providentially called out of the ordinary tumult to a life of discipline and order which marked them off from the masses of the damned. This godly elite was identified not by birth, but by their "reformed" morality. As one might guess, the conviction that one belonged to the elect brought self-confidence, energy, and enthusiasm in the performance of one's divinely appointed tasks. For the English Presbyterians, therefore, Calvinism was a revolutionary creed.

Its darker side, as we shall see, was the utter hopelessness to which this creed condemned the vast majority who were disenfranchised as well as damned. Calvin argued, as Walzer explains, that it was the responsibility of the godly to impose discipline upon those unregenerate masses incapable of self-control. God called his elect above all to magistracy, to sit in judgment upon the unredeemed and to maintain at least a minimal, external stability by controlling that "many-headed monster," the populace. Bereft of all virtue and reason, they were to be regimented by law and ruled by the whip.

The ideological spectrum in interregnum England can be seen to conform roughly to the social spectrum. Among the staunchest Presbyterians were employers and landlords.[24] When they moved against the monarchy, they always had one eye on the classes below them, whose independent activity in petitioning Parliament and in the army had always made them wary. The revolution had only sought to bring political mechanisms in line with economic realities, to establish government by men of substance in Parliament, while retaining the king as an authority symbol to awe the masses. The Puritans would retain the church as a coercive state apparatus, only transferring its governance to a Presbyterian assembly, that is, themselves. Far from intending greater liberty in religious affairs, they hoped thereby to overcome the moral laxity of a corrupt aristocratic church and impose a more rigorous discipline upon their employees and tenants. Strictures against idleness, vagrancy, and loose pleasures would strengthen the parish's hand against servants, day laborers, and recipients of the poor rates. Required attendance at services, censorship, and doctrinal uniformity would check popular rebellion by forbidding their seditious gatherings and preaching a gospel of obedience and subordination.

Against this program there was widespread resistance. For one thing, the rising (as opposed to the established) middle class had no enthusiasm for replacing the monopoly of the court with that of the Presbyterians. England had too many tradespeople, farmers, and intellectuals who held liberty too dear to exchange it so lightly.

Among these Independents were men who have achieved economic self-sufficiency in perhaps a single generation. Lifting themselves above the grind of coarse manual labor, acquiring literacy and some rational control over their lives had led them to begin to develop distinctive opinions and an unconventional culture. They felt like men who had been freed by a liberating Christ and were hardly about to surrender their newly formed consciences to new presbyters who were but old priests writ large. Their pride declared them a chosen people raised by God above the mass for great purposes. But, knowing their status also to be the fruit of their own diligent activity and dependent upon their freedom to mold their own circumstances, they were reluctant to accept any system which might officially designate a static elect. In this context, Milton's modification of ideas of election with an emphasis on the individual's free will does not seem unusual.

Acknowledging the Divine Word as the supreme authority, the Independents tended to favor religious toleration, a voluntary congregational church, republican government, and civil liberties. Their openmindedness was, however, to be tested when the de facto breakdown of religious and political discipline during the civil war allowed those liberties to be claimed by others who sought, rather than shared, their advantages. The Levellers, for example, hoped to reconstruct English government on an "Agreement of the People" which would establish a representative government elected upon a broad franchise. For John Lilburne, human beings still possessed the original rights endowed by their creator. He completely ignored the Fall and the distinctions it allowed between the redeemed and the reprobate.

The Levellers spoke for such artisans, yeomen, and apprentices as characterized the army rank and file.[25] They were men of little property, and their democratic demands terrified all people of means, providing the basis for an eventual rapprochement between those who had differed over toleration. As Colonel Ireton posed the problem, unless the vote be restricted to "the persons in whom all land lies, and those in corporations in whom all trading lies, . . . why may not those [propertyless] men vote against all property?"[26] As independent artisans and farmers, most Levellers probably hoped to create a situation in which they might acquire, not eliminate, property, so their disavowals of economic leveling were probably sincere. However, Ireton's point was well taken, as the Leveller spokesman Colonel Rainborough may have realized when he protested that then the soldier had apparently fought only "to enslave himself, to give power to men of riches, men of estates. to make him a perpetual slave." The alternatives laid out by these Putney debates were that either the poor would redistribute all wealth, or they would all become servants of the rich—which of course was exactly what happened, as the eviction of the peasantry turned England within a little more than a century into the "two nations" of capitalists and wage laborers. Rainborough's retort was to have a prophetic irony: "Sir, I see, that it is impossible to have liberty, but all propertie must be taken away."[27]

But property, as Milton might have pointed out, was also an inevitable consequence of the Fall, for since then,

> God suffer'd . . . all that which by Civilians is term'd the *secondary law of nature and of nations.* He suffer'd his owne people . . . to be som maisters, som servants, som to be princes, others to be subjects, hee suffer'd propriety to divide all things by severall possession, trade and commerce, not without usury; in his common wealth some to bee undeservedly rich, others to bee undeservingly poore. All which till hardnesse of heart came in, was most unjust; whenas prime Nature made us all equall, made us equall coheirs by common right and dominion over all creatures.   (YP II.661)

Early Christians, Milton admitted, had tried to live in a perfection that included community of goods; but, he asks, "who will be the man [who] shall introduce this kind of common wealth, as christianity now goes?" (YP II.666).

Who? According to Christopher Hill, this was the program of at least some of Milton's contemporaries, the "True Levellers" who may have provoked the army officers' alarm.[28] For around the same time that Lilburne's followers were pressing for democracy, a man named Gerrard Winstanley led a little band of impoverished "Diggers" to take back the commons at Saint George's Hill and to begin tilling it collectively. Not surprisingly, many of Winstanley's writings challenge the orthodox notion of the Fall. In his own version, quoted earlier, property was itself the Fall, and Eden might be recovered by restoring the earth to all men as a common treasury. All other so-called spiritual doctrine was, he taught, "the filthy Dreamer and the Cloud without rain," a trick of deceiving preachers who "lay claime to Heaven after they are dead, and yet they require their Heaven in this World too, and grumble mightily against the People that will not give them a large temporal maintenance. And yet they tell the poor People, that they must be content with their poverty, and they shall have their Heaven hereafter. . . . While men are gazing up to Heaven, imagining after a happiness, or fearing a Hell after they are dead, their eyes are put out, that they see not what is their birthrights."[29] The problem, as Winstanley analyzed it, was more than the monarchy; it encompassed a whole system of inequality which he called "kingly power," rooted in poverty and extending to politics, education, the courts, everything. Puritans often boasted that their material success was a sign of divine providence; Winstanley saw the reverse: election had not created classes, but the class system had created doctrines of election. "Kingly government," he wrote, "hath made the Election and Rejection of Brethren." Jesus Christ, who embraced all, was the "head Leveller."[30]

Lower-class sects were generally fond of denying the Fall. Socinians held that Christ's universal salvation had redeemed all people, without exception. George Fox, the Quaker, exulted in being renewed to "the state of Adam, which he was in before he fell."[31] Grindletonians and the Family of Love believed that prelapsarian perfection, including community of goods, were possible in this life. Many believed that Eden was about to be reestablished in England by God, or by revolution. The standards of this world would be turned upside down as God declined to act through the self-righteous elite, but appeared, as Jesus had, among sinners and the poor. William Erbery proclaimed that "God comes reigning and riding on an ass, that is, revealing himself in majesty and glory in the basest of men."[32]

Erbery appears among that vague conglomeration of self-appointed "mechanick preachers" reviled as Ranters by hostile contemporaries. They were condemned by the Blasphemy Act of August 9, 1650, for the antinomian heresy of denying "the necessity of moral and civil righteousness among men," a doctrine which "tended to the dissolution of all human society."[33] The bill made it illegal to claim to be God, to deny that there was such a thing as sin, or that adultery, drunkenness, and theft were sinful. The Ranters pursued the rights of individual conscience to extremes that horrified the respectable and the devout. Where Milton proclaimed the sonship of all believers, they claimed that God lives only in man. Here again is that old "everlasting gospel" with its third age of the spirit in which God has become fully immanent in humanity. "God is all in one, and so is in everyone," wrote Richard Coppin. The idea shaded off into lower-class materialism and atheism, with one allegedly postulating that God is in "this dog, this tobacco pipe, he is me, I am him."[34] Just as Calvin's transcendent Jehovah had conformed to an elitist social philosophy, so also these visions of radical immanence had democratic implications. All people were God; all were saved; all were equal; and the godly had no need for law. Coppin was arrested when a preacher attacked the political consequences of his creed. By arguing that "no man can be assured of his salvation, except he see the same salvation in the same Saviour for all men," the preacher contended, he had thrown himself "into the bosoms of (a many-headed monster) the rude multitude."[35]

Paradise Lost *and the Protestant Ethic*

What was at issue were two competing moral visions, each reflecting the experiences of a particular social group. Max Weber and R. H. Tawney have shown us how peculiarly suited the "Protestant ethic" was to the rising capitalists.[36] The key new concept was the "calling." Catholicism had seen a divine vocation as inspiring only those few monks and nuns who were called to abandon "the world" for a life of perfect poverty, chastity, and obedience. Protestantism taught, on the contrary, that God had assigned every Christian a specific life's task within the ordinary spheres of marriage and work. Thus the *Divine Comedy* concludes with Dante in rapt contemplation, while *Paradise Lost* shows Adam and Eve being dispatched to active work for their survival: "The World was all before them" (*PL* XII.646). Richard Rogers, the Puritan divine, reassured his brethren that "the saint has no reason to fear the world or run away from it," thus "by neglecting his necessary affairs cause poverty to grow upon the land."[37] God approved, above all else, of productivity. It was an ethic highly conducive to growing capitalism. Sermons abounded with attacks upon the idle, a category which William Perkins thought included monks, friars, and gentlemen "who live in no calling but spend their time in eating and drinking, sleeping and sporting," as well as beggars and vagabonds.[38] Cromwell, fired by this spirit, rallied his new recruits to the service of a God who says: "Up and be doing, and I will help you and stand by you." Cromwell added, "There is nothing to be feared but sin and sloth."[39]

Thus a medieval ethos encouraging resignation to one's condition, ritual piety, charitable alms, and heroic otherworldliness was abandoned by a middle class which instead emphasized energetic activity and the avoidance of extravagance and sensuous indulgence. Underlying this change was a vast economic and social revolution. In a feudal world, the absence of trade or opportunity for investment meant that produce had to be consumed immediately; hence the lords' opulent hospitality and the peasants' seasonal festivities— orgies of consumption blessed by the church. The aristocracy, freed from labor by their serfs, lived lives of leisure; they hunted, conquered, and patronized the arts. The peasants had little motivation to increase their productivity, since the gains would not be theirs anyway. Life was brutal and impoverished but not disciplined. Peasants enjoyed an erratic work rhythm regulated by the sun and the seasons and interrupted by numerous holy days. These patterns survived into the seventeenth century among cottagers eking out an existence from a little gardening, hunting, and day labor, working short-time whenever wages were high.

For the bourgeoisie, "reformation" largely meant repudiating this lackadaisical life style.[40] The creation of markets and the drive to rationalize production and accumulate profits for investment required a new breed, the "industrious sort of folk" for whom Slingsly Bethel spoke.[41] When he attacked popery in 1688, his charges were all fundamentally economic: monks live idly, making no contribution to production; an unmarried clergy means a declining work force; superstition supports the extravagant adornment of churches, wasteful pilgrimages, and other drains on capital; too many holidays interfere with work; almsgiving encourages idleness and begging among the poor. Christopher Hill calls this attack "an indictment of one system of ideas and social relations in terms of the values of another," explaining, "Popery is suited to a static agricultural society, which offers the mass of the population no possibility of becoming richer than their fellows, and in which poverty is a holy state. Protestantism is suited to a competitive society in which God helps those who help themselves, in which thrift, accumulation and industry are the cardinal virtues, and poverty very nearly a crime."[42]

Milton, obsessed with realizing his own vocation, "that one Talent which is death to hide" (sonnet 29), builds *Paradise Lost* around the Protestant ethic. Christ, the angels, and human beings all have their appointed tasks. God for the first time is imagined as a kind of cosmic foreman, "the great Work-Maister" (*PL* III.696), leaning down from his heavenly perch "His own works and their works at once to view" (*PL* III.59). His angels are no longer celestial forces but rather, as Michael Walzer tells us,[43] "a species of heavenly civil servants" at the bidding of an empyreal administrator, who "Stand ready at command" to "Bear his swift errands . . . O're Sea and Land" (*PL* III.650–53). Adam and Eve, traditionally distinguished from the beasts by their rationality, are now especially marked by their productivity:

> other Creatures all day long
> Rove idle unimploid; . . .
> Man hath his daily work of body or mind
> Appointed, which declares his Dignitie.   (*PL* IV.616–19)

They follow a methodical Puritan routine, only interrupting their work day for meals and sleep, and occasional religious instruction. The character of their work is also suggestive, their obligation to restrain a "wanton" nature serving as a metaphor and a means for their own self-discipline. As Adam and Eve bring order to the luxurious abandon of their sensuous wilderness, they also check the excesses of their own desires and channel overexuberant energies into systematic industry.

Max Weber calls this ethos "this-worldly asceticism," a sensuous self-denial geared towards storing up treasures on earth rather than in heaven. Adam and Eve are warned against uninhibited sensuality but succumb to "foul exorbitant desires" (*PL* III.177), Eve to gluttony and Adam to uxoriousness. Human history, as viewed by Milton, has been and will always be a cycle of repeated falls from discipline to dissoluteness, through which people "Shall change thir course to pleasure, ease, and sloth, / Surfet, and lust . . . So all shall turn degenerate, all deprav'd" (*PL* XI.794–95, 806). In fact, the choice between abstinence and abandon is presented as virtually the only moral issue and the sole motive force of all history. Milton even comments that physical suffering and death are to be attributed less to "Fire, Flood, Famin" (let alone poverty and war) than to "Intemperance . . . In Meats and Drinks, which on the Earth shal bring / Diseases dire" (*PL* XI.472–74), again referring to "th' inabstinence of *Eve*" (*PL* XI.476) as the cause of such misery. Who but a Puritan at war with a dissipated aristocracy and alienated from an impoverished populace could credit more misery to overeating than to starvation!

For Milton, the key to civilized life was a social discipline ultimately resting upon moral self-regulation. His Samson is torn between a divinely ordained mission and the temptations of sloth and seduction.[44] The analogy between military and moral discipline dramatized in *Samson Agonistes* is expressed in *The Reason of Church Government* as follows: "the flourishing and decaying of all civill societies, all the moments and turnings of humane occasions are mov'd to and fro as upon the axle of discipline. . . . Hence in those perfect armies of *Cyrus* . . . the excellence of military skill was esteem'd, not by the not needing, but by the readiest submitting to the edicts of their commander. And certainly discipline is not only the removall of disorder, but . . . the very visible shape and image of vertue" (YP I.751). We are spared an image of Adam and Eve engaging in military drill as a moral exercise, as the Puritan John Davenport had recommended, but Christ makes a good sergeant for angelic troops who demonstrate their inner virtue through martial order:

> At which command the Powers Militant
> That stood for Heav'n, in mighty Quadrate joyn'd
> Of Union irresistible, mov'd on
> In silence thir bright legions.
> . . . .

> On they move
> Indissolubly firm; nor obvious Hill,
> Nor streit'ning Vale, nor Wood, nor Stream divides
> Thir perfet ranks.   (*PL* VI.61–71)

Such discipline, granting the middle class an unprecedented mastery over nature and its own future, becomes synonymous with "reason." The laxity and indulgence which in a highly competitive, insecure, and still undeveloped world threaten destruction seem to portend all ruin. Thus, as critics have noted, *Paradise Lost* mounts its entire philosophic edifice upon the hierarchy of reason, which Raphael recommends to Adam, over "carnal pleasure" (*PL* VIII.593). Consequently, the Fall appears as a kind of upset victory for desire in the politics of the psyche;

> For Understanding rul'd not, and the Will
> Heard not her lore, both in subjection now
> To sensual Appetite, who from beneathe
> Usurping over sovran Reason claimd
> Superior sway.   (*PL* IX.1127–31)

For the poor, trapped in their condition, sweating for others, and accumulating nothing, this was a questionable rationality. The same freedom of Christian conscience which led Milton to reject customary ethics for a more demanding code of interior discipline allowed the Ranters to repudiate both in favor of a plebeian culture of immediate gratification. Tobias Crisp held that "sin is finished," for "If you be freemen of Christ, you may esteem all the curses of the law as no more concerning you than the laws of England concern Spain." "To be called a libertine," he thought, "is the most glorious title under heaven."[45] Another Ranter allegedly asserted that the only sin was a guilty conscience and "those are most perfect . . . which do committ the greatest sins with least remorse";[46] Lawrence Clarkson advised others to keep on sinning boldly until such uneasiness fell away. Since there was no sin, there could be no punishment. Heaven and hell could only describe earthly conditions; damnation was a "bugbear to keep men in awe."[47]

Nothing was finally more rational than the lower class's refusal to adopt a self-denial whose profits went to their superiors. Living miserable lives of no achievement, they resented righteous efforts to deprive them of the only enjoyments they could afford: drinking, dancing, games, sex, and other "idle pleasures." They were more likely to sympathize with a notion of sin that condemned the abuses of the middle class, which Abiezer Coppe decried as arrogance, greed, unmercifulness, tyranny, hypocrisy, and despising the poor: "The laying of nets, traps and snares for the feet of our neighbors is a sin, whether men imagine it to be so or no; and so is the not undoing of heavy burdens, the not letting the oppressed go free, the not healing every yoke, and the not dealing of bread to the hungry."[48] The more conscious plebeian rebels were sensitive to the hypocrisy involved when they were punished for poaching on lands legally wrested from them through the wholesale robbery of enclosure. "Covetousness" and "self-love" became catch-words for the sins of property. James Nayler, the Quaker, observed, "Saith God, Thou shall not covet . . . Saith Antichrist, Thou must live by the wits that God hath given thee, and this is not covetousness but a provident care."[49] Roger Crab asserted that it was impossible to love one's neighbor as oneself while accumulating private wealth: "All Our properties are but the fruit of God's curse."[50] Winstanley insisted that "the greatest sinne against universal Love" was "for a man to lock up the treasuries of the Earth in Chests and houses . . . while others starve for want to whom it belongs, and it belongs to all."[51] "The true communion amongst men," Coppe proclaimed, "is to have all things common and to call nothing one hath one's own."[52]

Blake's unique contribution to a reading of *Paradise Lost* lies in his perception that its confrontation of angelic and demonic forces embodies a conflict between social classes and the different values characterizing each. *The Marriage of Heaven and Hell* parodies Milton's allegory while reversing some of its allegiances. In the "Song of Liberty" Satan appears as the rebellious demon who challenges heavenly tyranny:

> On those infinite mountains of light now barr'd out by the atlantic sea, the new born fire stood before the starry king!
> Flag'd with grey brow'd snows and thunderous visages the jealous wings wav'd over the deep.
> The speary hand burned aloft, unbuckled was the shield, forth went the hand of jealousy among the flaming hair, and hurl'd the new born wonder thro' the starry night.   (*MHH* 25–26)

Against this rebellious son of fire, a caricature of Milton's God ranges his forces, "his grey brow'd councellors, thunderous warriors, curl'd veterans, among helms, and shields, and chariots[,] horses, elephants: banners, castles, slings and rocks" (*MHH* 26). As in Milton's poem, the conflict is fought out in moral as well as political terms, with "the gloomy king" seeking (through ethical authority) to preserve his power over his recalcitrant subjects: "With thunder and fire: leading his starry hosts thro' the waste wilderness he promulgates his ten commands, glancing his beamy eyelids over the deep in dark dismay" (*MHH* 26–27). But this ploy proves ineffectual when the fiery rebel renounces his moral tyranny and, "spurning the clouds written with curses, stamps the stony law to dust." Setting himself against both throne and pulpit, he cries, "Empire is no More! . . . Let the Priests of the Raven of dawn, no longer in deadly black. with hoarse note curse the sons of joy" (*MHH* 27).

These analogies were Milton's own; Blake had only shifted sides in the wars between heaven and hell, between the regenerate middle class and the reprobate masses, bourgeois discipline and plebeian desire. The hierarchy between reason and passion is reversed, since for Blake only fulfillment is rational. Milton's puritanical reason is seen simply as the repression imposed by a middle class which has subordinated pleasure to possession; hence it is designated elsewhere as "your reason" (Urizen), the attitudes of a single class posturing as universal value. In *Paradise Lost*, God, his Christ, and the angels embody this discipline and attempt to enforce it among others. Blake, therefore treats the poem as a parable for aggression: "Those who restrain desire, do so because theirs is weak enough to be restrained; and the restrainer or reason usurps its place & governs the unwilling. And being restrained it by degrees becomes passive till it is only the shadow of desire. The history of this is written in Paradise Lost & the Governor or Reason is call'd Messiah" (*MHH* 5). Milton's angels, as we have seen, perform their dubious tasks unquestioningly, like perfect soldiers, whenever God sends them "upon his high behests / For state, as Sovran King, and to enure / [their] prompt obedience" (*PL* VIII.238–40). Christ, their leader, is the prime exemplar of rational self-mastery and consequently, despite Milton's celebration of his mercy, is a rather bloodless figure bearing little resemblance to the human Jesus so loved by Blake, who comforted prostitutes, wept over a suffering Jerusalem, and raged at its rulers.

Blake's own faith, he tells us, was shared with the devils, whose creed, he intimates, he had learned in the streets and pubs of plebeian London: "As I was walking among the fires of hell delighted with the enjoyments of Genius; which to Angels look like torments and insanity" (*MHH* 6). The "Proverbs of Hell" which he collected there reject middle-class moralism, for "the fox condemns the trap, not himself." Repudiating the calculating bourgeoisie's obsession with industry and accumulation, he proclaims: "The hours of folly are measur'd by the clock, but of wisdom: no clock can measure. . . . Bring out number weight & measure in a time of dearth. . . . The fox provides for himself. but God provides for the lion." Blake celebrates instead a lower-class gospel of gratification and solidarity: "Damn.

braces: Bless relaxes. . . . The most sublime act is to set another before you" (*MHH* 7–9). Blake's ethic is an antinomian one, for when an outraged angel demands, "Has not Jesus Christ given his sanction to the law of the ten commandments and are not all other men fools, sinners, & nothings?" Blake retorts that "no virtue can exist without breaking these ten commandments" (*MHH* 23).

In the spirit of that seventeenth-century Ranter who "hoped to see the poor Devil cleared of a great many slanders that had been cast upon him," Blake puts this wisdom in the mouth of a demon. He may have been inspired to do so by the fact that Satan, Milton's symbol of unrestrained passion, speaks remarkably like a Ranter.[53] A "Rebel to all Law" (*PL* X.83) with his "Atheist crew" (*PL* VI.370), his temptation of Eve is a model of antinomian logic. In this little episode of consciousness-raising, Satan argues that human beings need obey no law that contravenes their own fulfillment, since they are "Deterrd not from atchieving what might leade / To happier life." Proceeding to question the moral law entirely, he adds, "if what is evil / Be real," and echoes the Ranter sentiment that rather the idea of evil is all a "bugbear to awe the ignorant": "Why then was this forbid? Why but to awe, / Why but to keep ye low and ignorant" (*PL* IX.696–99, 703–04). The idea of a God who opposes human fulfillment is a contradiction in terms: "God therefore cannot hurt ye, and be just; / Not just, not God; not feard then, nor obeid" (*PL* IX.700–01).

Satan urges Eve, as Clarkson might have done, to accomplish her own liberation by dismissing all authorities and following her own desires. When Eve then becomes convinced of the contradiction between freedom and law: "Such prohibitions binde not; . . . what profits then / Our inward freedom?" (*PL* IX.760–62), she breaks the divine command. Far from being a mere weakness of the flesh, her act is a political and ideological affirmation of the rights of the flesh, upholding the Ranter doctrine that all such inhibitions must be overthrown: "his forbidding / Commends thee more, while it inferrs the good / By thee communicated, and our want" (*PL* IX.753–55). In her alliance with the devil, Eve anticipates Blake's Jesus who "was all virtue, and acted from impulse, not from rules" (*MHH* 24). This heretical affirmation of human desire may have inspired Blake's transmutation of the tree of mystery from the test of obedience it represents in Milton to the obstacle to human self-determination that it becomes in *The Four Zoas*. It undoubtedly influenced his understanding of Satan as more than a perverse being of defective character and instead as the champion of a heretical ethic of gratification whose antinomian moral principles ("Evil be thou my Good," *PL* IV.110) had been deliberately misrepresented and maligned.

Where Merit Reigns

The positive value which infuses Satan's code is egalitarianism. Satan is continually pressing the issue, asserting that regardless of "Orders and Degrees" the devils remained "Equally free" (*PL* V.792): "Who can in reason then or right assume / Monarchie over such as live by right / His equals?" (*PL* V.794–96). "Our puissance is our own" (*PL* V.864), he states, recalling the left-wing tradition which had long held that a divinity immanent in all human beings established their equality:

> A third part of the Gods, in Synod met
> Thir Deities to assert, who while they feel
> Vigour Divine within them, can allow
> Omnipotence to none.   (*PL* VI.156–59)

The same claim inspires his proffering to Eve the title "Goddess humane" (*PL* IX.732). Her rebellion has been a quest for equality as well as freedom. In imitating one who had succeeded in "ventring higher then [his] Lot" (*PL* IX.690), she is explicitly rejecting all hierarchic systems, "for inferior who is free?" (*PL* IX.825).

The politics of this theology was of course perfectly familiar to Blake who emblazoned his faith that "All deities reside in the human breast" (*MHH* 11) and "every thing that lives is Holy" (*MHH* 27) in the republican manifesto of his *Marriage of Heaven and Hell*. Conversely, the exaltation of a transcendent God established a hierarchy between heaven and earth which easily might buttress social inequities, as the "godly" claimed a relationship to the Almighty that justified their hegemony over other human beings. When Blake observed that Christ was at once the Messiah, Reason and "Governor" (*MHH* 5), he recognized that *Paradise Lost* had built a political hierarchy upon theological and moral supremacy.

Milton had accepted the Calvinist conception that since the Fall a drastic inequality existed between the sinful and the saved. After the Fall, the common people, no longer capable of self-government, had delegated power to their superiors, "to one, whom for the eminence of his wisdom and integritie they chose above the rest" (YP III.199). Merging this theological notion with Aristotle's idea that a ruling class had emerged from natural inequalities, Milton came to see hierarchy as a cosmic principle no less than did the medieval philosophers.[54] The difference was that this hierarchy, based on inner virtues rather than birth, was not static or unchangeable.[55] Any person might be one of those few truly superior beings who were intended by God to rule rather than obey.

At times, Milton thought Cromwell to be such a leader.[56] His moral victories over his own impulses, the poet thought, had prepared him for rule over his spiritual inferiors: "Whatever enemy lay within—vain hopes, fears, desires—he had . . . long since reduced to subjection. Commander first over himself, victor over himself, he had learned to achieve over himself the most effective triumph, and so, on the very first day that he took service against an external foe, he entered camp a veteran and past-master in all that concerned the soldier's life" (YP IV.667–68). Such ethical purity had rendered Cromwell a fit agent for providence itself, and Milton shared the contemporary myth which interpreted his victories as proof of the Almighty's partisanship towards the Puritan cause. "For while you, Cromwell, are safe," Milton expostulated, "he does not have sufficient faith even in God himself who would fear for the safety of England, when he sees God everywhere so favorable to you, so unmistakably at your side" (YP IV.670).

Cromwell's merger of spiritual inwardness and worldly activity, finding in faith the ingredients of material and political power as well as moral rectitude, was characteristic of the Puritan forces in general. Of like-minded men, "who had the fear of God before them and made some conscience of what they did," Cromwell forged the first ideological army, proving that conviction and morale could win battles even with inferior numbers and arms.[57] With the Soldier's Pocket Bible at their breasts, this New Model Army marched forth to fight what it saw as the Lord's battles as well as Parliament's. In *Paradise Lost*, the uniting of moral virtue and military might is expressed in the heavenly hosts, when

> th' inviolable Saints
> In Cubic Phalanx firm advanc't entire,
> Invulnerable, impenitrably arm'd:
> Such high advantages thir innocence
> Gave them above thir foes, not to have sinnd.
>
> (*PL* VI.398–402)

These "Powers Militant" marching forth to "advent'rous deeds / Under thir God-like Leaders, in the Cause / Of God and his *Messiah*" (*PL* VI.61,66–68) unquestionably recall the "armed Saints" who fought with Cromwell against "that Godless crew" of royalists (*PL* VI.47,49).

The first principle of Milton's politics might thus be summed up by the title of a Puritan pamphlet, *Right and Might well met*.[58] As I have argued elsewhere, Milton dramatized the same interdependency of spiritual reformation and revolutionary power in Samson. He too had to defeat temptations to immorality and spiritual sloth before he might commence "By combat to decide whose god is god" (*SA* 1176) in a liberation struggle against a decadent and tyrannical Philistine aristocracy. If, as Wittreich argues, Blake repudiates this Samson as a false revolutionary, it may be that what he is rejecting is a Messiah figure who incorporates the principles of divine election and moral reformation which were so central to Milton's idea of revolution.[59]

That idea of election gave a rising class the confidence to dispense with all customary sanctions and strike out on completely unprecedented ventures. It could accept such acts as regicide only because it believed them authorized by divine providence. By merging God's will with their own deeply felt experience of conversion to a new faith, a new breed of men became capable of advancing onto the stage of history and pushing the kings, lords, and bishops, sanctioned by so many precedents, out of their way.

At the same time, these principles allowed them to halt the revolution short of real democracy by providing for a delegation of divine authority only to men like themselves, marked out from the mass by their superior discipline and their divinely ordained prosperity. Examined carefully, this is the import of the exaltation of Christ and God's proclamation, "This day I have begot whom I declare / My onely Son" (*PL* V.603–04).[60] In its ancient context, this had been the adoption formula by which kings had been elevated above their people to a semi-divine status, as literal heirs of the heavenly Father's prerogatives. While Milton rejected the divine right of kings, he retained a theocratic residue in his own conceptions, revering David and upholding an idea of divinely appointed leadership.

Where Milton's idea of providence differs from traditional concepts is in his conviction that since God has chosen to work through many virtuous persons and since hereditary rule fails to reflect his changing favor, a divinely inspired representative assembly is preferable to a monarchy. Milton's treatment of Christ's exaltation is designed to establish a hierarchy completely free of hereditary connotations. Playing havoc with orthodox notions of the Trinity, Milton infers that Christ was neither a part of the deity nor his eternal son, but rather had to be appointed to that role, like a prime minister. Scrambling chronology to place this investiture after Christ proves his worthiness by volunteering as redeemer (though humanity was not even created yet), Milton further emphasizes that his rule came as a consequence of superior virtue rather than family relationship. When Milton pronounces him "By Merit more then Birthright Son of God" (*PL* III.309), the psalmist's idea of adoption is neatly turned against its original celebration of dynastic rule into a nonhereditary concept of divine election.

In this manner also, Milton could oppose the egalitarian claims of lower-class rebels with the idea of an inequality of merit separating the sinful multitude from the few fit men who God had "chosen of peculiar grace / Elect above the rest" (*PL* III.183–84). Unlike the strict Presbyterians, he held that all people, granted by God the opportunity to be saved, required the freedom of conscience necessary to pursue their redemption. But, in opposition to the antinomians, he believed that only a few in fact achieved that moral liberty. These few, as Abdiel explains, rightfully ruled over their inferiors:

> Unjustly thou deprav'st it with the name
> Of *Servitude* to serve whom God ordains,
> Or Nature; God and Nature bid the same,
> When he who rules is worthiest, and excells
> Them whom he governs. This is servitude,
> To serve th' unwise.   (*PL* VI.174–79)

By the same principle, England was saved from both dynastic tyranny and popular elections. Milton's enormous pride and confidence in the existence of a class of men like himself prevented him from being perturbed by the question of who this moral aristocracy might be and by what standards they would be identified. At one point he himself blithely designated Cromwell in virtually the same language Abdiel applies to Christ, arguing that "there is nothing in human society more pleasing to God, or more agreeable to reason . . . than the rule of the man most fit to rule" (YP IV.671–72). The doctrine left Hobbes less sanguine; in his opinion, "Who hath that eminency of virtue above others, and who is so stupid as not to govern himself, shall never be agreed upon amongst men."[61] When Milton's Satan refuses to agree to his own disenfranchisement, the reign of merit turns to the rule of force, and Christ commences

> to subdue
> By force, who reason for thir Law refuse,
> Right reason for thir Law, and for thir King
> *Messiah,* who by right of Merit Reigns.   (*PL* VI.40–43)

For those who felt his heel, Milton's twin principles of virtue and liberty might appear, like Christ and Satan, to be warring principles.

Unholy Alliances: Satanic Freedom and Godly Repression

By the time the movement for liberty had revived in Blake's England, it had become a movement for democracy as well. That dialectic gives the Blake-Milton relationship the character of simultaneous unity and struggle which it retains throughout our reading of

Blake's poems, producing a reorientation of Miltonic symbols that inspires Blake's mythology. Under the pressure of historic events, however, the symbolism itself underwent certain alterations. In *The Marriage of Heaven and Hell*, when the bourgeois revolutions in America and France were still advancing, Blake could simply set the demons of revolution against the angels of the establishment. But as the limitations and class character of the French struggle began to assume primacy, Blake began to develop a critique which focused upon the devilish Orc himself. It will be useful to observe this analysis in the "Bard's Song" of *Milton* where it appears as an explicit historical commentary on the English Revolution, and then to show how the same understanding infuses the reconstructed Miltonic mythology of *The Four Zoas*.[62]

In the "Bard's Song," Milton returns after "One hundred years, pondring the intricate mazes of Providence" (*M* 2:17) to reevaluate the revolution he helped to make and to confess what terrible "acts have been perform'd" (*M* 13:49). In essence, his revelation is that "Satan is Urizen" (*M* 10:1)—the revolutionaries have by Blake's time become a new oppressor class. The plot revolves around a sequence of alliances and betrayals, with an original cooperation among Palamabron, Rintrah, and the Gnomes falling apart as Palamabron is drawn into a league with Satan against his former friends.

There is an interesting insight here into that civil war which had seen very disparate interests unite against the king and then fall into contention among themselves. The revolution, one might say, was waged by a fragile united front comprised of middle-class forces—the Presbyterian Parliament and Independent army officers—joined by humbler subjects whose needs were voiced by rank-and-file Levellers and radical, sometimes communist, propagandists. Christopher Hill goes as far as to describe it as two, overlapping revolutions:

> The one which succeeded established the sacred rights of property (abolition of feudal tenures, no arbitrary taxation), gave political power to the propertied (sovereignty of Parliament and common law, abolition of prerogative courts), and removed all impediments to the triumph of the ideology of the men of property—the protestant ethic. There was, however, another revolution which never happened, though from time to time it threatened. This might have established communal property, a far wider democracy in political and legal institutions, might have disestablished the state church and rejected the protestant ethic.[63]

The trajectory of the civil war saw these forces coalesce against the court and the prelates and then, once those enemies were eliminated, divide again over what was to replace them. The crucial splits came in

1648 and 1649. First the Presbyterians opposed the alliance of army officers and the rank and file over the regicide. Then this unity broke down over the question of democracy. From then on, no power was ever strong enough to govern, and the revolution could only drift back, under Presbyterian impetus, towards a settlement with the crown.

Blake does not delineate these exact forces, but he does point out that class differences were behind these shifting alliances. Palamabron, repeatedly linked to a "Solemn Great Assembly," seems to evoke liberal Parliamentary reformers, the progressive wing of the respectable class.[64] Thus he is in the class of "the Redeem'd / For he is redeem'd from Satans Law, the wrath falling on Rintrah" (*M* 11:22–23). Rintrah, "who is of the reprobate: of those form'd to destruction / In indignation . . . Flam'd above all the plowed furrows, angry red and furious" (*M* 8:34–36). Sharing the more total opposition of the outcast prophet, he appears here with Michael as a fomenter of apocalyptic revolution. Refusing "Satans soft dissimulation of friendship" (*M* 8:35), he is a revolutionary Orc who refuses to compromise with tyranny, even when it dons radical disguises. For his unrelenting struggle, he is relegated to damnation by his superiors.

Satan himself belongs to that class of the elect, the Calvinist bourgeoisie who believed their material power proved them predestined to rule "from before the foundation of the World" (*M* 7:1). According to Blake, however, it is they who are totally excluded from salvation "Except by Miracle & a New Birth" (*M* 25:34), since humanity's redemption really lies in the restoration of Brotherhood—that Jerusalem which Satan has left behind him in ruins (*M* 6:14–35).

A tendency to read the "Bard's Song" autobiographically, as a complaint against Blake's labors for Hayley, has tended to obscure Satan's role in dramatizing a more general exploitation. The entire episode bemoans the oppression of labor with Satan as the "Miller of Eternity" (*M* 3:42) whose "Work is Eternal Death, with Mills & Ovens & Cauldrons" (*M* 4:17). Behind the conflicts narrated here, there seems to have been an event similar to Urizen's abdication of the horses of light to Luvah in *The Four Zoas*. Palamabron and Los, his intellectual counterpart, have apparently allowed Satan to gain control over the productive forces, "the plow of Rintrah & the Harrow of the Almighty" (*M* 4:1) and place them in the sevice of capitalist England's "dark Satanic Mills" (*M* 1:8).

As a consequence, a fierce contention develops between Satan and the "Horses of the Harrow" (*M* 7:40) whose reduction to beasts of burden seems to convey the same image of slavery as we find in *The Four Zoas*. These raging beasts are repeatedly associated with working-class Gnomes, the "servants of the Harrow" (*M* 7:18) and "servants of the Mills" (*M* 8:12). The distinctions between Rintrah, the furious horses, and the Gnomes are somewhat unclear, although the fact that in its apocalyptic sense the harrow has military connotations might suggest an identification between horses and the army rank and file. At any rate, the central point seems to be that class oppression of the horses and the Gnomes has aroused Rintrah's anger. This opposition has divided him from the more conciliatory Palambron, who with Los's acquiescence has allowed his authority to be usurped by Satan:

> with incomparable mildness;
> His primitive tyrannical attempts on Los: with most endearing love
> He soft intreated Los to give him Palamabrons station.   (*M* 7:4–6)

Parliamentary power seems to have fallen into Satan's hands and the revolution under the dominion of a hypocritical class hiding its own self-interest under pretenses of reform:

> Next morning Palamabron rose; the horses of the Harrow
> Were maddened with tormenting fury, & the servants of the Harrow
> The Gnomes, accus'd Satan, with indignation fury and fire.
> Then Palamabron reddening like the Moon in an eclipse,
> Spoke saying, You know Satans mildness and his self-imposition,
> Seeming a brother, being a tyrant, even thinking himself a brother
> While he is murdering the just; prophetic I behold
> His future course thro' darkness and despair to eternal death
> . . . .
> My horses hath he maddend! and my fellow servants injur'd.
>   (*M* 7:17–27)

Blake's castigation of the revolutionaries for "Seeming a brother, being a tyrant" recalls Winstanley's charge at the time: "If thou consent to freedom to the rich in the City . . . to the Free-holders in the Countrey . . . [to] the Lords of Mannours, and Impropriators, and yet allowest the poor no freedome, then thou art a . . . hypocrite."[65]

Liberty and Property

More recently, a number of scholars have agreed with A. L. Morton that the civil war was fundamentally a bourgeois revolution in which "the divine right of kings was squarely opposed to, and finally broken upon, the divine right of private property."[66] This class analysis was anticipated at the time by observers from the right as well as the left. Hobbes, for example, complained that the whole tumult was instigated by London merchants "whose profession is their private gain

. . . their only glory being to grow excessively rich by the wisdom of buying and selling."[67] Moderates like Edmund Waller retreated from the opposition, lest an owning class find it has "as harde a task to defend our propriety [against the people's demands], as we have lately had to recover it from the prerogative."[68] By 1647, this note was being sounded by Presbyterians such as Thomas Case in opposition to freedom for the sectaries, who warned that "Liberty of conscience, falsely so called, may in good time improve itself into liberty of estates and liberty of houses, and liberty of wives and, in a word, liberty of perdition of souls and bodies."[69]

The 1650s saw men of property consolidating against lower-class radicalism. Cromwell had forcibly suppressed the Levellers; Diggers were persecuted and scattered; "mechanick" preachers were silenced and arrested under the Blasphemy Act. In Blake's poem, Palamabron collaborates; repudiating his former allies, he calls "A Solemn Great Assembly" in which "The Innocent should be condemn'd for the Guilty" (*M* 11:16). Then he calls no more assemblies at all, and parliamentary power yields to the superior might of arms. Milton confesses that he himself had been implicated in these events: "I in my Selfhood am that Satan" (*M* 14:30). His individualism had allied him with employers and landowners against the multitude; his class consciousness had blinded him to the crimes of exploitation:

> What could Los do? how could he judge, when Satans self, believed
> That he had not oppres'd the horses of the Harrow, nor the servants.
> (*M* 7:39–40)

Unwittingly Los-Milton had failed in his prophetic task, becoming the apologist for a new form of tyranny, negating human solidarity with providential hierarchies:

> So Los said, Henceforth Palambron, let each his own station
> Keep: nor in pity false, nor in officious brotherhood where
> None needs, be active. (*M* 7:41–43)

Blake's charge is founded in fact. Milton, living "out of the sweat of other men" (YP I.804), had made property rights the foundation of all liberties, insisting that they "are indeed under tyranny and servitude; as wanting that power, which is the root and sourse of all liberty, to dispose and *oeconomize* in the Land which God hath giv'n them, as Maisters of Family in thir own house and free inheritance" (YP III.236–37). Setting himself squarely against proposals for economic reform, he condemned such measures as Harrington's agrarian law as "the cause rather of sedition," convinced that England "requires no perilous, no injurious alteration or circumscription of mens lands and properties" (YP VII.445–46). To be free, Christopher Hill instructs us, in the seventeenth century literally meant to own property; the Latin *libertas* had implied the right to exclude others from one's estate, while the *Oxford English Dictionary* includes as a definition of free: "noble honourable. of gentle birth and breeding." Free men were "freeholders" whose property bore no restrictive feudal tenures.[70]

Milton's conception of liberty retains this class character. "To be free," he tells us, is not only "to be pious, wise, just, and temperate," but also "careful of one's property" and "aloof from another's" (YP IV.684). Liberty, he presumes, arises from the dignity, discipline, and responsibility of economic self-sufficiency and is foreign to both the parasitic nobility and the destitute and dependent populace. When Salamasius attacks the revolutionaries as blind and brutish men, Milton responds by defending not universal liberty but the honor and skill of his own class: "It may be true of the dregs of the population, but hardly of the middle class which produces the greatest number of men of good sense and knowlege of affairs. Of the rest, some are turned from uprightness and from their interest in learning their country's laws by excessive wealth and luxury, and others by want and poverty" (YP IV.471). Milton extols those of his class who, "befitting thir qualitie, may bear part in the government" (YP VII.459), for they "come not from the off-scourings of the mob . . . no random throng, but most of them citizens of the better stamp, of birth either noble or at least not dishonorable, of ample or moderate means" (YP IV.674).

Rude Multitudes

Milton's contempt for the wider population could not have been more virulent. Even in the early pamphlets where he allies with the sects against a snobbish episcopacy, upholding freedom of conscience among the lowliest, he betrays his social prejudices. Admitting that the poor are brutish, he chastises the bishops for failing in their reformation, "So little care they of beasts to make them men" (YP I.932). Later he will dismiss the greater part of his countrymen, bemoaning the "ignorant and Slavish mindes" of an "inconstant, irrational, and Image-doting rabble . . . a credulous and hapless herd, begott'n to servility" (YP III.399,691).

It must be granted that Milton was often more perturbed by the masses' conservatism than their extremism. But it never seems to have occurred to him that, among those whose burdens were overwhelmingly economic, there might be little cause for enthusiasm in substituting the rule of their employers for that of the lords. His own goals of a middle-class government, guaranteeing freedom of conscience and dismantling the state church, may have comprised the most progressive alternative at that time, but he could hardly have expected it to excite those whom it excluded. Milton's proposal for a commonwealth in 1659 would have set up an oligarchy of the propertied class in a perpetual senate which would "make the people fittest to chuse and the chosen fittest to govern," "not committing all to the noise and shouting of a rude multitude" (YP VII.442–43). Admittedly, he is anxious here to win the support of men of substance who were rapidly defecting to the monarchy, but his opposition to democracy expressed his own long-standing concern that "not wisdom and authority, but faction and gluttony would elect to Parliament in our name either inn-keepers and hucksters of the state from city taverns or from country districts ploughboys and veritable herdsmen" (YP IV.682).

The humble had had greater expectations of this revolution, for had not the Book of Revelation (19:6) prophesied their own exaltation when the Deliverer would be welcomed by "the voice of a great multitude . . . as the voice of many waters"? Many a radical preacher had built an egalitarian vision on that text, but not Milton. His God even takes time in heaven to avert erroneous attempts to make him champion of the lowly. When he sends his chosen Messiah out alone into what in many ways resembles the apocalyptic battle, God makes the point that "Number to this dayes work is not ordain'd / Nor multitude" (PL VI.809–10). The battle cry of popular revolution is muted to a mild angelic "*Halleluia,* as the sound of Seas, / Through multitude that sung" (PL X.642–43). They are singing, moreover, a hymn of praise to God who has just wisely exposed humanity to the ravages of sin and death. Otherwise, the multitudes in *Paradise Lost* are usually demons.

When Blake pronounces Milton a fallen prophet, he has him confess: "my multitudes are children of Care & Labour," having "piercd the Lamb of God in pride & wrath" (FZ 113:50,52). Milton's fault had been a class arrogance which made moral snobbery the covering cherub of social domination. When Los looks out at the people, all he can see, like Milton, is immorality: "The servants of the Mills drunken with wine and dancing wild" (M 8:8) in that inferno which is an English alehouse. He calls them to salvation through a Protestant ethic of obedient exertion: "And Los said. Ye Genii of the Mills! the Sun is on high / Your labours call you! . . . follow with me my Plow. . . . Resume your labours" (M 8:16–22). The slaves know that their real hell is this servitude. Milton's Jehovah is a metamorphosed

Moloch who sacrifices his children to capitalist slavery: "They Plow'd in tears! incessant pourd Jehovahs rain, & Molech's / Thick fires contending with the rain, thunder'd above rolling / Terrible over their heads" (*M* 8:27–29). Saying, "I am God alone / There is no other! let all obey my principles of moral individuality" (*M* 9:25–26), this god-devil invents damnation to terrorize his rebellious slaves:

> Satan astonishd, and with power above his own controll
> Compell'd the Gnomes to curb the horses, & to throw banks of sand
> Around the fiery flaming Harrow
>
> . . . .
>
> The Harrow cast thick flames & orb'd us round in concave fires
> A Hell of our own making. see its flames still gird me round [.]
> Jehovah thunder'd above! Satan in pride of heart
> Drove the fierce Harrow among the constellations of Jehovah
> Drawing a third part in the fires as stubble north & south
> To devour Albion & Jerusalem the Emanation of Albion.
>
> (*M* 12:16–27)

In a concatenation of apocalyptic images, Blake links the war in heaven with the day of judgment and the harrowing of hell when Jesus descended into the underworld to free the blessed and imprison the guilty. Blake finds this conjunction of apocalypse and fall, holiness and vengeance, salvation and damnation so offensive that he concludes that this Christ must be Satan, the evil one and the accuser. Like Milton's Messiah, who with pretensions of mercy imposed upon Adam and Eve the curse of miserable toil, so now this Satan, feigning kindness, works cruelty:

> The Gnomes in all that day spar'd not; they curs'd Satan bitterly
> To do unkind things in kindness! with power armd, to say
> The most irritating things in the midst of tears and love
> These are the stings of the Serpent!   (*M* 12:31–34)

Blake identifies him, as false Messiah and rebellious Satan, with the English Revolution and those Puritans who selfishly devoured Albion and Jerusalem as their own possession. Under the banner of liberty itself, they had imposed their own curses of terrible labor and had justified the whole hypocritical endeavor by a doctrine of original sin. The birth of this sin from the head of Satan signified for Blake that it was the tool of a self-serving elect, conceived out of "Cupidity unconquerable" (*M* 12:8) to compel the Gnomes to thraldom:

> The Gnomes labourd. I weeping hid in Satans inmost brain
> But when the Gnomes refus'd to labour more, with blandishments
> I came forth from the head of Satan! back the Gnomes recoil'd
> And call'd me Sin.   (*M* 12:36–39)

The Orc Cycle—Revolution Betrayed

The announcement that Milton was a false prophet appears in Night VIII of *The Four Zoas,* directly preceding a sketchy version of the events narrated above (*FZ* 113:48–115:40). Apparently at this point, with Blake's tale having reached contemporary England, the commentary on the Puritan bard, implicit throughout, begins to outgrow the form of this epic, inspiring the explicit treatment of *Milton.* The themes, however, are the same, with the French Revolution offering the same spectacle of a revolution betrayed. *The Four Zoas* had begun its modern phase in Night VI, where the reemergence of Urizen as both Milton's God and the author of modern industry had ushered us into the capitalist era. Urizen had commenced rebuilding civilization as a new form of tyranny:

> Here I will fix my foot & here rebuild
> Here Mountains of Brass promise much riches in their dreadful bosoms
>
> So he began to dig form[ing] of gold silver & iron
> And brass vast instruments to measure out the immense & fix
> The whole into another world better suited to obey
> . . . .
> And the Sciences were fixd & the Vortexes began to operate
> On all the sons of man & every human spirit terrified
> At the turning wheels of heaven shrunk away inward withring away
> Gaining a New Dominion over all his sons & daughters
> & over the Sons and daughters of Luvah in the horrible Abyss.
>
> (*FZ* 73:14–25)

Blake had not come to understand bourgeois politics from history books, for the same dynamics that Milton had faced in the civil war were at work in the 1790s both in the French Revolution and the English reform movement. As Erdman has demonstrated,[71] the latter nights of *The Four Zoas* focus on the dovetailing of English reaction with the degeneration of Napoleonic France "when Luvah in Orc became a Serpent" and "descended into / The State namd Satan" (*FZ* 115:26–27). The predominance of Miltonic images here reveals that ruminations over contemporary events are percolating in Blake's imagination while he continues to be absorbed in the politics of *Paradise Lost.* From the two, he manages to crystallize an analysis of bourgeois society and culture and the revolutions which gave it birth.

In England, enthusiasm for the French Revolution coincided with a resurgence of efforts to revive democratic aspirations buried by the Restoration and the compromise of 1688. Blake, in *The French Revolution,* anticipates a virtual return of Eden: "the ancient dawn calls us

/ To awake from slumbers of five thousand years" (*FR* 7–8). These hopes would be sadly disappointed, but Blake was probably more disillusioned by the revolution's abandonment than its pursuit. Unlike Wordsworth, who traced his disaffection to the Jacobin era, Blake was elated in 1793, castigating the moderate Fayette for deserting the revolution as it moved left. While for us counter-revolutionary myth has made the guillotine the consummate symbol of bloodthirsty radicalism, Blake may have had more in common with the popular tradition which cherished the "spirit of '93" as a time when the *menu peuple* of Paris had briefly wrested a universal franchise and a social program for themselves. From that perspective, the real betrayal came when the wealthy, having allowed the multitude to fight their battles against the king, decided that the time had come to put a halt to the democracy of the Parisian sections. What Saint-Simon once called "rule by the propertyless masses" gave way to Thermidorian reaction. By the time Blake began denouncing France in *The Four Zoas*, the republic had been completely dismantled, and Napoleon had embarked on imperialist wars.

"Liberalism and democracy," Eric Hobsbawm comments, "appeared to be adversaries rather than allies, the triple slogan of the French Revolution, liberty, equality, fraternity, to express a contradiction rather than a combination."[72] English events might have taught Blake the same lesson. As E. P. Thompson tells the story of those turbulent days, initial opposition to the oligarchy of landed and commercial wealth which had ruled England for over a century came from industrialists and dissenting tradesmen.[73] Soon, however, a far wider movement for reform was activated, with Paine's pamphlets being circulated in the thousands by the apprentices and mechanics of the London Corresponding Society and calls going forth for a national assembly in the French spirit to initiate a new government.

What was radical about this movement was its class base and its direct appeal to the masses—100,000 of whom could be mobilized for a demonstration in 1795. Moreover, it was a population that easily moved from political concerns to economic ones, from petitions to Parliament to bread riots. With Paine having leapt from constitutional to economic issues in the second part of his *Rights of Man* and the sansculottes enforcing their radical republicanism in Paris, the respectable recoiled from reform in fright. After 1792, Thompson tells us, "The French revolution *consolidated* Old Corruption by uniting landowners and manufacturers in a common panic."[74] Pitt passed antisedition acts barring all political activity by the masses; Paine was banned, run out of England; meetings were prohibited; radical publications were censored and taxed; trade unions were outlawed; radical leaders were arrested and deported. Blake himself was tried for sedition for having allegedly told one Private Schofield, "The king be damned" and "all soldiers [are] slaves." Thompson writes that "in the decades after 1795 there was a profound alienation between classes in Britain, and working people were thrust into a state of apartheid," with significant consequences for English radicalism: "Isolated from other classes, radical mechanics, artisans and labourers had perforce to nourish traditions and forms of organization of their own. So that, while the years 1791–95 provided the democratic impulse, it was in the repression years that we can speak of a distinct 'working class consciousness' maturing."[75]

It was in those years too that William Blake, brooding over Milton, English politics, and the lessons of history, came to reject not political action but the bourgeois assumptions that guided it, and to begin the enormous labor of refining out of the revolutionary—the Miltonic—tradition a vision purified of that egoism. At this time Satan ceases to be just the radical who upstages God in *Paradise Lost*. Blake still drew his materials from Milton's epic, but his work came to foreshadow modern readings which trace the decline of Satan from his heroic stature in the early books to his final complete degradation.[76] Taking his cue, perhaps, from the erstwhile rebel's ambitious ascent of his throne in Book X, proclaiming his intent to make all earth his empire and "over Man / To rule" (*PL* X.492–93), Blake parodies Satan's collapse as a symbol of revolution turning into its opposite. He captures the demon's grotesque metamorphosis: still vaunting, "he fell / A monstrous Serpent on his belly prone" (*PL* X.513–14) and slithered up into the branches of hell's own forbidden tree:

> No more remain of Orc but the Serpent round the tree of Mystery
> The form of Orc was gone he reard his serpent bulk among
> The stars of Urizen in Power rending the form of life
> Into the formless indefinite & strewing her on the Abyss.
> (*FZ* 93:24–27)

Erdman sees Bonaparte here having "strewn Liberty, Equality, Fraternity upon the winds and reared his head among the dynasts in his bid for imperial Power."[77] We should also note, however, that the context is explicitly anticapitalist. It immediately follows a lament over industrial slavery (*FZ* 91:17–33), with Orc's seduction by Vala suggesting a lust for material possession. We might reasonably conclude that for Blake the degeneration of Satan revealed the fate of bourgeois revolutions.

The same implication might be drawn from the reappearance at this moment of an apocalyptic chariot, perverted to plunder and war:

Arise O Vala bring the bow of Urizen bring the swift arrows of light
How ragd the golden horses of Urizen bound to the chariot of love
Compelld to leave the plow to the Ox to snuff up the winds of
   desolation
To trample the corn fields in boastful neighings.   (*FZ* 93:10–13)

Again we find the chariot a symbol alternately of creativity and
pillage, as instead of plowing the fields it comes to devastate them. As
the vehicle of the apocalyptic Christ in *Paradise Lost*, it also must
have struck Blake as conjoining revolution and conquest:

> Go then thou Mightiest in thy Fathers might,
> Ascend my Chariot, guide the rapid Wheeles
> That shake Heav'ns basis, bring forth all my Warr,
> My Bow and Thunder, my Almightie Arms
> Gird on, and Sword upon thy puissant Thigh;
> Pursue these sons of Darkness, drive them out
> From all Heav'ns bounds into the utter Deep:
> There let them learn, as likes them, to despise
> God and *Messiah* his anointed King.   (*PL* VI.710–18)

Modern society, like ancient society, is based upon conquest; and in
both Milton's England and insurgent France such spoils are taken
under the very banner of revolution. Thus Blake could recreate
Christ's advent to battle "Attended with ten thousand thousand
Saints . . . And twentie thousand . . . Chariots of God" (*PL* VI.767–70)
as the rampages of Luvah and Urizen:

> Ten thousand thousand were his hosts of spirits on the wind:
> Ten thousand thousand glittering Chariots shining in the sky:
> They pour upon the golden shore beside the shining ocean.
> Rejoicing in the Victory & the heavens were filld with blood.
> (*FZ* 12:32–35)

The development of revolution into reaction is symbolized by
Blake in the metamorphoses of Luvah and Orc. Satan becomes the
serpent just as Jesus when he died "became Jehovah" (*MHH* 6),
another starry tyrant in the heavens. The image of Satan as a rebel in
the earlier poems is also now replaced with a more unsettling reading
of *Paradise Lost* which anticipates Empson's allegations that God
was actually conniving with Satan, released from hell for the purpose of overthrowing the happiness of Eden.[78] This collusion reappears in *The Four Zoas* in the plots of Luvah and Urizen against
Albion, which cause humanity to fall "in Selfish cold repose / Forsaking Brotherhood & Universal love in selfish clay" (*FZ* 133:12–13). Like
Winstanley, Blake saw the rise of capitalism as continuing and inten-
sifying that primal catastrophe. Now as before Luvah ("I was love")

perpetuates this decline by turning solidarity into self-love through his lust for Vala. He is the arch-individualist whose boast, "I blotted out / That Human delusion to deliver all the sons of God / From bondage of the Human form" (*FZ* 27:16–18), indicates the liberation of individual aggrandizement from the bonds of common humanity, as well as the religious transcendence that has always acompanied and legitimized this division. Adam and Eve inhabit a garden of Vala because they are already fallen, isolated from all community in a bourgeois state of nature. Blake treats this myth much as Marx would when he observed:

> In this society of free competition the individual appears free from the bonds of nature etc., which in former epochs of history made him part of a definite limited human conglomeration. To the prophets of the eighteenth century . . . the eighteenth century individual, constituting the joint product of the dissolution of the feudal form of society and of the new forces of production which have developed since the sixteenth century, appears as an ideal whose existence belongs to the past; not as a result of history, but as its starting point.[79]

Blake's hatred of "nature" is a revulsion against this individualistic condition, more than a distaste for the pastoral.

Now Blake turns from the rebellious to the ambitious Satan as a model for Luvah. Protesting, "Dictate to thy Equals. am not I / The Prince of all the hosts of men nor Equal know in Heaven?" (*FZ* 22:1–2), he echoes his prototype who aspires "To set himself in Glory above his Peers" (*PL* I.38–39) and demands, "*who is our equal?*" (*PL* V.866). In branding as demonic all obstacles to his revolution, Milton had not spared the traitors within his own party who had placed their immediate personal gain above common political interests, "that therefor we must forgoe & set to sale religion, libertie, honor, safetie, all concernments Divine or human to keep up trading" (*YP* VII.462). Satan's colleagues in demonic council bear strong resemblances to enemies within the bourgeois revolution, and one of them, fittingly, is Mammon.[80]

Possessive Individualism and the Conflicts of Satan-Orc

What differentiates Milton's views from Blake's is that the socialist Blake cares little for Milton's distinction between respectable capitalist enterprise and greedy corruption, between a dignified and just individualism and its reactionary excesses. The middle class had accused the lords as conquerors; but to Blake's mind, the system they themselves built was just a legitimized form of depredation by which the owning classes despoiled the common people of their rights to the earth's resources. In *The Four Zoas,* the triumph of Luvah, with its ancient and Miltonic associations, suggests both conquests. Thus unrestrained competition is unleashed among the once fraternal Zoas until even Los has abandoned the divine vision of brotherhood: "Thou has Abundance which I claim as mine" (*FZ* 12:21). Accordingly, humanity falls into "Division" (*FZ* 4:4) in wars over possession: "Discord began & yells & cries shook the wide firmament" (*FZ* 22:15), "And the dark Body of Albion," the human community, was "left prostrate upon the crystal pavement / Coverd with boils from head to foot. the terrible smitings of Luvah" (*FZ* 41:15–16).

Satan's insatiable aspiration had similarly reduced the Miltonic cosmos to chaos, introducing, as Michael Walzer observes, a dynamism hitherto incompatible with the idea of an orderly chain of being. In the static hierarchy of the feudal cosmos, "the warfare of God and Satan, involving attack, military engagement, strategical maneuver and retreat—this was inconceivable. . . . Only in a Calvinist system could Satan be viewed dramatically as a rebel against the arbitrary sovereign of the universe." The opposition of God and Satan in the earlier view was "a mere function of the enormous, unbridgeable distance between them."[81] But whereas Dante's Satan is firmly lodged in icy hell at the base of the cosmic chain, Milton's is free on divine parole to roam about undermining creation. Emphasis has shifted from the stability of a social hierarchy sanctioned by God and nature to the disturbing potentialities of the individual bourgeois will. Chaos, no longer confined to the unformed elements, now penetrates the entire order of being, threatening heaven itself, as "Intestine War" (*PL* VI.259) provokes "horrid confusion heapt / Upon confusion" (*PL* VI.668–69). In an Empyrean previously held to be immutable, it now seems as "if Natures concord broke, / Among the Constellations warr were sprung" (*PL* VI.311–12).

This anarchic universe is Calvin's fallen world where every man, hoping to be a master, would scratch his neighbor's eyes out. Satan is engaged in Hobbes's "war of all against all" where "a perpetuall restless desire of Power after Power" provokes people "to invade and destroy each other."[82] In C. B. MacPherson's analysis, Hobbes's own society of "masterless men" provided the original of this brutish state which Christopher Hill calls "bourgeois society with the policeman removed."[83] Likewise, Blake perceived in these visions the disorder endemic to a system based upon exploitation and the restless competition and conflict of individual wills. In *The Marriage of Heaven and Hell* he proposes that there is no greater lawlessness than that of the present order. When a respectable angel denounces the chaos of revolution, he retaliates with a vision of the established hell in which there are a "number of monkeys, baboons, & all of that species . . . grinning and snatching at one another," where "the weak were caught by the strong and with a grinning aspect, first coupled with & then devoured, by plucking off first one limb and then another till the body was left a helpless trunk" (*MHH* 20).

Revolution would, in fact, restore order by rebuilding the bonds of community which had been shattered ever since the rise of class society when

> With trembling horror pale aghast the Children of Man
> Stood on the infinite Earth & saw these visions in the air
> In waters & in Earth beneath they cried to one another
> What are we terrors to one another. Come O brethren wherefore
> Was this wide Earth spread all abroad. not for wild beasts to roam
> But many stood silent & busied in their families
> And many said We see no Visions in the darksom air
> Measure the course of that sulphur orb that lights the darksom day
> Set stations on this breeding Earth & let us buy & sell. (*FZ* 28:11–19)

This fragmentation reaches its nadir in Night VI when Urizen explores the abyss which is his reconstructed capitalist order. It is a world in which all communication has broken down. His children, "Scard at the sound of their own sigh" (*FZ* 70:7), "every one wrapd up / In his own sorrow" (*FZ* 70:43–44), do not even realize they share a common predicament, as "in the regions of the grave none knows his dark compeer" (*FZ* 70:15). Yet they clearly suffer the common hell of a selfishly materialistic society which has turned life into torture, imprisoning an entire industrial army in the subhuman existence of its mines and furnaces:

> The horrid shapes & sights of torment in burning dungeons & in
> Fetters of red hot iron some with crowns of serpents & some
> With monsters girding round their bosoms. Some lying on beds of
>   sulphur
> On racks & wheels he beheld women marching oer burning wastes
> Of Sand in bands of hundreds & of fifties & of thousands
>   . . . .
>   till over rocks
> And Mountains faint weary he wandered. where multitudes were shut
> Up in the solid mountains & rocks which heaved with their torments
> Then came he among fiery cities & castles built of burning steel.
>   (*FZ* 70:18–30)

Urizen hopes to impose law upon this world, but he generates the very disorder he is anxious to control. Looking out upon human beings reduced to mutual war within the golden armor of a mercenary society, "scaled monsters or armd in iron shell or shell of brass / Or gold a glittering torment shining & hissing in eternal pain . . . He knew they were his Children ruind in his ruind world" (*FZ* 70:35–36,45). The relationships within society, as between societies, have reached the state of total war that characterizes the later nights of *The Four Zoas* where "Troop by troop the beastial droves rend one another . . . In dire confusion till the battle faints those that remain" (*FZ* 101:47–102:1).

Milton's God and the Centralized State

Ultimately it was Hobbes, and not Locke, who perceived the real implications of basing society on no firmer bond than the market mechanism. By seventeenth-century England, the solidarity of the clan was an ancient memory, and the hierarchic, personal ties characteristic of feudalism were rapidly falling before an onslaught of individual bourgeois wills. We must conjure up a moment when merchants were not entirely distinct from pirates, and trade on the high seas meant war. We have to imagine the chaos of this early capitalism as it depopulated villages, wrenching apart long-standing bonds and filling the roads with vagabonds and the cities with idle, desperate people. After sweeping away the whole system of personal authority resting in the aristocracy, the middle class faced total chaos unless they consolidated a state capable of replacing those ties. Capitalism required that a distinction be established between property and theft. There could be no market society unless people could be forced to honor contracts, no property while anyone capable of raising a private gang could seize whatever he wished. Confronted with the Hobbesian possibilities of unregulated accumulation, Locke maintained that "the great and chief end of Mens uniting into Commonwealths . . . is the Preservation of their Property."[84] Anxious to secure private wealth from the menace of overly powerful monarchs, lawless greed, and especially plebeian desires, Locke developed the model of a parliamentary state representing all and only propertied men. In this context one begins to understand why, as Walzer notes, Milton tended to transform the chain of being into a chain of command, and why, when he comes to express in *Paradise Lost* his peers' most heartfelt desires, they turned out to be a longing for a cosmic cop.

Similar political dynamics had occurred in the ancient world when an age of conquests gave way to the formation of the monarchy. Blake dramatizes this transition in Urizen's rise to sovereignty when

Enitharmon, terrified by the Eternals' tumultuous aggression, calls him to impose law and order:

Descend O Urizen descend with horse & chariots
Threaten not me O visionary thine the punishment
The Human Nature shall no more remain nor Human acts
Form the rebellious Spirits of Heaven. but War & Princedom & Victory
   & Blood.   (*FZ* 11:21–24)

When he does descend, however, it is as Milton's vengeful God, pronouncing, "Lo I am God the terrible destroyer & not the Saviour" (*FZ* 12:26); "Obey my voice young Demon I am God from Eternity to Eternity" (*FZ* 12:23). This metamorphosis achieved by Milton of the Jehovah of ancient empire ["Our Father Augustus Caesar" (PB 658)] into an omnipotent deity reflects the Puritan's own attempt to consolidate a centralized state. In his God Milton seeks a principle of authority upon which a new political order could base its claims. The despotism of that God—lawgiver, judge, general, policeman, and even executioner—must be commensurate with the disorder incorporated in his individualistic universe.

All societies have their authorities; the question always is whom they represent. What makes Milton's God so despotic, finally, is the undemocratic bias of his politics. With all voting and office holding restricted to a property-owning class, the government sought by Milton and his Puritan allies might be described with simple accuracy as a dictatorship of the bourgeoisie. Cromwell was in this sense no great aberration. It is just that when such power was briefly wielded against the upper class it was decried as a horrendous autocracy, while its subjugation of the laboring majority, à la Locke, was often viewed as sensible parliamentary politics.

Like Locke, Milton argues that the poor were fated to be ruled, rather than to rule, by their inferior rationality.[85] He never understood that his declaration "Reason is but choosing" ignored the fact that what the poor lacked was not intellectual potential but adequate choices. Looking out from a great social distance at his nation's shabby vagabonds, illiterate laborers, and peasants, Milton might well conclude that power should rest with a sober and educated middle class. What he, unlike Winstanley, never questions is whether that very hegemony prevents the poor for acquiring the material circumstances which might nurture their own intellectual ray. Having experienced no economic obstacles himself, Milton literally could not see them impeding the lives of others. Viewing all people, like Adam and Eve, as abstracted from the medium of their social conditions, he saw their destiny resting solely upon the wisdom of their moral decisions. That was how a self-made man understood the world. Unable to appreciate the tangled skein of circumstances which enmeshed the common people, Milton judged them by his own values, and when they did not measure up, he called it "sin."

This subjectivity, Blake had always pointed out, was the awful habit of Urizenic conscience. When he denounces "reason" and "virtue" it is because of the disastrous social consequences of using them as standards of one class to deny the rights of others. Such moral judgments led Milton to conclude both that tyranny was inevitable and that the people deserved it:

> Since thy original lapse, true Libertie
> Is lost, which alwayes with right Reason dwells
> Twinn'd, and from her hath no dividual being:
> Reason in man obscur'd, or not obeyd
> Immediately inordinate desires
> And upstart Passions catch the Government
> From Reason, and to servitude reduce.
> Man till then free. Therefore since hee permits
> Within himself unworthie Powers to reign
> Over free Reason, God in Judgement just
> Subjects him from without to violent Lords;
> Who oft as undeservedly enthrall
> His outward freedom: Tyrannie must be,
> Though to the Tyrant thereby no excuse.   (*PL* XII.83–96)

By the same moralistic logic, Milton always upheld the right of a virtuous minority to impose its rule upon inferiors: "More just it is doubtless, if it com to force, that a less number compell a greater to retain . . . thir libertie, then that a greater number for the pleasure of thir baseness, compell a less most injuriously to be thir fellow slaves" (YP VII.455). True, Milton is arguing here for a revolutionary dictatorship that would impose a wider liberty; but the same strictures would apply if the rabble threatened, for example, the economic liberties of their betters. The argument should by now be all too familiar, as again and again we see democracy entrusted to dictators for safeguarding against the "tyranny of the majority."

Throughout Milton's career, he always allowed for the repression of those whose radicalism exceeded his own definition of liberty. Even in *Areopagitica* when he shares with the sects a common opposition to censorship, he implies that the saints' liberty to abjure a religion of ritual in favor of true, self-imposed discipline must be distinguished from licentiousness and unbelief. Safeguards remain against what "is impious or evil absolutely either against faith or maners" which "no law can possibly permit, that intends not to unlaw it self" (YP II.565).

Later when he becomes England's censor himself and approves the Blasphemy Act as "that prudent and well deliberated Act. Aug. 9, 1650" (YP VII.246), he is not retreating from his principles but following their inevitable logic.

Similarly, Milton showed no reluctance in supporting right with might. Since the time when G. Wilson Knight applauded the wordly political virtue of *Paradise Lost,* there has been a countertendency to read Milton's rejection of Satan's military bravado and his disillusionment with Cromwell as the repudiation of martial for moral force.[86] The whole Puritan endeavor had presumed their congruity, had entailed a faith that God's own battles were being fought out in earthly confrontations. Throughout his prose, Milton supports the use of force, only concerned to inhibit from interference in matters of conscience "that law of terror and satisfaction belonging now only to civil crimes" (YP VII.265). The sword of truth could be a sword of iron as well, so long as it was wielded for the right cause. What the ironies of heavenly warfare indicate is Milton's disgust with those who would compensate with arms what they lacked in reason, with feudal chivalry on the right and army adventurism on the left. But as late as 1659 he is still advocating the use of force by those small in numbers but great in virtue; with General Monck marching on London, Milton was not one to rely solely on prayers and exhortations. Likewise, he never held back from either civil war or regicide; he sat in the Council of State the day Cromwell called for suppressing the Levellers and watched the army end its agitations for a democratic constitution with no dampening of his enthusiasm for Cromwell as an instrument of the Almighty. It is only later, when the army refused to abdicate its emergency powers in favor of his esteemed middle-class Parliament, that Milton turned against it.[87]

The contradictions in *Paradise Lost,* its despotic God and military Christ, reflect the dilemmas of this revolutionary, middle-class dictatorship poised simultaneously against a decadent feudalism and the "revolted multitudes" (*PL* VI.31). So too the ambiguities of Satan are inherent in his being a vehicle for all of Milton's enemies, right and left, the aristocratic tyranny and lower-class egalitarianism which threatened the saints' liberty to build a bourgeois paradise in England. Satan is a hybrid monster, and the fact that we find him so familiar demonstrates the profound hold upon us of our culture's central myth—that tyranny threatens as much from below as from above.

The reason Milton can deck his God in royal robes is that his revolution does not abolish the scepter but only internalizes it in a new elite. Kingship is rejected, Winstanley mourns, only so a "Kingly power" based upon "that Beast, Kingly propriety" can take its place.[88] Milton was libertarian enough to push these contradictions to the point where they are completely exposed. Orders and degrees, we feel, do jar with liberty; and Milton has aptly put his own credo in the mouth of the Father of Lies. We cannot help being offended by a deity who behaves like an insecure political boss, ever obsessed with defending his own power. His harshness, his predilection for blaming his victims, his delight in punishment, his complete lack of empathy revealed to Blake who he really was—the grand original of the self-righteous bourgeois who in the larger tyrannies of state and the petty tyrannies of landlord and employer would terrorize and harass the English people. Christ's patronizing mercy can hardly mitigate God's cruelty, for as Blake snorts sarcastically, "First God Almighty comes with a Thump on the Head   Then Jesus Christ comes with a balm to heal it" (PB 555).

The logic behind this repression, however inoffensive, is inescapable:

> Man disobeying,
> Disloyal breaks his fealtie, and sinns
> Against the high Supremacie of Heav'n,
> Affecting God-head and so loosing all,
> To expiate his Treason hath naught left
> . . . .
> Die hee or Justice must.   (*PL* III.203–10)

When the role properly belonging to the true moral aristocracy is usurped by a customary and hereditary elite, then Milton's God is on the side of revolution, but if it is challenged by such unworthies as the devils or the Levellers, then God sanctifies repression. Behind Milton's God is the firing squad which stands in the wings wherever governments rule without mass popular support. The real crime, it turns out, is no mere indulgence of the flesh, no subtle psychological self-alienation—it is treason, a challenge to the authority of those who make the rules: "Die hee or Justice must." Those who are uncomfortable with Milton's God should, like Winstanley and Blake, follow the logic behind his characterization into a scrutiny of the role of courts, prisons, and armies—the prevailing symbols of *Paradise Lost*—in any society based upon class rule.

The Creator of "This World"

Each historical epoch, it has been argued, invents a myth of origins congruent with its own social relations. In the beginning, according to the matrilineal peoples of many tribal cultures, Earth, the Great Mother, gave birth to all things out of her own body. Not so for the patriarchal class societies which succeeded them—their beginning portrays God, the royal Father, in an act of his all-powerful will, ordering nature, creating man and society according to his specifications. But for William Blake, heir to the industrial revolution and prophet of the socialist one, humanity implicitly begins with beings engaged in creating their own environment, their own relationships, and thereby their very selves. The mythology through which Blake expresses this vision was inspired by Milton's assimilation of Genesis and Revelation to the *Theogony*. Thus far we have been following the implications Blake drew from his forerunner's elevation of the Messiah into the chariot of warring Jove. Now we will consider his allegation that by presenting the demonic opposition as a band of energetic Titans, Milton unwittingly revealed his sense of the fundamental usurpation symbolized by his Creator-God.

The redeeming quality of Milton's problematic deity, it has been argued, is his creativity. As Joan Webber explains, "God's justification is the creative urge itself, and that finally is what *Paradise Lost* is all about."[89] Similarly, in his *Dialectics of Creation*, Michael Lieb documents extensively Milton's construction of his epic around the polarity between his creative God and the demonic forces of destruction and disorder.[90] Hence Uriel describes the formation of the universe itself as his infusing a magnificent design into the inchoate elements:

> I saw when at his Word the formless Mass,
> This worlds material mould, came to a heap:
> Confusion heard his voice, and wild uproar
> Stood rul'd, stood vast infinitude confin'd;
> Till at his second bidding darkness fled,
> Light shon, and order from disorder sprung.
>
> (*PL* III.708–13)

The image of light depicts creation emanating from God as an infinite fountain of dazzling intellect and "Answering his great Idea" (*PL* VII.557). At the same time, God is the source of unlimited fecundity, spawning innumerable creatures and impregnating the earth with so potent a spirit that everything he breathes upon itself becomes self-generating.

Creation Through Conquest

In projecting onto this God every image of energy and intelligence, Milton evoked ancient culture's consummate symbol of creative power, Ezekiel's winged chariot:

> The Chariot of Paternal Deitie,
> Flashing thick flames, Wheele within Wheele undrawn,
> It self instinct with Spirit, but convoyd
> By four Cherubic shapes, four Faces each
> Had wondrous, as with Starrs their bodies all
> And Wings were set with Eyes.   (*PL* VI.750–55)

From this image of Milton's Christ, Blake took his own image of creativity, for it was in this aerial form that the Messiah went forth to fashion the universe and "on the Wings of Cherubim / Uplifted, in Paternal Glorie rode / Farr into *Chaos*, and the World unborn" (*PL* VII.218–20).

"Thinking as [he did] that the Creator of this World is a very Cruel Being" (PB 555), Blake admired this creative imagery, but his admiration did not encompass the God it glorified. We can begin to grasp why by noticing that in *Paradise Lost* what creation is all about is power. The very language of its enactment is the language of command. At God's word, chaos "Stood rul'd" (*PL* III.711); when God demanded that earth bring forth creatures, "Earth obey'd" (*PL* VII.453). He orders the waters to disperse as "Armies at the call / Of Trumpet . . . Troop to thir Standard" (*PL* VII.295–97). Moreover, Christ's claims as creator lead to his investiture as king. His accomplishments are celebrated with the ancient Mesopotamian enthronement rite echoed in one of the royal psalms, Psalm 45:

> when at the holy mount
> Of Heav'ns high-seated top, th' Imperial Throne
> Of Godhead, fixt for ever firm and sure,
> The Filial Power arriv'd.   (*PL* VII.584–87)

The poet spares no ceremony. Christ reenters heaven heralded by a full angelic orchestra of harps, organs, and dulcimers, while clouds of incense engulf his mountain throne and choirs greet him with a hymn of kingship and creation:

> Great are thy works, *Jehovah*, infinite
> Thy power;
>   . . . .
>   greater now in thy return
> Then from the Giant Angels; thee that day
> Thy Thunders magnifi'd; but to create
> Is greater then created to destroy.
> Who can impair thee, mighty King, or bound
> Thy Empire?   (*PL* VII.602–09)

Milton reforges here the links between the myths of creation and cosmic war once severed by the priestly editors of Genesis. Christ

charges into the abyss like a sun god against Titanic foes, the erstwhile monsters of the deeps, and like those heroes rests upon this
victory over chaos his rights to empire. He drives the "Giant Angels"
out of heaven like a conquering Zeus in the same chariot in which he
fashioned the universe, making that vehicle a symbol of repression:

> His count'nance too severe to be beheld
> And full of wrauth bent on his Enemies
> At once the Four spred out thir Starrie wings
> With dreadful shade contiguous, and the Orbes
> Of his fierce Chariot rowld.
> . . . .
> Hee on his impious Foes right onward drove,
> Gloomie as Night.
> . . . .
> His arrows, from the fourfold-visag'd Foure,
> Distinct with eyes, and from the living Wheels,
> Distinct alike with multitude of eyes,
> One Spirit in them rul'd, and every eye
> Glar'd lightning, and shot forth pernicious fire.
>
> > (*PL* VI.825–32,845–49)

Here is Blake's source for the transformation of "the eternal wheels of
intellect" which raged in "the wars of eternal life" into "the wheels of
Urizen & Luvah," Milton's God and Christ, as they pursued their
enemies into the deep and as the wheels "back reversd / Downwards
& outwards consuming in the wars of Eternal Death" (*FZ* 20:14–15).[91]

What this narrative implied to Blake was that God was the cause
rather than the adversary of chaos. His commands had, after all,
provoked the conflict in heaven and for no imaginable reason. Moreover, creation and destruction seemed too closely related to his universe.[92] The motive for creating mankind seems to be the devastation
of the angelic legions. The "Womb of nature" in the "wilde Abyss"
(*PL* II.910–11) is closely associated with the hellish waste on which it
borders. And while it may have already existed, this source of all
being does not appear to us until Christ drives the falling devils
through a hole in the empyrean. Whatever Milton's intent, it is easy
to conclude that in his battle against those demons God has created
chaos. Blake so concludes, and in the *Book of Urizen* identifies God's
creation with his wars, which introduce disorder into the universe by
dissolving the primal unity of Eden. This God did not create the
universe, but only reduced it to his dominion. He is a great restrainer
who coerces its dynamic energies to his tyrannical will "in battles
dire / In unseen conflictions with shapes / Bred from his forsaken
wilderness" (*U* 3:14–16).

In this sequence of ironies, the various components of Blake's vision converge. The assimilation of Luvah to Urizen is foreshadowed in that of Christ to Zeus as Jesus to Jehovah. Now Creation, as earlier Salvation, is revealed as an ideology of power. Just as the Messiah wrapped the robes of royalist tradition over the simple garments of rebellion, so now as the world's great author he confounds the order of creation with an order of repression. The wheels of progress are reversed; and, in an obsession with control, he pushes his universe to the brink of chaos. To create is supposedly greater than [having] created to destroy (*PL* VII.606–07), but in *Paradise Lost* God's role in Creation also gives him the authority for destruction and despotism. In this vein, Abdiel rests his argument for Christ's assumed power over the angels upon his role in their creation and proclaims that it is as their maker that God commands complete obeisance:

> Shalt thou give Law to God, shalt thou dispute
> With him the points of libertie, who made
> Thee what thou art?   (*PL* V.822–24)

We are reminded here of the Babylonians' claim that the Code of Hammurabi was erected upon Marduk's creation, for, as Lieb demonstrates, Milton (employing the same analogies as are found in Mesopotamian myth) posits his creator as the antagonist of both natural disorder and political insubordination.[93] Thus every transgression of his rule involves cosmic as well as criminal anarchy. Satan's revolt threatens dissolution of the elements. Adam and Eve throw the whole world out of kilter. The immediate consequence of their sin is an ecological disaster which produces the climactic extremities of arctic and desert and the tempestuous winds that batter sea and shore.

This unification of the cosmic and moral orders with its chiaroscuro patterns of light and darkness, birth and dissolution, harmony and confusion, hierarchic symmetry and levelling disarray accounts no doubt for much of the brilliant architectonics of Milton's masterpiece. However, from the Mesopotamian affirmation of "the harmonious interlocking of nature and society in the person of the sovereign"[94] to the macrocosm-microcosm analogies of the medieval chain of being, the political consequences of such symbol systems have always been less fortuitous than the artistic ones. Once the cosmic and the social orders are equated, the latter, with all its injustices, is lifted above history and beyond criticism to become part of the eternal and unchangeable order of the universe.

Here, in Blake's mind, was that old marriage of Urizen and Vala, that age-old mythological trick which for millennia had kept the poor and uneducated bowing before their rulers, lest the rains not come. The same weltanschauung had caused the zodiac to trap humanity within its starry wheels of destiny, the gods rotating the stars and the stars controlling human fate. Blake tells us that Milton is in that starry heaven when he is called to awakening, for, although the great prophet had challenged many social shibboleths as mere "tyranny of custom" (YP III.190), he himself had worshiped at the shrine of necessity when he wrote his own social order into the structure of creation.

Milton's Satan consciouly rejects this ideology, dismissing Christ's claims as his maker as a "strange point and new" (*PL* V.855) and God's own title as creator as a ploy for asserting ownership and dominion. Creativity, he insists, is rather a virtue belonging to all and thus the angels are God's equals, "self-begot, self-rais'd / By our own quick'ning power" (*PL* V.860–61). His temptation of Eve, scarcely seductive, calls up the image of many a socialist orator, promulgating from his soapbox a dangerous materialist doctrine:

> The Gods are first, and that advantage use
> On our belief, that all from them proceeds;
> I question it, for this fair Earth I see,
> Warm'd by the Sun, producing every kind,
> Them nothing.   (*PL* IX.718–22)

Two hundred years would pass before Darwin threatened to topple Genesis's God from his throne with arguments like these, but Milton must have already heard them. One thinks at once of Winstanley's pantheism when he ruminates: "If you would know spiritual things, it is to know how the spirit or power of wisdom and life, causing motion or growth, dwells within and governs both the several bodies of the stars and the planets in the heavens above; and the several bodies of the earth below, as grass, plants, fishes, beasts, birds and mankind."[95] Winstanley's creator was a Reason which operated through humanity; in his commonwealth, Sunday sermons would bring scientific knowledge to the people. For a society which still based its political institutions on theological sanctions, the growth of such naturalistic attitudes was, as Christopher Hill tells us, quite frightening. Invariably, "mechanic atheism" was considered politically subversive.[96] And it was. When informed that his beliefs "will destroy all government, and all our Ministry and religion," Winstanley honestly acknowledged, "It is very true."[97] He refused to worship a creator who had become the court of appeal—against all reason—for the status quo, who was alleged, in fashioning human beings, to have designed them lords, knights, gentlemen, and landlords.

Divine Creator and Human Producers

The scientific attitudes of mechanics and artisans arose from work which was instructing them in a new faith—a belief that human beings created their own world through skill and ingenuity. But herein lay a new and even more dangerous materialism, one which would find its echo in Marx rather than in Darwin. For if humanity created the world, why did its actual builders have so little title to it? Mechanics who saw themselves "producing every kind / Them nothing" might draw menacing conclusions from Satan's picture of the "gods" who claimed ownership of a world they never created. Winstanley had already provided an allegorical reading of Creation and the Fall which linked both stories to the creation of private property and the exploitation of labor. Milton unintentionally inspires Blake to a similar interpretation when he links those biblical themes to the Promethean myth. In the story in which Prometheus is the cause of man's creation and his debacle, those events are associated with his confrontation with Zeus over the powers of production. Prometheus had supposedly stolen fire, and so the arts of civilization, from Zeus and had bestowed them on mankind. Consequently, he had been chained to a mountain precipice in a condition of perpetual torture and revolt. Like Shelley, Blake was impressed with the Promethean qualities of Milton's demons who are explicitly linked to that famous Titan in Milton's poem.[98] He forges both Prometheus and Satan into his own embodiment of plebeian rebellion, the fiery demon Orc.

Moreover, in *The Marriage of Heaven and Hell* Blake interprets Milton's heavenly feud as a Promethean conflict in which the "Messiah fell & formed a heaven from what he stole from the Abyss" (*MHH* 5–6). Hidden within the orthodox tale of creation, fall, and celestial combat which had been "adopted by both parties" (*MHH* 5) lay a popular history awaiting exposure by the prophet's corrosive imagination. In this version, real creativity proceeds from a Titanic class of laborers, but is repeatedly stolen by the governors, represented by Milton's Messiah, who make that misappropriated productivity the basis for their own realm. A later depiction of these events is even more explicit:

The Giants who formed this world into sensual existence and now

seem to live in it in chains, are in truth. the causes of its life & the
sources of all activity. . . .

   Thus one portion of being, is the Prolific. the other, the Devouring: to
the devourer it seems as if the producer was in his chains, but it is not
so, he only takes portions of existence and fancies that the whole.

   but the Prolific would cease to be Prolific unless the Devourer as a sea
recieved the excess of his delights.

   Some will say, Is not God alone the Prolific? I answer, God only Acts
& Is, in existing beings or Men.

   These two classes of men are always upon earth, & they should be
enemies; whoever tries to reconcile them seeks to destroy existence.
                                                                    (*MHH* 16–17)

"Messiah or Satan or Tempter," Blake adds, "was formerly thought to
be one of the Antediluvians who are our Energies" (*MHH* 17). We note
with Erdman "a substratum of reference here to the economic struggle of producer and exploiter or producer and consumer."[99] In Blake's
mythology, Milton's God does not create the world, but perpetually
wrests its fruits from the real producers whom he has enslaved and
"who now seem to live in it in chains."

   The God who appeared in Ezekiel's flaming chariot, drawn by
fantastic manlike creatures, was in Blake's mind the glorious image
of human intellect in its conquest of nature. However, an inversion
occurred when this metaphoric creator was said to be a separate
being. Then humanity began to worship an image of their own faculties as the source of their achievements and allowed to be undermined their own power to fashion their environment and history.
This doctrine had been imposed on the masses and was the self-
serving credo of a class of people in whose image this God was made.
The hegemony of this ruling class, like their God's, rested upon the
usurpation of others' productivity, a feat ultimately accomplished by
the yoke and the whip, but greatly facilitated when masters could
convince their servants that all goodness emanated from their
employers and all destruction from themselves. This mystification
was propagated by rites such as the enthronement ceremony which
presented the ruler as chosen by the creator from the foundation of
the world as the conduit of his power and the source of nature's life. It
was accomplished in Christian cultures by coupling praise of divine
creation with deprecation of worldly activity or by the self-approba-
tion of an elect which declared itself the agents of divine activity
while denigrating or openly condemning the contributions of others.
In *The Four Zoas*, Blake satirizes these conceptions by depicting
Urizen as a creator who commands slaves to construct his "mundane
shell" as both the natural universe and his earthly empire, and then

proclaims himself alone its maker and ruler. The erection of this monument to his omniscience thus becomes at the same time a detraction from its real builders.

This dialectic, we have tried to show, was also dramatized by Blake in Luvah's theft of the sun-chariot, which we can now recognize as Prometheus's alleged theft of fire seen from the opposite point of view. From this perspective, the event signifies the ultimate expropriation of science, knowledge, technology, and art from—not by—plebeian rebels. The real thieves are Zeus, Marduk, the God of Genesis, Milton's Messiah, and the exploiting classes whose rule they symbolized. In Milton's remarkable poetic polemic, Satan himself reveals to a sympathetic rebel like Blake the real meaning of the celestial chariot. Satan presents it to Gabriel, a loyal angelic subject, as an emblem of the angels' enslavement to a heavenly tyrant who would

> Ride on thy wings, and thou with thy Compeers,
> Us'd to the yoak, draw'st his triumphant wheels
> In progress through the road of Heav'n Star-pav'd.
>
> (*PL* IV.974–76)

Thus it is Milton's own image which redounds upon him in *The Four Zoas* and *Milton* as a condemnation of his God and of his class for perverting human intelligence and yoking Albion's children to servitude:

> When Luvahs bulls each morning drag the sulphur Sun out of the Deep
> Harnessd with starry harness black & shining kept by black slaves
> That work all night at the starry harness.   (*M* 21:20–22)

Blake must have been irked by the way in which *Paradise Lost*, in celebrating the Divine Architect, had rather denigrated his creatures' creativity. Yet by placing the most energetic productivity in hell Milton also lent credence to Satan's Promethean stance. For example, we learn that even heaven was designed by Mulciber, while God presumably looked on in idleness: "His hand was known / In Heav'n by many a Towred structure high, / Where Scepter'd Angels held thir residence" (*PL* I.732–34). Indeed, these demons are such an "industrious crew" (*PL* I.751) that they have barely arrived in exile when they attempt to reconstruct that heaven in hell. While Milton intends us to dismiss such efforts as vanity, we cannot help being impressed. With skill and imagination they raise a magnificent temple city, combining the grandeur of ancient art with the ingenuity of modern technology. Mining and metallurgy are both initiated, and as inventors, explorers, and energetic workers, the demons turn hell into a microcosm of Renaissance culture. With Mulciber serving as inventor, metalworker, and fire god, and with Satan hurling Promethean challenges at heaven, Blake might understandably conclude that they are contesting with the Almighty for the powers of civilization.

The contrast with heaven could not be more striking. The good angels appear to be founders of nothing. As William Empson indicates, they are kept busy running a series of fairly useless errands geared towards preventing a fall which God has already decided to let occur, chasing Satan around the outskirts of Eden while God lets him in a front window. Otherwise, the angels are left to amuse themselves with celestial adoration and sexy interpenetration. Apparently, with Mulciber's departure all heavenly construction is dismantled. Although the Creation presents marvelous possibilities for angelic participation, Milton does not even allow them to watch, but instead summarily dismisses them to "Mean while inhabit laxe, ye Powers of Heav'n" (*PL* VII.162). We need only recall the erection of the fallen world in *The Four Zoas*, where great winged spirits course the heavens, stretching gossamer firmaments across the poles of the universe, while thousands of Urizen's children busily carve out mountains and streams, towers and battlements, to compare what Blake could do with such a scene. By contrast, Milton's Creation, though the result is lush and awesome in its own way, seems terribly inhuman. Christ issues a series of divine edicts, and, for the rest, the show belongs to Mother Earth who brings forth mountains, trees and all living creatures out of "her fertil Woomb" (*PL* VII.454).

When Creation is dramatized as the product of the multifarious processes of human labor, a host of social questions concerning the condition of those laborers are immediately brought to the fore. These problems are completely avoided in procreative imagery, but so is the apocalyptic potential of human creativity. In Milton's myth, Blake sees Albion succumbing to Vala, abandoning the Eden which he would have to construct for Milton's "lower paradise," "a Soft Moony Universe feminine lovely, / Pure mild & Gentle given in Mercy to those who sleep / Eternally" (*FZ* 5:30–32). He designates Milton's garden as Beulah rather than Eden, a "married land" where human beings passively enjoy sensous nature and their own bodies in a respite from the more active pleasures of the imagination. It is no wonder that a modern critic like Tillyard might find it a fortunate fall that ends such passivity.[100] This deficiency of Milton's garden, according to R. J. Werblowsky, is all the more obvious in contrast to the "teeming activity" of hell. Milton's Eden "cannot but strike us as another Bower of Acrasia," he contends, "for what is going on in . . .

Paradise is rather sham activity."[101] We will have to postpone consideration of Milton's sexual Eden to a later chapter. For now, we may note that what is problematic is that Milton endows his primal pair with such dignified rationality and then gives them so little opportunity to actualize it. They live in an almost precivilized state, barely beyond food gathering. Eve works "with such Gardning Tools as Art yet rude, / Guiltless of fire had formd" (*PL* IX.391–92), and Milton speculates that even those implements have possibly been provided by a heavenly foreign aid. "Guiltless of fire," unlike the Promethean devils, humanity had not yet committed the crime of civilization. Passages like this one have led some critics to predicate an ambiguity in Milton's celebration of reason. Raymond Southall remarks that there is a tension between reason and faith in *Paradise Lost* which attests to Milton's participation in the "quietism that was invading Puritan ranks at the time," a quietism which extended to knowledge as well as to practical acitvity.[102] Hence Adam is warned against allowing scientific curiosity to intrude on paradise while Eve falls partly out of desire for a broader knowledge than was available through the Sunday school lessons of angelic missionaries.

How different were these two from humanity's original titanic energies! Adam and Eve appear in Blake's myth, therefore, as fallen Luvah and Vala, ensconced within an overgrown bower of fertility and trapped within the vegetative cycle of existence. This insight is provocative so long as the charge implies something other than literal inactivity. In fact, Milton goes out of his way to incorporate labor in paradise; the real problem lies in the nature of that work. The luxurious garden apparently is wildly prolific without human assistance, effortlessly dropping its fruits into their laps. Their task is simply to restrain an overabundant productivity in what we have seen is to a great extent a moral exercise. They work, like good Puritans, to avoid that idleness which is the devil's workshop, but they create nothing. Aptly, Milton has designated the first man a "domestick" Adam (*PL* IX.318) confined to those tedious activities which are necessary to sustain life without necessarily altering or improving it.

Milton's emphasis here cannot be attributed solely to his literal reading of Genesis, for he makes the same point in identifying civilization with the Fall in the final books of his poem. There, the origins of poetry, dance, music, cattle-breeding, and metallurgy are traced to the corrupt sons of Cain: "studious they appere / Of Arts that polish Life, Inventers rare, / Unmindful of thir maker" (*PL* XI.609–11). Werblowsky points here to the difference between "Cain's toiling iron-founding posterity, and the idyllic, extremely righteous, but rather unproductive Sons of Seth."[103] The prime virtue of Milton's biblical saints lies in their reliance on God, rather than on themselves. Their main contribution to history almost seems to be the seed of generation they contribute to the eventual propagation of the Messiah, the only man in history who will really make any difference. The only other human activity spared from contamination by hubris and worldly vanity is Milton's prayerful poetic search into the ways of God with man.

Although Blake's "mundane shell" shares the condemnation heaped upon Pandemonium, and he too identifies ancient civilization with a fall, his own conception must be distinguished from Milton's subordination of worldly activities to spiritual ones. The arts and sciences do not proceed from the Fall; on the contrary, "Nations are Destroy'd, or Flourish, in proportion as Their Poetry Painting and Music, are Destroy'd or Flourish! The Primeval State of Man, was Wisdom, Art, and Science" (*J* 3). Frequent demonic associations of science and industry in *The Four Zoas* might seem to render Blake a nostalgic primitivist, but in *Jerusalem* it will be Newton who blows the trumpet of the apocalypse. With Frye we must remember that "Blake, like Morris, ranks 'manufacture' with art rather than commerce."[104] The first principle of Blake's universe is that the existence of humanity as such presupposes the transformation of nature by culture and both into man himself. Milton's Christ notwithstanding, this creativity is inherently social, since only cooperation renders culture possible and lifts humanity above the condition of beasts. At the same time, human relationships cannot exist between disembodied intellectuals, much less between mankind and a disembodied God; they are rooted in a life of collective activity and mediated by its products. As Blake expressed it in *Jerusalem*, "Man cannot unite with Man but by their Emanations / Which stand both Male & Female at the Gates of each Humanity . . . When Souls mingle & join thro all the Fibres of Brotherhood" (*J* 88:10–14). Through such cooperative imagination, the whole world is transformed into an extension of humanity—Albion the community, lovingly united with Jerusalem, a city embodying his transformation of nature and society into a perfect expression of himself. It is an idea Marx himself would later express as follows:

> The human essence of nature first exists only for social man; for only here does nature exist for him as a bond with man—as his existence for the other and the other's existence for him—as the life-element of human reality. Only here does nature exist as the foundation of his own human existence. Only here has what is to him his natural existence become his human existence, and nature become man for him. Thus

society is the unity of being of man with nature—the true resurrection of nature—the naturalism of man and the humanism of nature both brought to fulfillment.[105]

What makes Milton's God, like Urizen, a destroyer is the fact that he symbolizes and upholds a stratification of the human community which abolishes all possibility for harmony between humanity and the world. Like Marx, Blake traces the idea of creation to the improverishment of the larger part of the human race:

A being only considers himself independent when he stands on his own feet; and he only stands on his own feet when he owes his existence to himself. A man who lives by the grace of another regards himself as a dependent being. But I live completely by the grace of another if I owe him not only the maintenance of my life, but if he has, moreover, *created* my *life*—if he is the *source* of my life, and it is not of my own creation. . . . The Creation is therefore an idea very difficult to dislodge from popular consciousness. The fact that nature and man exist in their own account is incomprehensible to it, because it contradicts everything tangible in practical life.[106]

Urizen declares himself the creator of all things, alluding to Psalm 104: "This Universal Ornament is mine & in my hands / The ends of heaven like a Garment will I fold them round me" (*FZ* 95:19–20), but he is only the "creator of this world," that is, of capitalism:

First Trades & Commerce ships & armed vessels he builded laborious
To swim the deep & on the Land children are sold to trades
Of dire necessity still laboring day & night till all
Their life exinct they took the spectre form in dark despair
And slaves in myriads in ship loads burden the hoarse sounding deep
Rattling with clanking chains the Universal Empire groans.
(*FZ* 95:25–30)

In this context we can understand the contradictions in Milton's attitude towards creativity and "the arts that polish life." Milton's God and Christ embody the virtues of his own bourgeois saints. They too achieve dominion as "the Worlds great Author" (*PL* V.188) because political systems generally triumph only insofar as they represent a superior mastery of nature. This was as true in capitalist England as it had been when ancient kings enabled the breakthrough to urban civilization by concentrating the surplus of many small producers. Their God, like Milton's, conquered a chaos identified with the backward, superseded order. From the triumphant perspective of the ancient empires (Babylon, Egypt, Greece, Israel, Rome, etc.), "chaos" meant the fertility-worshiping matrilineal tribes which they supplanted and the "barbarians" still existing on their fringes. From the perspective of the English middle class, spearheading by the seventeenth century the most extensive conquest of the material world yet, "chaos" now included both feudal backwardness and the vast "uncivilized" world still deprived of the benefits of English colonization.

For this reason, as we have seen, Milton could fruitfully pose his polemic against feudalism in terms of the old mythic attack on tribalism. His appropriation of the conquest-of-chaos motif reflects the fact that English capitalism in his day was the real heir to the ancient world's scientific and cultural advances, as the rising middle class, breaking the stranglehold of medieval attitudes and social relations, promoted a tremendous leap forward in culture and technology. It is in the historic context of this material renaissance that we must appreciate the grandeur of *Paradise Lost* which for sheer energy and encyclopedic scope is almost unparalleled in literary history. It is also in this context that we must appreciate the dazzling light of reason emanating from that amazing idealization of that victorious class—Milton's God.

Yet in his magnificent hymn to human freedom and intelligence Milton had remained ambivalent about whether civilization derived from Creation or the Fall. It was a schizophrenia not atypical of bourgeois prophets. In feudal society, dependence upon the creator and pessimism towards the fallen world had reflected mankind's real powerlessness before nature at a low level of production. The rise of capitalism seems both to intensify this despair and to contradict it. For the same developments that gave rise to the growth of science, trade, manufacture, and a self-confident middle class were shattering social bonds and creating an alarming social dislocation, filling the roads and cities with hordes of dispossessed peasants. Even middle-class spokesmen like Calvin were disturbed. Thus, while calling upon Protestant burghers to plunge into the mundane affairs of business and politics, Calvin expresses enormous pessimism, warning them to pursue such earthly salvation in constant fear and trembling. Their attempts to reform the world are necessary to halt its dissolution into total chaos, but, he warns, their city on the hill will be an armed camp against Satan's strongholds, not a bourgeois paradise on earth. The same divided consciousness characterizes enlightenment attitudes. On the one hand, the worldly philosophers sing a hymn to progress and the heavenly city to be built through empirical science and liberal politics. On the other hand, they pine nostalgically for the life of the noble savage whose psychic health and social harmony are incompatible with civilized existence.

Milton's vacillations are especially dramatic, for in two brief decades the English bourgeoise had seen its apocalyptic hopes chastened by the realities of class contradictions. In Blake's analysis, the problem ultimately proceeded from the monopoly over creativity and power symbolized by Milton's God and actualized in Blake's own society. Milton had lauded an elite of self-employed, productive citizens, masters of themselves and managers of others. These wisest and best of men he believed to have been providentially chosen to raise a New Jerusalem on English soil. Unfortunately, his celebration of transcendent goodness and its few earthly representatives left the unregenerate masses outside its gates, an ever present threat. When the multitude refused to recognize and follow their betters, he came to include among those demonic forces more and more of his countrymen. Long before Mary Shelley ever articulated it, the middle class had lived with this nightmare: that the price of all their advances was the creation below them of a social monster that would prevent their gains from ever being enjoyed in tranquility. Hence Blake's Urizen lives barricaded against a chaos of his own creation, insecure in his power and terrified of the future.

Labors of Art and Science

Blake did not associate such chaos with the sinfulness of the masses, as Milton did, but with the impoverished hell in which they were forced to live. Since the Renaissance, the expansion of science and education had primarily benefited a tiny elite. Social wealth accumulated alongside horrendous poverty; culture flourished amid mass illiteracy; the spires of London looked down on increasingly fetid slums until by Blake's day the working class stood more miserable than ever before a world of its own creation. The energy of Milton's poetry had captured the confidence of the middle class as it experienced unparalleled freedom and unleashed unheard-of powers of productivity. By the 1790s Blake saw bourgeois society as having come to thrive on a single industry—war—and having produced a life of ceaseless and unmitigated torture in the routine workings of its dark satanic mills:

> And Urizen gave life & sense by his immortal power
> To all his Engines of deceit that linked chains might run
> Thro ranks of war spontaneous & that hooks & boring screws
> Might act according to their forms by innate cruelty
> He formed also harsh instruments of sound
> To grate the soul into destruction or to inflame with fury
> The spirits of life to pervert all the faculties of sense

Into their own destruction if perhaps he might avert
His own despair even at the cost of everything that breathes.
                                        (*FZ* 102:14–22)

Among the worst of this system's offenses was its division of
humanity into warring classes and its obliteration of the divine
imagination in the vast majority. Much has been written about
Blake's concept of imagination, but it is not usually recognized as an
economic one, a celebration of the potential of human productivity.
Conversely, its denial implies the alienation of labor perpetrated by a
system which reduces a whole population to mindless robots:

Then left the Sons of Urizen the plow & harrow the loom
The hammer & the Chisel & the rule & compasses
. . . .
And all the arts of life they changed into arts of death
The hour glass contemnd because its simple workmanship
Was as the workmanship of the plowman & the water wheel
That raises water into Cisterns broken and burnd in fire
Because its workmanship was like the workmanship of the Shepherd
And in their stead intricate wheels invented Wheel without wheel
To perplex youth in their outgoings & to bind to labours
Of day & night the myriads of Eternity. that they might file
And polish brass & iron hour after hour laborious workmanship
Kept ignorant of the use that they might spend the days of wisdom
In sorrowful drudgery to obtain a scanty pittance of bread. (*FZ* 92:17–31)

Fifty years later, Marx would draw the same contrast between the
craftsman's simple implements and the machinery of modern industry: "In handicrafts . . . the workman makes use of a tool, in the
factory the machine makes use of him. There the movements of the
instruments of labor proceed from him, here it is the movements of
the machine that he must follow. In manufacture the workmen are
parts of a living mechanism. In the factory we have a lifeless mechanism independent of the workman, who becomes its mere living
appendage . . . it does away with the many sided play of the muscles
and confiscates every atom of freedom both in bodily and intellectual
activity."[107] It was this intellectual debilitation, more than just a
restricted consumption, that evoked Marx's hostility toward capitalist production. Like Blake, he saw it robbing humanity of its most
precious quality, a capacity for self-creation. The worker becomes
alienated from his own productive activity: "He does not affirm
himself but denies himself, does not feel content but unhappy, does
not develop freely his physical and mental energy but mortifies his
body and ruins his mind." Then Marx adds the remarkably Blakean

point that "just as in religion the spontaneous activity of the human imagination . . . operates independently of the individual—that is, operates on him as an alien, divine or diabolical activity—so is the worker's activity not his spontaneous activity. It belongs to another; it is the loss of his self."[108]

Blake understood this phenomenon so well because in a unique way he himself stood outside these divisions—a self-educated worker, a laboring artist, a highly skilled, creative, intellectual artisan—representative of a class which was rapidly becoming obsolete. His own experience taught him that human fulfillment, its Eden, lay in the process and the produce of creative work, while its true hell was servile toil, a slavery performed for no inherent worth to self or society but "in sorrowful drudgery to obtain a scanty pittance of bread."

The blind spot in Milton's vision lay in his acceptance of a demeaning division of labor and the class system on which it was based, and his reification of the distinctions between intellectuals and capitalists and their lowly laborers as a distinction between rationality and irrationality, and ultimately between the saved and the damned. Looking out upon the ignorant masses from his privileged height, Milton could envision no human solution to the conflict between a rational few and the mobs that had trampled their dreams. Although he knew that his own education and leisure had been based upon the sweat of other men, he never imagined that material progress might eliminate the obstacles to mass enlightenment. Unlike his friend Samuel Hartlib, he never even proposed universal education. The hierarchy of merit was too fundamental to his sense of reality for him to seek its abolition—at least in this world.

In Milton's defense, it must be recognized that to advocate an elite of talent, rather than birth, was truly revolutionary at that time, while technology had not even begun to reveal the potentialities that would inspire the egalitarian utopias of the nineteenth century. Nor was the illiterate, unorganized, and mostly rural lower class of his era the same force to be reckoned with as that emerging in Blake's London. Given who he was and when he lived, Milton's contradictions were unavoidable. Fearing the masses as demonic, he could find no resolution to the problems which perplexed him. For Milton, history becomes a standoff, a battleground where God's forces and Satan's would continue to clash until the Almighty, deciding that "Warr wearied hath perform'd what Warr can do" (*PL* VI.695), would step in to dismiss his beleaguered saints and put an end to it all. It is to Milton's credit that he never gives up his apocalyptic hope that God in his mysterious way would some day work the whole mess out—

although he has not the faintest idea how. He winds up in the wilderness among the "intricate mazes of Providence" (*M* 2:17) with barely a flickering candle to light the path ahead—a pretty disastrous end for a prophet.

Revolutionary Apocalypse

What distinguishes Blake's vision from Milton's is his far more democratic faith in the people themselves. The real hope for redemption, he believed, lay in the revolt of the enslaved masses, the rebirth of Luvah—Orc, "the Divine Lamb Even Jesus" (*FZ* 33:11) to abolish all class differences and reunite humankind. Unlike Milton, when Blake faced abortive revolution and the defection of the misguided masses to counter-revolution, his vision of the future was only further clarified. By the time Blake wrote Night VIII, recent revolutions had degenerated under the greed and amibtion of new elites. War unleased a universal terror, and Urizen, bent upon domestic repression, "called together the Synagogue of Satan in dire Sanhedrim / To Judge the Lamb of God to Death as a murderer & robber" (*FZ* 105:5–6). This repression of real prophets is accompanied by a revival of mystery in new and horrible forms to delude the people, to take Jerusalem "Captive by delusive arts impelld / To worship Urizens Dragon form to offer her own Children / Upon the bloody Altar" (*FZ* 111:2–4). The "Harlot of the Kings of Earth" (*FZ* 111:6) is communing with Orc in deceitful pity to debilitate his rebellious will and seduce him into a passive collaboration with his enemies. So Blake had watched the English people drawn by government propaganda from Jacobin fervor to patriotic enthusiasm for imperialist wars, while the French enlisted in Napoleonic legions to conquer Europe. Blake's concern with religious mystery may specifically refer to the Methodist campaigns of the period. Methodism may not be what prevented an English revolution in the 1790s, as historian Elie Halévy once argued, but Blake's perception of political significance in middle-class attempts to reform the poor is accurate.

However, avoiding Milton's idealism, Blake understood that it was not ideological faith alone that forged a revolutionary class; its opposition arose out of material realities too profound to be long avoided, no matter how great the confusion. Even as the history of tyranny and lies consolidates in a "Vast Hermaphroditic form" (*FZ* 113:20) outside Jerusalem's gates, the very misery of the Eternal Man awakens his sense of solidarity, and he reappears weeping:

That Man should Labour & sorrow & learn & forget & return
To the dark valley whence he came to begin his labours anew

In pain he sighs in pain he labours in his universe
Screaming in birds over the deep & howling in the Wolf
Over the slain & moaning in the cattle & in the winds
And weeping over Orc & Urizen in clouds & flaming fires
And in the cries of birth & in the groans of death his voice
Is heard throughout the Universe wherever a grass grows
Or a leaf buds.   (*FZ* 110:19–27)

Blake's revolution depends upon an alliance between Los and Orc, the visionary intellectual and the oppressed masses, whose interactions, as we saw in Night VII, are dialectically intertwined. Orc's sufferings, flaring repeatedly into revolt, can rekindle Los's idle furnaces. And the eternal prophet can provide the light which will enable the rebellious multitudes to penetrate all the ruses through which Urizenic enemies would pervert its liberating energies. Now the Lamb of God must rend the veil of mystery (*FZ* 110:1) and smash Milton's own idols of creation and moral righteousness, election and individual salvation, selfhood and holy war that have kept the people yoked to their foes:

> These two classes of men are always upon earth, & they should be enemies; whoever tries to reconcile them seeks to destroy existence.
>   Religion is an endeavour to reconcile the two.
>   Note. Jesus Christ did not wish to unite but to seperate them, as in the Parable of sheep & goats! & he says I came not to send Peace but a Sword.   (*MHH* 16–17)

In the spirit of a modern revolutionary hymn in which the working class proclaims that it wants "no condescending saviors," the aroused populace, directed by the true prophet to clarify its own consciousness, disavows those respectable allies who are corporeal friends but spiritual enemies and finally assumes responsibility for its own future. The one apocalyptic figure which therefore disappears from Blake's joyous consummation in Night IX is the Messiah, for the idea of just rulers has been totally absorbed in the communist vision of a people collectively developing the capacities of all.[109] In the final conflict which now commences, the transformation will be at once cultural, political and economic. Along with kings, generals, and taskmasters are overthrown the priests of mystery, the force and the fraud which have perpetuated subjection:

> Go down ye Kings & Councillors & Giant Warriors
>   . . . .
> Go down with horse & Chariots & Trumpets of hoarse war
>   . . . .

Lo darkness covers the long pomp of banners on the wind
And black horses & armed men & miserable bound captives
Where shall the graves recieve them all & where shall be their place
And who shall mourn for Mystery who never loosd her Captives

Let the slave grinding at the mill run out into the field
Let him look up into the Heavens & laugh in the bright air
Let the inchaind soul shut up in darkness & in sighing
. . . .
Rise & look out his chains are loose his dungeon doors are open
And let his wife & children return from the opressors scourge
. . . .
Are these the Slaves that groand along the streets of Mystery
Where are your bonds & taskmasters.   (*FZ* 134:7–26)

With the end of exploitation, repression, and the mystery which
disguised them, Urizen ceases to be a god, "anxious his Scaly form /
To reassume the human" (*FZ* 121:1–2). What remains of divinity
is a creativity which is democratized and incorporated in all human activity. The reunification of the four Zoas now occurs within a community of collaborative effort. Urthona's sons "ringing the
hammers sound . . . to forge the spade the mattock & the ax"
(*FZ* 124:20–21) and give them to the sons of Urizen. They finally
return to the plow and harness it again to the eternal horses who leave
off pulling the vehicles of war. Now the sun-chariot, traversing the
heavens, assists the harvest as Luvah's sons, no longer yoked to
slavery, lead golden wagons filled with grapes and corn:

His sons arising from the feast with golden baskets follow
A fiery train as when the Sun sings in the ripe vineyards
Then Luvah stood before the wine press all his fiery sons
Brought up the loaded Waggons with shoutings ramping tygers play
In the jingling traces furious lions sound the song of joy
To golden wheels circling upon the pavement of heaven.
                                                    (*FZ* 135:26–31)

Threshing the corn, Luvah gives it to Urthona to grind while Tharmas begins to bake the Bread of Ages. The time is arrived when "to
Labour in Knowledge. is to Build up Jerusalem" (*J* 77). No longer are
people divided by an alienating labor and a debilitating passivity;
rather a new rhythm is established, with Urizen "Calling the Plowman to his Labour & the Shepherd to his rest" (*FZ* 138:29). No more is
the culture of an elite set against the labor of the masses:

Then siezd the Sons of Urizen the Plow they polishd it
From rust of ages all its ornaments of Gold & silver & ivory

Reshone across the field immense where all the nations
Darkend like Mould in the divided fallows where the weed
Triumphs in its own destruction they took down the harness
From the blue walls of heaven starry jingling ornamented
With beautiful art the study of angels the workmanship of Demons
When Heaven & Hell in Emulation strove in sports of Glory.
(FZ 124:6–13)

The "study of angels" and "the workmanship of Demons"—heaven
and hell—are wed in the building of human civilization.

The disappearance of the Creator-God and his Messiah leaves all
humanity, now possessed of their world, creating and redeeming
themselves. For in the reconstruction of material and social relations
it is human beings themselves who are sown and harvested, vinted,
threshed, and forged anew. So Urizen begins "to sow the seed he
girded round his loins / With a bright girdle & his skirt filld with
immortal souls" until "from the hand of Urizen the myriads fall like
stars" (*FZ* 125:3–6), and Luvah waits to gather the "human harvest"
(*FZ* 125:20). As we reach the culminating image of Blake's epic,
humanity as earth-owner and craftsman, reunited with nature, is
recasting his own being in the furnaces of imaginative labor:

The hammer of Urthona sounds
In the deep caves beneath his limbs renewd his Lions roar
Around the Furnaces & in Evening sport upon the plains
They raise their faces from the Earth conversing with the Man.
(*FZ* 138:35–38)

The inhibiting walls of private property are finally left behind. And
now Blake's final vision casts a last fleeting dialectical glance backward to Milton, dismissing his repression and his dark religious world
view and fulfilling his revolutionary prophetic stance. Then mystery
is no more; and knowledge and technology, no longer perverted,
become tools of human liberation:

& Urthona rises from the ruinous walls
In all his ancient strength to form the golden armour of science
For intellectual War The war of swords departed now
The dark Religions are departed & sweet Science reigns.
(*FZ* 139:7–10)

9

The Politics of the Family

Is this thy soft Family-Love
Thy cruel Patriarchal pride
Planting thy Family alone,
Destroying all the World beside.

A mans worst enemies are those
Of his own house & family.
                                    (*J* 27:77–82)

Blake refused to take the Daughters of Memory for his Muses because for him history was not relegated to the past; it paraded outside his own window in the age-old conflicts which had been inherited, unresolved by English civilization. Among these was the battle of the sexes, for the clash between the mother-right of ancient tribes and the triumphant patriarchal order, memorialized in the overthrow of the goddesses of yore, had not been settled as conclusively as those myths claimed; the conflict had only been domesticated and incorporated into the squabbles within the monogamous family. Consequently, Milton can infuse that mythology, particularly as it appears in Genesis, with his own experience of the conflicts within contemporary love and marriage.

Blake finds Milton's accomplishment, in this regard, as inspiring and disturbing as his dramatization of bourgeois politics. When, in *Milton,* the later poet subjects his predecessor to criticism and self-criticism, he has Milton reject both aspects of false consciousness—his "selfhood" (bourgeois individualism) and the patriarchalism which induced his domination of the women in his household and the repression of his own sexuality. In plate 27 of *Jerusalem,* Blake links both errors—the denial of the human community and the repression of the individual by the patriarchal family.

Henry Crabb Robinson reports a conversation in which Blake announces, "I saw Milton in Imagination. And he told me to beware of being misled by his *Paradise Lost*. In particular he wished me to shew the falsehood of his doctrine that the pleasures of sex arose from the fall—The fall could not produce any pleasure." "And then," Robinson continues, "he went off upon a rambling state of a Union of Sexes in Man as in God—an androgynous state in which I could not follow him."[1] In *The Four Zoas* Blake performs the service of rewriting *Paradise Lost*, eliminating those errors with regard to sex and the family that derive from Milton's "Spectre."

"Imparadis't in one anothers arms"

In comparing the poems, we find that Milton anticipated Blake in associating Eden with erotic fulfillment and the Fall with sexual alienation. He presents Adam and Eve "Imparadis't in one anothers arms / The happier *Eden*" (*PL* IV.506–07). Sexual communion is at the essence of Eden, functioning as a kind of sacrament of universal harmony. The intense unity of the lovers, "one Flesh, one Heart, one Soule" (*PL* VIII.499), and their expanded senses, particularly of smell and touch, allow an erotic communion with Eden, itself an organic body of nature. When Adam and Eve embrace in its "sacred and sequesterd" bower (*PL* IV.706), all distinctions of self and other seem to disappear. Entering this veritable womb of nature, a floral cavern with walls delicate as human tissues, is like making love to the earth itself. As they embrace each other and their world, "on thir naked limbs the flourie roof / Showrd Roses" (*PL* IV.772–73).

Here is Blake's erotic Beulah, his "married land" where the same harmony exists between human beings and with their environment. Thus his primal lovers, Los and Enitharmon, are also a mythic evocation of the relationship between the human subject and the material world

> in those mild fields of happy Eternity
> Where thou & I in undivided Essence walkd about
> Imbodied. thou my garden of delight & I the spirit in the garden
> Mutual there we dwelt in one anothers joy revolving.   (*FZ* 84:4–7)

Blake's paradise underlines another aspect of Milton's as well, for it is also a playground where the pleasures of love are identified with the joys of childhood. Adam and Eve are first described as "two gentle Fawnes at play" (*PL* IV.404), while "About them frisking playd / All Beasts of th' Earth" (*PL* IV.340–41). We never forget that we are watching the childhood of the race. Similarly, Blake will present his innocents, Tharmas and Enion:

> Thus in Eternal Childhood straying among Valas flocks
> In infant sorrow & joy alternate Enion & Tharmas playd
> Round Vala in the Gardens of Vala.   (*FZ* 131:16–18)

So Blake identifies Milton's garden as a maternal paradise, and the Fall, simultaneously, as a loss of adult sexual fulfillment and infant joys.

"Torments of Love and Jealousy"

Blake also takes from his Puritan forebear the idea of a fall into the psychological fragmentation of sexual alienation, the "agonie of love till now / Not felt" (*PL* IX.858–59). When Blake cries out in *Jerusalem*, "Shame hath divided Albion in sunder!" (*J* 21:6), he is only following the implications of Milton's own association of the Fall with sexual guilt:

> Nor those mysterious parts were then conceald,
> Then was not guiltie shame, dishonest shame
> Of natures works.   (*PL* IV.312–14)

Milton's brilliant depiction of Adam and Eve, "wearied with thir amorous play" (*PL* IX.1045) in the first act of fallen sexuality, antici-pates not only Blake, but also the whole erotic wasteland in which clerks carbuncular and their unhappy girlfriends try to blot out the misery of their lives in joyless copulation. We pass from the tranquil, free and mutual communion of Edenic sexuality to a seduction whose wheedling, flirtatious tones all bespeak manipulation. Under the aphrodisiac influence of the forbidden fruit, the teasing, flattering lovers draw each other against the brakes of their resistant wills. Consciousness, which once expanded in the exultation of love, now appears only as a barrier that must be obliterated: "As with new Wine intoxicated both / They swim in mirth" (*PL* IX.1008). The language no longer expresses joy and communion, but hunger as the passive lovers become the objects of alien appetites. We have passed from the experience of cosmic unity to the mere alleviation of a genital itch.

The entire scene has an air of hasty, guilty satisfaction, with Adam acknowledging that now it is deprivation rather than fulfillment which turns him on: "if such pleasure be / In things to us forbidden, it might be wish'd, / For this one Tree had bin forbidden ten" (*PL* IX.1024–26). Desire and denial are now conjoined. The lovers have apparently succumbed to some internal ban on their own enjoy-ment. When they awake from an anxious sleep and feel themselves under a spotlight of cosmic judgment, it is only an extension of their disapproving self-consciousness in the act of love itself. They have become divided against their own feelings and against each other. Adam now assails Eve as the source of his own repudiated desires, the external source of his own alienated passion, a temptress "soild and staind" (*PL* IX.1076) by association with his sexuality.

Furthermore, the body is now divided from itself and from its environment. Adam and Eve seek to hide "The Parts of each from other, that seem most / To shame obnoxious, and unseemliest" (*PL* IX.1093–94). Here is the essence of what will in a later day be called the "castration complex": all erotic energies are concentrated in the genitals, which are then blocked off from the rest of the body. This repression stifles the whole flow of feeling, thus prohibiting full sensuous contact with the world. The environment, which once appeared as an extension of the human organism, embraced by its expansive senses, is now a covering for a naked human spirit couching in shame within the walls of its own skin. "Cover me ye Pines," cries Adam, "O might I here / In solitude live savage, in some glade / Obscur'd" (*PL* IX.1088,1084–86).

In *The Four Zoas*, Blake recapitulates these splits between man and woman, humanity and nature, mind and body. Milton's lament for a joy that has been lost is linked by Blake to the only paradise humanity ever had, its own unrepressed material life "In Eden; in the Auricular Nerves of Human life" (*FZ* 4:1). The Fall becomes in Blake's subtitle, "The torments of Love and Jealousy in The Death and Judgement of Albion the Ancient Man." In his version, humanity explicitly falls from the joys of love to the "lineaments of ungratified Desire" (*FZ* 48:1). Thus Los mourns on the dismal wind:

> Once how I sang & calld the beasts & birds to their delights
> Nor knew that I alone exempted from the joys of love
> Must war with secret monsters of the animating worlds.
>
> (*FZ* 82:5–7)

The monsters are of course his own alienated passions, for the Fall has been the fall of the human body,

> human bones rattling together in the smoke and stamping
> The nether Abyss & gnasshing in fierce despair panting in sobs
> Thick short incessant bursting sobbing. deep despairing stamping struggling
> Struggling to utter the voice of Man struggling to take the features of Man. Struggling
> To take the limbs of Man
>
> . . . .
>
> Crying. Fury in my limbs. destruction in my bones & marrow
> My skull riven into filaments. my eyes into sea jellies.   (*FZ* 44:15–24)

This fall of the body involves a general shrinking of the human senses: "two little orbs hiding in two little caves," "Two Ears in close volutions," "Two nostrils bent down to the deeps," "a red flame a tongue of hunger / And thirst," when "bones of solidness froze over all his nerves of joy" (*FZ* 54:21,25,29; 55:4–5; 54:14). As with Adam and Eve, the world divides into self and other, for the world cut off from desensitized human feelings becomes alien and opaque: "Thy roses that expanded in the face of glowing morn / Hid in a little silken veil scarce breathe & faintly shine" (*FZ* 81:34–82:1). Milton's picture of the fallen lovers hiding their genitals in shame becomes Blake's vision of the barriers to intercourse as the bars on the gates of paradise:

> Three gates within Glorious & bright open into Beulah
> From Enitharmons inward parts but the bright female terror
> Refusd to open the bright gates she closd and barrd them fast
> Lest Los should enter into Beulah thro her beautiful gates.
>
> (*FZ* 20:4–7)

On another level, the "fall into Division" (*FZ* 4:4) signifies the alienation of the sexes as Tharmas and Enion, Los and Enitharmon, Urizen and Ahania, Luvah and Vala each repeat the tragedy of Milton's lovers. *The Four Zoas* opens with Tharmas and Enion reenacting the agonies of Adam and Eve who "in mutual accusation spent / The fruitless hours" (*PL* IX.1187–88). Torn from each other by the conflicting demands of desire and denial, Enion cries, "Once thou wast to Me the loveliest son of heaven—But now / Why art thou Terrible and yet I love thee in thy terror"; and Tharmas replies in despair, "my Emanations are become harlots. . . . O Enion thou art thyself a root growing in hell / Tho thus heavenly beautiful to draw me to destruction" (*FZ* 4:20–21,35,38–39).

The conflict between the sexes, with its implications for an alienation of one's own sexuality, is also a self-division. Enion, in splitting off from Tharmas, divides him from himself, creating a "Spectre" (*FZ* 5:15). In fragmenting the Zoas into self and spectre, Blake dramatizes the psychological schizophrenia of a Christian doctrine articulated by Saint Paul: "We know that the law is spiritual but I am carnal. . . . For I do not do what I want, but I do the very thing that I hate. Now if I do what I do not want, I agree that the law is good. So then it is no longer I that do it, but sin which dwells within me. For I know that nothing good dwells within me, that is, within my flesh" (Rom. 7:14–18). In accepting a law of repression, one has to alienate the passionate side of the self. Hence the idea arose which Blake so despised, "That Man has two real existing principals Viz: A Body & a Soul. That Energy. calld Evil. is alone from the Body. & that Reason. calld Good. is alone from the Soul" (*MHH* 4). In this image, the

Christian soul is revealed as nothing other than that unhappy consciousness, the spectre that doubles back on the self when it becomes estranged from its own material life, for "Energy is the only life and is from the Body" (*MHH* 4).

It is here, of course, that Blake's analysis will begin to diverge from Milton's.[2] For although the poets concur in some respects in their description of human life before and after the Fall, Blake completely rejects Milton's belief that the "cause of all our woe" (*PL* I.1) is "sin," or that "sin" could in any way be an excess of desire. Attributing that doctrine to Milton's own spectre, Blake takes over his myth and builds his own vision on the cracks and contradictions in Milton's story. If we examine the original, there appears on the surface to be no immediate connection between the effects of the Fall—sexual neurosis, alienation from nature, servile toil, the battle of the sexes—and its causes. Those disorientations in human experience all appear as arbitrary punishments for an act of primal naughtiness in which the first children broke a parental command and dipped into a divine cookie jar. On closer examination, however, we discover that the prohibition against the Tree of Knowledge was not, as alleged, God's "sole command" (*PL* VIII.329). Rather, Milton portrays the Fall as the result of the breach of three separate laws written into the structure of Eden, the obligations to (1) restrain sexual desire, (2) maintain a sexual hierarchy, and (3) obey any other rules laid down by the Almighty Father. Since these assumptions are precisely those upon which the bourgeois family is built, they lead us into the heart of the contradictions within Milton's culture.

"Among unequals what societie?"

The most glaring of these contradictions lies in the fact, observed by numerous critics, that having identified paradise itself with erotic communion, Milton then has Adam fall not through pride or intellectual curiosity, as earlier commentators on Genesis had proposed, but through his love for Eve. "Fondly overcome with Femal charm" (*PL* IX.999), Adam is bereft of Eden in attempting to preserve the unity which had been its essence. "Flesh of Flesh, / Bone of my Bone," he cries at the moment of his fall, "How can I live without thee?" (*PL* IX.914–15,908). This conflict arises from an ambivalence towards sexual love which Milton displays throughout the poem. On the one hand, he celebrates "the Rites / Mysterious of connubial Love" (*PL* IV.742–43); on the other hand, he has Raphael warn Adam, in paradise, no less: "In loving thou dost well, in passion not" (*PL* VIII.588). Milton simultaneously elevates sexual love to a holy passion and denigrates it as an act of "Cattel and each Beast" (*PL* VIII.582). When later the forbidden fruit turns out to be an aphrodisiac, it becomes clear that the schizophrenic consciousness of the poet preceded that of Adam and Eve as the real serpent intruding upon Edenic bliss.

Adam's failure to put love in its proper place involves, moreover, a failure to put Eve in her proper place. In her article on kinship patterns in *Paradise Lost*, Marcia Landy indicates the whole system of sexual subordination built into Milton's poem.[3] Adam and Eve are "not equal, as thir sex not equal seemd; . . . Hee for God only, shee for God in him" (*PL* IV: 296,298), and Eve's fall takes on an aura of deliberate rebellion against this inferior status. Seduced by one who has succeeded in "ventring higher than [his] Lot" (*PL* IX.690), Eve then justifies her action as a means to equality: "for inferior who is free?" (PL IX.825). Adam's sin, on the other hand, is explicitly blamed upon the abdication of male supremacy for which Christ chastises him: "Was shee thy God, that her thou didst obey . . . that to her / Thou did'st resigne thy Manhood?" (*PL* X.145–48).

Blake captures Milton's dilemma in Enion's cry: "can Love seek for dominion?" (*FZ* 41:12). The problem was implicit in the Puritan conception of marriage, which, as William Haller summarizes it, stressed precisely this compatibility between love and power: "Though the wife was bound to obey the husband, the husband was bound to love the wife. . . . It was this relationship of love and obedience, reciprocal, inseparable, exclusive, and unique, which made marriage in truth the image, nothing less, of Christ's relation to his Church."[4] The source for this doctrine is Saint Paul, who insisted that "the husband is head of the wife" (1 Cor. 11.7), and it was elaborated endlessly by the church fathers. However, when the medieval church denounced "filthy woman, filthy matter," it was as an encouragement to celibacy. What was new in the seventeenth century was the attempt to reconcile the doctrine of feminine inferiority with the elevation of the married state.

In addition, it had formerly been assumed that love and marriage were probably incompatible. The Jewish patriarchs took wives to get sons in marriage deals of great complexity. Primitive myth reveals a world of eroticism completely unrelated to marriage; the ancient Greeks exalted a love which was both extramarital and homosexual, and the rules of medieval chivalry assumed love to be by nature adulterous. As C. S. Lewis demonstrates, the association of love with marriage began as late as the sixteenth century, with Shakespeare and Spenser leading their lovers to the altar rail in what became the ultimate happy ending.[5]

Milton and the Puritan preachers reflect this same historical phenomenon.[6] Although the Anglican wedding ceremony listed three objects of marriage: the procreation of children, the relief of concupiscence, and "the mutual help and comfort that one ought to have of the other,"[7] Puritan ministers now emphasized the last:

> They exhorted the young to choose helpmeets with godly companionship as the chief end to be desired. . . . They exhorted parents not to interfere with such promptings in the hearts of their children. A wife, they said, was to be regarded not simply as a bedfellow or a servant but as a spiritual equal and companion. The later preachers especially dilated upon the joys of spiritual union, sanctifying union of the flesh, and upon the misery of those who, coupled in body, were divided in soul. The most enthusiastic went so far as to say that husbands and wives, in thus communing with one another, came nearer to communion with God himself.[8]

These conceptions, usually traced back to the Edenic marriage of Adam and Eve, pervade *Paradise Lost*.

The Puritans' emphasis on voluntary marriage and its benefits to the individual was consistent with their general concern over freedom of conscience. We might expect, therefore, that such assumptions would be taken to their logical extreme by Milton, who applies libertarian principles to marriage in his *Doctrine and Discipline of Divorce*. There he upholds the argument of Paulus Fagius that "indisposition, unfitness, or contrariety of mind, arising from a cause in nature unchangeable, hindring and ever likely to hinder the main benefits of conjugall society, which are solace and peace, is a greater reason of divorce than naturall frigidity" (YP II.242). The problem however is that if these ideals were taken seriously, every marriage would be found to be hindered by such "contrariety of mind arising from a cause in nature unchangeable"—namely, the intellectual inferiority of all women. Milton faced this dilemma in his own marriage to Mary Powell when his high hopes for "the cheerfull conversation of man with woman" were dashed by the discovery that "the bashfull mutenes of a virgin may oftimes hide all the unlivlines and naturall sloth" (YP II.235,249) and, he might have added, an inferior education. When Milton banished Eve from angelic instruction (*PL* VIII.48–57), he failed to realize that with women rendered defective in reason, real communion between the sexes is impossible and all sexuality is degraded.

This is the hidden contradiction in Edenic love. Eve's love for Adam is a mixture of dependency and self-abnegation; Adam's love for Eve is perverted by arrogant superiority. Raphael recommends self-esteem to Adam—"weigh with her thy self; / Then value" (*PL* VIII.570–71)—but Eve must repudiate her own image in the pool as "excelld by manly grace" (*PL* IV.490). Her fall is an attempt to restore her injured self-love "so to add what wants / In Femal Sex," and by such improvement "the more to draw his Love" (*PL* IX.821–22). Like so many women after her, Eve's inferior position renders her dependent upon a man for her very identity at the same time that it makes her feel unworthy and insecure in his love. Caught in this double bind, she has to destroy the relationship in order to save it. Adam, on the other hand, finds himself torn between desire for a companion and contempt for an inferior. His fall conveys the experience of every man who passes from idealization of his woman as a goddess to contempt for her feminine limitations, spurning his previous love as mere lust for another beautiful object. But Adam should have anticipated this, for he had after all refused for similar reasons to find a companion among the animals, protesting, "Among unequals what societie?" (*PL* VIII.383).

"Among unequals what societie?" "For inferior who is free"—these lines which needle Milton's poem become the basis for Blake's reconstruction of it in *The Four Zoas*. Dominated by the patriarchal Urizen and his code of male supremacy, the poem captures the agony of a world divided between phallic aggression and feminine passivity. The "male forms without female counterparts" are "Cruel and ravening with Enmity & Hatred & War" in their obsessive "Domineering lust" (*FZ* 85:19–20,31). The females, conversely, are cunning in their subservience, "for [they] are weak women & dare not lift / [their] eyes to the Divine pavilions" (*FZ* 56:3–4). Each male Zoa, casting off his female Emanation, repudiates part of himself as Urizen rejects Ahania's feminine emotion for unrestrained power: "Shall the feminine indolent bliss. the indulgent self of weariness / The passive idle sleep . . . Set herself up to give laws to the active masculine virtue?" (*FZ* 43:6–8). In response, the females seek to control their masters through manipulation. Enitharmon declares to Los, "for thou art mine / Created for my will my slave tho strong tho I am weak" (*FZ* 34:45–46). Once restricted to a purely sexual function, women turn their sex into a source of power, asserting their will through denial until, in Enitharmon's words: "The joy of woman is the Death of her most best beloved / Who dies for Love of her / In torments of fierce jealousy" (*FZ* 34:63–65).

Blake's critique of sexual inequality roots the sexual politics of male domination in the very differentiation of male and female roles.[9] Milton assumed that unequal sex roles were natural and universal, divinely created in Adam and Eve: "For contemplation hee

and valour formed, / For softness shee and sweet attractive Grace"
(*PL* IV.296–97). Blake, however, takes the myth of woman created out
of man as a symbol of the Fall—the fragmentation of humanity came
from the creation of a separate female status:

> And Many Eternal Men sat at the golden feast to see
> The female form now separate　They shudderd at the horrible thing
> Not born for the sport and amusement of Man but born to drink up all
>　　his powers
> They wept to see their shadows they said to one another this is Sin.
> (FZ 133:5–8)

For man, as Blake had told Henry Crabb Robinson, was originally
androgynous, there being "a Union of Sexes in Man as in God." In
Jerusalem, Blake recounts the catastrophe in which "The Feminine
separates from the Masculine & both from Man, / Ceasing to be His
Emanations, Life to Themselves assuming!" (*J* 90:1–2). The poet
develops an old Neoplatonist motif, that Adam was androgynous
before the Fall:

> Wherefore in dreadful majesty & beauty outside appears
> Thy Masculine from thy Feminine hardening against the heavens
> To devour the Human! . . .
> . . . O Vala! Humanity is far above
> Sexual organization. (J 79:70–74)

"Haile Wedded Love"

In the prior passage from *The Four Zoas*, the Eternals go on to reveal
the cause of the Fall which established this sexual organization,
bringing forth human shadows clothed in sexual garments: "And One
of the Eternals spoke All was silent at the feast. . . . In families we see
our shadows born" (*FZ* 133:10,21). We can only comprehend sexual
repression and the division of the sexes in the context of the social
institution from which they emerge, the patriarchal family. Part of
the profundity of *Paradise Lost* lies in the fact that we are always
aware of Adam and Eve as simultaneously spouses and siblings, aware
that every conjugal embrace takes place under the watchful eyes of a
hovering parent. We are thereby led to experience the connection
between the relations of parent and child and the adult forms of
marriage and love.

We may now identify Milton's contradiction more sharply. We have
seen the ambivalence with which he approaches sexual communion.
If we actually analyze his praise of "Wedded Love," we find that in
those two words Milton has linked two quite separate phenomena,

on the one hand "love" as an experience of being-at-one-with-the-world and on the other hand the social institution of patriarchal monogamy:

> Haile Wedded Love, mysterious Law, true sourse
> Of human offspring, sole proprietie,
> In Paradise of all things common else.
> By thee adulterous lust was driv'n from men
> Among the bestial herds to raunge, by thee
> Founded in Reason, Loyal, Just, and Pure,
> Relations dear, and all the Charities
> Of Father, Son, and Brother first were known.
>
> (*PL* IV.750–58)

In this celebration of marriage, Milton identifies it with the end of sexual freedom, a foreshadowing of private property, and an expression of the male-oriented world of father, son, and brother.

Blake, as we have already seen, does not accept the assumption that before the imposition of patriarchal monogamy humanity lived only by brutal lust. Rather, in *The Four Zoas* he depicts the sexual liberty of primitive people as a tender, comradely affection, while marriage appears as the negation of love. The fall of the Zoas and their female Emanations is therefore also a wedding:

> And Los & Enitharmon sat in discontent & scorn
> The Nuptial Song arose from all the thousand thousand spirits.
>
> (*FZ* 13:19–20)

The poem begins with Tharmas falling as a result of Enion's demand that he become monogamous: "Lost! Lost! Lost! are my Emanations   Enion O Enion . . . Why hast thou taken sweet Jerusalem from my inmost Soul" (*FZ* 4:7–11). Connecting marriage with private property as arising from the same spirit of possessiveness, Blake makes this nuptial song a chant of war, slavery, and human misery.

A Little Commonwealth

The stern chastity of marriage, he claims, stems not from love but from jealousy and Urizen's patriarchal reign of repression:

> I whose labours vast
> Order the nations separating family by family
> Alone enjoy not   I alone in misery supreme [am]
> Ungratified.   (*FZ* 121:15–18)

Here is Milton's God, a sexless, loveless solitary who has inflicted his own deprivation upon his children.

The problematic relationship between Milton's Adam and Eve can best be understood in this patriarchal context. Much has been written about the poet's reorientation of the epic from ideals of martial valor to those of spiritual heroism. We may now note that Milton does so by telescoping an entire cosmic drama into the everyday conflicts of domestic relations. A child rebels against a parental command, induces a brother to share her naughtiness, and both are caught and punished. A lover is torn between his father and his wife. A disobedient son is disinherited, while a favored one is appointed heir. A young couple is banished from a parental estate. The message seems to be that it takes a certain amount of personal heroism just to seek psychological integrity within the patriarchal family. In centering his epic around an incident of filial and feminine rebellion, Milton exposed the "politics of the family" which the twentieth-century women's movement has unmasked behind the facade of domestic bliss. Although Milton sought to defend this family, the poem's triumphant moments remain not with God, the validator of hierarchy, but with a satanic son and a rebellious woman who in a moment of defiance cut through the righteous pretenses of heavenly paternalism to reveal the realities of power—that "great Forbidder, safe with all his Spies / About him" (*PL* IX.815–16).

Milton's sensitivity to these contradictions can be understood in the light of the seventeenth-century transformation of the family. Under feudalism, it had been submerged in a larger social formation, the manor. The peasant, whose family quarters comprised only a small hut, spent most of his life outdoors on the common fields. The primary unit was the manorial community where the serfs labored, worshiped, and played together. The nobleman's family was lost in a large castle retinue of soldiers, guests, kin, servants, and even animals. Personal ties between husband, wife, and children might be quite minimal.[10]

Marriage was primarily an economic affair.[11] For peasants it was a means of transferring rights to the land and begetting fellow laborers to help till it. The nobility married in order to unite adjacent estates or to forge diplomatic ties. With such weighty matters at stake, marriage could not be left to the vagaries of human emotions. Among the nobility, strict chastity was the rule for women, but men enjoyed the privileges of a double standard. About peasant relationships we know very little. Peer pressure and church law upheld the marriage bond, fornication and adultery were punished, and unwed fathers were forced to legitimize their offspring through marriage. But prudery was unlikely in a barnyard atmosphere, and numerous children might not have been unwelcome in a labor-scarce society. It is not clear how much clerical asceticism ever affected the lower classes. A cursory reading of Chaucer suggests the existence of two cultures persisting alongside one another, with the earthy sensuality of his fabliaux surviving behind the official ethos of monogamous chastity.

Proceeding from Chaucer's time to Milton's, one notices a drastic change. The rise of a new morality reflected the changing function of the family for the middle class. The middle-class farm and workshop had separated themselves from the collective production of the manor, sealing off its private property and establishing the "household" as the basic social unit. This household included, in addition to the nuclear family, those servants and apprentices bound within its economy. "Who anywhere," asked a London preacher in 1608, "but is of some man's family, and within some man's gates?"[12] The answer would be only the poor—day laborers, vagabonds, and those still trying to eke out a subsistence from the tiny plots that remained after the enclosure of once communal property had destroyed the village economy.

Within this system, the father as "householder" was quite literally the boss within his walls. These "chief fathers, ancients and governors of the parish,"[13] could alone own property, pay taxes, vote, and administer local affairs. As the personal administration of the lords declined in this period before the consolidation of a full-blown state, with police departments, public schools, and welfare commissions, communal obligations fell upon the parish and the household. Hence the dual obsession with church and family discipline. The breakdown of the feudal manor and the feudal church left the middle-class patriarch a magistrate and a minister in his own home. Eve is not far afield in identifying her "Almighty Father" as a kind of domestic cop. In 1659, for example, the mayor of London sought to prevent civil disturbances by having all heads of household police their servants and apprentices. William Gouge was to declare the family "a little church and a little commonwealth whereby tryall may be had of such as are fit for any place of authority,"[14] and Christopher Hill has concluded that "the household was almost a part of the constitution of the State."[15] "In the great conflict of [the] period, between the ethos appropriate to a society composed of feudal households and the ethos appropriate to an individualist society," he writes, "the puritan emphasis on the duties of small householders played an important transitional part."[16] This social reality was reflected in the theological vision of Milton and the preachers; "The word 'Father,' " Richard Sibbes proclaimed, "is an epitome of the whole Gospel."[17]

These changes in family functions created alterations in family relations. When the link between husband and wife ceases to be a formality uniting family lines and becomes the crux of the family economy, that relationship is redefined as a partnership, and woman gains in dignity as a "helpmeet." This cooperation requires a new marital stability which explains the preachers' emphasis on voluntary marriage and personal compatibility, and their condemnation of adultery and the double standard. Over this partnership, replacing all other ties of a shattered community, is raised the banner of love.

"Inferior who is free?"

The flaw in this harmony is the inferior social status of women. Their condition had been miserable ever since the development of the patriarchal family had relegated them to a subservient role in the social division of labor. Although during the medieval period aristocratic women could sometimes inherit land and power or even pursue independent careers in religious orders, they were largely pawns in the game of arranged marriages. Peasant women seem to have been terribly degraded as breeders and beasts of burden, though their crucial part in agricultural labor may have given them some say in family affairs. The greatest dignity acquired by women since primitive times seems to have been achieved in the early family economy of petit-bourgeois craftsmen, shopkeepers, and farmers. There a wife shared her husband's work and skill and was often able to join his guild and inherit his business. This golden age of small producers was, however, rapidly undermined by its development into a capitalist economy which turned a few men into employers and the rest of the work force into wage laborers. As Alice Clark documents in *The Working Life of Women in the Seventeenth Century,* the status that middle-class women had achieved by the early part of the seventeenth century was rapidly eroded by the time of the Restoration.[18]

As this capitalist economy replaced the cooperative labor of the family economy, transforming the husband from a producer into a boss, the middle-class wife lost her share in his trade and her relation to the means of production. A split occurred between the domestic and productive spheres, first expressed simply in removing the family quarters to a separate part of the house and pushing the wife off into the kitchen and nursery where she performed functions which, because they were unprofitable, were little valued. The situation for journeymen's wives was even worse; once the men could no longer become masters in their own shop, but had to labor permanently on their boss's premises, their wives lost economic participation in the trades and were forced onto the poor rates (parish welfare) or into low-paid textile work. At the same time, capitalist competition wiped out whatever independent roles women had once had. Women were forbidden to own property, squeezed out of the skilled trades, forced to lose their little markets to the merchants and denied an education; even their traditional service functions, such as teaching and tending the sick, were usurped as these became male professions closed to women. In the seventeenth century, according to Clark, there arose for the first time the notion of a woman being supported by a man.[19] Eventually, much production was moved out of the bourgeois home entirely, and among those who could afford servants, an idle wife became a status symbol; the bourgeois woman was thus transformed into that ornament and plaything known as femininity.

These conflicting tendencies underlie Milton's ambivalence towards Eve. She is Adam's beloved companion in a typical Puritan household, refuge against the loneliness of that isolation, sharing common labor and family piety, but she is also his inferior, restricted to a definitely subordinate place in the division of labor which accounts for the hierarchy of male over female character. This division of functions means that Adam alone is educated and does business with the outside world, while Eve is relegated primarily to the boudoir and the kitchen.[20] In this context, it is significant that Milton makes the immediate cause of the Fall Eve's assertion of her independence as a right to go off and work on her own. For it was, according to Clark, precisely the loss of such rights that so altered the character of women that we pass in a half-century from the vital and intelligent women of Shakespeare to the coy and insipid females who dominate literature from the moment of Eve's repentant surrender until the feminine rebellion of the nineteenth century. Moreover, the conflict dramatized here—between Adam's affirmation of his wife's freedom as a human being and his sense of her inadequacy as a woman to use it—is precisely the contradiction which we have found central to a class which proclaimed universal liberty and then undermined it through various forms of social stratification.

It is this socially imposed inferiority, dividing humanity into "active masculine virtue" and "indolent feminine bliss," that Blake identifies as the source of human misery in love and the family. Not only does it lead to the degeneration of men into petty tyrants, but also it leads women, denied creative self-actualization in the world, to try to turn their domestic and sexual spheres into outlets for power through sexual denial and maternal domination—the horrors of "female will." Blake prophesies, therefore, that the return to Eden must involve the return of women to participation in communal work:

Then Enion & Ahania & Vala & the wife of Dark Urthona
Rose from the feast in joy ascending to their Golden Looms

There the winged shuttle Sang the spindle & the distaff & the Reel
Rang sweet the praise of industry.   (*FZ* 137:11–14)

"Children of Care & Labour"

Blake also understands that the change in the bourgeois family
reflects a change in the nature of labor, as well as in the sexual
division of labor. We discussed in the previous chapter the social
transformation which led to the development of the Protestant work
ethic. The self-sufficient manorial community, with no need to produce a surplus, gave way to the pressures for capital accumulation for
trade and investment. The feudal ethos, as we pointed out, emphasized consumption, whether it be the lord's etiquette of hospitality,
the church's lavish expenditures on art and architecture, or the peasant's harvest cycle of fast and feast. Neither lord nor peasant sought
systematically to increase productivity. The nobility was a leisure
class traditionally devoted to religion, culture, or military affairs. The
peasant labored under minimal supervision in seasonal spurts of
effort and relaxation. Peasant labor was exhausting, but it was free
from the tyranny of the time clock. On an easygoing day, a peasant
might intersperse his labor with village gossip, chase a rabbit that
crossed his path, join in the amusements of his children who played
alongside him in the fields, or dally with a young woman on a village
path in the pleasant distractions of courtship. We should not under-
estimate the exactions of this life; it was hard, threatened by natural
catastrophe and coarsened by the brutishness of peasant labor. It
lacked the fullness that could only be made possible by education and
leisure, but by comparison to the factory routine that would come
later it had a wholeness rooted in the material character of the
undifferentiated working day.

The rise of capitalism, with its emphasis on accumulating a surplus, changed all this, replacing this life style with the work ethic
imposed by the Puritans. Milton captures the conflict in values in the
argument between Adam and Eve just before the Fall. Eve defends her
wish for separate employment with the argument of a good bourgeoise—that it will increase production:

> For while so near each other thus all day
> Our task we choose, what wonder if so near
> Looks intervene and smiles, or object new
> Casual discourse draw on, which intermits
> Our dayes work brought to little.   (*PL* IX.220–24)

Milton, labouring ever in his taskmaster's eye, was in *Paradise Lost*
primarily an exponent of the work ethic, embodied in God himself,

"the great Work-Maister" (*PL* III.696). However, in this scene he has Adam object that there are limits to the demands productivity can make in paradise:

> Yet not so strictly has our Lord impos'd
> Labour, as to debarr us when we need
> Refreshment, whether food, or talk between,
> Food of the mind, or this sweet intercourse
> Of looks and smiles,
>
> . . . .
>
> Love not the lowest end of human life.
> For not to irksom toile, but to delight
> He made us.   (*PL* IX.235–43)

Adam expresses a very un-Puritan attitude here, for it had been precisely the effort of these Protestants to refute the values of the leisured nobility which denigrated work as "the lowest end of human life." Milton's inconsistency—alternately praising work and, in the face of all tradition, incorporating it into paradise, yet elsewhere seeming to reject it—reflects a real ambivalence among his contemporaries regarding the significance of the new work ethic. On the one hand, this ethic marked an enormously progressive step, turning man's eyes away from contemplating the Empyrean to the possibilities of his own achievements and their potential for ending human want. Under the conditions of capitalism, however, production was guided neither by standards of human need nor by creativity, so the work ethic beame a religious rationale for the exploitation and alienation of labor. It is understandable, therefore, that even the enormously "productive" Milton could not decide whether to associate the Puritan ethic with Eden or the Fall. With work as with sex, he could not reconcile his Puritan principles with a state of supposedly ideal fulfillment. In linking the Fall to Eve's obsessive industry and in presenting it as a passage from a world of "pleasant labors" to one of unrelenting toil, Milton may have apprehended that human catastrophe which accompanied the rise of capitalism. His God, as a workmaster, oversees the banishment of human beings to a world in which production will not exist for humanity, but humanity for production. Thus he becomes the model for Urizen, the slave-master "Petrifying all the Human Imagination into rock & sand" (*FZ* 25:6).

The institution which had to effect the "reformation" of the human personality required by this new life style was the family. What the Puritans sought to achieve was the continuous subordination of all the vagaries of human impulse to the "godly discipline" of methodical labor. As Christopher Hill observes, the very language of the preachers indicates that they "knew what they were doing." In their attempt to destroy normal human inclinations towards pleasure and relaxation, "They were up against 'natural man.' "[21] Since the family was the agency for this transformation, it is significant that Milton presents the loss of paradise as a loss of childhood.

Phillipe Ariès notes a new attitude towards childhood arising with the bourgeoisie.[22] In the large medieval households and the village community, children grew up without special notice. Ages were not recorded, clothing was not distinctive, and children even played the same games as adults. Childhood was just a biological, not a social phase, and children began an early apprenticeship for their adult roles. This pattern was abandoned by the rising middle class. As they withdrew into their households, they tended also to become more child-centered. Children were kept back from wet nurses and masters to remain at home where they became the focus of much parental concern. This new attentiveness corresponded to the new economic interests. The child of an aristocrat had only to inherit the family name and to acquire from his peers the protocol appropriate to his status, while the education of the peasant child was labor. However, since the sons of the bourgeoisie had to preserve their wealth through industry and skill, they had to be severely trained to thrift and rationality, lest they squander the family capital on loose living, careless management, or foolish investments. Puritan families, like Milton's, sent their children to school and carefully supervised their progress. And this emphasis on education, Ivy Pinchbeck and Margaret Hewitt contend, pointed to more than merely a concern for knowledge; it was a testimony to a growing awareness of the desirability of "moulding the man."[23]

Since even Puritan babes seemed born with a penchant for self-gratification, the goal of Puritan child rearing was "breaking the will."[24] The infant was believed to be completely corrupted by original sin, as evidenced by what the Puritans appropriately called its "idle affections." "The young child which lieth in the cradle," a preacher wrote, "is both wayward and full of affections . . . he hath a great heart, and is altogether inclined to evil. . . . If this sparkle be suffered to increase, it will rage over and burn down the whole house."[25] Such measures were taken to suppress these inclinations as swaddling the child so it could barely move, denying it physical affection, depriving it the maternal breast, and allowing it when it protested to cry itself to exhaustion. The conduct books advised parents to avoid such familiarity with their children as might undermine discipline, and to forbid such idle pastimes as children's games and stories; instead they were urged to drill their children from birth in a routine of silent obedience and disciplined exertion.

This ethos involved a drastic intensification of moral training. Medieval morality had sought only negative restraints, the prevention of behavior deemed threatening to the social order. English Puritans believed that every motion of the human organism must be scrutinized lest it prove idle or indulgent. Phillipe Ariès documents a similar transition in their French equivalents to a new and more rigorous discipline under which children were subjected to the constant supervision of parents and mentors; as one seventeenth-century teacher's manual recommended: "A close watch must be kept on the children, and they must never be left alone anywhere. . . . This constant supervision should be exercised gently and with a certain trustfulness calculated to make them think that one loves them. . . . This will make them love their supervision rather than fear it."[26]

In this context we can understand how Milton can rest the entire human tragedy upon a breach of paternal authority. His patriarchal God, leaning down from heaven to monitor his children, is the parental surrogate whose ever watchful eye the Puritans had taught their children to fear, the superspy against whom Eve is so defiant. Likewise, Puritan socialization accounts for Milton's obsession with temptation. A human organism, contorted into the unnatural rhythms of inordinate labor and denied basic material gratification, experiences a continual temptation to return to a more normal condition. The children of the thrifty, ascetic bourgeoisie, deprived in the midst of plenty, must steal their simple pleasures, like the disobedient Eve, behind their fathers' backs.

This intrusion of Puritan discipline, idealized as the subjugation of passion to reason, completely undermines Milton's Eden. His attempt to reconcile the fulfillment of human desires and their submission to patriarchal moral restraint in paradise proves impossible, as Blake insists all efforts to join a "contrary" to its "negation" always must. Consequently Adam and Eve are never really innocent; their unfallen impulses are suspect even in paradise. An interesting psychological dialectic therefore follows. A deity who is himself a projection of the judgmental paternal eye must be internalized in their own consciousness as a psychic inhibitor: God says, "I will place within them as a guide / My Umpire *Conscience*" (*PL* III.194–95). The angelic moralists dispatched to hem them in with warnings and prohibitions attempt to develop in Adam and Eve a reason which will serve as a mental referee between the ways of God and man, parent and child, desire and artificial restraint.

We have already seen that Blake recognizes this reason as little more than bourgeois repression: "the restrainer or reason usurps its [desire's] place & governs the unwilling" (*MHH* 5). Thus we can understand Blake's contention in *The Four Zoas* that the Fall, on the psychological level, is a self-division, the splitting off of this rational spectre, a kind of superego formed by the hostile demands of society. The idea is supported by later studies of Puritan psychology: "Demanding supervision," G. Rattray Taylor argues, "tends to create the schizophrenic (or 'split') type of personality . . . that is, the child constructs a screen-personality which satisfies the parents' demands, while continuing to live its own life in fantasy behind the screen."27

In his analysis of *Paradise Lost*, Blake's identification of "the restrainer or reason" with the Messiah suggests that Milton's separation of reason and desire has resulted in the splitting of a single personality into the characters of Christ and Satan. Christ's entire identity is contained in his "Filial obedience" (*PL* III.269). This filial piety, moreover, involves a masochistic willingness to sacrifice his own identity to his father's will and be reconstructed as a "Divine Similitude" (*PL* III.384), thereby becoming the worthy heir of the Almighty Father's realm. This gruesome process is in fact the essence of Puritan child rearing. This emphasis on Christ as a self-sacrificial son (rather than cosmic world-soul, humanitarian lover, etc.) was a particular orientation of Protestant theology developed by Luther. Interestingly enough, the doctrine had roots in Luther's own experience of the bourgeois family.28 His father was an upwardly mobile, dispossessed peasant who had become a small mine owner. He had hoped to secure his new class status by educating his son as a lawyer, but Luther revolted against his father's harsh discipline and expectations by running away to a monastery. His spiritual life thereafter was torn between feelings of submission and rebellion and by the anguish of being unable to believe in God as a loving father. Ever fearful for his salvation, Luther finally resolved his doubts through the doctrine that God's love, like a stern father's, is shown through his wrath, and that Christian conversion therefore consists in internalizing Christ as the suffering son. The other side of this theology of submission, however, was Luther's increasing obsession with Satan. According to Erik Erikson, that cosmic rebel was to Luther a projection of his own suppressed filial revolt, continually threatening to destroy his uneasy peace with his Father-God.29 Milton's Satan expresses a similar alter ego. In contrast to Christ, Satan's entire self-definition requires his being the disobedient son who disdains "feign'd submission" (*PL* IV.96) and who denies the fatherhood of God by proclaiming the angels "self-begot" (*PL* V.860).

The repression of children is a central theme throughout Blake's works. In *The Four Zoas* the patriarchal Urizen announces:

For labourd fatherly care & sweet instruction. I will give
Chains of dark ignorance & cords of twisted self conceit
And whips of stern repentance & food of stubborn obstinacy
. . . .
Go forth sons of my curse. Go forth daughters of my abhorrence.
(FZ 68:21–23,27)

The family's assault upon its children continues to be symbolized, as it was in "A Little Boy Lost," by the barbaric practice of infant sacrifice:

> The weeping child could not be heard.
> The weeping parents wept in vain:
> They strip'd him to his little shirt.
> And bound him in an iron chain.
>
> And burn'd him in a holy place,
> Where many had been burn'd before.   (PB 29)

Blake argues that this abhorrent primitive practice is the essence of the Puritan doctrine of atonement. By raising to a religious ideal Christ's sacrifice to his father's sadistic will, this tenet had both reflected and rationalized existing social practice. Thus in Blake's version of the crucifixion, Los, in "Love of Parent Storgous Appetite Craving" (*FZ* 61:10) with Enitharmon's reluctant assistance chains his son to a mountain of obdurate rock, a symbol of stern, hard-hearted parental discipline. The shackles which identify this torture as slavery point to the socialization of children to the cruelties of capitalist production as well. Such immolation, although exalted by self-abnegating piety, produces a fall rather than a redemption, so Blake merges the cross with the snake-entwined tree of mystery whose proscription recreates the crucifixion in every human being. The suffering but rebellious Orc thus reunites the twin aspects of the Miltonic psyche: Christ's masochistic obedience and Satan's irrepressible rage, the inevitable concomitants of a paternal love which is expressed in prohibition and punishment.

"To sulk upon my mothers breast"

In order fully to comprehend this division, we must turn to the ambivalence towards the mother which is also expressed in Milton's poem. It might seem that Blake falls under his precursor's patriarchalism in this respect, for he blames the Fall as much upon a tyrannical female will as on the Father of Jealousy. Milton's misogyny at times might even seem to pale before Blake's complaints at having been "Woman-born / And Woman-nourishd & Woman-educated & Woman-scorn'd" (*J* 64:16–17). These antifeminist allegations can perhaps be seen as compatible with Blake's endorsement of woman's freedom in *Visions of the Daughters of Albion* if they are understood to be directed not at woman but at the female role under patriarchy.

We have already observed that an intensified division of labor produced the complete economic dependence of the middle-class woman and her constriction within the functions of wife and mother in a household where her husband was also her boss. "Within the family," Engels writes, the husband "is the bourgeois, and the wife represents the proletariat."[30] Milton espouses the doctrine of feminine inferiority that such conditions create, not including woman in the "Charities / Of Father, Son, and Brother" (*PL* IV.756–57). Adam, although he is born reeking with the moisture of the womb (*PL* VIII.253–56), has no mother, and Eve is born out of the body of a man. One might dismiss all this as required by Milton's sources, but it was precisely this patriarchal element that Puritans dwelled upon in the Genesis text, forcing some women to remind the preachers that Eve was, after all, only taken from Adam's side as a "fellow feeler" and not "out of his foote to be trod upon."[31]

The paradoxical result of woman's exclusion from the wider social world was in fact her growing domination of the life of the child. The isolation of the family and the imprisonment of mother and children together in the domestic realm made her the child's sole source of satisfaction and survival. This situation intensified certain qualities endemic to infancy anyway. Norman O. Brown describes the babe, unable to distinguish its pleasurable feelings from the source of its care, as in a state of "being-at-one-with-the-world." Since in our society that world is usually its mother, the infant, totally absorbed in its own bodily sensations, exists in a kind of sensuous harmony with an entire world mediated by her. "Reality," Brown writes, "is [its] mother; . . . infantile sexuality affirms the union of the self with a whole world of love and pleasure."[32]

Milton's epic is caught in that paradox; thus his patriarchal subordination of the mother coexists with an extensive substratum of maternal allusions pervading the poem. In his *Dialectics of Creation*, Michael Lieb has documented procreative and nurturant images in *Paradise Lost* too numerous to recount here.[33] We should notice however the maternal aspects of Milton's garden, which associates "Earth, all bearing Mother," and Eve, "Mother of Mankind," in an image of primal maternal benevolence ministering to the sensuous needs of her children. The Song of Songs had made the *hortus conclusus* a woman's body, and Milton makes it a maternal one. His Eden veritably flows with mother's milk, offering Adam and Eve "nec-tarous draughts" from a "milkie stream" (*PL* V.306). Maud Bodkin recognizes his garden as one of those many "blessed spots of repose amidst the sandy wastes of life, the plots green and fountainous, unviolated of the Earthly Paradise" where "poets have felt . . . Harsh step-dame Nature has shown them the breasts of mother's tenderness."[34]

Milton's Eden, furthermore, has such womblike qualities that when Adam makes love to "our General Mother" in their sacred and sequestered bower, their sexual desires seem impelled by the pursuit for infantile harmony. These incestuous undertones are brought out as a grotesque parody in the full-blown oedipal relations of Satan, Sin, and Death. The image of Sin, raped by her own son, perpetually engendering a pack of monsters who crawl in and out of her womb unable to be fully born, expresses the simultaneous repulsion and attraction of the maternal bond. This same ambivalence is drama-tized in Satan's relationship to the Mother of All Mankind. In that marvelous passage in Book IX when he first discovers her, for a moment he is transported by nostalgic odors (significantly, of fresh milk) beyond the hell that rages within him to taste the pastoral delight of Eden:

> The smell of Grain, or tedded grass, or Kine,
> Of Dairie, each rural sight, each rural sound;
> If chance with Nymphlike step fair Virgin pass,
> What pleasing seemd, for her now pleases more,
> She most, and in her look summs all Delight.
> . . . .
> Her graceful Innocence, her every Aire
> Of gesture or least action overawd
> His Malice, and with rapine sweet bereav'd
> His fierceness of the fierce intent it brought:
> That space the Evil one abstracted stood
> From his own evil, and for the time remaind
> Stupidly good, of enmitie disarm'd,
> Of guile, of hate, of envie, of revenge;
> But the hot Hell that alwayes in him burnes,
> Though in mid Heav'n, soon ended his delight,
> And tortures him now more, the more he sees
> Of pleasure not for him ordain'd: then soon
> Fierce hate he recollects.   (*PL* IX.450–54,459–71)

For an instant, Satan makes contact with a deeper self, the feeling of tranquility and joy which prevails before the first harmony with the mother is perverted and destroyed. Adam's wife is suddenly transfigured into a virgin Madonna through that sexual ambivalence towards the mother which must divide all women into either virgins or whores. Satan approaches her with childlike innocence—"with rapine sweet bereav'd" (*PL* IX.461) until the experience of prohibited gratification turns his vision of pleasure back into the rage of frustration.

Frustrated passion is the very essence of Satan's character; he suffers "fierce desire, / Among our other torments not the least, / Still unfulfill'd with pain of longing pines" (*PL* IV.509–11). The consequence of this obstructed feeling is the perversion enacted in his relations with Sin and Death. With his contorted sexuality and his diversion of unspent passion into hellish rage, he is the model for Blake's Luvah, whom Jean Hagstrum has shown expressing love gone amuck. The "sexual Babylon" which he inhabits with Vala is "A Cavernd Universe of flaming fire" (*FZ* 77:6), "a place of both (1) raging fiery passion and (2) caverned restraint." As Hagstrum describes this Luvah-Orc, we clearly hear the Miltonic echoes "of an obsessive phallic passion that burns alone, unattached to any love object, and that then stalks abroad seeking whom it may devour. Destructive, it is also nasty; and scaly monsters, bred in the swamps of Orc-country, vomit up creatures that 'annoy the nether parts / Of Man' " (*FZ* 108:28–29).[35]

Satan's vacillation between anger and nostalgic longing for the mother can be traced to the mother's function in the family. For one thing, in bourgeois society the period of maternal indulgence is very short; then the child begins preparation for a vocation under supervision of the father or the school. John Locke remarked that it pained him to see a child above the age of three idle, and John Robinson wrote in his treatise, "Of Children and Their Education": "Children in their first days have the greater benefit of good mothers. . . . But afterwards when they come to riper years, good fathers are often more behoveful for their forming in virtue and good manners, by their greater wisdom and authority, and oftimes also by correcting the fruits of their mother's indulgence by their severity."[36] Puritan austerity, moreover, "extended itself to the total sphere of bodily living . . . spreading its frigidity over the tasks of pregnancy, childbirth, nursing and training."[37]

This frustration is intensified by the fact that the mother is often made responsible for rebuking the child and casting him out from the "Short pleasures" (*PL* IV.535) of infancy. Levin L. Schücking remarks that "so delicately minded a writer as Rogers can find no better way of expressing the spiritual harmony . . . of husband and wife than the following: '[she] holdes not his hands from due stroakes, but bares their skins with delight, to his fatherly stripes'."[38] Taylor comments that, as slaves themselves, women become the ideal perpetuators of slave mentality: "It is not difficult to appreciate that women deprived of almost every other outlet for constructive and manipulative activity, and themselves dominated by their husbands, must have found in the domination of their children an outlet for their pent-up frustration."[39]

Another paradox implicit in the bourgeois family was that the goal of this authoritarian child rearing is to produce autonomy rather than servility. The task facing the son in the quest for his inheritance is to deny the mother and to internalize the father, and through self-discipline to become a master in his own right. Thus a filial theology allows Luther and Milton, as sons of an almighty father, to scorn the powers of pope and king. The price is the sacrifice of maternal affection and indeed all capacity for unity with another. Hence, as does not happen in primitive cultures whose initiations lead a child from identification with specific mothers to dependency upon the community as a whole, the bourgeois child is weaned from all human bonds whatsoever and delivered into the wilderness of "every man for himself." The hero of this culture is invariably the man without roots, the motherless man, John Henry, Paul Bunyan, "Raised in the backwoods, suckled by a polar bear."[40] Dickens reveals the social genealogy of the type in Bounderby, the banker who cannot stop vaunting himself as a self-made man. Devotee of laissez-faire economics, contemptuous of his employees' neediness, he eliminates his mother rather than let the admission of that first dependence undermine his philosophy of total self-reliance:

> "My mother? Bolted, ma'am!" said Bounderby. . . . My mother left me to my grandmother . . . the wickedest and worst old woman that ever lived. . . . She kept a chandler's shop," pursued Bounderby, "and kept me in an egg box." . . . As soon as I was big enough to run away, of course I ran away. Then I became a young vagabond; and instead of one old woman knocking me about and starving me, everybody of all ages knocked me about and starved me.[41]

Capitalism not only dishonored its mothers; as Alice Clark remarks, it also renounced mothering: "Thus it came to pass that every womanly function was considered as the private interest of husbands and fathers, bearing no relation to the life of the State, and therefore demanding from the community as a whole no special care or provision."[42]

The irony, as Blake understood, is that the inhumanity and loneliness of such a society creates an emotional regression to unfulfilled infantile desires, a frustrated longing for maternal love. His poem therefore expands the incestuous suggestions of Milton's. Los will begin his son's initiation by wresting Orc from the bosom of Enitharmon. Blake's concept of female will, moreover, encompasses both Enitharmon's collusion in binding Orc into those societal chains and the excessive hold of maternal love in an otherwise atomistic society. Perceiving the maternal character of Milton's Eden, Blake recreates it as the garden of Vala where Enion and Tharmas stray in eternal childhood. This paradise of passive, sensuous gratification is benevolent as a passing respite, but any attempt to dally there longer propels a fall from Beulah into Ulro: "Among the Flowers of Beulah walkd the Eternal Man & Saw / Vala the lily of the desert. . . . Upon her bosom in sweet bliss he fainted   Wonder seizd / All heaven. . . . they built a golden wall / Round Beulah" ·(*FZ* 83:7–11). The ancient world's entombment within the maternal womb of procreative nature provides at the same time the symbolism for the contemporary retreat from the horrors of the anarchic capitalist world into the refuge of domesticity and its psychological concomitant, a romantic love based upon infantile fantasies. That fixation of desire on a return to infant eroticism's "moony sleep" becomes as awful an abdication of human creativity as the Urizenic world of repressive labor from which one flees. Vala is the harlot of Urizen because all escapist visions—religious, sexual, or psychological—serve only to maintain the contradictions of the status quo.

Lacking a social analysis of the family, Freud misconstrued all these conflicts in biological terms, positing a universal "birth trauma," "incest wish," and "oedipal conflict." The original Oedipus myth, however, reflected the transition from matrilineal to patrilineal society with its consequent conflicts of loyalties and confusions over descent. The only analogy in modern experience is a distant one—the passage of the child from a mother-dominated to a father-dominated phase. The incest wish thus ceases to be universal and appears as the creation of a patriarchal nuclear family which allows the individual one brief sensuous relationship with a mother before requiring two decades of deprivation. A person then remains fixated emotionally upon the mother in longing for the environment of infant joys, requiring society to counter the intensity of that relationship with strenuous taboos. The conflict between father and child lies not so much in sexual competition for the mother but in the child's attempt through the mother to hold onto its sensuous and emotional life in the face of pressures towards socialization.

Chains of Generation

In addition, Satan's transmutation of love and desire into egotistical aggression is the emotional process required for the son's
initiation into adult male power. He is compensated for his loss by
promotion from victim to tyrant as his pent-up childhood rage is
channeled into the legitimized aggression of father and boss. Before
acceding to his inheritance, however, every Adam, emulating the
divine son, must exchange fraternal solidarity for an identification
with his father's authority. On one level, the Fall is a crisis of solidarity, of brotherly love. Adam is faced with the choice of abandoning
Eve and facing the consequences of total isolation or allying with her
wholeheartedly in repudiation of their "great forbidder." He can do
neither. His loyalty to her is undermined by his disapproval, for he
joins her in sin but not in revolt. In accepting Christ's partiarchal
allegation that he has valued her overmuch and in approving the
judgment passed upon her, he begins to change before our eyes from a
fraternal lover to a pompous patriarch. From then on, paradise is lost,
for Adam is self-divided. His condition is never better expressed than
at the moment when he stands at the borders of Eden, torn between a
sad nostalgia for the paradise of loving union that he leaves behind
and eager anticipation for the active power which now becomes his
birthright in the world which lies before them, where to choose.

Within the dynamics of the family we can thus understand
Milton's characterizations. If Christ and sometimes Adam appear
stiff, it is because they are mere dramatizations of the conduct books,
like the screen personalities children throw up to placate their parents. The psychic reality behind their double bind lies in Satan's
emotional torment—"Infinite wrauth, and infinite despaire / Which
way I flie is Hell; my self am Hell" (PL IV.74–75). Schizophrenia has
become the normal condition of the bourgeois psyche. Blake understands this when he adopts from Milton that seminal image of the
preachers in which Christ and Satan are psychic powers clashing
upon the battlefield of every Christian soul. Now we can see the
multiple dimensions of Blake's mythology—social, psychological,
and ideological—converge. On one level, Urizen, as the ruler of an
exploitative society, is actually at war with Luvah whom he has
enslaved, but that conflict has emotional and ideological consequences as well. In order to maintain its dominion, that elite must
repress its own desires till they are "weak enough to be restrained"
(MHH 5) and then must govern the unwilling by imposing its stifling
ethos upon its reluctant slaves. Thus within the bourgeois family the
wars between Urizen and Luvah, reason and desire, appear as the

struggle of patriarchal restraint against infant affections. Those conflicts are internalized within the bourgeois character itself where a power-hungry rationality battles emotions which, though subdued, often survive to take a pathological revenge. At the same time, this reason is sanctified as an ascetic ideology which rationalizes the deprivations required for the preservation of the status quo by denigrating the passions of the masses.

Recognizing the multiple ways in which the family reinforces society's repressive institutions, Blake names his fallen state "Generation." Through the "bloody chain" of the family cycle, each newborn child is constricted by the aims of a fallen society. History is bound by Urizenic social structures, but also by the process through which each generation internalizes the limits of the past in its own character. The child inherits its mother's repression; the son hoards his rebellious anger for future expression as legitimized aggression towards subordinates. Brother and sister, separated by the sexual division of labor into roles of loveless power and powerless love, pursue a lost wholeness through the clumsy refitting of the marriage bond. Los and Enitharmon, born of the division of the fraternal Tharmas and Enion, are "link'd in the marriage chain" to reduplicate their tragedy. Male and female spectres, isolated by an individualistic society, seek the fulfillment of all their needs in a desperately possessive monogamy with a single mother substitute. The family which splits home and work, feminine and masculine, also creates a fundamental divide in the life of every human being, a chasm separating one permanently from the spontaneity of childhood, finishing off the "auricular nerves of human life" and transforming the body from an organ of experience into a mere implement of production. Through its systematic repression, the family reproduces fallen man as that human zero perfectly malleable to the needs of capitalism, turning bourgeois sons into sober employers while at the same time delivering up a whole class of chimney sweepers as a sacrifice to their employers' greed.

Cruelties of Moral Virtue

It was this latter social disaster, the ideological role of the family in constraining the lower classes, that was Blake's primary concern. The world view that facilitated the self-transformation of the middle class also justified the exploitation of their employees. Discipline within the early capitalist household had always been a two-headed monster, providing for the moral edification of the middle class and the policing of their servants and dependents. For, as Gouge writes, a family is "a school wherein the first principles and grounds of government and subjection are learned."[43] This twofold effect was implicit in Calvinism which, Michael Walzer tells us, "brought conscience and coercion together."[44]

The Fall, Calvin had argued, was a political as well as a spiritual disaster, leaving human affairs in such disarray that only Christian "reformation," permanent and unrelenting discipline, could prevent regression to total anarchy. This discipline was to be found in the self-subordination of the elect to a regime of sober living and methodical labor—an ethos which dovetailed nicely with the material interests of the bourgeoisie. Upon those outside this elite, Calvin maintained, they would have to impose their God-given authority and superior moral standards—by any means necessary. This justification of class rule was enormously beneficial to the new masters, particularly in giving religious sanction to the authority of the patriarchal employer over his employees; for as Henry Bullinger admitted, "The good man of the house, by planting godliness in his family, doth not a little advance and set forward his private profit and own commodity."[45]

This emphasis on paternal responsibility within the household served also to exonerate the bourgeoisie's disregard for the community and their assault on the fabric of rights and duties by which feudal society had sought to preserve its members. In that world, survival had depended on the possession of neither property nor employment. The peasant's subsistence rested in his rights to till the earth, hunt in the forest, and graze animals on the village commons. In times of trouble, he turned to the collective resources of the manor and the church. Under the onslaught of capitalism, all this began to crumble. Thousands were dispossessed from the land which was gradually enclosed as private property. Artisans were destroyed when guild regulations were no longer allowed to protect them against the competition of cheap labor. The world divided into those possessing property, who could support their families, and the poor who could not. As Marx describes it in *Capital*, "They were turned *en masse* into beggars, robbers, vagabonds" and then subjected to "a bloody legislation against vagabondage. . . . Legislation treated them as 'voluntary' criminals, and assumed that it depended on their good will to go on working under the old conditions that no longer existed."[46]

The chaos that so terrified Calvinists was largely caused by the fall into an unregulated market economy, but from the individualistic bourgeoisie came an individualistic ethos; those whom they destroyed they also condemned. Similarly, Milton, unable to explain the social causes for the failure of the Puritan Revolution, had retreated to the denigration of depraved humanity and the blaming of tyranny upon its victims. Since man "permits / Within himself unworthie Powers to reign . . . God in Judgement just / Subjects him from without to violent Lords" (*PL* XI.83–94). When Milton must explain political oppression, all he can point to is sin, and that particular sin, "passion." It is this ethic, rationalizing all the injustice of history by a failure of human self-control, proclaiming the cruel and unusual sentence of capital punishment for an impulse of childish indulgence, that makes Milton's God so offensive. He speaks of man in the unmistakable tones of the self-righteous English bourgeois pouring scorn on the heads of those he has ruined: "Whose fault? / Whose but his own?" God carps; "ingrate, he had of mee / All he could have" (*PL* III.96–98).

The ideology of the middle-class family made people completely responsible for their own survival. The wealthy hedged in their estates and then from the comfortable vantage point of their hearths condemned those they had locked out for failing to achieve their standards of domesticity. The preachers blessed the selfish accumulation of wealth, declaring that "grace in a poor man is grace and 'tis beautiful; but grace in a rich man is more conspicuous, more useful."[47] Almsgiving, on the other hand, was no longer advocated but condemned for encouraging idleness: "No parcel of God's law doth bind or bid thee to distribute to other men the wealth which thou thyself doth need. . . . It is sufficient for thee to provide that they of thine own household be not a burden to other men's backs."[48] The wealthy household became a sign of election, while the man who could not provide for his family was considered "worse than an infidel."[49]

The monogamous sexual standards of the middle classes, as we have seen, served their economic interests. They promoted the orderly transmission of property, stability within the household economy, the saving of money that would be wasted on bastards and time that might be wasted on love. "It was especially in sexual behaviour," Christopher Hill notes, "that the standards of the bourgeoisie differed from the aristocracy."[50] Their morality distinguished them no less from the lower classes who lacked the resources to maintain stable families, or often, even to pay for a marriage license.

In this period the middle classes, reluctant to lose their growing resources to those below them, passed poor laws that made indigence a crime punishable by the shame of the workhouse and illegitimacy an offense justifying the transformation of orphanages into penal institutions. Like contemporary politicians, they watched procreation among the lower classes with their eyes on the poor rates and harangued about how "the poor when their bellies were filled . . . fell to lust . . . and brought forth basterdes in such quantity that it passed belief."[51] It was a peculiar but convenient logic: when the children of the poor starved, one could blame them for having children; because like Adam and Eve they overvalued their appetites, one could believe that they deserved to go hungry. The condemnation of appetite and passion that pervades *Paradise Lost*, Blake recognized, was inseparable from this class ethos of righteous angels who built their heaven on what they stole from those in the abyss.

Out of the lower classes themselves arose an alternative tradition, the context in which Blake must ultimately be placed. Hill documents it in the ideology of the lower-class Protestant sects which espoused equality of women, sexual freedom, and communal cooperation:

> Labour is one thing for small masters whose wealth is directly related to their labour; if they do not work neither shall they eat. But the wage labourer works in part, at least, that another may eat. So long as he gets his wages, he is not interested in what he produces or how much. The inner voice speaks differently to communities drawn from the lowest classes. Idleness is not a sin; adultery is no sin to the pure in heart. Love is more important than faith.[52]

Thus the Ranter Abiezer Coppe decries the "stinking family duties"[53] of the middle class, recording an encounter with a poor vagabond in a field in which his true Christian generosity must triumph over a nagging Puritan conscience that selfishly admonishes him: "It's a poor wretch, give him 6d; and that's enough. . . . Besides (saith the holy Scripturian whore) he's worse than an infidel who provides not for his own family. True love begins at home etc. . . . Have a care of the main chance."[54] Coppe follows this advice but, upon riding away is so miserable that he returns and gives the man all that he has, blessing God and proclaiming this his true Christian conversion. On the one hand condemning the ethics of heartless self-interst, the Ranters on the other hand saw no harm in sexual enjoyment, only praise of their maker, leading Coppe to exclaim: "Kisses are numbered among transgressors—base things—well! . . . by base impudent kisses . . . my plaguey holiness hath been confounded . . . and external kisses have been made the fiery chariot to mount me into the bosom of . . . the King of Glory. . . . I can . . . kiss and hug ladies, and love my neighbor's wife as myself, without sin."[55] In proclaiming "the right of natural man to behave naturally," Hill writes, these sects "gave ideological form and coherent expression to practices which long had been common among vagabonds, squatter-cottagers, and . . . migratory craftsmen."[56]

Although these radical sects were silenced in the restoration of law and order after the civil war, their values survived in the lower classes whence they came. In eighteenth-century England, the various classes retained their distinctive cultures. The bourgeoisie may have controlled their workers by force, but they had not yet "reformed" them; Blake inherited these traditions from the London streets. In *Songs of Innocence and of Experience,* he had already drawn the connection between Puritan religion, parental repression, and the joyless labor of an exploited working class. "The Chimney Sweeper" tells of a child who has been sold into labor by parents who "are gone to praise God & his priest & King / Who make up a heaven of [his] misery" (PB 23). The new masters defend this system as rescuing the child from idleness and sin; thus the factories are aided in their oppression by the Sunday schools which are erected in their shadows. This change is reflected in "The Garden of Love":

> I went to the Garden of Love,
> And saw what I never had seen:
> A Chapel was built in the midst,
> Where I used to play on the green.
>
> . . . .
>
> And Priests in black gowns, were walking their rounds,
> And binding with briars, my joys & desires.   (PB 26)

The poet witnessed the direct relationship between the accumulation of capital and an accumulation of misery that grew from hard work and restricted consumption of the lower class. He also saw the hypocrisy with which the bourgeois ethos, particularly that of family respectability, was used to rationalize a system of repression and greed. While the middle classes were retreating into comfortable domesticity and proclaiming the virtues of sexual denial, child discipline, and family self-sufficiency, they were creating for others conditions inimical to those objectives. According to Engels, "Family life for the worker is almost impossible. . . . All he has is a dirty and comfortless hovel."[57] The conditions which Engels described in mid-century had already begun to appear by Blake's era. Low wages and casual labor made it impossible for men permanently to support a family, so their women were abandoned to the sweated trades or to "sin," and their children to the workhouse. Child and female labor meant that family members seldom saw each other, and children grew up without care or control. Soon Dickens would be describing a London overrun by orphans abandoned by their indigent parents, bringing each other up in the city's streets. In his "Holy Thursday" poems, Blake exposed the callousness of a society which thus impoverished its children and herded them into workhouse slavery to be "Fed with cold and usurous hand" (PB 19). The "aged men, wise guardians of the poor" (PB 13) who oversaw these prisons were undoubtedly of that same class of employers whose greed had driven these innocents into such asylums, gilded with ideals of "charity" and "holy Christian asceticism."

Monogamy, moreover, was often difficult for the poor. Edward Shorter documents that between 1790 and 1860 illegitimacy among the lower classes rose to unprecedented heights.[58] We find in the sympathetic journalism of Henry Mayhew a pathetic picture of factory girls disabused of their morals by intimidating employers, forced by their low wages to drift to any man who could temporarily provide a roof over their heads.[59] Poor pay and irregular employment also drove them to the streets, so that, as Blake recognizes in "London," the chastity of the middle-class wife came to be built upon the degradation of a whole army of prostitutes. At any rate, monogamous morality was unlikely when people lived with no privacy—several generations crowded into a single room and even a single bed. Working mothers had little time for the moral instruction of their young, who were often on their own at an early age in the chaotic moral environment of slum rooming houses. And given the misery and hopelessnes of working-class life, a "catch-as-catch-can" attitude towards any kind of immediate gratification was inevitable.

The Gradgrinds could therefore look out from beside their domestic hearths at the broken families of their employees and blame their poverty on their "low morals." Robert Malthus even went so far as to assign all the evils of capitalism to an overpopulation caused by the laborers' excessive procreation. Parodying Milton's God in Urizen, Blake grasped how the Puritan tendency to reduce all social questions to individual morality had turned into the righteous hypocrisy of industrialists whose Ten Commandments were indistinguishable from their laws of political economy:

> Listen O Daughters to my voice   Listen to the Words of Wisdom
> So shall [you] govern over all let Moral Duty tune your tongue
> But be your hearts harder than the nether millstone
>   . . . .
> Compell the poor to live upon a Crust of bread by soft mild arts
> Smile when they frown frown when they smile & when a man looks
>   pale
> With labour & abstinence say   he looks healthy & happy
> And when his children sicken let them die there are enough
> Born even too many & our Earth will be overrun
> Without these arts   If you would make the poor live with temper

With pomp give every crust of bread you give with gracious cunning
Magnify small gifts reduce the man to want a gift & then give with
   pomp
Say he smiles if you hear him sigh   If pale say he is ruddy
Preach temperance   say he is overgorgd & drowns his wit
In strong drink tho you know that bread and water are all
He can afford.
                                                      (*FZ* 80:2–4,9–20)

Defending the Garden of Love

Blake's vision of his society is incisive and comprehensive. Like
Los in *Jerusalem*, "Striving with Systems to deliver Individuals from
those Systems" (*J* 11:5), he draws the connections among the economics, religious values, family ethos, and psychology of industrial capitalism. What constitutes his real uniqueness and underlies the
originality of his symbol system is that, standing out in the long
history of elite culture as the spokesman of the masses, Blake uses
their point of view to reorganize their masters' categories. His ability
to render so thorough an analysis lies in the fact that he did so at a
time when before his very eyes capitalism was drastically altering
English society, environment, and culture, visibly eliminating former
modes of existence. As he himself testifies in "The Garden of Love,"
"I saw what I never had seen" (*PB* 26).

   That transformation included the intrusion of the dreary values of
the chapel on the merrier ones of the village green. G. R. Taylor has
argued that whereas in the eighteenth century the landed, moneyed,
and working classes each retained its own life style, and middle-class
sobriety had little influence on those above or below them, in the
years 1790–1810 all that changed. Suddenly the pall of bourgeois
morality seemed to fall over the whole culture, and we pass from
"merrie olde England" to a foreshadowing of Victorian reserve. Taylor
points to a growth in public adherence to religion, increased prudery
in speech, and a general chilling of the atmosphere. E. P. Thompson
tells the same sorry tale—of Hannah More's tracts and Wilberforce's
Society for the Suppression of Vice; arrests for "lewd" behavior;
legislation against the amusements of the poor, against two-penny
hops, gingerbread fairs, "obscene" pictures; penalties imposed upon
Sabbath breakers, stage dancers, ballad singers, and nude sea
bathers.[60] The middle class, having grown in numbers, wealth, and
education, had become the arbiters of literary taste and manners.
They controlled local government, education, and welfare. With this
power they were able to force an upper class increasingly dependent
upon their wealth to "shape up," and through the Methodist cam-

paign they hoped finally to exact godliness from their employees. Dickens's "hard times" had come upon England.

Blake witnessed with horror the inroads that these attitudes made in the working class. Turning some chimney sweepers against themselves and creating a dominant atmosphere against which workers had to struggle to retain their own sense of reality, this ideological offensive threatened, in Blake's words, to "bring the shadow of Enitharmon beneath our wondrous tree / That Los may Evaporate like smoke & be no more" (*FZ* 80:5–6). In fact, as Blake's apocalyptic vision proclaims, Urizen can never entirely eradicate his opposition. Blake captures in his own "intellectual War" (*FZ* 139:9) a class warfare that continued throughout the era in culture and in consciousness itself.

He turned to the crude existence of working people for the sources of an alternative vision. Laborers with nothing to gain from denial clung to a healthy affirmation of pleasure and demands for material improvement, an earthly and palpable paradise. Households in which everyone worked for the survival of all presented a democratic contrast to the patriarchal tyranny of the bourgeois home. From them, Blake took a vision of a world where feminine passivity would be replaced by the cooperation of Los and Enitharmon in building Jerusalem and in which they would no longer indoctrinate their children in servility:

> But Los loved them & refusd to Sacrifice their infant limbs
> And Enitharmons smiles & tears prevaild over self protection
> They rather chose to meet Eternal death than to destroy
> The offspring of their Care & Pity.   (*FZ* 90:50–53)

The logic of that refusal would demand revolution. Short of that, Blake understood that the family which had risen upon the ruins of the primitive community was a defense as well as a disaster:

> Forsaking Brotherhood & Universal love in selfish clay
>   . . . .
> With windows from the inclement sky we cover him & with walls
> And hearths protect the Selfish terror till divided all
> In families we see our shadows born.   (*FZ* 133:13,19–21)

So long as the anarchic individualism of class society prevailed, the family would remain a refuge for all classes. Material necessity, the failure of capitalist society to guarantee children's survival, to provide birth control, equal employment for women, or communal child care, would force workers also to rely upon the monogamous family as their only semblance of security. Hence, by the end of the nineteenth century, failing to make a revolution, workers had won only through their trade unions a breadwinner's wage enabling men to support a family based upon the traditional sexual division of labor.

When analysts like Edward Shorter celebrate the laborers' lack of sexual inhibition, such romanticization of that liberty often overlooks the fact that its context was grinding poverty. Blake's view is different because of his understanding that a really free sexuality requires a new world. However, since he remains an antinomian up until *The Everylasting Gospel,* he never seems to have observed that other twist of the dialectic noted by E. P. Thompson in which the very discipline imposed upon the workers by capital would come to serve their struggle against it.[61] Still, Blake's rather more somber depiction of sexuality in passages of *The Four Zoas* suggest a premonition that in a world otherwise characterized by egoism and dominion, the energies of Luvah might find perverse expression as well as cruel restraint. Blake's total social vision allows us, who have been released from a collapsing family and driven to solace our loneliness in an emotionally defused sexuality, to find in him more than the exhausted apocalypse he himself found in Milton.

It was from the men and women of the working class, linked to each other in the social ties of production, their mutual-aid societies and trade unions, that Blake took his inspiration for a vision of a world beyond the selfish bourgeois family, a world in which repression is overcome through cooperation and solidarity, where "Man subsists by Brotherhood & Universal Love" (*FZ* 133:22). It was also from the perspective of workers who knew that human beings energetically build their world that he rejects the boundaries of Milton's Eden. While finding in that paradise of pleasure a profound critique of a regimen of joyless repression, Blake rejects the dichotomy, from which Milton could never escape, between a primitive, childhood paradise and the fallen world of adult civilization. He characterizes his garden, Beulah, as a retreat from full humanity into a worship of Vala, the goddess who reigns over the world of natural sensation, sexual love, domestic security, and the unconscious dreams of a lost infantile bliss ("the caves of sleep"). Subtitling *The Four Zoas* "Rest before Labour," he assigns these passive, personal delights their rightful place but distinguishes them from Eden, the apocalyptic transformation of nature and society. Similarly, he rejects the identification of paradise with the dependent securities of mother and child or man and wife for a vision of Eden as an eternal brotherhood, the interdependence of equals in a communal society. Blake's Eden must be "Jerusalem," the common, historically constructed world in which a divine humanity, undivided by sex or class, will see its energies flow both in unhibited affection and collective creativity.

10

Epilogue

Really to do justice to Milton's great epic, I have always thought, one must become engaged with the question which that work so provocatively poses and so inadequately answers—namely, what was lost? On one level, of course, what was lost was Milton's revolution and the dream of a liberty to be achieved by allowing free men to decide their own affairs without interference from a monarchic state or an established church. However, since that good old cause was defeated as much by contradictions within as by enemies without, the question of why it was lost immediately demands consideration of the problems inherent in the history which it culminated and the future which it sought to inaugurate. Struggle though he did with this dilemma, Milton, given the idealist and individualistic bias of his Puritan Christianity, could only conclude that humanity had once again been defeated by an inherent predilection to personal immorality. This was the only import he could find in that intriguing biblical myth which located a fall at the very beginning of human history no less disastrous than that which he had suffered in 1660.

Facing Milton's experience of failed revolution again in his own day, Blake drew a very different inspiration from the congruence between that event and the fall of Adam. The merger of his more collectivist, plebeian tradition with a growing historicism enabled him to give new answers to Milton's troubling questions. Transmuting the fall of Adam into the division of Albion, he concluded that what humanity had forfeited in modern times as in the days of old was the strength and joy of its own unity, a disaster which resulted from the community's shattering into antagonistic classes.

The consequence of this division, by the seventeenth and eighteenth centuries, had been the "liberation" of bourgeois individualism. This "freedom" was a very contradictory phenomenon, bringing power to a middle class released from feudal strictures but various forms of economic and cultural immiseration to their employees. Thus it is appropriate that the event is simultaneously mourned and celebrated in *Paradise Lost* where Adam's emergence from his paradisal womb suggests the historic birth of the individual from a disintegrating feudal society. The process begun when the first Adams severed the umbilical cords which bound them to the matrilineal clan is completed. Adam's appearance as an unconditional self in an original state of nature is accomplished as he is "self-begotten," like Satan, through a sin of self-assertion and left alone with his wife in an uninhabited universe where the world is all before them, where to choose.

At that point, the myths which celebrated a collective human experience, the products of a common, folk imagination, cease to be the main focus of literature. Adam emerges from the dramatic sequences of *Paradise Lost* to begin his career as hero of the novel. In the following centuries the literary imagination will be primarily absorbed with a sequence of new Adams whose societies are mere foils for their individual trajectories and whose choices are more important than their contexts. With the romantics the old tribal myths will be given a basis in individual psychic experience; Wordsworth will even turn the epic, the great historical genre, into a vehicle for autobiography.

The autonomy of the individual celebrated by bourgeois literature has always been something of a mirage, however. For humanity, as Blake uniquely understood, continues to live in society, not in nature. The freedom into which modern man was initiated was never an unrestricted power for self-realization, but only the far more modest mobility which became possible when face-to-face community relationships gave way to the invisible collisions of the market.

Moreover, the conditions for even this limited autonomy would soon disappear. In our own century we have passed from the age of free enterprise and vaunted individualism to a new era in which giant monopolies face an increasingly socialized working population. Not surprisingly, therefore, by World War I the Wordsworthian impetus had been reversed, as the novel in Joyce's hands tried to turn itself back into epic. The European artist had been shocked by cataclysmic wars into confrontation with Europe's collective history, although—significantly—what Joyce gives us is not historical vision but individual personages who are parodies of mythic heroes, speaking as their own heart's truth the now fractured phrases of a dismembered tradition. In America, the cultural crisis had not set in fully until after World War II. By then the frontier had grown sufficiently crowded for the bourgeois self, although still isolated, to begin to recognize its own voice as merely an echo of the voices of others. The system which had once released the individual from communal bonds now seemed to be dissolving that sublime ego into a host of fragmentary personae which simply reflect the various social forces by which that self is buffeted and molded.

It is no wonder that at this point literary criticism might begin to supplement its aesthetics of the performing self with an interest in influences and codes. Nor is it inconsistent that the acknowledgment of influence should be perceived as an agonizing loss of ego, the submission to demonic forces which is illustrated in the recent works of Harold Bloom. As I read him, Bloom seems to assume that a quest for originality, for individual proprietorship, is somehow fundamental to art. He traces the failure of this endeavor to the "belated" romantics in whom we might rather see its origin. Personally, I find little profundity in his pseudo-mystical psychologisms but instead just another example of the tendency of bourgeois thought, as history increasingly challenges its categories, to retreat into obscurantism. Nevertheless, Bloom directs our attention to an important phenomenon—the decay of the myth of individual creativity which arose as the aesthetic counterpart of the Lockean world view which had planted the self alone in nature and had attributed production to private persons. These ideas must inevitably suffer from the elimination of the last vestiges of petit-bourgeois property ownership and the reduction even of intellectuals to paid laborers. Bloom offers little useful analysis, but he does make a contribution to our understanding by demonstrating that at the heart of bourgeois poetry there had always been an anxiety, an awareness that its exalted claims to individual creativity were illusory.

Bloom errs particularly in misreading Blake and his concept of imagination. Blake rejected the myth of the individual from the start as the form assumed by mystery in his time. At the center of his poetry is a historical awareness of the interactions of continuity and change. His epics demonstrate how innovation always builds upon the legacy of not only intellectual tradition but also the whole productive achievement of humanity. They also unveil the way each new cultural formation of class society has partly been a covering cherub to hide an ultimate reliance upon barbaric anachronisms which it cannot relinquish. What I have been trying to show is that Blake's whole effort has been to separate the wheat from the tares, to distinguish between two traditions, the rationalizations through which elites have defended their power against change, and the vision upon which the people might construct their future.

In doing so, Blake follows in the steps of Milton who built a mythology for the revolutionary bourgeoisie upon the various legacies of Western civilization. This study has maintained that Milton's vision nevertheless reproduced the three major splits which had yielded the dynamics of his culture: (1) the symbolic reversals which proceeded from the overthrow of Goddess-worshiping egalitarian tribes by class societies devoted to the royal Father-God; (2) the conflict which emerged within those triumphant cultures between the traditions of the masses and those of their rulers, between prophecy and state religion, prophecy and mystery, particularly within the Judeo-Christian heritage; (3) the social contradictions within bourgeois society and its Protestant, liberal ideology.

Blake understood with Hegel that all cultures are *aufgehoben*— negated and absorbed by those which succeed them. He also grasped that differences between his and Milton's stances toward tradition arose from differences in the societies each was trying to build. Both would return to primitivist myth for an image of harmony between humanity and nature, man and woman. Both would also reject the backward nature cult with which primitive culture was actually associated. However, Blake would espouse only the knowledge and technology of civilization, while Milton would embrace its social institutions—the family, private property, and the state. Hence Milton would celebrate a Jove-like Jehovah while Blake looked to a rebirth of the overthrown Titans to restore an Eden of sexual liberty and equality, social equality and cooperation. The irony is that Milton, accepting the rise of class society, would tend to blame human misery on all man's worldly creations and would indulge a regressive nostalgia in creating his garden paradise. In contrast, Blake, by identifying the Fall with social decline rather than material advance, could look forward to a reestablished golden age in an urban Atlantis-Jerusalem.

Similarly, while both incorporated prophetic resistance to a sanctified king-worship, Milton could never fully relinquish the images of theocratic hierarchy. His deity, as a guarantor of class rule, would retain a kinship with Solomon, Zeus, and all those conquerors whose religion was a worship of plunder and power. For this reason, Blake would charge Milton with having been "curbd by the general malady & infection from the silly Greek & Latin slaves of the Sword" (*M* 1). Milton's Christ would display the same ambiguity, appearing as both the Messiah who led the Puritans in battle against feudal enemies and a Zeus who established their tyranny over Promethean rebels in their own lower classes. The great Puritan prophet had in the end been unable to sever Prophecy entirely from state religion and mystery.

Blake perceived culture as an arena where a people and their rulers contested to impose their own sense of reality. The powerful sought to impress upon their subjects emblems of their rule. They even coopted popular images and fed them back in a distorted form, as the priests transformed Yahweh into a Mesopotamian King of Kings. Thus in *The Four Zoas* Urizen continually entangles Los and Orc in his cruel tree of mystery. The people had various options for resisting this hegemony. They could reassimilate an experience which had been given an alien form, or they could simply invert the values and symbols erected by their masters. As an example of the first process, the Hebrew tribal covenant, after having been turned into an endorsement of the Davidic dynasty, was reclaimed in a new form by plebeian Christians who professed themselves the true heirs of a kingdom of God, no longer a literal monarchy. Similarly, radical Christians like the Ranters would appropriate for humanity as a whole a concept of divinity which once expressed their subordination to theocratic rulers. Blake simply continues this process when, for example, he severs the sun-chariot's image of intellectual mastery from its use as a weapon of domination and transforms it from the image of a god and of deified rule into a vision of the four Zoas, the cooperative humanity from which creation really derives. On the other hand, Blake also espoused the second method of resistance. Like his antinomian antecedents, he simply reversed the virtues and vices of the established order, celebrating its outlaws and demons as his own heroes. Much of Blake's notorious originality actually stemmed from his espousal of a tradition out of power, one which was politically inclined to reinterpret and reverse the dominant ideologies.

In Western culture this adversary tradition had primarily survived in the prophetic-apocalyptic strain of the Bible which Blake had inherited from Milton. They adopted that tradition with different emphases, however. For example, Milton's notorious Hebraism is explained by the fact that he found in the Hebrew testament a confirmation of his own espousal of the values of small, patriarchal, independent property owners, a legacy to which he added his own bourgeois deformations. When Blake sought to purify that heritage, he did so by reemphasizing the collective, plebeian values of the greatest prophet of all, the Jesus who had dwelt with paupers and sinners and promised a kingdom of equality and solidarity to the humble and despised. Blake's goal was to pass that last judgment on his culture which occurs when "Men of Real Art Govern & Pretenders Fall" (PB 551), gathering together all the Error of tyrants to be burned as mystery and incorporating into Jerusalem all the real achievements of the past—primitive harmony and shamanic vision, the arts of civilization, prophetic justice, the brotherly love of lower-class Christianity, antinomian mysticism, scientific enlightenment, and Milton's legacy of liberty and revolution.

It would not be sufficient, however, merely to reorient old categories, for they often had built-in biases. For example, the symbol of woman-as-nature resisted successful adaptation and in some respects undermined Blake's vision of sexual harmony. The image of the Christ, even as a revolutionary leader, failed to express a people's collective power and had to be excluded from Night IX. Blake's real innovation would not lie in reworking these images, but in delineating the social history from which they emerged. His own revolutionary myth is nothing less than a fully conscious realization of the actual history of mankind. His central symbols—Babylon, Egypt, Albion, America, France, Jerusalem—do not represent values; they evoke events and historical processes.

Blake inherited his method of having events stand for each other from the typological exegesis of the Bible which Milton had employed. Biblical commentators had presumed that all history could be read as a single drama of salvation in which God was the prime actor. This epic was not without a plan; rather, a pattern of redemption had been revealed in the Bible where critical events in the interactions of God and human beings had prefigured future events, the Old Testament, for example, foreshadowing the New. A Christian artist like Milton undertook to envision all human life and history in terms of these paradigms, incorporating, for instance, the battles of the New Model Army into those of God's chosen against the pagans. *The Four Zoas* adopts this historical poetry, extending the revelatory nature of biblical events to all temporal incidents. Biblical typology had found the coherence of history in its relationship to divine agency. Milton can see Moses, Samson, and Cromwell as all carrying on the same work of liberation because he sees God working through them all. When Blake replaces divine with human agency, he is proposing to outline the actual historical relationships through which many human actors were joined in a common process.

Herein lies the real significance of Blake's "allegory." The reason why the poet alternately espouses this method as "the Most Sublime Poetry"[1] and eschews it as "a totally distinct & inferior kind of Poetry" (PB 544) is that he is anxious to distinguish his vision of the sum and continuity of human action—"A Representation of what

Eternally Exists" (PB 544)—from the substitution for it of conceptual abstractions. Northrop Frye is correct in warning us against associating Blake's allegory with that which "points away from itself towards something else" or demands "the continuous translation of poetic images into a series of moral and philosophic concepts."[2] He is also right in attributing to Blake a search for "the universal significance in the artist's creation of particular things."[3] Where Frye errs, abandoning Blake for Plato, is in assuming that this significance is "the whole of life seen in the primary outlines of the human and divine mind,"[4] for Blake is not presuming a pattern which inheres in "primary outlines" or eternal forms; he is exploring the design which conscious human activity has given to history.

The hero of *The Four Zoas*, Albion, the Eternal Man, therefore should not be construed either as a philosophic construct, a Hegelian world-spirit, or a universal psyche formed according to eternal spiritual principles or the changing psychobiology of birth, death, and procreation. *The Four Zoas* cannot simply be read, as is common, as a psychomachia whose giant forms are personifications of psychic faculties because "reason" does not exist, nor does "desire"; only thinking, feeling human beings exist. Still less can Blake's epic figures be identified with individual experience. Individuals become spectral when isolated from the relationships through which their existence is actualized. It must be noted that in no corpus of work since the myths projected from the collective experience of primitive peoples has the role of individuals been so minimized. When men like Milton or Locke do appear, it is in terms of the broader cultural significance they had for other men. Thus Blake rejects Reynolds's claim that "A History-painter paints man in general; a Portrait-painter a particular man," insisting on the contrary that "A History Painter Paints The Hero, & not Man in General. but most minutely in Particular" (PB 641).

Blake's epic characters do not represent either abstractions from real people or suprahuman forces. They embody particular human beings, united as by life in social bodies with historic continuity or, as Blake once put it, "Kingdoms . . . represented . . . as Single Personages" (PB 547). For that reason his paintings of these giants often turn out upon closer examination to be composed of multiple human bodies, as "States I have seen in my Imagination when distant they appear as One Man but as you approach they appear Multitudes of Nations" (PB 546). Viewed at a distance, "Multitudes of Men in Harmony appear like a single Infant sometimes in the Arms of a Female . . . the Church" (PB 546) because collective humanity is the real mother of each individual person. When Blake proclaims that man is his own creation, it is this social birth to which he refers; his view has nothing to do with Frye's aesthetic idealism in which "words are of the pattern of the human mind"[5] and art sings only of itself, for Blake's "art" includes all human activity. These remarks appear in his comments on *The Last Judgment* which is the visual equivalent of *The Four Zoas*, attempting as it does to present a vision of history from that perspective of apocalyptic hindsight in which all its processes are comprehended: "Thus My Picture is a History of Art & Science the Foundation of Society Which is Humanity itself" (PB 551).

The concept is simple enough: there is no thread upon one's back, no thought, no feeling, which does not incorporate in some way a legacy from other people. We are not the children of Vala (nature), or Urizen (God), but Jerusalem; we produce ourselves, and Blake's idea of imagination shows he was one of the first to understand that who we are has a great deal to do with how we produce ourselves. In asserting these continuities, Blake's prophetic art provides a sharp contrast to the novelistic realism or psychoanalytic solipsism of much modern art. Artists with an individualistic bias stand too close to their subjects to perceive the wider relationships which determine their meaning. Where they would trace a woman's coy smile to the man who just walked out the door or a remembered paternal rebuke, Blake could elaborate its relation to the whole panorama of human frustration, from the deformed relationships of an impoverished England down through the whole history of Christian asceticism back to the dissolution of primitive society. His historical allegory can turn any particular into a living metaphor by making it reveal its relation to all interconnected human action, for the "Spectres of the Dead" (*FZ* 87:54) live on in us—in our social institutions, our consciousness, and even our technical capabilities. It was in this sense that humanity, taken collectively, was eternal, for "not one Moment / Of Time is lost, nor one Event of Space unpermanent. / But all remain. . . . The generations of men run on in the tide of Time / But leave their destind lineaments permanent for ever & ever" (*M* 22:18–25).

Anyone who has ever tried to communicate historical process with its multiple levels of human experience—cultural, political, economic—its complex interweavings of events and all their dialectical inter-relationships will appreciate the advantages of Blake's suggestive prophetic structures over the linear narrative of chronological realism. Moreover, while biblical typology offered him a method for depicting continuities, the metamorphoses and genealogies of ancient myth provided a means of expressing the way historical contradictions involve the continual transformation of everything into its opposite. The *Theogony* had articulated the evolution of prehistoric society through the births, deaths, marriages, and transmutations of its mythic figures. By wedding Hesiod and the Bible, Blake hoped to depict through the interactions of his four Zoas, their Spectres, Emanations, and offspring, the whole convoluted process of history.

We have traced a number of these figures. For example, we have seen how Luvah, when the harmonious tribe degenerated into conquering chieftaincies, exchanged his chariot of mercies for a chariot of wrath and the power of magic for the magic of power. As the lost brotherhood survived in the enslaved masses, so the sacrificial lamb that once symbolized a communion with natural forces came to signify a humanity sacrificed in propitiation of angry authorities. The destitute now sought communion in mysteries of their own death and resurrection, and Christianity identified the Lamb of God with the crucified Jesus. But Luvah-Jesus appeared also as a rebellious Orc, the antecedent of those revolutionaries who would rise up against Empire in 70 A.D. and in the prophecies of Revelation. Soon however, Blake thought, Jesus would be elevated into another king-god by the feudal aristocracy, while the peasants reverted to worshiping him once again as a dying and rising god of nature. Through the peasant revolts of the later Middle Ages, however, the vision of the deliverer would again be revived, until eventually that prophecy would be adopted as the justification of the revolutionary middle classes, particularly in England. Watching revolution itself turn against them, the plebeian masses would look on in dismay as "Luvah in Orc became a Serpent and descended into / That State calld Satan" (*FZ* 115:26–27). Satan and Messiah, Christ and Zeus, heir of both lower-class rebels and conquering tyrants, Blake's Luvah would be forged out of the paradoxes of *Paradise Lost* into a lucid symbol of that mass of contradictions which was the bourgeois revolution. Nor would his revolt terminate in the wars of Cromwell or Napoleon. For while the theologian might find in history the unifying power of a mystic Christ and the empiricist might only see innumerable discrete rebellions, short-lived and ineffectual, Blake would see in the epic heroism of Luvah-Orc the antiquity, continuity, and inevitability of class struggle.

In this sense Blake did not invent his characters but rather brought out the unity of images cast up by popular experience, reproducing in Luvah an actual historical amalgamation of Adonis, Christ, Prometheus, and Satan, embodiments of the masses in different times and under different conditions. We can observe the same dialectical involutions of a popular image in Vala. Originally a projection of the fertility-worshiping matrilineal clan, she and her serpent lover came to be maligned in the Bible as the Beast and the Whore by a civilization that repudiated their association with backwardness and female power. However, it took more than ideological slander to accomplish this inversion; it reflected an actual evolution of the nature cult into the rites of Mesopotamian theocracies where the priestesses of the Goddess actually became the temple prostitutes of theocracy. Hence, the Great Mother had come to serve the very empires which had obliterated the tribal world of her origins. As Blake puts it, Vala became "Urizens harlot . . . & the deluded harlot of the Kings of Earth" (FZ 91:14–15). He inherits the symbol from Revelation which recorded the identification, by nationalistic Jewish insurgents, of the Babylonian Whore with a new Roman tyranny, fixing her thereafter as a popular image of oppression. So the symbol of heavenly war by triumphant chiefs against the egalitarian clan with its Great Mother had now been totally inverted to express the longing of the downtrodden for the victory of their deliverer over the Beast and Whore as reversal of that class oppression.

Vala came to represent for Blake a kind of continuity that was reactionary and regressive, the way in which all stratified societies cling to backward formulations to mystify their power. The victorious Mesopotamian civilizations had consequently erected their monarchies upon the most archaic aspects of the nature cult, a panoply of generative cycles, astrological determinism, sexual magic, and bloody sacrifices. At the height of its cosmopolitan glory, Israel had introduced Canaanite fetishes into its worship, so Blake symbolized such regression by its seclusion of a despotic law within the wings of covering cherubs behind veils of secrecy in the temple's holy of holies.

The primitive Vala had reflected humanity's real helplessness before nature in a pretechnological state in which an obsession with procreative nature was inevitable. The priest's Vala indicated the savage conditions in which tyranny kept the enslaved and ignorant people at a brutish level of existence. A similar regression later characterized feudal Catholicism when it sanctified rites of pagan superstition in its magnificent cathedrals and tried to gloss with sophisticated metaphysics its worship of the Great Mother and her son, the dying and rising god of nature. Milton had attempted to purge religion of this paganism and substitute morality for magic, but he too clung to an outmoded supernatural mumbo-jumbo. For although he could kill a king he could not abandon the worship of the anachronistic king-god who validated the power of his own oligarchic elite. Nor would the English bourgeoisie through two centuries of scientific development relinquish the piety with which they hoped to sanctify their abuses and bemuse their victims. And in Blake's mind, those who did, the rationalist deists, had only devised a new religion of Vala, reviving the old fertility cult's fatalistic subordination of humanity to natural cycles as a rationale for the misery to which progress had reduced the populace. Capitalism, despite the untold power within its grasp, promoted passivity before the laws of nature rather than liberate the people's creativity for a real mastery of their world. And so it continues to our own day. On the one hand we are encouraged to worship a technology which threatens to subject us to ever new forms of barbarism. On the other hand the rags of mystery are dipped in the colors of modish psychologies by new priests who hope to divert us from taking real imaginative control of our lives. "Luvah & Vala ride / Triumphant in the bloody sky. & the Human form is no more" (*FZ* 15:7–8).

Through delineating the social origins of the Mother Goddess's nature cult and the Father God's state cult, Blake hoped to enable us to recognize mystery in all its forms and cast it off forever. Now he could celebrate that new hero whose growing strength had just been glimpsed in the French and industrial revolutions—the people whose story is history, the unacknowledged authors of the universe who would be its real redeemers. The image of the four Zoas acquires a significance which goes beyond anything in its biblical or mythical sources. In the epic of Albion's "Fall into Division & his Resurrection to Unity" (*FZ* 4:4), Blake creates a new protagonist who is neither the idealization of an elite, the individual of bourgeois realism, nor the abstract "humanity" of philosophy. Albion is alternately a single hero and a community of variously allied and warring beings. As such, he expresses the interdependence of all human beings in history, a unity that would finally become conscious with the emerging power of a majority class which must abolish with its own subjection all divisions and hierarchy. Now all mythology and literature appear as the world of our dreams, the illusions through which we have perceived our lives. (At the heart of literature there is also myth, since artists always work with the images generated by a popular imagination which have erected the canons of the novel as well as the figures of ancient ritual).

In Blake's epic, Albion is awakening to a comprehension of what all those dreams have been about. Only a few decades after Blake's Eternal Prophet had left off constructing Golgonooza as a total vision of history, Karl Marx would arrive in London to pick up his hammer and rekindle his furnaces. History, he would announce, is the history of class struggle. Blake had anticipated that manifesto and had begun to analyze culture as a reflection of that strife, though sometimes, as in a pool, somewhat darkly and often inverted by the perspective of the perceiver. He did so by claiming art, as Milton had done for "intellectual war," to be a conscious weapon in that struggle.

At the same time, taking up a battle that went beyond Milton's, Blake's work is the culmination of a tradition which began with the first lament for paradise and initiated a direction in art whose full potential we have not yet seen. In this tradition, the *labors* of art and science would direct all human activity toward building up Jerusalem in fact as well as in vision, toward replacing the rule of human beings over each other with the reign of cooperation and the liberation of an Imagination whose full powers we have scarcely begun even to conceive.

Notes

Index

Notes

Chapter 1. Critical Introduction

1. Walter A. Raleigh, *Milton* (New York: Putnam, 1900), p. 85.

2. Joseph A. Wittreich, *The Romantics on Milton* (Cleveland: Case Western Reserve University Press, 1970), p. 8.

3. Christopher Hill, "Milton the Radical," *TLS*, 29 Nov. 1974, p. 1330.

4. The phrase is taken from Harold Rosenberg, *The Tradition of the New* (New York: Horizon, 1959).

5. Harold Bloom, *The Anxiety of Influence: A Theory of Poetry* (New York: Oxford University Press, 1973), p. 32.

6. M. H. Abrams, *Natural Supernaturalism: Tradition and Revolution in Romantic Literature* (New York: Norton, 1971), pp. 17–70.

7. Bloom, *Anxiety of Influence*, p. 96.

8. Ibid., p. 32.

9. A. L. Morton, *The Matter of Britain: Essays in a Living Culture* (1966), quoted in Joseph A. Wittreich, *Angel of Apocalypse: Blake's Idea of Milton* (Madison: University of Wisconsin Press, 1975), pp. 186, xvi, xvii.

10. Denis Saurat, *Blake and Milton* (London: Stanley Nott, 1935).

11. Northrop Frye, *Fearful Symmetry* (Princeton, N.J.: Princeton University Press, 1947), "Notes for a Commentary on Milton," in *The Divine Vision: Studies in the Poetry and Art of William Blake*, ed. Vivian de Sola Pinto (London: Victor Gollancz, 1957), pp. 97–138.

12. Harold Bloom, *Blake's Apocalypse* (Garden City, N.Y.: Anchor, 1963); *Anxiety of Influence*.

13. John Beer, *Blake's Humanism* (New York: Barnes & Noble, 1968), esp. pp. 23–57; *Blake's Visionary Universe* (New York: Barnes & Noble, 1969).

14. Leslie Brisman, *Milton's Poetry of Choice and Its Romantic Heirs* (Ithaca, N.Y.: Cornell University Press, 1973), pp. 151–212.

15. Florence Sandler, "The Iconoclastic Enterprise: Blake's Critique of Milton's Religion," *Blake Studies* 5 (1972), 13–57.

16. Joseph A. Wittreich, ed., *Calm of Mind: Tercentenary Essays on "Paradise Regained" and "Samson Agonistes" in Honor of John S. Diekoff* (Cleveland: Case Western Reserve University Press, 1971), p. 93; for Wittreich's discussion of Blake's Miltonic sources, see "Blake's Philosophy of Contraries: A New Source," *ELN* 4 (1966), 105–10; "Blake and Milton," *Blake Newsletter* 2 (1968), 17–18, "The Satanism of Blake and Shelley Reconsidered," *SP* 65 (1968), 816–33; "Opening the Seals: Blake's Epics and the Milton Tradition," in *Blake's Sublime Allegory: Essays on "The Four Zoas," "Milton," "Jerusalem,"* ed. Stuart Curran and Joseph A. Wittreich (Madison: University of Wisconsin Press, 1973), pp. 23–58.

17. Northrop Frye, *The Stubborn Structure: Essays on Criticism and Society* (Ithaca, N.Y.: Cornell University Press, 1970), p. 160.

18. S. Foster Damon, "Milton," in *A Blake Dictionary: The Ideas and Symbols of William Blake* (New York: E. P. Dutton, 1971), pp. 274–75. For Damon's work on Blake's Miltonic sources, see "Blake and Milton," in *The Divine Vision,* ed. de Sola Pinto, pp. 89–96; see also Harold Fisch, "Blake's Miltonic Moment," in *William Blake: Essays for S. Foster Damon,* ed. Alvin Rosenfeld (Providence, R.I.: Brown University Press, 1969), pp. 36–56.

19. Kathleen Raine, *Blake and Tradition,* Bollingen Series 35:11 (Princeton, N.J.: Princeton University Press, 1968), I.xxxii.

20. Blake's remark to Henry Crabb Robinson, in G. E. Bentley, Jr., *Blake Records* (Oxford: Clarendon Press, 1969), p. 322.

21. Herbert Grierson, *Milton and Wordsworth: Poets and Prophets* (London: Chatto & Windus, 1963); see also William Kerrigan, *The Prophetic Milton* (Charlottesville: University Press of Virginia, 1974).

22. The tradition is explored in Joseph A. Wittreich, ed., *Milton and the Line of Vision* (Madison: University of Wisconsin Press, 1975).

23. Abrams, *Natural Supernaturalism,* p. 38.

24. Bloom, *Blake's Apocalypse;* Sandler, "Iconoclastic Enterprise"; A. L. Morton, *The Everlasting Gospel* (London: Lawrence & Wishart, 1958); William F. Halloran, "The French Revolution: Revelation's New Form," in *Blake's Visionary Forms Dramatic,* ed. David V. Erdman and John E. Grant (Princeton, N.J.: Princeton University Press, 1970), pp. 30–56; Michael Fixler, "The Apocalypse Within *Paradise Lost,*" in *New Essays on "Paradise Lost,"* ed. Thomas Kranidas (Berkeley and Los Angeles: University of California Press, 1969), pp. 131–78; Austin Dobbins, *Milton and the Book of Revelation,* Studies in the Humanities, no. 7 (University, Ala.: University of Alabama Press, 1975); Wittreich, "Opening the Seals," in *Blake's Sublime Allegory;* "A Poet Amongst Poets: Milton and the Tradition of Prophecy," in Wittreich, ed., *Milton and the Line of Vision,* pp. 97–142; and *Visionary Poetics: Milton's Tradition and His Legacy* (San Marino, Calif.: Huntington Library, 1979).

25. Percy Bysshe Shelley, "A Defence of Poetry," in *Shelley's Prose or The Trumpet of a Prophecy,* ed. David Lee Clark (Albuquerque: University of New Mexico Press, 1954), pp. 296–97.

26. Marcia Pointon, *Milton and English Art* (Toronto: University of Toronto Press), p. xxvii.

27. K. L. Sharma, *Milton Criticism in the Twentieth Century* (New Delhi: S. Chad, 1973), p. v.

28. Wittreich, *Angel of Apocalypse,* p. 163.

29. Douglas Bush, *"Paradise Lost" in Our Time: Some Comments* (Ithaca, N.Y.: Cornell University Press, 1945); B. Rajan, *"Paradise Lost" & the Seventeenth Century Reader* (London: Chatto & Windus, 1962).

30. Edgell Rickword, "Milton, the Revolutionary Intellectual," in *The English Revo-*

lution, ed. Christopher Hill (London: Lawrence & Wishart, 1940), p. 102; primarily responsible in defining this image of Milton was Thomas B. Macaulay, "Milton," *Edinburgh Review* 84 (1825), 304–46.

31. Percy Bysshe Shelley, "A Defence of Poetry," p. 290.

32. The phrase is Samuel Johnson's in "Life of Milton," *The Works of the Most Eminent English Poets, with Prefaces, Biographical and Critical* (London, 1770–81); the issue is most provocatively discussed by William Empson in *Milton's God* (London: Chatto & Windus, 1961).

33. See E. M. W. Tillyard, *Milton* (New York: Barnes & Noble, 1967); A. J. A. Waldock, *"Paradise Lost" and Its Critics* (Cambridge: Cambridge University Press, 1947); John Peter, *A Critique of "Paradise Lost"* (London: Longmans, 1960); and Raymond Southall, *Literature and the Rise of Capitalism* (London: Lawrence & Wishart, 1973), pp. 121–33.

34. In Tillyard, *Milton*; and R. J. Zwi Werblowski, *Lucifer and Prometheus: A Study of Milton's Satan* (London: Routledge, 1952).

35. See Southall, *Literature and the Rise of Capitalism*; Maurice Kelley, *This Great Argument: A Study of Milton's "De Doctrina Christiana" as a Gloss upon "Paradise Lost"* (Princeton, N.J.: Princeton University Press, 1941).

36. Harold Fisch, *Jerusalem and Albion: The Hebraic Factor in Seventeenth Century Literature* (London: Routledge, 1964).

37. Waldock, *"Paradise Lost" and Its Critics*, pp. 145, 65.

38. Basil Willey, *Seventeenth-Century Background: Studies in the Thought of the Age in Relation to Poetry and Religion* (London: Chatto & Windus, 1934).

39. Tillyard, *Milton*, p. 234.

40. Kelley, *This Great Argument*, p. 212; Hill, "Milton the Radical," p. 1332.

41. Stanley E. Fish, *Surprised by Sin: The Reader in "Paradise Lost"* (New York: St. Martin's, 1967).

42. However, in *Angel of Apocalypse*, pp. 148–49, Wittreich does explain to what great an extent this distortion occurred.

43. Hill, "Milton the Radical," p. 1332.

44. Arthur Barker, *Milton and the Puritan Dilemma, 1641–1660* (Toronto: University of Toronto Press, 1942); Edgell Rickword, "Milton, the Revolutionary Intellectual," pp. 100–32; George Sensabaugh, *That Grand Whig Milton* (Stanford, Calif.: Stanford University Press, 1952); William Haller, *The Rise of Puritanism* (New York: Columbia University Press, 1938); Zera S. Fink, *The Classical Republicans: An Essay in the Recovery of a Pattern of Thought in Seventeenth Century England* (Evanston, Ill.: Northwestern University Press, 1945); Don M. Wolfe, *Milton in the Puritan Revolution* (New York: Thomas Nelson, 1941); Florence Sandler, "Icon and Iconoclastes," in *Achievements of the Left Hand: Essays on the Prose of Milton*, ed. Michael Lieb and John Shawcross (Amherst: University of Massachusetts Press, 1974); A. S. P. Woodhouse, "Milton, Puritanism and Liberty," *University of Toronto Quarterly* 4 (1935), 485–513.

45. Malcolm M. Ross, *Milton's Royalism: A Study of the Conflict of Symbol and Idea in the Poems* (Ithaca, N.Y.: Cornell University Press, 1943); G. Wilson Knight, *Chariot of Wrath: The Message of John Milton to Democracy at War* (London: Faber & Faber, 1942); Michael Fixler, *Milton and the Kingdoms of God* (London: Faber & Faber, 1964); Wittreich, *Angel of Apocalypse*. See also Joan Bennett, "God, Satan and Charles I: Milton's Royal Portraits," *PMLA* 92 (1977), 44–57; Boyd M. Berry, "Puritan Soldiers in *Paradise Lost*," *Modern Language Quarterly* 35 (1974), 376–402; Stella Revard, *War in Heaven: "Paradise Lost" and the Tradition of Satan's Rebellion* (Ithaca, N.Y.: Cornell University Press, 1980); Merritt Y. Hughes, "Milton as a Revolutionary," *Ten Perspectives on Milton* (New Haven, Conn.: Yale University Press, 1964).

46. Christopher Hill, *Milton and the English Revolution* (New York: Viking, 1978), p. 249.

47. Frank Kermode, *Romantic Image* (New York: Vintage, 1964), p. 165.

48. David Erdman, *Blake: Prophet Against Empire*, rev. ed. (Garden City, N.Y.: Anchor, 1969).

49. Christopher Hill, "Milton and Bunyan: Dialogue with the Radicals," *The World Turned Upside Down: Radical Ideas in the English Revolution* (New York: Viking, 1972), pp. 320–27; Edward P. Thompson, letter to *TLS*, 7 Mar. 1975, p. 253.

50. Clark Emery, *Blake's "The Marriage of Heaven and Hell"* (Coral Gables, Fla.: University of Miami Press, 1963), p. 43.

51. John Broadbent, *"Paradise Lost": Introduction* (Cambridge: Cambridge University Press, 1972).

52. Fred Whitehead, "William Blake and the Radical Tradition," in *Weapons of Criticism*, ed. Norman Rudich (Palo Alto, Calif.: Ramparts Press, 1976). In "Studies in the Structure of European History in Blake's Epics" (Ph.D. diss., Columbia University, 1972), Whitehead develops a historical interpretation of all Blake's epics and interprets *The Four Zoas* as being located in ancient history. This interpretation is summarized in "Visions of the Archaic World," in *Sparks of Fire: Blake in a New Age*, ed. James Bogan and Fred Goss (Richmond, Calif.: North Atlantic Books, 1982).

53. Friedrich Engels, Letter to H. Starkenberg, 25 Jan. 1894, *Selected Correspondence* (Moscow: Foreign Languages Publications, 1953), p. 549.

Chapter 2. Milton and the Line of Prophecy

1. Karl Marx, "Contribution to the Critique of Hegel's Philosophy of Right," introduction to *Marx and Engels On Religion* (New York: Schocken, 1964), p. 41.

2. Ibid., p. 42.

3. Ibid.

4. William Haller, *The Rise of Puritanism* (New York: Columbia University Press, 1938), pp. 150–60.

5. Richard Bernard, *The Bible Battells or the Sacred Art Military for the Rightly Waging of War According to the Holy Writ* (London, 1629); John Downame, *Christian Warfare* (London, 1609); William Gouge, *The Whole Armour of God* (London, 1622).

6. Bernard, *Bible Battells*, p. 25.

7. Thomas Brightman, *The Revelation of St. John Illustrated*, 4th ed. (1644); Joseph Mede, *The Key of the Revelation*, 2nd ed., trans. Richard More (London: Printed for Phil. Stephens, 1659).

8. Christopher Hill, *Antichrist in Seventeenth-Century England* (London: Oxford University Press, 1971).

9. Richard Baxter, *The Holy Commonwealth* (London, 1659), p. 92.

10. T. Hall, *Vindiciae Literarum* (1655), quoted in Christopher Hill, *The World Turned Upside Down* (New York: Viking, 1972), p. 302.

11. *Regii Sanguinis Clamor ad Coelum adversus Parricides Anglicanos*, quoted in William Riley Parker, *Milton, A Biography* (Oxford: Clarendon Press, 1968), vol. 1, p. 421.

12. Joseph Jane, *Salamasius His Dissection and Confutation of the Diabolical Rebel Milton* (1660).

13. Quoted by Edward P. Thompson, *The Making of the English Working Class* (New York: Vintage, 1963), p. 114.

14. John Toland, *The Life of John Milton* (1698), in *The Early Lives of Milton*, ed. Helen Darbishire (London: Constable, 1932), p. 182.

15. *The London Chronicle*, 12–13 Nov. 1763, pp. 12, 468.

16. Ibid., 7 June 1764, pp. 12, 627.

17. Karl Marx, *Preface to a Contribution to the Critique of Political Economy*, in *Selected Works* (New York: International Publishers, 1968), pp. 182–83.

18. Max Weber, *The Protestant Ethic and the Spirit of Capitalism* (New York: Scribner's, 1958); R. H. Tawney, *Religion and the Rise of Capitalism* (New York: Harcourt Brace, 1926); C. H. George and Katherine George, *The Protestant Mind of the English Reformation* (Princeton, N.J.: Princeton University Press, 1961); Michael Walzer, *The Revolution of the Saints* (New York: Atheneum, 1968); Keith Thomas, *Religion and the Decline of Magic* (New York: Scribner's, 1971); Christopher Hill, *Puritanism and Revolution* (New York: Schocken, 1964); *Society and Puritanism in Pre-revolutionary England* (New York: Schocken, 1964); *The World Turned Upside Down: Radical Ideas in the English Revolution* (New York: Viking, 1972); *Change and Continuity in Seventeenth-Century England* (Cambridge, Mass.: Harvard University Press, 1975).

19. Anon., *Animadversions Upon Those Notes Which the Late Observator Hath Published* (London, 1642), quoted in Ernest Sirluck, introduction to *Complete Prose Works of John Milton* (New Haven, Conn.: Yale University Press, 1959), vol. 2, p. 8.

20. William Dell, *Several Sermons and Discourses* (London, 1709), p. 144.

21. Ibid., p. 109.

22. Oliver Cromwell, *The Writings and Speeches of Oliver Cromwell*, ed. W. C. Abbott (Cambridge, Mass.: Harvard University Press, 1937–47), vol. 1, p. 256.

23. Hill, *The World Turned Upside Down*, pp. 88–90.

24. John Robinson, *Works* (1851), quoted in Don M. Wolfe, introduction to *Complete Prose Works of John Milton*, ed. Don M. Wolfe et al. (New Haven, Conn.: Yale University Press, 1953–82), vol. 1, p. 14.

25. Hill, *The World Turned Upside Down*, p. 271.

26. Ibid., p. 73.

27. Ibid., p. 76.

28. John Selden, *Table Talk* (London, 1847), p. 185.

29. Thompson, *The Making of the English Working Class*, p. 30.

30. A. L. Morton, *The Everlasting Gospel* (London: Lawrence & Wishart, 1958), p. 11; Thompson, *The Making of the English Working Class*, p. 31.

31. Quoted in Thompson, *The Making of the English Working Class*, p. 36.

32. Hill, *The World Turned Upside Down*, pp. 307–08; see also E. D. Andrews, *The People Called Shakers* (New York: Diver, 1953), pp. 13–20, 27–28.

33. Thompson, *The Making of the English Working Class*, p. 48.

34. I Kings 12:16,19, quoted in ibid., p. 51. Unless otherwise noted, biblical references are to the King James Version.

35. Morton D. Paley, "William Blake, the Prince of the Hebrews, and the Woman Clothed with the Sun," in *William Blake: Essays in Honour of Sir Geoffrey Keynes* (Oxford: Clarendon Press, 1973), p. 268; Clarke Garrett, *Respectable Folly: Millenarians and the French Revolution in France and England* (Baltimore: Johns Hopkins, 1975); John F. C. Harrison, *The Second Coming, Popular Millenarianism 1780–1850* (New Brunswick, N.J.: Rutgers University Press, 1979).

36. Richard Price, "A Discourse on the Love of Our Country," in *British Radicals and Reformers 1789–1832*, ed. Wilfried Keutsch, *English Texts* (Tubingen: Max Niemeyer, 1971), p. 108.

37. Hill, *The World Turned Upside Down*, p. 306.

38. Thompson, *The Making of the English Working Class*, p. 108.

39. Henry Parker, *The Case of Shipmony Briefly Discoursed* (London, 1640), p. 35.

40. Thomas Goodwin, *A Glimpse of Sion's Glory*, in *Puritanism and Liberty, Being the Army Debates (1647–9) from the Clarke Manuscripts, with Supplementary Documents*, ed. A. S. P. Woodhouse (London: J. M. Dent, 1938), p. 234.

41. Richard Overton, *An Appeale* (1647), in *Leveller Manifestoes of the Puritan Revolution*, ed. Don M. Wolfe (New York: Nelson, 1944), p. 188.

42. David Erdman, *Blake: Prophet Against Empire*, rev. ed. (Garden City, N.Y.: Anchor, 1969), esp. pp. 433–61.

43. G. Rattray Taylor, *The Angel-Makers* (London: Heinemann, 1958).

Chapter 3. Blake's Philosophy:
A "New Church" of the "Active Life"

1. David Erdman, *Blake: Prophet Against Empire*, rev. ed. (Garden City, N.Y.: Anchor, 1969), p. 134.

2. See for example Friedrich Engels, introduction to *Socialism Utopian and Scientific*, in Karl Marx and Friedrich Engels, *Selected Works* (New York: International Publishers, 1968) pp. 378–98; *Ludwig Feuerback and the End of Classical German Philosophy* in ibid., pp. 596–632; and introduction to *Dialectics of Nature*, in ibid., pp. 342–57.

3. Northrop Frye, *Fearful Symmetry* (Princeton, N.J.: Princeton University Press, 1947), p. 117.

4. Ibid., p. 255.

5. Christopher Caudwell, *Studies and Further Studies in a Dying Culture* (New York: Monthly Review, 1971), p. 206.

6. J. H. Randall, *The Making of the Modern Mind* (New York: Houghton Mifflin, 1940), p. 270.

7. John Stuart Mill, *Mill on Bentham and Coleridge* (New York: George W. Stewart, 1950), p. 41.

8. Christopher Hill, "Protestantism and the Rise of Capitalism," *Change and Continuity in Seventeenth-Century England*, (Cambridge, Mass.: Harvard University Press, 1975), pp. 81–102.

9. Nassau Senior, *An Outline of the Science of Political Economy* (New York: Augustus M. Kell, 1938), p. 27.

10. Alasdair MacIntyre, "Egoism and Altruism," in *The Encyclopedia of Philosophy* (New York: Macmillan, 1967), vol. 2, p. 466.

11. Richard D. Altick, *Victorian People and Ideas* (New York: Norton, 1973), p. 119.

12. Mark Shorer, *William Blake: The Politics of Vision* (New York: Vintage, 1959), pp. 277–78.

13. Friedrich Engels, *Selected Works*, p. 345.

14. Charles Dickens, *Hard Times* (New York: New American Library, 1961), p. 64.

15. Ibid., p. 160.

16. Karl Marx, *Capital* (New York: International Publishers, 1967), vol. 1, p. 72.

17. Ibid.

18. Ibid.

19. Marx, "Theses on Feuerbach," *Selected Works*, p. 28.

20. Ibid.

21. Engels, letter to J. Bloch, 21 Sept. 1890, *Selected Works*, pp. 692–93.

22. Marx, *Selected Works*, p. 28.

23. See, for example, Frye, "The Case Against Locke," *Fearful Symmetry*, pp. 3–29; Peter Fisher, "The Critique of Vision," *The Valley of Vision* (Toronto: University of Toronto Press, 1961), pp. 102–21; Kathleen Raine, *Blake and the New Age* (London: Allen Unwin, 1979).

24. Frye, *Fearful Symmetry*, p. 21.

25. Several recent books examine the implications of a non-Newtonian physics for ideas of consciousness; see Fritjof Capra, *The Tao of Physics* (New York: Random House, 1975); Donald Ault, *Visionary Physics: Blake's Response to Newton* (Chicago: University of Chicago Press, 1974).

26. Thomas J. Altizer, *The New Apocalypse: The Radical Christian Vision of William Blake* (East Lansing: Michigan State University Press, 1967), esp. pp. 57–68.

27. M. H. Abrams, *Natural Supernaturalism* (New York: Norton, 1971), p. 49.

28. Ibid.

29. Ibid.

Chapter 4. "Historical Facts . . . Written by Inspiration"

1. Harold Bloom, *Blake's Apocalypse* (Garden City, N.Y.: Anchor, 1963), pp. 266–80; D. J. Sloss and J. P. R. Wallis, *William Blake's Prophetic Writings* (Oxford: Clarendon Press, 1926), vol. 1, p. 143; vol. 2, p. 184; John Sutherland, "Blake and Urizen," in *Blake's Visionary Forms Dramatic*, ed. David V. Erdman and John Grant (Princeton, N.J.: Princeton University Press, 1970).

2. Northrop Frye, *Fearful Symmetry* (Princeton, N.J.: Princeton University Press, 1947), p. xiii; H. M. Margoliouth, *"Vala": Blake's Numbered Text* (Oxford: Clarendon Press, 1956), p. xiii.

3. David Erdman, *Blake: Prophet Against Empire*, rev. ed. (Garden City, N.Y.: Anchor, 1969), pp. 377–89.

4. Frye, *Fearful Symmetry*, p. 292.

5. Ibid., pp. 292, 295–96.

6. Erdman, *Blake: Prophet Against Empire*, pp. 316–17.

7. M. H. Abrams, *Natural Supernaturalism* (New York: Norton, 1971), p. 145.

8. Bloom, *Blake's Apocalypse*, p. 221.

9. Abrams, *Natural Supernaturalism*, pp. 21–32.

10. Ibid., p. 443.

11. Frye, *Fearful Symmetry*, p. 295.

12. Karl Marx, *Selected Works* (New York: International Publishers, 1968), p. 29.

13. The phrase, taken from Frank Kermode, *Sense of an Ending: Studies in the Theory of Fiction* (New York: Oxford University Press, 1967), pp. 8, 18, was applied to Milton by Joseph A. Wittreich in "Opening the Seals: Blake's Epics and the Milton Tradition," in *Blake's Sublime Allegory*, ed. Joseph A. Wittreich and Stuart Curran (Madison: University of Wisconsin Press, 1973), p. 54.

14. Bloom, *Blake's Apocalypse*, p. 183.

15. Samuel Taylor Coleridge, letter to Rev. Geo. Coleridge, *Letters of Samuel Taylor Coleridge* (New York: Houghton Mifflin, 1895), vol. 1, p. 243.

16. Abrams, *Natural Supernaturalism*, pp. 368, 357.

17. Frye, *Fearful Symmetry*, p. 298.

18. Erdman, *Blake: Prophet Against Empire*, p. 255.

19. Ibid.

20. For the historiography of the period, see Harry Elmer Barnes, *A History of Historical Writings*, 2nd rev. ed. (New York: Dover, 1962), esp. "The Rise of Social and Cultural History," pp. 136–77.

21. Friedrich Schiller, *Something Concerning the First Human Society, According to the Guidance of the Mosaic Records* (1790); universal histories had also appeared in England, such as *Universal History from the Earliest Account of Time to the Present* (1736–1765), compiled by John Campbell, George Sale, John Swinton, Archibald Bower and George Psalmanazar; John Adams, *View of Universal History* (1795); and Alex-

ander Tytler, *Elements of General History*; see Abrams, "The Paradox of the Fortunate Division: Schiller and Universal History," *Natural Supernaturalism*, pp. 201–16.

22. Adam Ferguson, *An Essay on the History of Civil Society*, ed. Duncan Forbes (1767; rpt. Edinburgh: Edinburgh University Press, 1966); see also Abrams, *Natural Supernaturalism*, pp. 210–11; and Gladys Bryson, *Man and Society: The Scottish Inquiry of the Eighteenth Century* (Princeton, N.J.: Princeton University Press, 1945).

23. Augustin Thierry, *History of the Conquest of the English by the Normans* (London: Bohn's Standard Library, 1856); François Pierre Guillaume Guizot, *Outline of the History of France from the Earliest Times to the Outbreak of the Revolution* (Boston: Estes & Lauriat, 1883); François Auguste Alexis Mignet, *The French Revolution from 1789 to 1814* (London: G. Bell, 1906).

24. James Barry, *An Inquiry into the Real and Imaginary Obstructions to the Acquisition of the Arts in England* (London, 1774), pp. 132–44; Horace Walpole is quoted on Barry's project by Erdman, *Blake: Prophet Against Empire*, p. 40.

25. Eric Hobsbawm, *Revolutionaries* (New York: Pantheon, 1973), p. 138.

26. Florence Sandler, "The Iconoclastic Enterprise: Blake's Critique of Milton's Religion," *Blake Studies* 5 (1972), 15.

27. Ibid.

28. John Beer, *Blake's Visionary Universe* (New York: Barnes & Noble, 1969), p. 114.

29. E. O. James, *The Beginnings of Religion* (New York: Hutchinson's University Library, 1950), pp. 137–38.

30. Bronislaw Malinowski, *Magic, Science and Religion* (New York: Doubleday, 1954), pp. 101, 84.

31. French Fogle, introduction to *The History of Britain, The Complete Prose Works of John Milton* (New Haven, Conn.: Yale University Press, 1971), vol. 5, pt. 1, pp. xix, xxxii.

32. Eric Auerbach, *Scenes from the Drama of European Literature* (New York: Peter Smith, 1959), p. 53.

33. J. M. Evans, *"Paradise Lost" and the Genesis Tradition* (Oxford: Clarendon Press, 1968), p. 100.

34. Fogle, introduction to *The History of Britain*, p. xx.

35. Frye, *Fearful Symmetry*, pp. 9–11; Abrams, *Natural Supernaturalism*, p. 47.

36. Joseph Campbell, *Occidental Mythology* (New York: Viking, 1964), p. 95.

37. Sandler, "The Iconoclastic Enterprise," p. 14.

38. Joan Webber, "Milton's God," *ELH* 40 (1973), 515.

39. George Thomson, *Studies in Ancient Greek Society* (New York: Citadel, 1965), vol. 1, p. 578.

40. Joseph A. Wittreich, *Angel of Apocalypse: Blake's Idea of Milton* (Madison: University of Wisconsin Press, 1975), pp. 158–60.

Chapter 5. Milton and Genesis: Mythological Defamation

1. Joan Webber, "Milton's God," *ELH* 40 (1973), 514.

2. Joseph Campbell, *Occidental Mythology* (New York: Viking, 1964), p. 17.

3. Joseph E. Duncan, *Milton's Earthly Paradise* (Minneapolis: University of Minnesota Press, 1972), pp. 241, 238.

4. Isabel MacCaffrey, *"Paradise Lost" as "Myth"* (Cambridge, Mass.: Harvard University Press, 1959), p. 145.

5. Northrop Frye, *The Stubborn Structure* (Ithaca, N.Y.: Cornell University Press, 1970), p. 139.

6. Noted by John Carey and Alastair Fowler in *The Poems of John Milton* (London: Longmans, 1968), p. 899.

7. This theme is also discussed in Merritt Y. Hughes, "Milton's Celestial Battle and the Theogonies," *Ten Perspectives on Milton* (New Haven, Conn.: Yale University Press, 1965), pp. 196–219.

8. MacCaffrey, *"Paradise Lost" as "Myth,"* p. 145.

9. Robert Graves, *Adam's Rib* (Boissia, France: Trianon, 1955), p. 15.

10. In S. G. Brandon, *Creation Legends of the Ancient Near East* (London: Hodder and Stoughton, 1963), p. 94; Joseph Campbell, *The Flight of the Wild Gander* (Chicago: Henry Regnery, 1972), pp. 130–50.

11. E. O. James, *The Ancient Gods* (New York: Putnam's, 1960), p. 77; Campbell, *Occidental Mythology.*

12. Jane Ellen Harrison, *Themis* (Cambridge: Cambridge University Press, 1903), pp. 268–71.

13. Ibid., pp. 166, 165.

14. George Thomson, *Studies in Ancient Greek Society* (London: Lawrence & Wishart, 1972), vol. 2, pp. 88–89.

15. Vera Gordon Childe, *Man Makes Himself* (New York: New American Library, 1951), p. 38.

16. Gerhard von Rad, *Genesis* (Philadelphia: Westminster Press, 1972), p. 17.

17. T. H. Robinson, "Hebrew Myths," in *Myth and Ritual of the Hebrews,* ed. S. H. Hooke (Oxford: Oxford University Press, 1933), pp. 172–96; Raphael Patai, *The Hebrew Goddess* (New York: Ktav, 1967).

18. For mythical sources of Genesis, see George Buttrick, *The Interpreter's Bible* (Nashville, Tenn.: Abingdon Press, 1952), vol. 1, pp. 441–57; Theodor H. Gaster, *Myth, Legend, and Custom in the Old Testament* (New York: Harper & Row, 1969), esp. pp. 3–50; Raphael Patai and Robert Graves, *Hebrew Myth* (New York: McGraw-Hill, 1966); Patai, *The Hebrew Goddess.*

19. J. B. Pritchard, ed., *Ancient Near Eastern Texts Relating to the Old Testament* (Princeton, N.J.: Princeton University Press, 1955), pp. 60b–61a.

20. Joseph Campbell, *Occidental Mythology,* p. 146.

21. Ibid., pp. 17, 70. The idea of a transition from female to male gods has received much discussion recently; see Merlin Stone, *When God Was a Woman* (New York: Harcourt Brace, 1976); *Ancient Mirrors of Womanhood* (New York: New Sibylline, 1980); Carol Ochs, *Beyond the Sex of God* (Boston: Beacon, 1977); Eleanor Leacock and June Nash, "Ideologies of Sex: Archetypes and Stereotypes," *Annals of the New York Academy of Science* 285 (1977), 618–45; Ann Barstow, "The Uses of Anthropology in Women's History: James Mellaart's Work on the Neolithic Goddess at Catal Huyuck," *Feminist Studies* 4 (1978), 7–18; Rayna Rapp, "Women, Religion and Archaic Civilizations," *Feminist Studies* 4 (1978), 1–6; Judith Ochschorn, *The Female Experience and the Nature of the Divine* (Bloomington: Indiana University Press, 1982); and Marija Gimbutas, *The Gods and Goddesses of Old Europe* (Berkeley: University of California Press, 1974). An alternative approach to myth which argues against historicity is found in Claude Lévi-Strauss, "The Structural Study of Myth," *Structural Anthropology* (New York: Basic Books, 1958). Lévi-Strauss believes all variants of a myth should be considered equivalent, rather than derivative, and that myths attempt resolutions of philosophical conflicts rather than expressions of historical ones. For critiques of Lévi-Strauss, see Eleanor Leacock, *Myths of Male Dominance: Collected Articles on Woman Cross-Culturally* (New York: Monthly Review, 1981), pp. 209–21; L. L. Thomas, J. Z. Kronenfeld and D. B. Kronenfeld, "Asdiwal Crumbles: A Critique of Lévi-Straussian Myth Analysis," *American Ethnologist* 3, no. 1 (1976), 147–74; and Marvin Harris, *Cultural Materialism* (New York: Random House, 1978).

22. Campbell, *Occidental Mythology,* p. 80; Robert Graves, *The White Goddess* (New York: Noonday, 1954), p. 219.

23. Robert Graves, *The Greek Myths* (Baltimore: Penguin, 1955), vol. 1, p. 124.

24. Jane Ellen Harrison, *Prolegomena to the Study of Ancient Greek Religion* (Cambridge: Cambridge University Press, 1903), p. 309; *Themis*, p. 500.

25. Thomson, *Studies in Ancient Greek Society*, vol. 1, p. 268. For the argument that Goddess worship reflected an elevated female status, see also Jacquetta Hawkes, *Dawn of the Gods* (London: Chatto & Windus, 1968); and Stone, *When God Was a Woman*.

26. Graves, *Adam's Rib*, p. 13.

27. Wilhelm Schmidt, *Der Ursprung der Gottesidee*, quoted in Campbell, *Primitive Mythology* (New York: Viking, 1959), p. 322; see Theodore Reik, *The Creation of Woman* (New York: McGraw-Hill, 1960), pp. 133–48.

28. John Weir Perry, *Lord of the Four Quarters: Myths of the Royal Father* (New York: George Braziller, 1966), p. 3.

29. Friedrich Engels, *The Origin of the Family, Private Property and the State* (New York: International Publishers, 1974), p. 120; for reassessments of Engels, see Eleanor Leacock, introduction to ibid.; Kathleen Gough, The Origin of the Family," in *Toward an Anthropology of Women*, ed. Rayna R. Reiter (New York: Monthly Review, 1975), pp. 51–76; *Sisters and Wives: The Past and Future of Sexual Equality* (Westport, Conn.: Greenwood, 1979); Ann J. Lane, "Women in Society: A Critique of Frederick Engels," in *Liberating Women's History*, ed. Berenice A. Carroll (Urbana: University of Illinois Press, 1976); and Elizabeth Fee, "The Sexual Politics of Victorian Social Anthropology," *Feminist Studies* 4 (1978), 23–29.

30. See, for example, Judith K. Brown, "Iroquois women: An Ethnohistoric Note," in *Toward an Anthropology of Women*, ed. Reiter, pp. 235–51; and Sacks on four African societies at different stages of development, in "Engels Revisited," in ibid.; Peggy R. Sanday, "Female Status in the Public Domain," in *Woman, Culture and Society*, ed. Michelle Z. Rosaldo and Louise Lamphere (Stanford, Calif.: Stanford University Press, 1974), pp. 189–206; this last collection generally argues for a universal female subordination, and has been countered more recently by *Nature, Culture and Gender*, ed. Carol McCormack and Marilyn Strathern (Cambridge: Cambridge University Press, 1981); and by *Women and the State in Pre-Industrial Societies*, ed. Christine Gailey and Mona Etienne, forthcoming, which includes arguments relating the decline of female status to economic stratification and political centralization by Gerald Sider on Mesopotamia, Christine Gailey on the Tongan Islands, and Connie Sutton on the Yoruba; see also Irene Silverblatt, "Andean Women in the Inca Empire," *Feminist Studies* 4 (1978); Viana Muller, "The Formation of the State and the Oppression of Women: Some Theoretical Considerations and a Case Study in England and Wales," *Review of Radical Political Economy* 9, no. 3 (1977), 7–21; Ruby Rorlich-Leavitt, "State Formation in Sumer and the Subjugation of Women," *Feminist Studies* 6 (1980), 76–102; and *Woman and Colonization: Anthropological Perspectives*, ed. Mona Etienne and Eleanor Leacock (New York: Praeger, 1980); Leacock, *Myths of Male Dominance*; Martin King Whyte, *The Status of Women in Pre-Industrial Societies* (Princeton, N.J.: Princeton University Press, 1978).

31. Jacquetta Hawkes and Leonard Wooley, *Pre-History and the Beginnings of Civilization* (New York: Harper & Row, 1963), pt. 1, p. 264.

32. Gough, "The Origin of the Family," pp. 54, 69.

33. Ibid., p. 73; see also David F. Aberle, "Matrilineal Descent in Cross-Cultural Perspective," in *Matrilineal Kinship*, ed. Kathleen Gough and David M. Schneider (Berkeley and Los Angeles: University of California Press, 1961).

34. Gordon Childe, *Man Makes Himself*, p. 71; Fritz M. Heichelheim, *An Ancient Economic History* (Leiden: A. W. Stijthoff's, Uitgeversmaatschaapij N.V., 1958), p. 31.

35. Sally Slocum, "Woman the Gatherer: Male Bias in Anthropology," in *Toward an*

Anthropology of Women, ed. Reiter, pp. 36–50; see also Frances Dahlberg, ed., *Woman the Gatherer* (New Haven, Conn.: Yale University Press, 1981).

36. E. G. Payne, *History of the New World*, in Harrison, *Prolegomena*, p. 272.

37. Aeschylus, *The Oresteian Trilogy*, trans. Phillip Vellacott (Baltimore: Penguin, 1956), pp. 172, 169.

38. Ibid., pp. 173, 174, 176.

39. Thomson, *Studies in Ancient Greek Society*, vol. 1, p. 142.

40. Eleanor Leacock, "Women in Egalitarian Societies," in *Becoming Visible: Women in European History*, ed. Renate Bridenthal and Claudia Koonz (Boston: Houghton Mifflin, 1977), p. 14.

41. Ruby Rorlich-Leavitt, "Women in Transition: Crete and Sumer," in ibid., p. 50.

42. Leacock, "Women in Egalitarian Societies," p. 31.

43. Demosthenes, *Contra Neara* (1386), in Robert Briffault, *The Mothers* (New York: Macmillan, 1927), vol. 11, p. 337.

44. Gough, "The Origin of the Family," p. 73.

45. Briffault, *The Mothers*, vol. 2, p. 254.

46. Christopher Dawson, *The Age of the Gods* (New York: Sheed and Ward, 1933), pp. 242–43.

47. Engels, *The Origin of the Family*, pp. 121, 128.

48. Elise Boulding, *The Underside of History: A View of Woman Through Time* (Boulder, Colo.: Westview Press, 1976), pp. 153–54.

49. Rorlich-Leavitt, "Women in Transition," p. 50.

50. Dawson, *The Age of the Gods*, p. 243.

51. Graves, *The Greek Myths*, vol. 1, pp. 17–19; see also Stone, *When God Was a Woman*, pp. 62–102.

52. Norman O. Brown, introduction to Hesiod, *Theogony* (Indianapolis: Bobbs-Merrill, 1953), p. 17.

53. Harrison *Prolegomena*, p. 73.

54. Campbell, *Occidental Mythology*, p. 22.

55. David Bakan, *And They Took Themselves Wives: The Emergence of Patriarchy in Western Civilization* (New York: Harper & Row, 1979).

56. Louis Wallis, *A Sociological Study of the Bible* (Chicago: University of Chicago Press, 1912).

57. Ibid., pp. 213–14.

58. Keith Thomas, *Religion and the Decline of Magic* (New York: Scribner's, 1971), p. 27.

59. Jackie DiSalvo, "In narrow circuit strait'n'd by a Foe: Puritans and Indians in *Paradise Lost*," in *Ringing the Bell Backwards: The Proceedings of the First International Milton Symposium* (Kittanning, Pa.,: Indiana University of Pennsylvania Press, 1982), pp. 19–33.

Chapter 6. Blake's Genesis: Eden

1. George Thomson, *Studies in Ancient Greek Society* (New York: Citadel, 1972), vol. 1, p. 57.

2. Ovid, *The Metamorphoses*, trans. Mary M. Innes (Baltimore: Penguin, 1955), pp. 31–32.

3. Virgil, *Georgics* I.125–8.

4. Pompeius Gnaeus Trogus, *Juniani Justini Epitoma Historiarum Phillipicarum Pompei Trogi*, quoted in Norman Cohn, *The Pursuit of the Millennium*, 2nd ed. (New York: Harper & Row, 1961), p. 196.

5. Diodorus Siculus, *Bibliothecae Historicae libri qui supersunt* (1746), quoted in ibid., pp. 197–98.

6. Seneca, *Epistoles Morales*, quoted in Arthur O. Lovejoy and George Boas, *Primitivism and Related Ideas in Antiquity* (Baltimore: Johns Hopkins, 1935), p. 273.

7. Jacquetta Hawkes and Leonard Wooley, *Pre-History and the Beginnings of Civilization* (New York: Harper & Row, 1963), pt. 1, p. 231.

8. Louis Wallis, *Sociological Study of the Bible* (Chicago: University of Chicago Press, 1912), esp. pp. 154–58, 181.

9. Augustine, *The City of God Against the Pagans*, trans. Marcus Dods (New York: Modern Library, 1950), book 19, p. 693.

10. Ambrose, *De officiis ministrorum*, quoted in Cohn, *The Pursuit of the Millennium*, p. 203.

11. Ambrose, *In Psalmum CXVIII exposito*, quoted in ibid., p. 203.

12. Clement, *Recognitiones (S. Clement Romani)*, quoted in ibid., p. 204.

13. Christopher Hill, *The World Turned Upside Down* (New York: Viking, 1972), p. 124; Hill also discusses these traditions in "The Norman Yoke," *Puritanism and Revolution* (New York: Schocken, 1958), pp. 50–57.

14. William Perkins, *The Workes of the Famous and Worthey Minister of Christ William Perkins* (London, 1616–18) vol. 3, p. 398.

15. Jean Froissart, *Chronicles*, ed. and trans. by John Jolliffe (New York: Modern Library, 1968), p. 237.

16. Sebastian Franck, *Chronica, Zeybuch, und Geschychtbibel* (1531), quoted in Cohn, *The Pursuit of the Millennium*, p. 280.

17. Jan van Ruusbroec, *Werken* (1350–1372), quoted in ibid., p. 182.

18. Cohn, *The Pursuit of the Millennium*, p. 234; the "delight of Paradise" is mentioned in *Errores sectae hominum intelligentiae*, in E. Baluze, *Miscellanea* (1683), quoted in ibid., p. 189.

19. The story appears in Alexander Gilchrist, *Life of William Blake*, ed. Ruthven Todd (New York: E. P. Dutton, 1942), pp. 96–97.

20. See Richard Schlatter, *Private Property: The History of an Idea* (New York: Russell & Russell, 1973), esp. pp. 124–61.

21. John Locke, *Second Treatise, Two Treatises on Civil Government*, ed. Peter Laslett (New York: New American Library, 1965), p. 327.

22. Ibid., p. 332.

23. Ibid., p. 362.

24. Ibid., p. 364.

25. David Erdman, *Blake: Prophet Against Empire*, rev. ed. (Garden City, N.Y.: Anchor, 1969), p. 352.

26. Ibid., p. 259.

27. Jean-Jacques Rousseau, *Discourse on the Origins and Foundations of Inequality, The First and Second Discourses*, trans. Roger Masters and Judith Masters (New York: St. Martin's, 1964), p. 144.

28. Ibid., p. 112.

29. Ibid., p. 137.

30. Gerrard Winstanley, *The Works of Gerrard Winstanley*, ed. G. H. Sabine (Ithaca, N.Y.: Cornell University Press, 1941), pp. 251–52.

31. Ibid., pp. 203, 210–18, 446, 457.

32. Schlatter, *Private Property*, p. 79.

33. A. L. Morton, *The Everlasting Gospel* (London: Lawrence & Wishart, 1958).

34. Marjorie Reeves, *The Influence of Prophecy in the Later Middle Ages* (Oxford: Clarendon Press, 1969), pp. 243–48.

35. Hill, *The World Turned Upside Down*, p. 307.

36. *The Four Zoas* has also been read as the myth of a fall from an egalitarian tribal golden age by Fred Whitehead in "Studies in the Structure of European History in Blake's Epics," (Ph.D. diss., Columbia University, 1972), and "Visions of the Archaic World," in *Sparks of Fire: Blake in a New Age*, ed. James Bogan and Fred Goss (Richmond, Calif.: North Atlantic Books, 1982).

37. Leslie White, *The Evolution of Culture* (New York: McGraw-Hill, 1959), p. 141; E. B. Tylor, in ibid. Marx's description of tribal society as "primitive communism" has, with some qualifications, been sustained by later scholars such as White, Jacquetta Hawkes, Fritz Heichelheim, and by recent anthropology. According to Eleanor Leacock ("Introduction to Lewis Henry Morgan, *Ancient Society*" and "Women's Status in Egalitarian Society," *Myths of Male Dominance* [New York: Monthly Review, 1981], p. 101), the trend led by Robert Lowie's *Primitive Society* (New York: Liveright, 1947) to demonstrate the universality of private property and social classes was not upheld by later studies. With regard to egalitarian band society, Leacock writes, "It is common knowledge that there was no differential access to resources through private land ownership and no specialization of labor beyond that by sex, hence no market system to intervene in the direct relationship between production and distribution" (p. 139).

38. Roy Harvey Pearce, *The Savages of America*, rev. ed. (Baltimore: Johns Hopkins, 1965), p. 68; see also H. C. Porter, *The Inconstant Savage: England and the North American Indian 1500–1660* (London: Duckworth, 1979).

39. Jacob Baegert, "An Account of Aboriginal Inhabitants of the California Peninsula," in *A Reader in General Anthropology*, ed. Carleton S. Coon (London: Jonathan Cape, 1950), pp. 77–78.

40. A. de Lahontan, *Travels in North America* (1735), quoted in Robert Briffault, *The Mothers* (New York: Macmillan, 1927), vol. 2, pp. 496–97, along with others making the same point.

41. Samuel de Champlain, *Oeuvres*, quoted in ibid., vol. 2, p. 33.

42. See John Ferguson, *Utopias of the Classical World* (Ithaca, N.Y.: Cornell University Press, 1975), pp. 19–21.

43. G. E. Bentley, *Blake Records* (Oxford: Clarendon Press, 1969), p. 548.

44. Pearce, *The Savages of America*, pp. 84, 93, 156.

45. Eleanor Leacock, introduction to Friedrich Engels, *The Origin of the Family, Private Property and the State* (New York: International Publishers, 1972), p. 43.

46. Briffault, *The Mothers*, vol. 2, pp. 253–54; Leacock has written extensively on the relationship between female status and productivity; see *Myths of Male Dominance*.

47. Paul Lejeune, *The Jesuit Relations and Allied Documents* (1636), quoted in Eleanor Leacock, "Women in Egalitarian Society: The Montagnais-Naskapi of Canada," *Myths of Male Dominance*, p. 50.

48. Bentley, *Blake Records*, p. 450.

49. Erdman, *Blake: Prophet Against Empire*, pp. 226–42.

50. Ibid., p. 239.

51. A similar point can be drawn from *Woman and Colonization: Anthropological Perspectives*, ed. Mona Etienne and Eleanor Leacock (New York: Praeger, 1980), which documents recent interventions at the expense of tribal mores.

52. Rousseau, *Discourse on Inequality*, p. 152.

53. Hawkes and Wooley, *Pre-History and the Beginnings of Civilization* pt. 2, p. 378; see also Ruby Rorlich-Leavitt, "Women in Transition: Crete and Sumer," In *Becoming Visible: Women in European History*, ed. Renate Bridenthal and Claudia Koonz (Boston: Houghton Mifflin, 1977); Joseph Campbell, *Occidental Mythology* (New York: Viking, 1964), p. 62.

54. Robert Graves, *The Greek Myths* (Baltimore: Penguin, 1955), vol. 1, pp. 146-48.

55. S. Foster Damon, "Albion," *A Blake Dictionary* (New York: E. P. Dutton, 1971), p. 9.

56. Schlatter, *Private Property,* pp. 151–273.

57. Northrop Frye, *Fearful Symmetry* (Princeton, N.J.: Princeton University Press, 1947), pp. 292–94.

58. Ibid., pp. 127, 135, 136.

59. Thomson, *Studies in Ancient Greek Society,* vol. 2, p. 50.

60. Ibid., pp. 36–52; see also George Thomson, *Aeschylus and Athens* (London: Lawrence & Wishart, 1966), pp. 9–20, 42–48.

61. Jane Ellen Harrison, *Epilogomena to the Study of Ancient Greek Religion* (Cambridge: Cambridge University Press, 1921), pp. xxx–1.

62. Thomson, *Studies in Ancient Greek Society,* vol. 2, p. 45; David Aberle, "Matrilineal Descent in Cross-Cultural Perspectives," in *Matrilineal Kinship,* ed. David M. Schneider and Kathleen Gough (Berkeley and Los Angeles: University of California Press, 1962), p. 702; Elise Boulding, *The Underside of History: A View of Woman Through Time* (Boulder, Colo.: Westview Press, 1976), pp. 148–49.

63. Joseph Campbell, *Primitive Mythology* (New York: Viking, 1959), p. 322; see also Joan Bamberger, "The Myth of Matriarchy: Why Men Rule in Primitive Society," in *Woman, Culture and Society,* ed. Michelle Z. Rosaldo and Louise Lamphere (Stanford, Calif.: Stanford University Press, 1974), pp. 263–80.

64. Campbell, *Occidental Mythology,* p. 62; see also Leacock's arguments for egalitarianism in *Myths of Male Dominance.*

65. Paul Friedrich, *The Meaning of Aphrodite* (Chicago: University of Chicago Press, 1980) explores the imposition of patriarchal themes such as chastity and woman as temptress on the goddess of sex and maternity.

66. For a recent debate on the identification of woman with nature and how limiting her reproductive role was, see Sherry Ortner, "Is Female to Male as Nature Is to Culture?" in *Woman, Culture and Society,* ed. Rosaldo and Lamphere (pp. 67–87), and other essays in that volume; rebuttals are found in *Nature, Culture and Gender,* ed. Carol McCormack and Marilyn Strathern (Cambridge: Cambridge University Press, 1980).

67. Leacock, "Women in Egalitarian Societies," in *Becoming Visible,* ed. Bridenthal and Koonz, p. 30.

68. Jane Ellen Harrison, *Themis* (Cambridge: Cambridge University Press, 1903), p. 460; for a similar admonition to contemporary devotees of goddess and fertility myth, see Rosemary Ruether, *New Woman—New Earth* (New York: Seabury, 1975).

69. Li Feng-Lan, "How I Began to Paint the Countryside," *China Reconstructs* 23, no. 1 (Jan. 1974), 21; see also Fred Whitehead's materialist reading of the conquest of the dragon motif in "William Blake and the Radical Tradition," in *Weapons of Criticism,* ed. Norman Rudich (Palo Alto, Calif.: Ramparts Press, 1976), pp. 206–07.

70. Karl Marx, *Capital* (New York: International Publishers, 1967), vol. 1, p. 334.

Chapter 7. Blake's Genesis: The Fall

1. William Empson, *Milton's God* (London: Chatto & Windus, 1965), p. 13.

2. Fred Whitehead, "William Blake and the Radical Tradition," in *Weapons of Criticism: Marxism in America and the Literary Tradition,* ed. Norman Rudich (Palo Alto, Calif.: Ramparts, 1976), pp. 193–94. In "Visions of the Archaic World," in *Sparks of Fire: Blake in a New Age,* ed. James Bogan and Fred Goss (Richmond, Calif.: North Atlantic Books, 1982), p. 240, Whitehead writes: "The main narrative of the poem follows the course of ancient civilization through . . . what Childe called the Urban Revolution,

characterized by . . . hierarchies of kings and priests, the classes of workers and slaves, the accumulation of economic surpluses on a large scale, the formation of cities as such, and, eventually the imperial phases with their inevitable emphases on war and conquest. We may see this process sweeping westward from Mesopotamia to Greece, and thence to Rome. . . . Night the Ninth has many parallels with the Book of Revelation, the definitive mythic vision of the collapse of the Roman Empire."

3. J. M. Evans, *"Paradise Lost" and the Genesis Tradition* (New York: Oxford University Press, 1968), p. 9.

4. Ibid.

5. Cuthbert A. Simpson, introduction to *The Interpreter's Bible*, ed. George Buttrick (Nashville, Tenn.: Abingdon Press, 1952), vol. 1, pp. 445–46.

6. N. P. Williams, *The Idea of the Fall and of Original Sin* (n.p., 1927), chs. 1–2.

7. *The Book of the Secrets of Enoch*, in *Apocrypha and Pseudographia of the Old Testament*, trans. R. H. Charles (London: Oxford University Press, 1913), vol. 2, pp. 447, 451.

8. Evans, *"Paradise Lost" and the Genesis Tradition*, pp. 81–88.

9. Norman O. Brown, introduction to Hesiod, *Theogony* (Indianapolis: Bobbs-Merrill, 1953), p. 22.

10. Gilbert Murray, *Five Stages of Greek Religion* (New York: Doubleday, 1951), pp. 46–47, 57.

11. George Thomson, *Studies in Ancient Greek Society* (New York: Citadel, 1965), vol. 1, pp. 327–31.

12. Homer, *Iliad* 12:310–21, trans. and quoted by Thomson, ibid., p. 331.

13. *Theogony*, 512; Brown, in his introduction (pp. 32–35), analyzes the Prometheus myth; Fred Whitehead points out its social significance in Blake in "Studies in the Structure of European History in Blake's Epics" (Ph.D. diss., Columbia University, 1972).

14. On Jewish history in the biblical era, see R. H. Harrison, *Introduction to the Old Testament* (Grand Rapids, Mich.: Eerdman's, 1969); J. N. Schofield, *Historical Background of the Bible* (New York: Thomas Nelson, 1938); H. Keith Beebe, *The Old Testament: An Introduction to its Literary, Historical and Religious Traditions* (Encino, Calif.: Dickinson, 1970); Louis Wallis, *Sociological Study of the Bible* (Chicago: University of Chicago Press, 1912); Harry M. Buck, *People of the Lord: The History, Scriptures and Faith of Ancient Israel* (New York: Macmillan, 1966); Buttrick, ed., *The Interpreter's Bible*, vol. 1; and Jacob Bryant, *A New System or An Analysis of Ancient Mythology* (New York: Garland, 1979).

15. See Whitehead on the horses of light incident and the rise of private property in "Visions of the Archaic World," p. 237.

16. Jacquetta Hawkes and Leonard Wooley, *Pre-History and the Beginnings of Civilization* (New York: Harper and Row, 1963), pt. 2, p. 484.

17. George Thomson, *Aeschylus and Athens* (London: Lawrence & Wishart, 1966), pp. 91–118.

18. Vera Gordon Childe, *Man Makes Himself* (New York: New American Library, 1951), p. 86.

19. Eleanor Leacock, "Women in Egalitarian Societies," in *Becoming Visible: Women in European History*, ed. Renate Bridenthal and Claudia Koonz (Boston: Houghton Mifflin, 1977), p. 15; for other studies of the evolution of private property, classes, the state and ancient theocracy, see Leslie White, *The Evolution of Culture* (New York: McGraw-Hill, 1959), pp. 303–28; Thomson, *Studies in Ancient Greek Society*, vol. 2, pp. 71–95; Henri Frankfort, *The Birth of Civilization in the Near East* (Bloomington: Indiana University Press, 1951); Morton Fried, *The Evolution of Politi-*

cal Society: An Evolutionary View (New York: Random House, 1967); Robert M. Adams, *The Evolution of Urban Society* (Chicago: Aldine, 1971); Ruby Rorlich-Leavitt, "State Formation in Sumer and the Subjugation of Women," *Feminist Studies* 6 (1980), 76–102; and *Women and the State in Pre-Industrial Societies,* ed. Christine Gailey and Mona Etienne, forthcoming.

20. Thomson, *Studies in Ancient Greek Society,* vol. 1, p. 49; Jane Ellen Harrison, *Epilogomena to the Study of Ancient Greek Religion* (Cambridge: Cambridge University Press, 1921), p. xxxiv.

21. Paul Radin, *Primitive Religion* (New York: Dover, 1957), pp. 256–57.

22. Thorkild Jacobsen, in Henri Frankfort et al., *The Intellectual Adventure of Ancient Man* (Chicago: University of Chicago Press, 1946); and Henri Frankfort, *Kingship and the Gods: A Study Ancient Near Eastern Religion* (Chicago: University of Chicago Press, 1948); and Bryant, *Ancient Mythology.*

23. S. H. Hooke, ed., *Myth and Ritual: Essays on the Myth and Ritual of the Hebrews in Relation to the Culture Pattern of the Ancient East* (London: Oxford. University Press, 1933).

24. J. B. Pritchard, ed., *Ancient Near Eastern Texts Relating to the Old Testament* (Princeton, N.J.: Princeton University Press, 1955), p. 65b.

25. Jacobsen, in Frankfort et al., *The Intellectual Adventure,* p. 173.

26. Quoted in Alexander Heidel, *The Babylonian Genesis* (Chicago: University of Chicago Press, 1942), p. 48.

27. Robert F. Harper, ed., *The Code of Hammurabi, King of Babylon* (Chicago: University of Chicago Press, 1904), p. 3.

28. Wallis, *Sociological Study of the Bible,* pp. 88–98.

29. Florence Sandler, "The Iconoclastic Enterprise: Blake's Critique of Milton's Religion," *Blake Studies* 5 (1972), esp. 24–28, 36–43. Sandler points out Blake's identification of the ideological sources of Milton's religion in the Hebrew incorporation of Canaanite politics and ritual.

30. John Weir Perry, *Lord of the Four Quarters: Myths of the Royal Father* (New York: Braziller, 1966), pp. 98–99.

31. The royal psalms are analyzed by Aage Bentzen, *King and Messiah* (Oxford: Blackwell's, 1970); and by Aubrey Johnson, *Sacral Kingship in Ancient Israel* (Cardiff: University of Wales Press, 1967).

32. Heidel, *The Babylonian Genesis,* p. 48.

33. Perry, *Lord of the Four Quarters,* p. 22.

34. Buttrick, ed., *The Interpreter's Bible,* vol. 1, pp. 441ff.

35. F. J. Hollis, "The Sun Cult and the Temple at Jerusalem," in S. H. Hooke, ed., *Myth and Ritual,* pp. 104–05.

36. Ibid., pp. 87–110; see also Buck, *People of the Lord,* pp. 77–97.

37. Buck, *People of the Lord,* p. 80.

38. Heidel, *The Babylonian Genesis,* p. 47.

39. Thompson, *Studies in Ancient Greek Society,* vol. 1, p. 24.

40. Wallis, *Sociological Study of the Bible,* pp. 190–93.

41. Whitehead views the division of Albion similarly as a psychic split, a class division, and a division of labor in "William Blake and the Radical Tradition," p. 201.

42. Gordon Childe discusses the development of the wheel in *Man Makes Himself* (p. 100) and the solar calendar (p. 111).

43. J. H. Adamson recounts the history of the winged chariot symbol in theology and myth in "The War in Heaven: The Merkabah," *Bright Essence: Studies in Milton's Theology,* with C. A. Patrides and W. B. Hunter (Salt Lake City: University of Utah Press, 1971), pp. 103–14.

44. Northrop Frye, *Fearful Symmetry* (Princeton, N.J.: Princeton University Press, 1947), pp. 272–73.

45. Gordon Childe, *Man Makes Himself,* p. 187.

46. Frye, *Fearful Symmetry,* pp. 288–89.

47. Thomson, *Studies in Ancient Greek Society,* vol. 2, p. 238; for an analysis of the mystery cults, see also Thomson, *Aeschylus and Athens,* chs. 7–9.

48. Thomson, *Studies in Ancient Greek Society,* vol. 2, p. 239.

49. Ibid. pp. 240–45; Christopher Caudwell, "The Breath of Discontent," in *Studies and Further Studies in a Dying Culture* (New York: Monthly Review, 1971), pp. 17–20, 44–49.

50. G. W. F. Hegel, "Self-Consciousness," *The Phenomenology of Mind* (New York: Harper & Row, 1967), p. 251; Thomas J. Altizer discusses the "unhappy consciousness" in relation to Blake in *The New Apocalypse: The Radical Christian Vision of William Blake* (E. Lansing: Michigan State University Press, 1967), pp. 43–47, 61, 71, 85.

51. T. H. Robinson and W. O. Oesterly, *A History of Israel* (Oxford: Oxford University Press, 1932), vol. 1, p. 325.

52. Frank Moore Cross, *Canaanite Myth and Hebrew Epic* (Cambridge, Mass.: Harvard University Press, 1973), ch. 1.

53. Thomson, *Studies in Ancient Greek Society,* vol. 2, p. 100.

54. For the political significance of Jesus, see Archibald Robertson, *The Origins of Christianity* (New York: International Publishers, 1965); S. G. F. Brandon, *Religion in Ancient History* (New York: Scribners, 1969), pp. 223–67; and Caudwell, "Breath of Discontent," pp. 54, 63.

55. Ernest Renan, quoted in Friedrich Engels, "On the History of Early Christianity," in *Marx and Engels on Religon* (New York: Schocken, 1964), p. 318.

56. G. E. Bentley, *Blake Records* (Oxford: Clarendon Press, 1969), p. 540.

57. Frye, *Fearful Symmetry,* p. 213.

58. Ibid., p. 220.

59. Jean Hagstrum, *William Blake, Poet and Painter: An Introduction to the Illuminated Verse* (Chicago: University of Chicago Press, 1964), p. 126; Joseph Anthony Wittreich, Jr., *Angel of Apocalypse: Blake's Idea of Milton* (Madison: University of Wisconsin Press, 1975), p. 287, n. 43.

60. M. H. Abrams, *Natural Supernaturalism: Tradition and Revolution in Romantic Literature* (New York: Norton, 1971), p. 47.

Chapter 8. The Politics of Paradise Lost *and* The Four Zoas

1. Malcolm Mackenzie Ross, *Milton's Royalism* (Ithaca, N.Y.: Cornell University Press, 1943), pp. 75–76.

2. See the summary in chapter 2 of the debate in the *London Chronicle,* 12–13 Nov. 1763.

3. A. S. P. Woodhouse, *The Heavenly Muse: A Preface to Milton* (Toronto: University of Toronto Press, 1972), p. 290.

4. Joseph Wittreich analyses this aspect of Blake's view of Milton in *Angel of Apocalypse* (Madison: University of Wisconsin Press, 1975).

5. E. M. W. Tillyard, *The Elizabethan World Picture* (New York: Vintage, 1943).

6. Christopher Hill studies this myth in *Puritanism and Revolution* (New York: Schocken, 1958), pp. 50–122, and notes its relevance to *Samson Agonistes* in "Milton the Radical," *TLS,* 29 Nov. 1971, p. 1332.

7. Florence Sandler discusses Milton's view of monarchy as idolatry in "Icon and

Iconoclast," in *Achievements of the Left Hand*, ed. Michael Lieb and John Shawcross (Amherst: University of Massachusetts Press, 1974), pp. 160–84.

8. Arthur Barker had explicated the relationship between Milton's concept of reason and his politics in *Milton and the Puritan Dilemma 1641–1660* (Toronto: University of Toronto Press, 1942), pp. 48–122.

9. For analyses of Milton's politics I have relied primarily upon the excellent introductions to Don M. Wolfe et al., eds., *Collected Prose Works of John Milton* (New Haven, Conn.: Yale University Press, 1953–82); and Don M. Wolfe, *Milton in the Puritan Revolution* (New York: Humanities Press, 1963).

10. Balechandra Rajan, *"Paradise Lost" and the Seventeenth-Century Reader* (London: Chatto & Windus, 1962), p. 63.

11. Quoted in Don M. Wolfe, introduction to volume 1 of *Collected Prose Works*, vol. 1, p. 44.

12. Barker, *Milton and the Puritan Dilemma*, p. xix.

13. For Milton's view of the Hebrew monarchy, see Sandler, "Icon and Iconoclast," pp. 163–64; Merritt Y. Hughes, introduction to volume 3 of *Collected Prose Works*, ed. Wolfe et al., vol. 3, pp. 67–80.

14. Quoted in Don M. Wolfe, introduction in volume 1 of *Collected Prose Works*, ed. Wolfe et al., vol. 1, p. 185.

15. Michael Walzer, *Revolution of the Saints* (New York: Atheneum, 1968), pp. 151–52.

16. Robert West discusses Milton's tampering with the angelic hierarchy in *Milton and the Angels* (Athens: University of Georgia Press, 1955), pp. 133–36.

17. Sandler discusses the political significance of Christ's kingship for Milton in "Icon and Iconoclast," pp. 165–68.

18. *A Short History of the Anabaptists of High and Low Germany* (1642), quoted in Barker, *Milton and the Puritan Dilemma*, p. 140.

19. The phrase is Merrit Hughes's, introduction to volume 3 of *Collected Prose Works*, ed. Wolfe et al., vol. 3, p. 27.

20. Christopher Hill discusses the political significance of concepts of sin and the Fall in *The World Turned Upside Down* (New York: Viking, 1972), pp. 121–47.

21. Walzer, *Revolution of the Saints*, pp. 31–45.

22. John Calvin, *Sermons Upon the Book of Job* (London, 1574), sermon 136, p. 718; *Sermons Upon the Fifth Book of Moses* (London, 1583), sermon 142, p. 872.

23. Walzer, *Revolution of the Saints*, pp. 45–57.

24. The class analysis of the ideology of the Puritan revolution which I am assuming here has been developed in several other works by Christopher Hill in addition to those already cited: *Century of Revolution 1603–1714* (New York: Norton, 1961); *Society and Puritanism* (New York: Schocken, 1967). See also Don M. Wolfe, *Milton in the Puritan Revolution*; and introductions to volumes 1 and 4 of *Collected Prose Works*, ed. Wolfe et al.; R. H. Tawney, *Religion and the Rise of Capitalism* (New York: New American Library, 1954).

25. For the Levellers, see H. N. Brailsford, *The Levellers and the English Revolution* (London: Cresset, 1961); W. Haller and G. Davies, *The Leveller Tracts* (New York: Columbia University Press, 1934); Don M. Wolfe, *Leveller Manifestoes of the Puritan Revolution* (New York: Nelson, 1944); A. S. P. Woodhouse, *Puritanism and Liberty* (London: J. M. Dent, 1938).

26. Quoted in Woodhouse, *Puritanism and Liberty*, pp. 54, 63.

27. Ibid., p. 71.

28. For the Diggers and True Levellers, see Hill, *The World Turned Upside Down*, pp. 86–120.

29. In *The Works of Gerrard Winstanley*, ed. G. H. Sabine (Ithaca, N.Y.: Cornell University Press, 1941), pp. 409, 569.

30. Ibid., p. 276.

31. George Fox, *Journal*, ed. Norman Penney (New York: Octagon, 1973), p. 28.

32. William Erbery, *The Testimony of William Erbery* (London, 1658), p. 40.

33. Quoted in Hill, *The World Turned Upside Down*, p. 167.

34. Richard Coppin, *Divine Teachings*, 2nd ed. (London, 1653), p. 8; a Ranter remark reported by Edward Hide, *A Wonder, Yet No Wonder* (London, 1651), pp. 35–41.

35. Richard Coppin, *A Blow at the Serpent* (London, 1656), p. 52; John Thurloe, *State Papers*, ed. Thomas Birch (London, 1742), vol. 4, p. 486.

36. Max Weber, *The Protestant Ethic and the Spirit of Capitalism* (New York: Scribner's, 1958); Tawney, *Religion and the Rise of Capitalism*, pp. 164–209; Hill, *Society and Puritanism*, pp. 124–44, and *The World Turned Upside Down*, pp. 261–77.

37. Richard Rogers, *Seven Treatises* (London, 1603), p. 577.

38. William Perkins, *Workes* (London, 1616), vol. 1, pp. 755–56.

39. In *Letters and Speeches of Oliver Cromwell*, ed. W. C. Abbott (Cambridge, Mass.: Harvard University Press, 1937), vol. 1, p. 245.

40. For the changing sense of time, see Hill, *Puritanism and Revolution*, p. 130; and on a later period, E. P. Thompson, "Time, Work Discipline and Industrial Capitalism," *Past and Present* 38 (1967), 56–97.

41. Slingsley Bethel, *The World's Mistake in Oliver Cromwell*, in *Harleian Miscellany, A Collection of . . . Pamphlets Found in the Late Earl of Oxford's Library*, ed. R. Dutton (London, 1809–1815), vol. 7, pp. 358–59.

42. Hill, *Society and Puritanism*, p. 132.

43. Walzer, *Revolution of the Saints*, p. 164.

44. I treat the politics of *Samson Agonistes* at greater length in "The Lord's Battells: *Samson Agonistes* and the Puritan Revolution," *Milton Studies* 4 (1972), 39–62.

45. Tobias Crisp, *Christ Alone Exalted in Seventeen Sermons* (London, 1643), pp. 87, 156–59; cf. pp. 276–77.

46. According to Hide, *A Wonder, Yet No Wonder*, pp. 36–38.

47. Hill, *The World Turned Upside Down*, p. 166.

48. Abiezer Coppe, *Copps Return to the wayes of Truth* (London, 1651), pp. 19–21.

49. James Nayler, *The Old Serpent's Voice* (London, 1656), p. 6.

50. Roger Crab, *Dagon's Downfall* (London, 1657), pp. 5–6.

51. Sabine, ed., *The Works of Gerrard Winstanley*, p. 496.

52. Abiezer Coppe, *A Fiery Flying Roll, Part II*, p. 21.

53. Quoted in A. L. Morton, *The Everlasting Gospel* (London: Lawrence & Wishart, 1958), p. 45. Hill notes Satan's affinity to the Ranters in "Milton the Radical," *TLS*, 29 Nov. 1974, p. 1332.

54. Milton's hierarchic principle is discussed by Barker, *Milton and the Puritan Dilemma*, esp. pp. 174–92, 260–90.

55. For Milton's aristocratic moralism, see Malcolm MacKenzie Ross, *Milton's Royalism*, pp. 57–67, 78–82.

56. For Milton's changing attitude toward Cromwell, see Austin Woolrych, "Milton and Cromwell: 'A Short But Scandalous Night of Interruption'?" in *Achievements of the Left Hand*, ed. Lieb and Shawcross, pp. 185–218.

57. Abbott, ed., *The Writings of Cromwell*, vol. 4, p. 471.

58. John Goodwin, *Right and Might well met* (London, 1648).

59. Joseph Wittreich, *Angel of Apocalypse: Blake's Idea of Milton* (Madison: University of Wisconsin Press, 1975) pp. 57–67.

60. A theological interpretation of the exaltation is offered by W. B. Hunter, "The

War in Heaven: the Exaltation of the Son," in W. B. Hunter, C. A. Patrides, J. H. Adamson, eds., *Bright Essence* (Salt Lake City: University of Utah Press, 1971), pp. 115–30.

61. Thomas Hobbes, *De Corpore Politico or The Elements of Law Natural and Politic*, ed. F. Tonnies (London, 1889), p. 88.

62. David Erdman reads the "Bard's Song" as "an indictment of the revolution for which Milton bears bardic responsibility" in *Blake: Prophet Against Empire* (Garden City, N.Y.: Anchor, 1969), p. 426.

63. Hill, *The World Turned Upside Down*, p. 12.

64. Erdman identifies Palamabron with Parliament, as I do, in *Blake: Prophet Against Empire*, p. 424; his identification of Satan with Cromwell does not necessarily conflict with the interpretation I give here.

65. Sabine, ed., *The Works of Gerrard Winstanley*, p. 316.

66. A. L. Morton, *A People's History of England* (New York: International Publishers, 1938), p. 228.

67. Thomas Hobbes, *Behemoth*, ed. F. Tonnies (London, 1889), p. 126.

68. Edmund Waller, *Mr. Waller's Speech in Parliament . . . 6 July 1641*, quoted in Don M. Wolfe, introduction to volume 1 of *Collected Prose Works*, ed. Wolfe et al., vol. 1, p. 131.

69. Thomas Case, *Spirituall Whordome discovered in a sermon before the House of Commons* (26 May 1647), p. 34.

70. Hill discusses this meaning in *Century of Revolution*, pp. 43–46; and in *Change and Continuity in Seventeenth-Century England* (Cambridge, Mass.: Harvard University Press, 1975), pp. 226–31.

71. Erdman, *Blake: Prophet Against Empire*, pp. 294–358, esp. pp. 316–17.

72. Eric Hobsbawm, *The Age of Revolution: 1789–1848* (New York: New American Library, 1962), p. 284.

73. E. P. Thompson, *The Making of the English Working Class* (New York: Vintage, 1963), pp. 17–188.

74. Ibid., p. 178.

75. Ibid., pp. 177, 181.

76. Aileen Ward draws this parallel in "The Forging of Orc: Blake and the Idea of Revolution," in *Literature and Revolution*, ed. George Abbott White and Charles Neiman (New York: Holt, Rinehart and Winston, 1972), pp. 204–27.

77. Erdman, *Blake: Prophet Against Empire*, p. 317.

78. William Empson, *Milton's God* (London: Chatto & Windus, 1965), pp. 117–18.

79. Karl Marx, *The Grundrisse*, trans. David McLellan (New York: Harper & Row, 1971), p. 17.

80. Hill identifies Satan with the bourgeois revolutionaries in *The World Turned Upside Down*, p. 327.

81. Walzer, *Revolution of the Saints*, p. 154.

82. Thomas Hobbes, *Leviathan*, ed. W. G. Pogson Smith (Oxford: Oxford University Press, 1929), p. 75.

83. C. B. MacPherson, *The Political Theory of Possessive Individualism* (New York: Oxford University Press, 1962), pp. 17–46; Hill, *Society and Puritanism*, p. 242.

84. John Locke, *Second Treatise on Civil Government*, ed. Peter Laslett (New York: New American Library, 1965), p. 395.

85. For Locke's views on the class differential in rationality, see *Some Considerations of the Consequences of the Lowering of Interest, The Works of John Locke, Esq.* (London: A. Churchill and S. Manship, 1759), vol. 2, pp. 580–85; and MacPherson's discussion, *The Political Theory of Possessive Individualism*, pp. 222–38.

86. G. Wilson Knight, *Chariot of Wrath* (London: Faber & Faber, 1942); see also Arnold Stein's antimilitaristic reading of the war in heaven in *Answerable Style: Essays on "Paradise Lost"* (Minneapolis: University of Minnesota Press, 1953), pp. 17–38; and Stella Revard, "Milton's Critique of Heroic Warfare in *Paradise Lost* V and VI," *Studies in English Literature* 9 (1967), 119–30.

87. For Milton's criticisms of the army, see Austin Woolych, "Milton and Cromwell," pp. 185–218.

88. In Sabine, ed., *The Works of Gerrard Winstanley*, p. 385.

89. Joan Webber, "Milton's God," *ELH* 40 (1973), 526.

90. Michael Lieb, *The Dialectics of Creation* (Amherst: University of Massachusetts Press, 1970).

91. Florence Sandler's article, "The Iconoclastic Enterprise: Blake's Critique of Milton's Religion," *Blake Studies* 5, no. 1 (1972), 13–57, discusses Blake's criticism of the war in heaven motif in Milton. Although Sandler sees it as a political criticism, she interprets it as a rejection of revolutionary violence rather than as a class critique of the revolution.

92. In "Milton's God" (pp. 519–22), Joan Webber treats this affinity as Milton's affirmation of a creativity which necessarily proceeds amid disorder. Blake's ironic reading questions whether that disorder is really necessary.

93. Lieb, *The Dialectics of Creation*, passim.

94. Henri Frankfort, *Kingship and the Gods: A Study of Ancient Near Eastern Religion* (Chicago: University of Chicago Press, 1948), p. 190.

95. Winstanley, *Law of Freedom*, p. 112.

96. Hill, *Change and Continuity*, pp. 257–60.

97. In Sabine, ed., *The Works of Gerrard Winstanley*, p. 471.

98. Percy Bysshe Shelley, *Shelley's Prometheus Unbound: A Variorum Edition*, ed. Lawrence John Zillman (Seattle: University of Washington Press, 1959), pp. 120–21; the Promethean theme was also the subject of a book by R. J. Werblowsky, *Lucifer and Prometheus* (London: Routledge & Kegan Paul, 1952).

99. Erdman, *Blake: Prophet Against Empire*, p. 179.

100. E. M. W. Tillyard, *Milton* (London: Chatto & Windus, 1930), p. 242.

101. Werblowsky, *Lucifer and Prometheus*, p. 70.

102. Raymond Southall, *Literature and the Rise of Capitalism* (London: Lawrence & Wishart, 1973), p. 123.

103. Werblowsky, *Lucifer and Prometheus*, p. 83.

104. Northrop Frye, *Fearful Symmetry* (Princeton, N.J.: Princeton University Press, 1947), p. 297.

105. Karl Marx, *Economic and Philosophic Manuscripts of 1844* (New York: International Publishers, 1964), p. 137.

106. Ibid., p. 144.

107. Marx, *Capital* (New York: International Publishers, 1967) vol. 1, p. 422.

108. Marx, *Economic and Philosophic Manuscripts*, pp. 110–11.

109. Florence Sandler has also noted the disappearance of the Messiah from Blake's *Milton* in "The Iconoclastic Enterprise," p. 24.

Chapter 9. The Politics of the Family

1. Henry Crabb Robinson, in *Blake Records*, ed. G. E. Bentley, Jr. (Oxford: Clarendon Press, 1969) p. 317.

2. For Blake's attitude toward the matter/spirit dualism, see Stuart Curran, "Blake and the Gnostic Hyle: A Double Negative," *Blake Studies* 4 (1972), 117–33; since this

work was completed, Blake's attitude has been discussed extensively by Leopold Damrosch, Jr. (*Symbol and Truth in Blake's Myth* [Princeton, N.J.: Princeton University Press, 1980]), who finds the poet struggling with a fundamental contradiction which he cannot resolve. Milton, it has been noted, leans toward a less dualistic view in his prose, particularly in *De Doctrina Christiana;* see, for example, Denis Saurat, *Milton, Man and Thinker* (London: J. M. Dent, 1925), pp. 116–18; and Arthur Sewell, *A Study in Milton's Christian Doctrine* (London: Oxford University Press, 1939), pp. 180–81.

3. Marcia Landy, "Kinship and the Role of Women in *Paradise Lost,*" *Milton Studies* 4 (1972), 3–18; see also Barbara K. Lewalski, "Milton on Women—Yet Once More," *Milton Studies* 6 (1974), 3–30; Joan Webber, "The Politics of Poetry: Feminism and *Paradise Lost,*" *Milton Studies* 14 (1980), 4.

4. William Haller, "Hail Wedded Love," *ELH* 13 (1946), 84.

5. C. S. Lewis, *The Allegory of Love: A Study in Medieval Tradition* (London: Oxford University Press, 1953).

6. William Haller and Malleville Haller, "The Puritan Art of Love," *Huntington Library Quarterly* 5 (1942), 239.

7. John Halkett offers an extensive study of Milton's relationship to these traditions in *Milton and the Idea of Matrimony* (New Haven, Conn.: Yale University Press, 1970). See also David Aers and Robert Hodge, "Rational Burning: Milton on Sex and Marriage," *Milton Studies* 13 (1979), 3–33; Edward Le Comte, *Milton and Sex* (New York: Columbia University Press, 1977); for Milton's heterodox views, see Leo Miller, *John Milton Among the Polygamophiles* (New York: Loewenthal, 1974).

8. Haller, "Hail Wedded Love," 84–85.

9. For Blake's attitude towards the female role, see Irene Tayler, "The Woman Scaly," *Bulletin of the Midwest Modern Language Association* 6 (1973), 74–87. See also Susan Fox, "The Female as Metaphor in William Blake's Poetry," *Critical Inquiry* 3 (1976), 507–19; David Aers, "William Blake and the Dialectics of Sex," *ELH* 44 (1977), 500–14; Margaret Storch, "Blake and Women: 'Nature's Cruel Holiness,' " *American Imago* 38 (1981), 221–46; Damrosch, *Symbol and Truth;* Alicia Ostriker, "Desire Gratified and Ungratified: William Blake and Sexuality," *Blake Quarterly* 16, no. 3 (1982–83); and Ann Mellors, "Blake's Sexism," ibid.

10. The development of the nuclear family has been the subject of wide research which is summarized by Christopher Lasch in "The Family and History," *New York Review of Books* 18 (1975), 33–39. See also Peter Laslett, *The World We Have Lost* (New York: Scribner's, 1971); Peter Laslett and Richard Wall, eds., *Household and Family in Past Time* (Cambridge: Cambridge University Press, 1972); William J. Goode, *World Revolution and Family Patterns* (New York: Free Press, 1963); Theodore K. Rabb and Robert I. Rotberg, eds., *The Family in History: Interdisciplinary Essays* (New York: Harper & Row, 1971).

11. For the class differences in sexual ethos, see Sheila Rowbotham, *Hidden from History* (London: Pluto Press, 1973); Eli Zaretsky, *Capitalism, the Family and Personal Life* (New York: Harper, 1976); Christopher Hill, *Puritanism and Revolution* (New York: Schocken, 1958), pp. 367–94; Edward Shorter, *The Making of the Modern Family* (New York: Basic Books, 1975), pp. 79–119.

12. Quoted in Keith Thomas, "Women and the Civil War Sects," in *Crisis in Europe 1560–1600,* ed. Trevor Aston (Garden City, N.Y.: Anchor, 1967), p. 332.

13. William Stoughton, *An Assertion for True and Christian Church-Policie* (London, 1604), pp. 246–47.

14. William Gouge, *Domesticall Duties* (London, 1622), pp. 17–18.

15. Christopher Hill, *Puritanism and Society in Pre-Revolutionary England,* 2nd ed. (New York: Schocken, 1967), p. 448.

16. Ibid., pp. 463–64.

17. Richard Sibbes, *Works*, ed. A. B. Grosart (Edinburgh, 1862–64), vol. 1, p. 25.

18. Alice Clark, *The Working Life of Women in the Seventeenth Century* (New York: A. M. Kelley, 1968).

19. Ibid., p. 12.

20. Lewalski sees Milton giving Eve a much broader role in "Milton on Women—Yet Once More."

21. Christopher Hill, *The World Turned Upside Down* (New York: Viking, 1972), p. 262.

22. Phillipe Ariès, *Centuries of Childhood* (New York: Random House, 1965).

23. Ivy Pinchbeck and Margaret Hewitt, *Children in English Society* (Toronto: University of Toronto Press, 1969), vol. 1, p. 297.

24. See ibid., p. 274; Phillip Greven, *Child-Rearing Concepts 1628–1861* (Itasca, Ill.: Peacock, 1973); and G. Rattray Taylor, *The Angel-Makers* (London: Heinemann, 1958).

25. John Dod and Richard Cleuer, *A Godlye Forme of Household Government* (London, 1630), sig. S_8–S_8 verso.

26. Jacqueline Pascal, *Reglements pour les enfants* (appendix to the Constitution of Port Royal, 1721), quoted in Ariès, *Centuries of Childhood*, p. 115.

27. Taylor, *The Angel-Makers*, p. 318.

28. Erik Erikson, *Young Man Luther* (New York: Norton, 1958), pp. 201–22.

29. Ibid., p. 247.

30. Friedrich Engels, *The Origin of the Family, Private Property and the State* (New York: International Publishers, 1972), p. 137.

31. *The Women's Sharpe Revenge* (London, 1640), p. 77.

32. Norman O. Brown, *Life Against Death* (Middletown, Conn.: Wesleyan University Press, 1959), p. 45.

33. Michael Lieb, *Dialectics of Creation* (Amherst: University of Massachusetts Press, 1970), pp. 18–86.

34. Maud Bodkin, *Archetypal Patterns in Poetry* (London: Oxford University Press, 1934), p. 109.

35. Jean Hagstrum, "Babylon Revisited, or the Story of Luvah and Vala," in *Blake's Sublime Allegory*, ed. Stuart Curran and Joseph Wittreich (Madison: University of Wisconsin Press, 1973), pp. 110, 111.

36. John Locke, "Of Children and their Education," in Greven, *Child-Rearing Concepts*, p. 11.

37. Erik Erikson, *Childhood and Society* (New York: Norton, 1963), p. 293.

38. Daniel Rogers, *Matrimoniall Honour* (1642), quoted in Levin L. Schücking, *The Puritan Family* (New York: Schocken, 1969), p. 75.

39. Taylor, *The Angel-Makers*, p. 316. Taylor also points out that in Blake's period women such as Mrs. Pennington, Mrs. Chapone, Miss Edgworth, and Mrs. Trimmer were the leading moralists, publishing books on the proper conduct for women and children which ran through several editions.

40. Quoted in B. A. Botkin, ed., *A Treasury of American Folklore* (New York: Crown, 1944), p. 64.

41. Charles Dickens, *Hard Times* (New York: New American Library, 1961), p. 25.

42. Clark, *The Working Life of Women*, pp. 307–08.

43. Gouge, *Domesticall Duties*, pp. 16–17.

44. Michael Walzer, *Revolution of the Saints* (New York: Atheneum, 1968), p. 47.

45. Henry Bullinger, *The Decades of Henry Bullinger* (London: Parker Society, 1849–52), vol. 1, p. 258.

46. Karl Marx, *Capital* (New York: International Publishers, 1967), vol. 1, p. 734.

47. H. Peter, *Good Work for a Good Magistrate* (London, 1651).

48. Bullinger, *Decades*, vol. 3, p. 58.

49. William Temple, quoted in Hill, *The World Turned Upside Down*, p. 265.

50. Hill, *Puritanism and Revolution*, p. 372.

51. *Records of the City of Norwich 1570*, ed. John Cottingham Tingey and the Rev. William Hudson (Norwich: E. Burgess, 1898), p. 344.

52. Hill, *The World Turned Upside Down*, p. 271.

53. Abiezer Coppe, *A Fiery Flying Roll* (1649), reprinted in Norman Cohn, *The Pursuit of the Millennium* (New York: Harper, 1957), p. 376.

54. Ibid., pp. 371–73.

55. Coppe, *A Fiery Flying Roll*, quoted in ibid., pp. 376–77.

56. Hill, *The World Turned Upside Down*, p. 258.

57. Friedrich Engels, *The Condition of the Working Class in England* (Palo Alto, Calif.: Stanford University Press, 1948), p. 145. At any rate, one is forced to speculate from evidence on conditions after 1830. Little research has been done on the working-class family in the 1790s and the early nineteenth century because of the scarcity of records for that time.

58. Edward Shorter, "Illegitimacy, Sexual Revolution and Social Change in Modern Europe," in *The Family in History*, ed. Rabb and Rotberg, pp. 48–54.

59. Henry Mayhew, *The Unknown Mayhew*, ed. E. P. Thompson and Eileen Yeo (New York: Schocken, 1972), pp. 147–52.

60. E. P. Thompson, *The Making of the English Working Class*, (New York: Vintage, 1963), pp. 401–17.

61. Ibid., pp. 418–29.

Chapter 10. Epilogue

1. Letter to Butts, 6 July 1803, in Geoffrey Keynes, ed., *Complete Writings of William Blake* (Oxford: Oxford University Press, 1966), p. 825.

2. Northrop Frye, *Fearful Symmetry* (Princeton, N.J.: Princeton University Press, 1947), pp. 116, 117.

3. Ibid., p. 121.

4. Ibid.

5. Ibid., p. 115.

Index